AF369736

THE FENRIS WOLF

ISSUE NO. 8

EDITED BY CARL ABRAHAMSSON

TRAPART*books*

The Fenris Wolf, issue no 8
Trapart Books 2021
Originally published by Edda Publishing 2016

ISBN 978-91-986243-5-9

Trapart Books
P.O. Box 8105
SE-104 20 Stockholm
Sweden

info@trapart.net
www.trapart.net
www.patreon.com/vanessa23carl

The Fenris Wolf, issue no 8

Contents

Editor's Introduction

> "I should find it difficult to say which of these people annoy me most, those who would have us know nothing or the ones who refuse even to leave us the small satisfaction of knowing that we know nothing."
> – Seneca

And so it howls again.

It is with great pride and joy that I present yet another issue of *The Fenris Wolf*. Again, we are in the midst of an eclectic jamboree of ideas and people that I hope will inspire you to study further and lay your own existential puzzles. I often hear from readers that the best thing about this publication is the fact that you can always return to it to find new things, or re-find things you'd forgotten about. If that's the case, which I hope, here's some more fuel to the intellectual and open-minded fire. Enjoy it now, enjoy it later. Or, preferably, do both.

It's been two years since issue number seven was published, which is a little bit confusing for an annual journal. There is a remedy of course: 2016 will see two issues. Number nine will consist of all the papers and talks from the symposium *Psychoanalysis, Art & the Occult*, which was held in London in May 2016.

This was a wonderful event, filled with panels, an art exhibition, film screenings and musical entertainment by living legend Val Denham. I worked together with the brilliant American psychoanalyst (and *Fenris Wolf* contributor) Vanessa Sinclair on this attempt to have three esoteric and quite often conservative environments meet and talk. Judging from people's reactions post-conference we succeeded very well. When *The Fenris Wolf 9* is published (late 2016) considerably more people will be able to take part of what was said and discussed.

Another noteworthy conference was *Here To Go 2014*, which I co-arranged with Martin Palmer in Trondheim, Norway. It was the second time we did it, and it also felt like a big step forward. The participants Vicki Bennett, z'ev, Peter Grey, Alkistis Dimech, Jesper Aagaard Petersen, Angela Edwards, Martin and me succeeded in creating an occultural boucquet "live", which was also captured in printed form.

In the summer of 2014, shortly after the release of the seventh issue, *Fenris Wolf* contributor Patrick Lundborg died at age 47. Patrick was an old friend of mine and a true gnostic labourer and philosopher. His illuminating research within psychedelia culminated in a masterpiece of a book called exactly that: *Psychedelia: An Ancient Culture, A Modern Way of Life* (Lysergia, Stockholm, Mojave, Lhasa, 2012). This extensive study of the development of inner refinements – lysergic and other – in cultural history has since gained a cult following, and is absolutely a must-read for anyone with even the slightest interest in the subject. Patrick's bright mind, sardonic humour and well-written texts will be sorely missed. It is more than appropriate that I dedicate this issue to his loving memory.

I rarely like to comment on contemporary issues on these pages, but one thing that's struck me during this past year is that there's been an increase – in attention and focus if nothing else – of political correctness paradoxically masquerading as "liberal" or well-meaning insinuations. I won't waste too much effort or space on that here, but suffice to say that it is fully my intention to leave a whole row of Fenris Wolves behind to combat these tendencies. When a vague, collective consensus tries to define basically what's "good" or "bad", and what should be accepted or not, self censorship is never far away. And whenever imposed self-censorship pops up, the real deal usually follows suit.

One absolute core of a healthy intellectual environment (and thereby a healthy culture in general) is an open-minded tolerance. The stronger the dynamic and diametrics, the more vital the playground. It's also very much a prerogative and a challenge based in fundamental moral philosophy: Can you tolerate and allow a person who can't tolerate and allow you? If your answer is yes, you'll always have the upper hand.

What bugs me the most is the hypocriosy surrounding the phenomenon itself. Most of these benevolently moralistic termites are just that: termites. They will gnaw away at individual liberties and responsibilities until nothing remains, simply to paradoxically secure the rights of those who *might possibly* be hurt or offended by your point of view. This is a bitter, speculative and destructive legacy stemming from the *absolutely justified* battle of securing rights for minorities of various kinds. But once these have been established, all that is left are usually self-proclaimed spokespeople in league with greedy lawyers equally befuddled opinion-makers. Add some social media impoliteness to that putrid hooligan's brew and you have an apparent army of self-hating do-gooders willing to be manipulated by anyone who smoothly lies to them about lofty and egalitarian mirages. Quite often, their outlook is so narrow and prejudiced that they can't even understand the damage they actually do.

There is, however, a great remedy. That is to expose them and to continue to be brave and free in your own expressions of your own feelings and views. If these don't happen to be in line or resonant with the politically correct status quo, good for you. More power to you.

Thanks and praise to the following: All the contributors, without whom... Thanks also to Fredrik Söderberg for some great years under the Edda umbrella, Andreas Kalliaridis for the amazing cover art, the Odrörer Oasis of OTO Sweden, Vera & Stojan Nikolic of Aleph in Skopje, Bjarne Salling Pedersen of Nekropolis in Copenhagen, Lea Porsager and the Overgaden Institute for Contemporary Art in Copenhagen, the Society of Sentience, Henrik Bogdan and to all the supportive Trapart-friends, customers and booksellers. And most of all to inspiratrix extraordinaire Vanessa Sinclair for showing up at exactly the right time.

An editorial note: As the texts in this issue stem from various minds from various cultures, there are obviously some stylistic inconsistencies. I have chosen to keep these, including possible "magical" language quirks and experiments, in the name of heterogeneous and creative integrity. However, for any spelling or typographical errors, pure and simple, I assume full responsibility.

Finally, I would like to say that the views and values expressed in the various texts in this eclectic anthology are those of the respective authors, and do not necessarily represent my own views, those of Trapart Books or any kind of general "Fenris Wolfean" perspective.

Vade Ultra!

Carl Abrahamsson
Stockholm-Monstropolis, Summer Solstice 2016

Polymorphous Perversity and Pandrogeny

Vanessa Sinclair

"Never before has a generation felt such a rage to live, destroy gender, destroy the control of DNA and the expected. Every man and woman is a man and woman." – Breyer P-Orridge

We are born into a story, an already existing narrative. Even before we are born, our parents, family and society have ideas of who we will be, what we will do, how we will succeed, and what trials we may face, all before we have even left our m/others' body. We are subjugated *in utero*. Our identity is prescribed, and not with us in mind. It is mapped out for us, structured, put into play, and is largely based on gender. The first question asked of us, "Is it a boy or a girl?", leaves no room for ambiguity – boys have penises, girls do not. We are all well aware of the atrocities that have taken place in the early assignment of gender to children born intersex and what catastrophic repercussions this often has. Yet rather than exalt the hermaphroditic, as has been done in times past, we continue to force people into categories we've deemed socially acceptable. The system is built on dichotomy: male/female, active/passive, 1/0, master/slave. But what happens when we begin to break down this system, push boundaries, surpass borderlines and transgress limits?

Gender and sexuality are not simply determined by biology. Judith Butler revolutionized the academic discourse surrounding gender and gender identity in 1990 with her book *Gender Trouble* in which she introduces the idea of gender as performance, utilizing drag kings and queens as overt examples. Taking this a step further, not only is gender a performance but our entire identity could be seen in this way: our gender, race, class, profession, ethnicity. This is how a white, middle class, female professor at the New School for Social Research acts. So if gender and overall identity is a performance, or at least has a heavy performative aspect, it should be essentially malleable, not only varying from person to person but evolving over a person's life span, from situation to situation or even from day to day if one so desires.

Sigmund Freud stated in 1923 that our ego is first and foremost a body-ego. We learn about ourselves and the world via our bodies, especially through our orifices as these are the spaces where we exchange inside and out, ingest and discharge, are penetrated and expel. These sites are holes, openings, gaps, but also limits, boundaries and surfaces; the rim of the mouth, anus, urethra, vagina, nostrils, eyes and ears. What is the difference between those that seal versus those that remain open or rather, unable to close? We may even consider the pores of the skin to be countless numbers of orifices, tiny mouths opening and closing more quickly or slowly depending on our state, mood, level of stimulation or relaxation.

Around the turn of the twentieth century, Freud released his seminal work, *Three Essays on the Theory of Sexuality* (1905), in which he introduced his theory of childhood sexuality outlining the oral, anal and genital stages for the first time, claiming we are all born bisexual and intrinsically polymorphously perverse. The expert on sexuality and perversions at the time was Richard von Kraft-Ebbing, who believed – as did society at large – that sex is solely for procreation and any sexual act falling outside of the reproductive intention was considered to be perverse. Freud actually agreed with this definition of perversion but stated that perversion is our natural inclination and is the norm, even precedes the norm. Humans are sexual beings. Children are sexual beings. We are all perverse, and the entire body is sexual, not just the genitals and erogenous zones. Any part of the body can become eroticized, as can the gaze, smell or voice.

In the sexual relation, no matter if it is overtly sadomasochistic or not, there is always an inevitable element of dominance and submission. Even in the sexual relation with oneself, in masturbation, we are the one doing the beating as well as the one being beaten. We are performing the act on ourselves and therefore occupy both positions – dominant and submissive. We gain pleasure engaging in this activity, which is nonetheless an aggressive action. Furthermore, we are witnessing the act being done by ourselves to ourselves, thereby entering a third position as well, the witness. So no matter if it is auto-erotic, homosexual, heterosexual, transsexual, queer, top/bottom, S/M, 1/0, adult/child, D/s, oral, anal, polyamorous, orgiastic, and/or anything in between – no matter in which position we might be, we may concurrently take the stance of the other(s) as well, and therefore occupy both (and all) positions at once. We are voyeur and exhibitionist. We are being seen while enacting and observing the scene, exposing ourselves as we bear witness to the exposure.

Lady Jaye and Genesis Breyer P-Orridge have explored these concepts at a depth few have dared to traverse. They have taken contemporary ideas of identity, the body, consciousness, gender and sexuality that much further in a process they deemed *Pandrogeny*, undergoing a series of medical, chemical, psychological, spiritual and behavioral procedures intended to break down prescribed conceptions of themselves as individuals so that they may come together more fully as one to create a third being they called the *Pandrogyne*. Influenced by the work of Brion Gysin and William Burroughs, the pair chose to apply the cut-up method to their selves with the intention of creating a Third Mind – in this case a Third Being.

In *The Pandrogeny Manifesto* (2006), Breyer P-Orridge state, "Some people feel they are a man trapped in a woman's body. Some people feel they are a woman trapped in a man's body. Breyer P-Orridge just feel trapped in a body." Lady Jaye likened the human body to a cheap suitcase in which we carry around our consciousness. "I'm limited by time, by gravity, by all these physical forces when really I wish my consciousness could be liberated completely free to go everywhere, to be everywhere, to do everything, to be everyone that I've ever dreamed of being."

Genesis has been exploring identity, pushing limits and breaking boundaries since he/r earliest work with the Exploding Galaxy commune in 1969, where any semblance of routine or structure was completely dismantled. The walls of the building were literally torn down as much as possible, including the walls surrounding the bathrooms. Members were not to sleep in the same location two nights in a row. Meals were cooked at irregular times throughout the day. No one had he/r own money. All clothing was kept in the center of the room with a 'first come, first served' policy each morning. This disrupted attachment to material possessions, personal space, privacy, as well as separation between self and other. When it was discovered that leaders were not abiding by the same rules as the others in the house, Genesis left and founded COUM Transmissions. As part of COUM, Genesis developed a practice of adopting various identities and living fully as each character for days on end, whether or not s/he liked or agreed with the belief system of the person chosen.

This greatly influenced the performance art of Genesis and early collaborator Cosey Fanni Tutti. For example, the pair's *Orange and Blue* performance pieces began with the male-bodied person dressed from head to toe in orange with all of his orange belongings on one side of the room, while the female-bodied person dressed in all blue with her collection of blue items. Throughout the course of the performance, Genesis and Cosey would slowly exchange items and clothing with one another over several hours, until they had switched over to the other's attire and accoutrements completely. In this way, Genesis was already exploring the idea of gender and identity as performative in 1969, something which was not brought to the fore in academia until decades later (Butler, 1990).

In an interview in 1982 with UK television program *Riverside*, Genesis was questioned about he/r use of the pronoun *we* when referring to he/rself:

> GBP-O: Well the *I* is what we call the flat people, who assume that the person that they've be donated by social conditioning is a one-dimensional actual person. The *We* is how we see the world, which is that everybody is made up of lots and lots of different personalities, fantasies, attitudes, and that the multi-personality is in fact the reality, not the *I* personality, and that where those two things meet is the position that we're trying to work at, to break people across from seeing themselves as one-dimensional and having no potential to seeing themselves as being almost anything they want to be, and that those different things don't have to always agree in the usual accepted way.

> Interviewer: Sex and sexuality seem to be the more obvious subject matters that you're dealing with. Why sex and sexuality?

> Peter Christopherson: Because it's the area that most people would like to make greater progress with than they are at the moment.

> GBP-O: And because we feel that it's no mistake that in every society and in every tribal structure there are laws governing sexuality, and to us that suggests that sexuality has in itself some power and energy which

these societies and those in control have a vested interest in suppressing. That freedom is taken away when there is a threat, therefore there is a threat to control from sexuality, therefore it ought to be investigated and liberated.

As with every aspect of he/r work, the use of the pronoun *we* has evolved over time, currently representing the union of Breyer P-Orridge as Pandrogyne. As Lady Jaye dropped he/r body in 2007, Genesis embodies the Pandrogyne in this world, while Lady Jaye represents in the next.

In psychoanalysis, sexuality and the unconscious are one and the same. Sexuality is intrinsically subversive and sexual identity can change over a person's lifetime or circumstances. There is only one libido, meaning that there is no psychic representative of the opposition masculine-feminine in the unconscious. The subject is inserted into h/er sexual nature, with sexuality preceding the *I*. Attempts to grasp onto an identity can be seen as one grappling with sexuality, with one's intrinsic sexual nature, attempting to categorize it, restrict it, contain it, and give it a limit in an effort to control it.

The effort to normalize is itself pathological. Normalization fixes desire. It constrains the mobility of desire, orienting it in increasingly limiting ways – you must desire persons, specifically persons of the opposite sex, then only certain sexual acts with a certain person of the opposite sex. This freezes fragments of the unconscious evermore into an identity. What are you? Who are you? How can we categorize you so that we can separate ourselves from you? The over-pathologization of the human experience. You are not like us, you have an illness, a disease, you are an addict, an other. If we pin down the problem, we can prescribe a solution. However, normalization fails. All paths that sexuality may take are equally valid and complex. In fact, Jaques Lacan called the hetero-normative prototype, "the delusional normality of genital relations."

In his paper, *Gender, Sex and the Sexual* (2003/2011), Jean Laplanche differentiates gender, sex and sexuality in the following way: Gender is plural. It is oftentimes seen as dual, as in masculine-feminine, but it is not so by nature. It is actually plural, existing on a continuum. Sex is dual. It is so by virtue of sexual reproduction and also by virtue of its human symbolization, which sets and freezes the duality as presence/absence or phallic/castrated. The sexual is multiple, polymorphous. The fundamental discovery of Freud: it is based on repression, the unconscious and fantasy. It is the object of psychoanalysis.

Laplanche feels the displacement of the question of sexual identity onto the question of gender identity conceals the fundamental Freudian discovery, which does not lie in gender identity but in the question of the sexual, sexuality. Laplanche would like to distinguish between the sexual and the sexed. It has been claimed that the etymology of sex is cut from the sexed, clearly delineating the difference of the sexes within the sexual relation. When Freud speaks of enlarged sexuality, the sexuality of the *Three Essays*, it is always the sexual. It is a sexuality that has been called polymorphously perverse, non-procreative, and even non-sexed, as distinguished from what is called sexual reproduction or in these terms would be more precisely called sexed reproduction. The sexual then is not the sexed, it is essentially perverse infantile sexuality, which is our unconscious.

Sexuality is fluid and does not have a prescribed object, objective or path. In a 1972 essay entitled *Panthropology* – an apparent precursor to Pandrogeny – Genesis writes, "We are not heterosexual, homosexual, bisexual or transsexual. We are simply sexual." For Lacan, sexuality is not in the realm of nature or nurture, as it is not constricted to nor constructed by either. The unconscious shows how both society/culture and biology are limited, how they fail. We are situated in the space, the gap between nature and nurture. Deconstructionists argue that as bodies, corporeal matter must be realized through the social process of embodiment. And even though Butler, amongst others, utilizes Lacan's theories in her argument, Lacan does not authorize the constructionist nor deconstructionist argument any more than the biological. He insists that psychoanalytic logic remains fundamentally irreducible to these terms (Dean, 2006).

The concept of the individual is a product of power. Identity is a regulatory norm. Freud's conceptualization of the subject as divided (conscious/unconscious) undermines the possibility of a seamless identity, sexual or otherwise. Psychoanalysis views identity as illusory. Historicism relegates identity to cultural and social practices. A society's ideology of individuality ensures maximum freedom as long as one conforms. The ego is the internalized ideals of our parents, as was theirs and those before that, connecting one dimension of social identification/exclusion with another through generations. Queer theory and politics began with a critique of identity and identity politics. Queer is opposed to normalization and attempts to evade the impasse of identity politics.

Sexuality is key to subverting control.

BREAKING DNA

In his essay *The Supreme Homage,* Jean-Pierre Turmel describes the ritual of coming on a partner's face. While this is seen by society as perverse, and in our definition certainly is, we are made to feel that such an action is somehow debasing to our partner and possibly ourselves. However, as Turmel points out, the insistence that the sperm enter the hole is actually the base animal instinct. One may be honoring one's partner by coming on he/r face, beholding the image of the beloved rather than attempting to instinctually reproduce the species. Society holds procreation in esteem while encouraging us to feel deviant if we should harbor a desire to engage in sexual acts for other reasons. This example illustrates how the hetero-normative ideal of genital intercourse with procreation as the ultimate goal might be seen as the base animal instinct, while the ability to utilize our sexuality in more creative and (in my view) productive ways may be more in line with spirituality and evolution as a species.

In his essay *Instincts and their Vicissitudes* (1915), Freud states, "Biology teaches that sexuality is not to be put on par with other functions of the individual and have as their content the production of new individuals – that is, the preservation of the species. It shows, further, that two views, seemingly equally well founded, seem to take place between sexuality and the ego. On the one view, the individual is the principle thing, sexuality is one of its activities and sexual satisfaction one of its needs; while on the other view the individual is a temporary and transient appendage to the quasi-immortal germ-plasm (DNA), which is entrusted to him by the process of generation."

Breyer P-Orridge believe, "DNA is an evolutionary parasite, and our bodies are merely the host environment in a symbiotic relationship with it. Our species replicates as much to perpetuate DNA as it does to perpetuate the species." They go on to state, "In fact we see the *I* of our consciousness as a fictional assembly or collage that resides in the environment of the body. One of the central themes of our work is the malleability of physical and behavioral identity. The body is used by the mind as a logo for the self before we are able to speak language."

For Lacan, identity/ego is first formed during the mirror stage. During this time (ages 6-18 months), the child experiences he/r self and body as fragmented, but when s/he sees he/r self in the mirror, the mirror image appears to be whole. As the child's experience of he/r own body/self is fragmented, there seems to be a disconnect between one's experience of one's self and the image in the mirror. This experience of disconnect continues throughout life. This process of identification is similar to that of identification with the m/other, only this time identification occurs with one's own mirror image, the child is able to internalize the cohesive sense of self that s/he imagines the mirror image to have, which thus forms the ego/identity. We identify with what we imagine ourselves to experience. The ego/identity is therefore an identification with a fantasy. However, the position of what would more accurately be considered to be the true self, what Lacan calls the subject, is not equivalent to the ego/identity but rather is situated in the gap that exists between consciousness and matter, the ego and the real of the body, perception and the unconscious.

Breyer P-Orridge seem to have recreated this experience of the origin of the formation of identity by cutting up their own selves as individuals, thereby recreating this fragmentation, while concurrently creating a mirror image in one another. Through this they could more fully identify with the wholeness of the mirror image in each other, creating a new sense of identity for the pair, facilitating their union as Pandrogyne. Lady Jaye writes, "I am making a mirror, something to see myself in." The experience of such a union went well beyond what the artists anticipated. "We are also beginning slowly to explore the surprisingly profound effects of being lost so totally and lovingly in the mirror of another being."

Gysin and Burroughs show that the cutting up of language creates the space for something new to form. Breyer P-Orridge illustrate that this also occurs with the cutting up of bodies and behavior. The cut of the scissor or surgeon is not just aesthetically uniting the two but also creates the gap/space in which something new can grow. Just the way ritual cuts us out of our day to day narrative, creating room for us to imagine a new reality.

Psychoanalysis does the same. By breaking the mindless replication of DNA, we are also creating a space where we are able to produce something new. We are situated in the gap. We may fill this space with our self, consciousness, creative energy, Will, intention. The cut-up has proven to be effective not only when applied to word, image and sound but also to self, identity, gender and sexuality. People should be able to create themselves in any way they imagine themselves to be. Why experience oneself as limited, one-dimensional? Sexuality is inherently subversive and is at our core. It is foundational to the essence of every subject. Anti-normalization is achieved by disruption of the narrative. So as Alain Badiou (2000) states, "Persevere in the interruption."

"This is the final war. A jigsaw. A war to repossess your self. There is no gender anymore. Only p/androgyny is divine. Sexuality is a force of nature that cannot be contained… As a being possessed, repossess yourself. Be possessed by your self, any self, every self you were ever afraid of… Identity is theft." – Breyer P-Orridge

REFERENCES

—≈— Badiou, A. (2000). *Ethics: An Essay on the Understanding of Evil.* New York: Verso.
—≈— Bornstein, K. (1994). *Gender Outlaw: On Men, Women, and the Rest of Us.* New York: Vintage Books.
—≈— Breyer P-Orridge, G. (2010). *Thee Psychick Bible: The Apocryphal Scriptures ov Genesis Bryer P-Orridge and Thee Third Mind ov Thee Temple ov PsychickYouth.* Washington: Feral House.
—≈— Butler, J. (1990). *Gender Trouble: Feminism and the Subversion of Identity.* London: Routledge.
—≈— Dean, T. (2006). Lacan meets queer theory. *Perversion: Psychoanalytic Perspectives, Perspectives on Psychoanalysis,* Dany Nobus & Lisa Downing (Eds.) London: Karnac Books. 261-322.
—≈— Freud, S. (1905). Three essays on the theory of sexuality. *SE* 7:123-246.
_________ (1923). The ego and the id. *SE* 19: 1-66.
—≈— Laplanche, J (2011). *Freud and the Sexual.* International Psychoanalytic Books.
—≈— Verhaeghe, P. (1997). *Does the Woman Exist? From Freud's Hysteric to Lacan's Feminine.* New York: Other Press.

ALCHYMIA

Charles Stansfeld Jones

In 1922 Charles Stansfeld Jones (1886-1950) – Grand Master (X°) for O.T.O. North America and Aleister Crowley's "Magical Child" – joined the Universal Brotherhood, a highly secretive and obscure organisation. As Jones gradually drifted away from Crowley, he became increasingly involved in the Universal Brotherhood and eventually became its Mahaguru or leader. This first publication of Jones' short essay on alchemy was written exclusively for Universal Brotherhood members on December 12, 1929. A few notes, identifying quoted sources, have been added for this publication.
– Professor Henrik Bogdan.

Only the slightest and most indirect references to the Science of Alchemy are to be found in the documents of G.T.

The Historical Studies occasionally refer to men who have transmitted certain aspects of Alchemical tradition but they give little or no detail of the nature of Alchemy itself.

Lesson 17, *The Sciences*, makes a single reference to Hermetic Philosophy under which Alchemy subsumed.[1] It indicates that the subject of the formal or ideal science of Symbology (including Hermetic Philosophy) is the mystical significance and esoteric correspondences of mental processes, mathematical elements and corporeal things and attributes.

It may also be gathered from this lesson that Symbology may be subsumed under the science of Ontology (the subject of which is *Being* as such) in its larger sense.

Also, it informs us that many sciences have thus far been very little or very ineffectively cultivated, especially in the world of exoteric learning, and that this particularly true of Symbology, which, taken with certain other sciences, is of special importance to the mystic.

Mystical science, it states, is the highest of the special sciences. It focuses all the light of all the sciences upon the Supreme Object of spiritual consciousness, as manifested in and by the Macrocosm, with a view to enabling man to attain to the vision of the whole through its Archetypal Idea.

Alchemy insofar as it even in directly contributes towards that end, must, therefore,

---

1 'Sutra Saptadashan: The Sciences'. This is one of the sutras or instructional papers given to members of the first grade of the Universal Brotherhood.

be considered as of importance and value, especially to the mystic.

One of the Integral Gurus makes certain references to Alchemy in his Responsa to a Quaerenda submitted by a Neophyte. He informs us that the subject discussed under that name in such periodicals as *The Occult Review* and *Le Voile d'Isis* is merely a jumble of chemistry with the superstitions connected with its origin. This, he states, is as much as can easily be learnt from the profane history of chemistry and Alchemy.

Genuine Alchemy, he continues, is not experimental, but symbolical. He further states, "The subject of Alchemy, is of much less importance to a Neophyte, and even to a Chela and Mahachela than the faithful carrying out of his own proper duties, and the thorough study and assimilation of the instruction which the Integral Wisdom has provided for him.

It is evident, therefore, that Alchemy is not to be considered as of great importance for study in the lower stages of advancement, unless perhaps it be for those whose aspiration is particularly directed toward the Mystical Goal.

On the other hand, Lesson 7 informs us: "Since every idea, theory or doctrine must, in the very nature of things, have some truth at its basis, it happens that the difficult, unreasonable or even absurd, any idea seems to be, the more illuminative does it become when thoroughly understood; for only some very important truth could have availed to give currency to a teaching of extreme incredibleness and difficulty.

A short examination of the literature of Alchemy cannot fail to convince the student that much that has been written upon the subject fails to be comprehensible and appears quite unreasonable and absurd, while, at the same time, it cannot be denied that during certain periods of history, Alchemy has been very widespread and that since its roots are in the far distant past it is part of tradition which has persisted for many ages despite its incredibleness and apparent absurdity.

Alchemy may therefore, be considered as concealing beneath the mass of symbolism which covers its essential doctrine, some very important truth.

Although, while lacking the Integral Teaching on this subject, we may find it beyond our power to discover just what that very important truth is, it may be possible for us to eliminate some of the graver sources of error which detract from such a possible discovery, and such a course appears to be in conformity with the principles of Alchemy itself, if the meaning of the term be rightly understood.

Reference to an ordinary dictionary gives the definition as: "Medieval chemistry, especially the pursuit of the transmutation of base metals into gold." The Standard Dictionary gives: "Alchemy, the immature chemistry of the middle ages, characterized by the pursuit of the transmutation of base metals into gold, and the search for the alkahest and the panacea." These further terms are defined as follows: "Alkahest: An imaginary liquid, reputed to be universal menstruum, capable of resolving all bodies into their constituent elements.

Panacea: A remedy or medicine proposed for, or professing to cure all diseases; cure-all; catholicon; hence a remedy or cure for all ills, mental or physical.

It would however, appear to be wiser to refer to a dictionary published at a time when Alchemy was in less ill-repute than it is at the present day, if we are to discover what the meaning of the word was considered to be by those who practiced the Art.

Turning to a "Chemycal Dictionary, explaining Hard Places and Words met with in the Writings of Paracelsus and other Obscure Authors", London, 1674, we find a great consistency in the definitions given of various words relating to Alchemy.[2] Thus:

ALCHYMIA is the separation of that which is impure from a purer substance.

CHYMIA is the art of Separating pure from impure and making essences.

SPAGIRUS or SPAGIRICUS is he who knows to distinguish between good and bad, to separate pure from impure; a CHYMIST or ALCHMIST.

SPAGIRIA is commonly taken for ALCHEMY

YSOPUS is the art of Alchemy to separate pure from impure

Of the above definitions CHYMIA alone appears to denote the making of anything (essences). The others all refer exclusively to the SEPARATION OF THE PURE FROM THE IMPURE – THE GOOD FROM THE BAD.

These older definitions throw quite a different light upon what was meant by Alchemy by those who practiced the Art. They supply the Key to the study of the subject, the student who is a true Son of the Science must learn to distinguish between the good and the bad alchemist, to separate the pure from the impure symbolism, as well as to discover the essence of the subject

A certain author (not writing for the *Occult Review*) makes the following remarks which may be of service to the true student and save him much useless labor and research. He writes: "Modern research by profane scholars leaves it still doubtful as to whether Alchemical treatises should be classified as mystical, magical, medical or chemical. The most reasonable opinion is that all these subjects formed the preoccupation of the alchemists, in varying proportions

"The literature of alchemy is immense. Practically the whole of it is wholly or partially unintelligible

"We do not propose any of the actual processes. Most readers will be already aware that the main objects of alchemy were the Philosopher's Stone, the Medicine of Metals, and various tinctures and elixirs possessing diver's virtues; in particular, those of healing diseases, extending the span of life, increasing human abilities, perfecting the nature of man in every aspect, conferring magical powers and transmuting material substances, especially metals, into more valuable forms.

"The subject is further complicated by the fact that many authors were unscrupulous quacks. Ignorant of the first elements of the Art, they plagiarized without shame, and reaped a harvest of fraudulent gain. They took advantage of general ignorance, and the convention of mystery, in just the same way as their modern successors do in the matter of the Occult sciences generally.

"But despite all this, one thing is abundantly clear: all serious writers, though they seem to speak of an infinity of different subjects, so much so that is has proved impossible for modern analytic research to ascertain the true nature of any single process, were agreed on the fundamental theory on which they based their practices. It appears at first sight as if hardly any two of them were in accord as to the nature of the "First Matter

---

2 First published in English as Sendivogius, Michael, *A New Light of Alchymie: Taken Out of the fountaine of Nature, and Manuall Experience. To which is added a Treatise of Sulphur... Also a Chymicall Dictionary explaining hard places and words met withall in the writings of Paracelsus, and other obscure Authors.* London: Printed by Richard Cotes, for Thomas Williams, at the Bible in Little-Britain, 1650.

of the Work". They describe this in a bewildering multiplicity of unintelligible symbols. We have no reason to suppose that they were all talking of the same thing, or otherwise. The same remarks apply to every reagent and every process, no less than to the final product or products.

"Yet, beneath this diversity, we may perceive an obscure identity. They all begin with a substance in nature which is described as existing almost everywhere, and as universally esteemed of no value. The alchemist is in all cases to take this substance and subject it to a series of operations. By so doing, he obtains his product. This product, however named or described, is always a substance which represents the truth or perfection of the original "First Matter", and its qualities are invariably such as pertain to a living being, not to an inanimate mass. In a word, the alchemist is to take a dead thing, impure, valueless and powerless, and transform it into a live thing, active, invaluable and thaumaturgic."[3]

The above quotation should be sufficient to help the student over many difficulties by enabling him to separate that which is essential from that which is inessential in alchemical writings and symbols.

A few further hints may be obtained from one of the best of the Alchemical treatises written by an Adept whose name is unknown but whose work is held in high esteem.

"I protest unto you, (he writes) before God, and upon the eternal Salvation of my Soul, with a sincere Heart, touched with compassion for those who have been a long while in this great Search; and I give you notice, all you who Esteem this wonderful Art, that our whole work takes its Nativity from one only thing, and that in this thing the Work finds its Perfection, without need of any other thing whatsoever, but to be dissolved and coagulated, which it must do itself, without the assistance of any foreign Thing."[4]

He also gives this further piece of advice which should in no wise be neglected: "But remember, ye Sons of the Science, that the knowledge of our Magistry comes rather by the Inspiration of Heaven, than from the Lights which we can get ourselves. This Truth is acknowledged by all Philosophers; 'tis for that reason that it is not enough to Work; Pray daily, read good books and meditate Night and Day on the Operations of Nature, and on what she may be able to do when she is assisted by the help of our Art, and by these means you will succeed, without doubt, in your Undertaking."

From all of which we may gather in some manner, not perhaps clearly known to us as yet, the Art of Alchemy serves to raise Nature above Herself, and this the Integral Teaching tells us, is one of the great privileges and duties of Man.

December 12, 1929

---

3 The Master Therion [Aleister Crowley], *Magick in Theory and Practice* (Paris, Lecram Press, 1929), pp. 183-185.

4 *The Hermetical Triumph: or, The Victorious Philosophical Stone. A Treatise more compleat and more intelligible than any has been yet, concerning The Hermetical Magistery.* London: Printed ; and Sold by P. Hanet, at the Sign of the *Black-Spread-Eagle*, near *Somerset-House* in the *Strand*, 1723, p. 2.

Black Lodge/White Lodge

Notes toward a Symbology of Secret Societies and Gnosis in Recent Drama

Timothy O'Neill

It is no secret that I am fascinated with the whole world of secret societies and conspiracies. It stems back to a childhood visit to Rosicrucian Park in San José one rainy day in November, 1962. I recall or perhaps imagine seeing a figure in a monk's robe going into a back entrance of the Planetarium building where I later worked after a very long and strange journey of writing and art. I am still not certain that I saw that event, but it left an indelible impression as one of those life-defining moments. My whole experience with the Order is worthy of recounting someday, but for now the chain of events leads to that leviathan of good and evil: Facebook. I have joined many groups on FB with gnostic or illuminist themes, including the AMORC and Martinist groups, but one of the most interesting is the Gnostic Movie group:

https://www.facebook.com/groups/gnosticmovies/

The focused discussion of films with gnostic content or symbology is something new to me and has sparked many thoughts about my history as a student of film. I have naturally gravitated toward films, television drama and books that contain such material but the revelation that others are thinking along similar lines is inspiring. One of the treasures found in that group is reference to a blog that delves into the depths of symbolism in such works:

http://themaskofgod.blogspot.com/2012/01/death-is-road-to-eleusis.html

Films like *Agora* and *The Fountain* demonstrate that the gnostic current is alive and well in contemporary cinema if we know where to look. The idea of secret orders seeding cultural references to the Gnosis is something that has also fascinated me. In a culture of oppression and greed, it is often popular entertainment where the Gnosis can find a foothold: simple fortune telling cards, tales of mythical Grails and heroes searching for the impossible. This is the world that we are examining here in several films, books and even television dramas, released since the late 1980's. I should mention that I have attempted to avoid spoilers wherever possible, but this article is about insights so I can only forewarn that there may be some secrets revealed!

Twin Peaks: Mark Frost and David Lynch. April 8th, 1990 to June 10th, 1991

(The White Lodge, the Black Lodge)

The List of 7 and *The Six Messiahs:* Mark Frost 1993 and 1995

(The Dark Brotherhood)

Along the line of secrets, it is also no secret that I am fascinated with the work of David Lynch, particularly the vast and sprawling symbolism of *Twin Peaks*. I am quick to add that *Twin Peaks* is equally the creative work of Mark Frost, whose writings I have also delved into with gusto. *Twin Peaks* has become a cottage industry for film scholars, but few have understood or delved into the deeply theosophical background of the drama. The first clue I had that something deeper was going on was a peculiar reference to a regular weekly meeting of the *Theosophical Society* in Twin Peaks in one of those ephemeral books released around the time of the series: *A Town Guide to Twin Peaks*. It's a silly book full in in-jokes and tidbits, most of which are simply there to add some atmosphere. The reference to Theosophy made me stop, because one of the key scenes of Season Two includes a discussion between Dale Cooper and Deputy Hawk about *The White Lodge*. The discussion even features a mention of *The Dweller on the Threshold*. So, the supposed Blackfoot legend of the White Lodge as recounted by Hawk shares something in common with the thought of Madame Blavatsky! As Season Two continues, the search for the Black Lodge becomes a race to the death between former FBI agent/Project Bluebook member Windom Earle and the erstwhile FBI agent, Dale Cooper. Another character, Air Force Major Garland Briggs, also a member of the Bluebook investigation, is abducted, UFO style, into the White Lodge during all of this. What is interesting is that the White and Black Lodges are described more as *places* than as organizations. They are embodiments, in some other place and timelessness, of pure goodness and evil.

The local secret society in Twin Peaks is revealed to be the *Bookhouse Boys*; a semi-chivalric group of men dedicated to fighting the evil of the Black Lodge in the woods surrounding Twin Peaks. They are clearly a human society that has existed for many decades, probably back to the founding of the town, but they are not overtly working on the behalf of the White Lodge. There is mention in the shooting script of the penultimate episode, number 29, of a scene in which Sheriff Harry Truman would have had a vision of an angelic figure with a sword out in the woods. As leader of the Bookhouse Boys, this vision would have tied them firmly to the Grail Knights and to the White Lodge, but this interesting aside never made it into the actual shooting.

So, where does this complex symbology of the eternal battle between good and evil secret organizations come from? It is not exactly alien to David Lynch's worldview. *Eraserhead* featured a gnostic style "engineer" figure on a strange planetoid, played by Jack Fisk, who becomes the Demiurge of Henry's world and experience. The fact is, though, that most of the *Twin Peaks* Black Lodge/White Lodge symbolism comes from Mark Frost. Frost is a Sherlock Holmes fanatic and even wrote two Holmesian novels:

The List of 7 and *The Six Messiahs*. Madame Blavatsky is a minor character in *The List of 7*. Clearly, Mark Frost was very aware of the role of Theosophy in the rise of modern occultism. The occult forms a key force in *The List of 7*, wherein a group called "The Dark Brotherhood" is attempting to infiltrate the British Royalty and install their own dark Lord, the Dweller on the Threshold!

The essential idea of a disembodied group of occult adepts inspiring and guiding their human followers is of course something that can be traced to ancient gnostic groups, but the modern form of that idea is found in Karl von Eckartshausen's classic *Cloud upon the Sanctuary*, published in 1795:

http://www.adepti.com/docs/eck.pdf

That this work was a seminal influence for Madame Blavatsky is beyond doubt. Her description of the Great White Brotherhood occupies a central role in her works and explains how those books came to be through the mysterious influence of the invisible adepts supposedly guiding her.

So, through Mark Frost and his knowledge of Victorian culture, these ideas came to be embodied in *Twin Peaks*. I should say that looking at the wider circle of books and films in the *Twin Peaks* cycle (which even includes a reference to King Arthur and the Grail) includes David Lynch's feature film *Fire Walk with Me* and the book, *The Autobiography of Dale Cooper*. The recently released Blu-Ray edition of *Twin Peaks* and *Fire, Walk with Me* features the long sought deleted scenes from *Fire Walk with Me* which nail home the idea that what *Twin Peaks* was really about was the gradual infiltration of high levels of the FBI and international government by the Black Lodge. It is apparent from all of the sources, that Dale Cooper was groomed from birth to become the vessel of the parasitic demon serial killer Bob. It was no accident that two other FBI agents were abducted by the Black lodge in the course of *Fire Walk with me*. Much like Frost's story in *The List of 7*, the forces of darkness aim for the highest levels of power and influence in human society. This vast conspiracy roams around the globe, from Buenos Aires to Hong Kong in the course of the *Twin Peaks* cycle.

The recent revelation that there will be a third season of *Twin Peaks*, directed by David Lynch and co-written by Mark Frost, as well as a book by Mark Frost about the history of the town during the intervening twenty five years between the original events and now, indicates that we are in for some fascinating gnostic story telling during the next two years. The whole gnostic back-story of *Twin Peaks* deserves a full book and I am hoping that this might spark some thought out there.

Millennium: Chris Carter, 1996 to 1999

(The Millennium Group (Owls and Roosters))

During the hey-day of *The X-Files*, Chris Carter was approached by Fox to do another series. This was during the period when millennial obsessions were running high and books like *Apocalypse Culture* were being produced. Carter had his own fascinations with millennial thought, so he agreed to do the series, again, featuring an ex-FBI profiler, named Frank Black. The prevalence of the FBI in conspiratorial stories is of note. For three seasons, Frank Black used his semi-psychic abilities as a profiler to stop serial killers and save the innocent, but a larger theme emerged. At first, Black was approached by a mysterious group called "The Millennium Group", which funded his activities and groomed him for eventual initiation. Yes, the group may have been composed of ex-FBI agents and other government types, but a strongly gnostic religious strain of thought ran through their beliefs and those accepted were initiated by a sacrifice of their own blood during an elaborately symbolic ceremony. Over the course of the three seasons, it is revealed that the Millennium group has been around for centuries and was originally a secret society within the body of the Catholic Faith that focused on the Apocalypse and the second coming of Christ.

By the time of the contemporary *Millennium*, the group has split into two factions: The *Roosters*, who believe that the coming Millennium will trigger a theological apocalypse, while the *Owls* believe that the end of the world will be a secular, scientific and material event. The reference to the Owls should trigger a few raised eyebrows, since it is a clear reference to the Illuminati, who are associated emphatically with the scientific and reason-based approach to mystical experience. The dynamic in the Millennium group is complex and full of the twists and turns associated with the warfare common to opposing secret societies.

These secret societies are coincidentally obsessed with fragments of the True Cross and the hand of Saint Sebastian, which is an amazing thing to run into on American television! Naturally, portions of the group start taking more pro-active steps toward *causing* the Millennium through terrifying research into bio-engineering and weapons of mass destruction. In a final episode which was actually aired through the X-Files, the group resorts to attempting to raise the Four Horsemen of the Apocalypse through the dead bodies of four FBI agents. It is all very heady, very deep and takes on more and more significance as times go on. The idea of high levels of government actively engaged in such activities is becoming less and less bizarre with every moment. As is the case with *Twin Peaks*, a large fandom is actively promoting a return to *Millennium* through a new film or TV series. We can only hope.

Carnevale: Daniel Knauf, September 14th, 2003 to March 27th, 2005

(The Knights Templar and the Sacred Bloodline)

http://en.wikipedia.org/wiki/Mythology_of_Carniv%C3%A0le

Carnevale is set during the Dustbowl era of 1934 and is an amazingly open gnostic story firmly anchored in the symbol of the Tree of Good and Evil. The first episode reveals that in every generation, men who are the very embodiments of good and evil are born to do battle around the Tree of Good and Evil. What distinguishes *Carnevale* is that these beings, "avatars" as we learn during a feature segment on the last DVD, literally carry a special blood, which is colored blue and called the *Vita Divinae*. This blood is the source of their amazing powers to heal or destroy. These avatars are not rooted in either good or evil, but grow toward their final incarnation of those forces through twists and turns. Ben Hawkins, who is a fugitive from a chain gang and wanted as a murderer, joins the wandering Carnevale at a tragic moment. He slowly learns of his destiny as a healer and avatar of goodness in the search for his long lost father. Brother Justin, a minister and man of good works slowly becomes the embodiment of a demon. From the gnostic perspective, it is no accident that a third figure, a Roma fortune teller in the Carnevale named Sofie (Sophia) is a third avatar, called the Omega. She plays a decisive role in the drama of light and dark during the final episode.

There is also an interesting character, named Wilfrid Talbot Smith, who is described as an *Occultist*. He introduces the lost Gospel of Matthias and other volumes of hidden lore that describe the succession and prophecies regarding the avatars throughout history. The hidden gospel is also linked the Knights Templar, who appear both in their original form during visionary flash-backs and in their contemporary form as members of a seedy masonic lodge in New Mexico. That they have these prophetic gospels buried in their library and do not even realize their significance is telling. Ben Hawkins' father, Henry Scudder, who is also an avatar in the blood succession, joins the Templars specifically to steal these holy books out from under their noses. The Knights Templar play a peripheral role in the drama of the Avatars as guardians of the sacred bloodline, but their symbols and history are everywhere in the background, influencing the course of events. This also implies that this secret history goes back to the beginning of creation and that there have always been secret societies who served as guardians.

For a show that runs the gamut from the nuclear bomb tests at Alamogordo to the Middle Ages, *Carnevale* sums up the hidden history of the avataric bloodline in wonderfully coherent terms. The background of life in the Carnival forms the perfect story telling matrix for a complex and powerful human drama. I cannot really do justice to the breadth of the story, so I include the Wikipedia article link above in the hopes that you will read it and watch and learn from Carnevale. As was the case with *Twin Peaks, Carnevale* was cut short after only two seasons although we know that Season Three would have focused on Sofie and the battle between good and evil raging in her soul. I always stop to think that it is amazing that any of these shows saw the light of day and managed to show what they did on American television.

Marebito: Takashi Shimizu 2004

(The Deros and the Men in Black)

Marebito is a film which focuses upon the underworld visions of Richard Sharpe Shaver, who should be no mystery to anyone who has read my previous articles. The story begins with a television news cameraman who is locked in ennui and a sense of hopelessness. He happens to film a bizarre scene in the Tokyo Underground with a man committing suicide by stabbing himself in the eye. The man's gaze is focused upon something that no one else can see. The cameraman is fascinated and becomes obsessed with finding out what the suicide was looking at that could have caused him to take his own life in such a bizarre way. Slowly but surely, the cameraman uncovers hidden layers of experience that lead him downward into the underground world described by Shaver and even highlighted by the cameo appearance of H.P Lovecraft's *Mountains of Madness*. Shaver and Lovecraft drank from the same fountain of inspiration in many ways and this merging of mythos is a wonderfully creative moment. Deep inside the Hidden World, the cameraman discovers a young woman, shackled and seemingly in a coma somewhere in the mountains of madness. He brings her back to his apartment and the rest of the story focuses upon his growing thralldom to her and his horrendous discovery when she awakes. Throughout the film, he starts seeing bizarre creatures, part animal, part human, whom he learns to be the Dero of Shaver Mystery lore. They do not interact with him, but gradually lead him to a terrifying encounter with an otherworldly Man in Black, who confronts him with the threat that he must continue with the woman or he will be killed. *Marebito* is a very personal vision of the Shaver Mystery and the works of Lovecraft and it rewards repeated viewing with more and more layers of meaning. It is also a genuinely disturbing film that perfectly captures the intensely paranoiac feelings that the Shaver books engender. There is the unmistakable feeling that everything we experience in day to day life is simply a smokescreen or a dream. This same sentiment is expressed in *Twin Peaks* in many ways and is a common denominator for many gnostic films and books. I would even say that it is a central idea for gnostic art as a whole and a way to distinguish the genuinely gnostic work of art. True gnosis sees the reality that we shy away from in our daily lives and it is a mixed reality of inspiration and horror.

Beyond Lemuria: Poke Runyon, 2007

(The Draconians and the Lothinians)

Again, the works of Richard Sharpe Shaver form the perfect backdrop for a gnostic tale of Light and Dark; Dero and Tero. Poke Runyon has done a wonderful job of pulling together many disparate strands of occult history into a story of two secret societies at war for the human soul. The Draconians are serpent worshippers who are in contact with the Dero civilization of the Underworld. They travel to Mount Shasta to meet with the Dero in the flesh and their experience is more than what they had bargained for. Interestingly, the Draconians have been infiltrated by high level intelligence agents from the US government, who have their own agenda in finding and testing weapons that can be used against the Dero. This reaches into the whole UFO-Intelligence question from an interesting perspective. Again, this is something that we found in *Twin Peaks* with the Project Bluebook connection. I might suggest that this purely conspiratorial element finds a perfect matrix in the wider gnostic battle between Light and Dark, since the Outsiders may be Angels, Demons, Tero, Dero, Aliens or who knows what! During an episode in the earlier parts of the film, a professor who has learned too much about the Draconians dies in an episode of spontaneous human combustion, generated by the Dero rays. The lesson that seeking hidden wisdom can be dangerous is a universal in the gnostic tradition.

Meanwhile, as the Draconians descend into the depths, the Lothinians or followers of the Light ascend Mount Shasta and receive visions that are inspired by the famous 19th Century occult classic, *Phylos the Thibetan: A Dweller on Two Worlds* by Frederick Spenser Oliver. What is central to the film is that the same actors play *both* the Draconians and Lothinians. The hero of the story, young William Morgan (need I remind you of the role of that name in Masonic history?) must choose between Light and Dark. The setting of the Holy Mountain in Shasta along with the Shaver Mystery was a stroke of inspiration. The themes coalesce perfectly. For a semi professional production, *Beyond Lemuria* has its moments of cheesiness, but as a whole, it is well worth viewing as a gnostic film.

The Banshee Chapter: Blair Erickson 2013

(MKUltra, the CIA and Other-Dimensional creatures)

I include *The Banshee Chapter* since it touches upon several of the themes we have already explored. The story is about a young man exploring the research into psychedelic drugs undertaken during the MKUltra experiments, funded by the CIA during the 1960's. What he discovers is that the drug he is taking is not what it seems to be. Rather than a psychedelic trip, he encounters a being from another dimension. His subsequent disappearance becomes an obsession for a young woman whom he had known in college. During her search for him, she uncovers the secret research, the lab where it was done and the whole story of how the US Government secretly bought into contacting an other-dimensional race of beings who, yes, actually wish to infiltrate human society. The story is loosely based upon H.P. Lovecraft's short story, "From Beyond" in which a scientist discovers a way to contact and touch other dimensions, to the detriment of Humanity. The Banshees of the story are not unlike the Deros of Shaver and their quest to inhabit the upper echelons of the Government is not unlike the story of the Black Lodge in *Twin Peaks*. Echoes of "The Body Snatchers" and questions of identity theft mesh strongly with contemporary fears and paranoia. Again, as a micro-budget horror film, The Banshee Chapter manages to impress with its vision of an alien invasion. The entry of the *Other* is central to the Gnostic story, since in the presence of *Otherness* and the *Anomalous* we touch upon the central Mysteries of Creation. High Strangeness shows us that we are on the trail!

True Detective: Nic Pizzolatto January 12th, 2014 to March 9th, 2014

(The Order of the Yellow Sign (Based on Robert W. Chambers *The King in Yellow*))

As my final entry, I am going to pitch the idea that the first season of *True Detective* was not only a compelling story based on *The King in Yellow* but that it expressed even deeper levels of gnostic experience. I can barely go into the complexity of the series but suffice it to say that it is, like *Twin Peaks*, rooted in the investigation of the ritual murder of a young woman with aspects so bizarre that only an otherworldly source could suffice to explain them. By the end of the last episode, the two detectives have uncovered a secret society called the Order of the Yellow Sign, which is attempting to reveal the other-worldly City of Carcosa from the Robert W. Chambers' book *The King in Yellow*. The Order is literally trying to make the City of Darkness manifest on our planet, in order to descend the entire World into Chaos, Decay and Madness.

These powerful members of Louisiana government and society who form the Order desire to gain the power of being followers of the King in Yellow through child abuse, murder and torture. The chief character who is the serial murderer behind many of these acts mentions during the last episode that he could "almost feel the infernal levels" descending to earth. That chilling statement defines what the Order of the Yellow Sign was aiming at. As is the case with almost all of these stories, the Orders of darkness seek to bring the Darkness here as something tangible and powerful; as an *embodied force* that roams the Earth at will and destroys it in an apocalyptic nightmare. In this case, as in many others we have seen, the King in Yellow is actually not native to the Earth but dwells in the alien worlds of the star cluster known as the Hyades:

> Along the shore the cloud waves break,
> The twin suns sink behind the lake,
> The shadows lengthen
> In Carcosa.
>
> Strange is the night where black stars rise,
> And strange moons circle through the skies,
> But stranger still is
> Lost Carcosa.
>
> Songs that the Hyades shall sing,
> Where flap the tatters of the King,
> Must die unheard in
> Dim Carcosa.
>
> Song of my soul, my voice is dead,
> Die thou, unsung, as tears unshed
> Shall dry and die in
> Lost Carcosa.
>
> – "Cassilda's Song" in *The King in Yellow*, Act 1, Scene 2. From
> Robert W. Chambers' *The King in Yellow*, published in 1895.

It is the *Other*; the *Alien* that embodies the gnostic darkness in so many of these stories. Chambers book is a collection of short-stories through which runs the theme of a French play entitled "The King in Yellow" set in an alien world. Merely reading or watching the second act of the play is reputed to be enough to create madness, despair and decay. H.P. Lovecraft would incorporate that idea into his famous *Necronomicon* of the mad poet Abdul Alhazred. Nic Pizzolatto, the series writer and producer, is a writer of Weird stories in the Chambers-Lovecraft tradition and clearly understands the ripeness of the moment for revealing that dark gnosis to contemporary popular culture. What makes the Weird Story both gnostic and unsettling in general is that it reveals the uncomfortable truth that we are not alone in the Universe and that we are, indeed, a barely significant scrap of life on a tiny dirtball in a neglected corner of a galaxy in the middle of an infinite nothingness.

This is the gnostic quest then as defined in these stories we have discussed: to discover meaning and the precious link to the Absolute that burns within each of us as a tiny spark. Each of these works of art depicts a battle that each of us faces daily. Fanning the tiny spark to a flame is the work of Gnosis but it is constantly intruded upon by the Dark and those who would seek to delude or confuse us. There are those who follow the Dark to the Light and those who pile Light upon Light. Each of these stories teaches us to find ourselves in that struggle for there is no guarantee that the Light will prevail unless it is the individual who embodies it. What is heartening is that these stories universally focus upon the humanity of the individual and the strength of the Light regardless of the depth of the Dark.

Bosie and The Beast

Nina Antonia

Wait and watch and watch and wait,
He shall pay the half and the whole,
Now or then, or soon or late,
(Steel or lead or hempen cord,
And the devil take his soul!)

"A Ballad of Hate", Lord Alfred Douglas, September 1894

Each century has its spirits of disturbance, those beings whose actions affect the very fabric of society either by default or design. In the case of Lord Alfred "Bosie" Douglas, a mutually impassioned attachment with Oscar Wilde created a maelstrom. However, Douglas did not consciously pursue controversy. A man of unguarded passions, Lord Alfred came from an ancient if aristocratic lineage descended from blood-thirsty Scottish chieftains and blighted with instability; 'The mad, bad line' as Oscar Wilde once referred to the Douglas clan, who at the time were presided over by the fearsome John Sholto Douglas, the eighth Marquess of Queensberry. His title alone would have guaranteed Lord Alfred social renown unlike his shadowy *bête noire* Aleister Crowley, who of less eminent birth-right had to create his own mythology as "The Great Beast, 666" a.k.a "The Wickedest Man In The World." No one worked harder for infamy's crown than Crowley, yet Douglas hardly had to break a sweat to utterly annihilate his own reputation whilst being universally condemned for ruining Oscar Wilde and all before turning 25. In the spring of 1895, when Wilde was put on trial and crucified in the dock for homosexuality, Lord Alfred was cast in the role of temptation, forever taking his place in history. Amongst the Douglas related evidence used against Wilde was the "Red Rose-Leaf" letter which commences:

My own Boy,

Your sonnet is quite lovely, and it is a marvel that those red rose-leaf lips of yours should have been made no less for music of song than for madness of kisses. Your slim gilt soul walks between passion and poetry. I know Hyacinthus, whom Apollo loved so madly, was you in Greek days...

Always with undying love.
Yours
Oscar

Aleister Crowley would later turn at least some of the "Red Rose-Leaf" contents against L.A.D, trying him through literary means. Though now regarded as Wilde's "Homme Fatale", Douglas was not the lone component that brought about the playwright's imprisonment on charges of gross indecency, a legal immolation that showed both justice and Britain at its very worst. The terrible series of events that led to Oscar Wilde's trial is too complex for easy deduction, at least for the purpose of this essay, but it placed Bosie in a scapegoat's spotlight. Following Wilde's incarceration, Lord Alfred Douglas was socially ostracised, deemed the masculine equivalent of a scarlet woman and A.C. sharpened his claws. What is surprising about Aleister Crowley's particularly virulent attacks upon Lord Alfred is his unusual readiness to align himself with public opinion. A.C. after all loathed convention, venerated intrigue, and had relationships with both men and women. In his excellent book *Alfred Douglas – A Poet's Life and His Finest Work*, biographer Caspar Winterman's succinctly notes:

> Envy! One cannot wholly rid oneself of the impression that the mud which over the years had been slung at Lord Alfred derives in part, consciously or unconsciously, from this feeling. After all, most of us aren't really beautiful. Most of us are not of noble birth. Most of us are not so charming as to be capable of charming charming people like Oscar Wilde – *if* we ever meet them that is. And then we cannot write poetry – at least not as well as to gain the praise of masters like Stéphane Mallarmé. Bosie was extremely privileged. That irked and continues to irk.

Although my favourite of Aleister Crowley's aliases has always been "Little Sunshine" – produced during a 1934 libel case – he was usually prone to loftier titles, assuming at different times the aliases of Laird Boleskine, Lord Boleskine and Lord Lockey. Crowley's predilection for pseudonyms probably dates back to childhood, when his mother, inspired by the *Book of Revelations*, bestowed upon him the soubriquet of "The Beast"; Lord Alfred had to make do with the rather less imposing pet name of "Bosie". Only five years in age separate the two; Lord Alfred having arrived via gilded stalk on October 22nd, 1870, whilst Aleister descended upon Warwickshire on October 12th, 1875, later commenting, "It has been remarked a strange coincidence that one small county should have given England her two greatest poets" – this of course is not a reference to Bosie who alighted in Worcester, home of the sauce – but to Shakespeare. The early flowering of both Aleister and Alfred's poetic talents bloomed whilst at university. Douglas being the elder was always one dainty leap ahead, entering Magdalen College, Oxford, in 1889. Making up for a fragrantly lackadaisical approach to his studies, Bosie drew praise for a melancholy poem, "Autumn Days", which was published in the *Oxford Magazine*. The lilt of regret that runs through "Autumn Days" is at odds with the daring and frivolous image of Douglas as a young man and could be considered a prelude to the catastrophe that was to follow. The stage was set in the summer of 1891, when the poet Lionel Johnson introduced Lord Alfred Douglas to Oscar Wilde and a love missile was unwittingly aimed at polite society. It would take four years to detonate, creating the greatest scandal of fin de siècle England and decimating Wilde and Douglas in the process. But foresight – much like hindsight – is the tidy province of casual bystanders and historians. Oscar Wilde, married with children and approaching middle age, became infatuated by Bosie who at 20 possessed a "flower-like" beauty (according to George Bernard Shaw) and thus commenced one of the most complex liaisons of all time. The relationship bore elements of co-dependency; being both rapturous and fraught, not to mention dangerous as to be homosexual made them sexual outlaws. Douglas was needy, Wilde besotted, reconciliations inevitably followed rows but the poetry was unsurpassable, the love letters sublime, O.W.'s plays hugely successful, the highs greater than heaven and the lows more desolate than the grave. Under Wilde's spell, Lord Alfred emerged as one of the most promising poets of the age, although his university education went up in a blaze of blackmail threats and red rose leaves.

In December 1894, *The Chameleon*, a student magazine started by John Francis Bloxam that promised "A bazaar of dangerous and smiling chances", published "Two Loves" and "In Praise of Shame", by Lord Alfred Douglas, which were to be raked over at Wilde's trial. In the latter, Bosie employed a lyrical, symbolism, in which "shame" – an allusion to homosexuality – is exalted. In this he was utterly fearless as "In Praise of Shame" demonstrates:

> Last night unto my bed methought there came
> Our lady of strange dreams, and from an urn
> She poured live fire, so that mine eyes did burn
> At sight of it. Anon the floating flame
> Too many shapes, and one cried: I am Shame
> That walks with Love, I am most wise to turn
> Cold lips and limbs to fire; therefore discern
> And see my loveliness, and praise my name.
>
> And afterwards, in radiant garments dressed
> With sound of flutes and laughing of glad lips,
> A pomp of all the passions passed along
> All the night through; till the white phantom ships
> Of dawn sailed in. Whereat I said this song,
> Of all sweet passions Shame is loveliest.

In the year of Wilde's trial, Aleister Crowley entered Trinity College, Cambridge. Certain aspects of Crowley's university life – occult awakenings aside – bear a similarity to those of another poet. Whilst at Trinity College, Crowley embarked on a relationship with an older man, Herbert Charles Jerome Pollitt, who introduced him to the world of decadent literature and influenced his poetic craft. A friend of Aubrey Beardsley and a keen art collector, Pollitt also performed female roles, including that of "Diane D'Rougy" at Cambridge's Footlight Club. They enjoyed a passionate affair during which Crowley dashed off several poems praising shame, including "The Ballad of Passive Pederasty":

> Of man's delight and man's desire
> In one thing is no weariness –
> To feel the fury of the fire,
> And writhe within the close caress
> Of fierce embrace, and wanton kiss
> And final nuptial done aright,
> How sweet a passion, shame, is this...

During his courtship with Pollitt, A.C also penned a scathing offensive against a Cambridge homosexual who supported Wilde's cause, which was issued in "Mysteries, Lyrical and Dramatic" (1898). There was an unexpected incongruity in Crowley's feelings towards Wilde. The Beast's ambivalence to O.W is adroitly summarised by Timothy D'Arch Smith in the pamphlet, *Bunbury*, in which he explains:

> Crowley was not wholeheartedly in favour of Oscar Wilde. He found his behaviour snobbish, his writings second-rate and his amatory alignment fraudulently irresponsible in that Wilde failed to grasp the enormous, if limited, on occasion dangerous, spiritual forces to which he was exposed. He particularly objected to Wilde's addiction to irrumation which, in magical terms, he condemned as vampiric. Parallel, however, to this disapproval – the fact, doctrinally, that Wilde disobeyed his True Will – ran Crowley's abhorrence of British hypocrisy which had led to Wilde's downfall...

A.C was to find himself on the fringes of the Wilde coterie, courtesy of Pollitt who introduced him to Oscar's publisher, Leonard Smithers. The association not only provided a home for his poetry, under the title of *White Stains* but as part of a literary milieu, Crowley also became privy to certain anti-Bosie inferences.

White Stains was issued in a limited edition of 100 copies in May 1898. Exactly one year later, in May 1899, Lord Alfred's second collection of poetry *The City of The Soul* was published. Neither *White Stains*, due to its contents, nor *The City of The Soul*, because of L.A.D's reputation, bore the name of the author, Crowley plumbing for a pseudonym, George Archibald Bishop, whilst Douglas settled on the more classic "anonymous". It is unlikely that A.C rejoiced in the publication of *White Stains* with Pollitt as by then they had gone their separate ways. To Crowley's regret, Pollitt had no interest in the Magickal workings that he had begun to pursue, having been initiated into the Golden Dawn. Bosie, however, celebrated the publication of *The City of The Soul* in the company of Oscar Wilde, their glasses tilted to the stars under the Parisian night.

One of the great mysteries to "Bosie Bashers" (a term devised by L.A.D. biographer

Caspar Wintermans) has always been the continuation of relations between O.W. and Lord Alfred after the playwright was released from prison but perhaps Wilde's words "I cannot live without you", sent to Bosie in a note, might in some way explain this. Their reunion overrides the scourging tones Wilde employed in his prison letter "De Profundis" to Bosie. Written in Reading Gaol, in the most dreadful conditions, O.W. was under the misconception that his "graceful boy with a Christ-like heart" had abandoned him and did not hold back. "De Profundis", sadly, was to prove the whammy from beyond the grave but that was as yet come. A distraught Bosie led the mourners at Wilde's funeral on December 3rd, 1900, at Bagneux on the outskirts of Paris. How bleak the thought of one of life's most extravagant peacocks being interred in a pauper's grave. Douglas, in a letter to his friend More Adey, would write, "I am miserable and wretched about darling Oscar… what is to be done with one's life? I simply don't know." By the time Wilde was reinterred at Père-Lachaise, a decade later, Lord Alfred had found the answer, having embraced Catholicism with a zealousness that would match Crowley's occult devotion and like The Beast, he had also married. However, Lady Olive Douglas (née Custance) a colonel's daughter, kept the ring on her finger longer than Lady Rose Boleskine (née Kelly.) Having obtained a divorce, Rose departed from Crowley's life in November, 1909, coinciding with the intensification of the relationship between The Beast and the visionary poet Victor Neuburg. A superlative account of their union is given by Jean Overton Fuller in *The Magical Dilemma of Victor Neuburg*. With A.C. acting as Guru to Neuburg's student/seer, their Magickal workings were potent enough to break the devotee's mental and physical health, ably abetted by beatings with gorse and nettles; "A homosexual sadist" was how Victor affectionately referred to his esoteric master in his notes. Although Crowley berated Neuburg for his Jewish ancestry, The Beast nonetheless remained in touch with his family, issuing a telegram that read "Send £500 or you will never see your son again." Unsurprisingly, this brought about the desired results. There is no doubt that Aleister Crowley was a mystic and magician who sought to rip asunder the confines of life but there was a price to pay as Jean Overton Fuller attested: "If ever a man went off his head through the occult sciences, it was Crowley." Many years after Neuburg had cut ties with The Beast, cowed by the belief that A.C. had cursed him, Lord Alfred Douglas paid a visit to Victor's home on the Sussex Downs. The reason for the call is not specified in Overton Fuller's book but he never got over the threshold, Victor's wife, Kathleen, unceremoniously shutting the door in his face. Perhaps she feared it was in some way connected to The Beast's anti-Bosie poems dating back to 1910, when Neuburg had still been in Crowley's thrall. The poems, "The Child" and "A Slim Gilt Soul" dedicated to "Lord A" had appeared in a collection of The Beast's work under the title *The Winged Beetle*. In a handsome 1992 facsimile edition of *The Winged Beetle* (Teitan Press) editor Martin P. Starr makes a curious observation in the introduction, stating that "A Slim Gilt Soul" … "Is alleged to have provoked the highly litigious Douglas to pursue Crowley in court but to no avail." Though eminent in his Beastly knowledge, Starr's wording is evasive and misleading. Some clarity is shed upon the matter in *Oscar Wilde and The Black Douglas* (1949). Written by Bosie's nephew, the book does Lord Alfred few favours save for this one: "In 1910 that enigmatic and somewhat sinister personage, the late Aleister Crowley, honoured Bosie – whom one gathers he did not like – with a lampoon in the best eighteenth-century manner. For once Bosie did not take action. In this he was well advised. Aleister Crowley was a rich man and an experienced litigant, with a power of invective that left nothing to be desired." One has the sense that The Beast was chomping at the bit for Bosie to take the bait and "A Slim Gilt Soul" was the opening salvo – as the first three verses establish.[1]

> Few men are given, 'twixt heaven and hell,
> To play one part supremely well.
> On all time's tablets there are few
> Who make a first-rate show of two,
> While those who perfectly play three
> We knew not, until you were he.
>
> For what were lovelier on the lawn
> Than you, pearl-naked to the dawn,
> Wrapped in a scarlet dressing-gown
> Not thirty miles from London town,
> That "observed of all observers" – save
> That Scotland Yard, serene and suave,
> When trouble came, went tramping by;
> Closed one, and winked the other eye.
>
> How pleasantly you must have smiled:
> "I left them, and I left them wild":
> Though certainly they had abhorred
> The task of locking up a lord.
> For a more tragic role you played
> Your master neatly you betrayed.
> His shame and torture, turned your leer
> To a snarl – your drab's smile to a sneer,
> Quickened, when afterwards your help
> He needed to a currish yelp…

In *The King of the Shadow Realm*, John Symonds, biographer of The Beast and his literary executor, observed:

> Early in his life, Crowley made the discovery that he could say untruthful
> and horrid things about people – that they were prostitutes or drug
> addicts or thieves or cowards or just "unimaginable shits" – and there

---

1 Given that A.C sometimes liked to play games and scatter clues in his poetry, he surely cannot have overlooked that in "A Slim Gilt Soul" he imbues L.A.D. with qualities usually attributed to the triple faced moon Goddess – maid, mother and crone – whose consort is the horned God. Coincidentally, or perhaps not, Wilde gave Douglas the title "The Triad of The Moon" for three incomparably beautiful sonnets that appeared in "The City of The Soul."

the slander would remain or quietly evaporate in the air. Who was to deny it? He did not say these things of course to the person herself. Against the defenceless or those whom he knew were not going to get themselves embroiled with so shocking a person as Aleister Crowley, he would sometimes say malicious things in a letter or in print. It was a characteristic he shared with the paranoid Lord Alfred Douglas.

Was it any wonder Bosie was paranoid? Unfortunately, it was a Douglas family trait, the Marquess of Queensberry suffering from delusions that the "Oscar Wilders" were after him shortly before the end of his life. As well as acting as Crowley's biographer, Symonds also wrote a mischievous book entitled *Conversations with Gerald* (Duckworth 1974.) A playful account of Gerald Hamilton's adventures, the book not only explores Hamilton's recollections of lodging with The Beast in Berlin but also covers his friendship with Lord Alfred Douglas. Early on in *The Conversations*, the subject of L.A.D.'s mental instability is raised, Hamilton remarking, "Bosie Douglas was a perfect client for a first-class psychiatrist, but in those days psychology had hardly been invented, at least in England." Symonds seeks to elicit further information: "Apart from his somewhat obvious persecution mania, were there other symptoms that you noticed?" "Symptoms of what?" "Of peculiar behaviour." "Isn't persecution mania enough?" said Gerald...

Lord Alfred Douglas was not an astute man and possessed an uncanny knack for acquiring enemies, which grew as the years darkened. George Bernard Shaw noted the split in Bosie's persona, "There is Douglas the poet and the hereditary Douglas." Lord Alfred was a creature of extremes, the louche youth transforming into an ardent Roman Catholic which informed an incipient homophobia and with it a sense of moral righteousness that had Crowley rearing up on his hairy haunches. The irony is that The Beast was just as devout, albeit to different Gods, whilst in his *Confessions* he refutes the sexual aspect of his relationship with Pollitt, stating, "To him I was a mind – no more..." Though A.C. speaks of his former Cambridge lover with immense affection, the negation of the erotic elements of the relationship is explained by Lawrence Sutin in *Do What Thou Wilt*... "Crowley was willing to be iconoclastic when it came to Christianity, but he felt compelled to take a virulent stance against the effeminate decadence as perceived by late Victorian society – of homosexuals." (St. Martin's Press, 2000) The second of The Beast's anti-Bosie pieces, "The Child", an acrostic ode written a year before Bosie's full conversion to the Church of Rome, references one of L.A.D.'s earlier poems, "Rejected." Composed in 1896, "Rejected" finds the poet abandoned by Wilde in the guise of Apollo whilst renouncing Christ and is beautifully wrought, concluding; "And now I am lost in the mist. Of the things that can never be. For I will have none of Christ. And Apollo will none of me." Crowley lacerates the sentiments; "Cry out on Apollo; he laughs at the whine. Evoke we a soul nor of man nor divine. Deep-throned in a darker, unspeakable shrine."

To venerate Wilde's final resting place at Père-Lachaise cemetery, the sculptor Jacob Epstein designed a controversial monument featuring an exotic winged chimera that manifested facets of Wilde's poem "The Sphinx"... "Whose pallid burden, sick with pain, watches the world with wearied eyes, And weeps for every soul that dies, and weeps for every soul in vain." To preserve the statue's modesty and protect the general public, a tarpaulin was erected to obscure the sphinx's sex. This attempt at art censorship was a red rag to The Beast. On November 5th, 1911, A.C., having notified the press of his intentions, visited Père-Lachaise and whipped away the offending tarpaulin. Epstein was less than pleased. To maintain the sphinx's privacy, a butterfly was placed over the offending organ, which The Beast swiped. Returning to London, his appearance at the Café Royal, sporting the butterfly, fig-leaf style, brought a rapturous response from onlookers. The Café Royal, incidentally, had been a favourite rendezvous of Wilde and Douglas but fortune's wheel had long since turned.

In the poem "Beauty and the Hunter", Bosie had mused, "Where lurks the shining quarry, swift and shy, Immune, elusive, unsubstantial? In what dim forests of the soul, where call, No birds and no beasts creep?" But The Beast still had his quarry in his sight, though he would remain dormant until the baleful contents of "De Profundis" was revealed to Lord Alfred during a court case in February, 1913. From beyond the veil, Douglas was convicted of crimes against the soul by the man he had loved, when the unexpurgated prison letter was made public knowledge. For the second time, Bosie's life went up in flames along with many of the more tender notes that Wilde had written to him, which he burned. Crowley energetically reaped a harvest of withered red rose leaves, including a hypothesis of the events that led to Wilde's trial, which he called "The Danger of Bunburying" in a correspondence with Robert Hamilton Bruce Lockhart, the British vice-consul in Moscow. The subject is incisively covered by Timothy D'Arch Smith in his leaflet *Bunbury* which contains notes on the subtext of Wilde's play "The Importance of Being Earnest." A play upon a play upon a play… Crowley's account to the vice-consul alleges that Oscar one day took the train to Banbury and on the journey encountered a young man who he arranged to meet in Sunbury and thus "Bunbury" came to be. The Beast's theory as explained to Lockhart, continues… "For our author (Wilde) began a series of frequent and unexplained absences. The talented author of so many sonnets (Bosie) the same who is now the consummation of purity in English morals, found these absences suspicious and jumped as women (sic) will to a correct conclusion although without definite evidence. There was a tremendous row, and in the event he determined to ruin his friend." As the author of *The Book of Lies*, Crowley once remarked: "Keep people ignorant of the facts of nature and make them fighting drunk on bogey tales." Or should that have been Bosie?

Amongst the many mysteries in the life of Lord Alfred Douglas, perhaps the greatest is why no one gently escorted him to a secluded secret location where he could have concentrated on his consummate poetry and prayed in private, gently sequestered from worldly woes. In the aftermath of the "De Profundis" court case his paranoia would have understandably reached a nadir but it was also well-founded as outside contrivance had played a part in his public humiliation. Unfortunately, with little impulse control, Lord Alfred was an unmitigated public relations disaster, more often than not tumbling into the claws of his enemies of whom none was archer than The Beast. The idiosyncratic decision to make a gruff tabloid hack, Thomas William Hodgson Crosland, his left-hand man when he became the editor of *The Academy* newspaper in 1907, might be attributed to the irresistible pull between the aristocratic and those of a knavish disposition. However, it could also have been a misconception of masculinity, Bosie's father having been a rough-hewn lout that caused Douglas to appoint as his deputy an irascible unkempt, alcoholic whose tie he used to straighten prior to social occasions. How far from the days of the finely dressed decadents had Douglas wandered? In its initial phase, *The Academy* had a literary bias, but as time passed and the fading scent of sin was supplanted by papal incense, the paper became political and censorious; "It has become more than ever important that literature should be kept free from viciousness, prurience and improper suggestion" piped the former pin-up boy of the aesthetic movement. Bosie's poetry also altered, the wonder that he had experienced in the era of Wilde succeeded by religious reveries that on occasion verge on idolomania. Even at their strangest, as "Prayer for Protestant Children" verifies, fearing as it does for the little darlings "doomed to keep close company with darkness"… Douglas could still turn a perfect phrase. The quiet beauty of his finest poetry was now hidden behind the besieged fortress of his heart, whilst his mind fought a thousand screaming battles, just as his blood-maddened ancestors had once done. Crosland became Bosie's attack dog and vicious was he. Worn down by court cases and having lost custody of his son, Raymond, to Colonel Custance, his father-in-law, Bosie foolishly let Crosland loose across the pages of an "autobiographical account" entitled "Oscar Wilde and Myself" (1914) a bitter rebuke to "De Profundis." The dark ink of hurt was once again made public, with Crosland as uncouth emissary and Wilde ridiculed and denounced. All was manna to Crowley but it was a book solely credited to Crosland, *The First Stone*, that saw The Beast return in fevered pursuit of Lord Alfred Douglas and his sidekick.

Under the auspices of society hostess, Elizabeth Gwendolen Otter a.k.a "E.G.O.", two editions of a privately issued pamphlet, *The Writing on The Ground* was produced in 1913. Displaying the quote "Whosoever is without sin amongst you let him cast the first ston'" on the cover, *The Writing on The Ground* ably demonstrates The Beast's aptitude for rip-roaring malevolence. Both versions of the pamphlet are prefaced by a brief introduction that whilst avoiding naming Douglas, sites Crosland and fangs bared, rounds on the "Master and his Jackal." "A Slim Gilt Soul" is represented in the first and subsequent edition but Crowley's critique of "The City of The Soul" (TITEL??), which he dubbed "A Galahad in Gomorrah," only appears in volume one. Presented in the manner of a spoof, "A Galahad in Gomorrah" beseeches Lord Alfred Douglas to condemn the works of an anonymous decadent poet, which commences:

> It is very fortunate that even in times when the greatest laxity of morals prevails, in England at least there is always found some austere and noble soul to protest against decadence; to be a witness in the midst of corruption, that there is a standard of pure and lofty thought, a City of the Soul, fortified against all evil, and whose artillery can overwhelm the savage hordes of impurity. We do not think anyone will accuse us of flattery in saying that Lord Alfred Douglas is just such a person, and this is the more striking phenomenon as it so rare to find the true moral greatness associated with poetical genius…

Rarely has anyone pursued their prey with such ardent devotion as Aleister Crowley. With *The Writing on The Ground*, The Beast had hoped to incite Bosie into a courtroom punch-up but was to be sorely disappointed. Proceedings got no further than the somewhat disgruntled aristocrat taking a disconsolate mooch around a block of flats in Chelsea. Unsurprisingly, Crowley's version of events differs from those of Lord Alfred. After Bosie failed to react, A.C. continued to work thematically, penning "The Writing on The Wall":

> In its (sic) book *Oscar Wilde and myself* it professes itself very anxious to persecute the author of *The Writing on The Ground*. The initials of the author were given and her address; my name is also given… "A Galahad in Gomorrah" was republished by Wieland & Co, 33 Avenues S.W. in the *Equinox Vol 1 No IX*. It took no action. Will it return to England to prosecute ME for criminal libel? "Bosie" is a common prostitute, blackmailer, sodomite, and swindler; and my name is Aleister Crowley, and my address 33 Avenue Studios London S.W.

Paranoid though he might have been, and with due cause in this particular instance, Douglas, who refers to the pamphlet as "The Writing On The Floor" makes no mention of seeking legal recourse in *Oscar Wilde and Myself*:

> … Nobody who lived on any of the floors of these flats, from the basement upwards, would own to the slightest connection with it. I mention these facts not because I attach any importance to the pamphlet but because they show to what extraordinary courses my enemies will have resort when their malice gets the better of them…

Having failed to drag to Bosie into the dock, from 1913 onwards The Beast employed different and more subtle tactics, including the covert use of names in his fictional works, as if needing to remind Lord Alfred that he was still on his case. A short story, "The Ideal Idol" (1918), written under the pseudonym of Cyril Custance, is particularly creative. Let us not forget that Custance was the maiden name of Bosie's now estranged wife, Olive. Prefaced as "Two Stories in One, But With Only One Moral", "The Ideal Idol" relays the quest of a 42 year old bachelor called Reggie who goes to the States in search of a bride. This is precisely what Douglas had done until his prior association with Wilde had caused yet another scandal, whereupon he returned to England and married Olive Custance. By calling the main character Reggie, we again return to Bosie, who was parodied by Robert Hichens in the book *The Green Carnation* (1894) as Lord Reggie Hastings. Though Hichen's satire on the vain young aristocrat, Lord Reggie Hastings and his decadent friend, Mr Esme Amarinth, is relatively good hearted, it was withdrawn when the Wilde trial commenced as the comparisons were all too obvious. *The Green Carnation* concludes with Reggie having a marriage proposal declined and much the same happens in "The Ideal Idol." However, Crowley's narrative sees the spurned Reggie receiving a magical stone from a witch that ensures he will indeed find a bride. The lady in question is one Nina Yolande de Montmorency de Carbajal y Calvados. Retiring to the boudoir after the wedding, the bride screams when she sees the bible and transforms into Mephistopheles, who delivers a sermon: "Young man!' he said to the astounded Reggie, 'learn that humanity implies imperfection; those who are not content with the ordinary limitations of life, demand perfection, are liable to find the ideal idol an illusion created by the Devil. However, you have willed it, so if you would be so kind as to throw that book out of the window, I will turn back into Nina Yolande (and all the rest of it) and we can get to bed…" Bosie, the unwilling muse was once again at the mercy of The Beast.

The case of "Bosie and The Beast" must surely be the strangest and most protracted unrequited literary stalking, lasting almost forty years and peaking with *Diary of A Drug Fiend*. Published in 1922, The Beast commits to posterity a pen caricature of Lord Alfred Douglas as "The Earl of Bumble" described as "The slight figure of a young-old man with a bulbous nose to detract from his otherwise remarkable beauty, spoilt thought it was by years of insane passions." At the Earl's heels is his "jackal", T.W.H. Crosland, depicted as "… a huge, bloated, verminous creature… in shabby black clothes, ill-fitting, unbrushed and stained." Though designated a walk on part in the first chapter, the Earl and the Jackal's entrance causes a stir as The Beast continues: "The café sizzled as the men entered. They were notorious, if nothing else and the leader was the Earl of Bumble. Everyone seemed to scent some mischief in the air. The earl came up to the table next to mine, and stopped deliberately short. A sneer passed across his lips. He pointed to the two men. 'Drunken Bardolph and Ancient Pistol,' he said, with his nose twitching with anger. Jack Fordham was not behind with the repartee. 'Well roared, Bottom,' he replied calmly, as pat as if the whole scene had been rehearsed beforehand. A dangerous look came into the eyes of the insane earl. He took a pace backwards and raised his stick…" Needless to say the Earl is given a swift thrashing and ends up prostrate on the floor. Perhaps The Beast felt that by continuing to channel pent-up energies they would impact on Bosie, whose star was not the most stable despite his Christ passion. In religion, Douglas searched for the sanctuary that a turbulent life had failed to offer and with A.C working his tricks, Bosie would have needed one. In pairing the "Earl of Bumble" with his "creature", *Drug Fiend* commemorates an alliance that was already over, Douglas having finally written off his tempestuous friendship with Crosland in a poem entitled "The Unspeakable Englishman":

> You were a brute and more than half a knave,
> Your mind was seamed with labyrinthine tracks
> Wherein walked crazy moods bending their backs
> Under grim loads. You were an open grave
> For gold and love…

Between the seven years that separated the publication of *Diary of A Drug Fiend* and *Moonchild* which, though written in 1917, wasn't issued until 1929, Aleister Crowley took his foot off the accelerator as far as Lord Alfred Douglas was concerned; or perhaps his machinations finally manifested when Bosie, riven with paranoia, published a leaflet accusing Winston Churchill of participating in a Jewish conspiracy. For reviving gibberish that had long been debunked by those of right minds, Douglas ended up being sentenced to six months stir in Wormwood Scrubs. The Beast meanwhile swanned off to Sicily and founded the Abbey of Thelema, where he honed his now famous credos "Do What Thou Wilt Shall Be The Whole of The Law. Love Is The Law, Love Under Will." Lord Alfred Douglas and Aleister Crowley were polar opposites – Bosie a ruined aristocrat from a bygone era struggling with modernity, The Beast a creature of an aeon that had not yet dawned. Both in their own way predicted the future; Douglas as a youth anticipating an impending century of more liberated sexuality while The Beast unapologetically ushered in the Aquarian age. *Moonchild* was to be the penultimate sputtering of the taper in the one-sided feud that never was. In the novel's brief introduction, A.C concludes, "Need I add that, as the book itself demonstrates beyond all doubt, all persons and incidents are purely the figment of a disordered imagination!" The majority of the characters that populate *Moonchild* are drawn from old friends and foes. While the main villain of the piece, who is based on Macgregor Mathers, the former head of The Golden Dawn, bears no resemblance to Bosie, The Beast kept enmity's flag flying and called him "Douglas." This may also be a reference to the journalist James Douglas who slated *Diary of A Drug Fiend*, thus two birds are killed with one stone. But who threw the first?

As the long night drew closer, Lord Alfred Douglas retired to Hove, where he lived in financial penury but not obscurity. Of superfine manners, Bosie still attracted moths to the myth and made his peace with Oscar Wilde. In his autobiography *A Touch of The Memoirs* (1982) actor Donald Sinden fondly evokes his friendship with Bosie. One rarely mixes with "dead" people, for the youthful Sinden had initially assumed Douglas deceased but happily discovered otherwise though their time would be short: "So began a series of visits", wrote Sinden of Bosie, "during which he would talk of his childhood, his time in Oxford, the actors he had known – not many – his court cases, books and writers, and gradually the subject of Oscar Wilde, whom he always recalled with great affection. Sometimes tears welled in his eyes." On March 20th, 1945, Sinden recollects the arrival of a telegram; "'Lord Alfred Died Early This Morning.' Not more than ten of us gathered at his graveside in Crawley as we buried Oscar's 'Rose-lipped youth.' To me, a very kind old man."

No one could have written a finer elegy better than Bosie himself:

> …How sweetly, forged in sleep, some dreams that make
> Swift wings and ships that sail the estranged sea,
> Less roughly than blown rose-leaves in a bowl,
> To harboured bliss. But oh! The pain to wake
> In empty night seeking what may not be
> Till the dead flesh set free the living soul.

> – Second verse, "The Wastes of Time", Lord Alfred Douglas, 1934

The Beast felt compelled to leave a final mark in his last collection of poetry, *Olla,* published in 1946, shortly before his own passing. Dedicated to the "Divine Oscar", the six line poem entitled "The Spring of Dirce" does not wax lyrically in its allusion to Lord Alfred Douglas:

> The purple pageant of my incommunicable woes
> Was painted by the hand of gin-and-water on my nose.
> The mellow gold that filters through my rich autumnal style
> Is minted in me by a superfluity of bile.
> The feet of Christ I worship at appear so thin and pale
> Because of all the skilly that I ate in Reading Gaol.

Aleister Crowley departed from the world on December 1ˢᵗ, 1947, to the blustery serenade of a thunderstorm as the Old Gods beckoned. Multiple accounts of his death from the average to the mythic circulate, as he would have wished. The Beast was far more astute at engineering a public image than Lord Alfred Douglas. Creator of an "anti-religion," The Beast's devotees are legion and he enjoys a prolific cultural afterlife buoyed by an unceasing flow of books, films and articles, whilst the majority of his poetry has been reissued. At Crowley's funeral service, Louis Wilkinson read selected extracts from The Beast's best poem "Hymn To Pan." A.C had specifically requested that his old friend recite the piece for the past is never far from hand and the circle is unbroken. At the age of 16, Wilkinson who also wrote under the name "Marlow" had begun a correspondence with Oscar Wilde that was to last until the playwright's death in 1900. Bosie is now regarded as Saint Oscar's scarlet shadow, his poetry more often than not forgotten in the lost dust of dreams.

Many Thanks to Sandy Robertson, Timothy D'Arch Smith, Clive Harper and with special gratitude to Caspar Wintermans. – NA

FESTIVALS OF SPRING

Aki Cederberg

This text is a chapter from a forthcoming, soon-to-be published book titled Pilgrimage: Journeys in the Kali Yuga. – *Ed.*

Transcendent manhood is the immanent cause of creation; transcendent womanhood is the efficient cause. There cannot be procreation without such union and there cannot be divine manifestation without their cosmic equivalent.

– Shiva Purana

It was twilight as we wandered in the silent forest. Although it was spring, the snow still covered all things as a serene white shroud. We were on a path to a secluded place in the woods close to my home. I had visited that place for several years, albeit before in solitude. As we made our way through the forest, the sky turned dark, glistening with stars, and a sense of vastness overtook me, as I remembered it from my early childhood. And there we stood, under the northern constellations, our breath turning into frost in the cold night air. We were as trembling trees, our roots deep in earth and our arms as branches reaching skyward.

One day later, that heartland in the north was very far away, as were the stars and silence. It was early morning and we were dodging rickshas in the notorious Pahar Ganji area of Delhi, while a legless half-man somehow shuffled past us on the street. Once again, I was among the chaos, the heat and the unrelenting holy madness that is India. We walked up a narrow, run-down staircase to a restaurant on the rooftop of a house. Drinking beer and watching the dirty sunset over this seemingly hopeless city, something familiar came over me. I wondered what the hell I was doing here – again.

After my last journey in Hardwar during the Kumbh Mela festival, I thought I would never return. The unfolding of the events at the Mela had showed me a line in the sand which was not to be crossed. I had explored the Indian esoteric tradition of knowledge as far as I could, and found both wisdom and folly; it had been a process of learning and un-learning. I had come to the conclusion that the esoteric path of India was not one to embarked upon by a European such as myself, who would ultimately remain a foreigner in its realms. At best, what could be found was a new way to see one's own hereditary spiritual landscape in the light of an ancient tradition. Drawing from these experiences and realizations, I had written a book that had recently been published in the Finnish language[1], and I thought the story had come to an end.

Yet, divinely ironic as it was, here I was again. The story had come back to life. My fate seemed somehow entwined with this land and its ancient gods, with the figure of Shiva at the helm. However, this time it was not some forgotten god or mythic longing that had led me back to India, but my new lover: a student of yoga and ayurveda.

As night fell, we headed to the train-station. Our destination was Khajuraho, the remote temple town known throughout the world for its ancient erotic sculptures. As the train took off, a smiling Indian couple offered to share their dinner of rice, dal and chapati with us. I climbed to the top bed of the three-tier sleeper and sipped whiskey from my flask, listening to the all-too familiar sound of the train as it raced through the night. Like the mythic Siren calls that lured sailors toward shipwrecks, this was the sound that always accompanied me during my travels, toward something beautiful perhaps, and dangerous certainly.

As the sun rose next morning, we got in a small riksha and bounced along the country lanes, crossing fields lined with palms trees, eventually passing distant temples and rickety houses in the chilly morning air. I put an ochre colored cloth around my lover's face and shoulders, as the sweet dew of dawn mixed with the smell of burning garbage.

It was still early morning as we walked down the already bustling dirt road of the town. From a shoddy looking seller on the street I bought a paperback called the "Kama Sutra", which was not the ancient text of same name. Obviously geared toward sexual interest, it mostly contained erotic Indian art, along with prudish and unintentionally humorous descriptions. Based on the *Kama Sutra*, but retold here with much less finesse, it described various form of "congress" (sex), along with methods and advice on "striking, biting and quarreling". For instance, it told that for the sake of "mouth congress" (oral sex), courtesans abandon men of high value and become attached to "low persons, such as slaves and elephant drivers." Low persons take note.

The erotic in all its forms, from profound to banal, seemed to underlie everything in Khajuraho. Vendors were selling souvenirs and art of an overwhelmingly amorous nature. We purchased an ornately carved wooden statue of a pair of hands against each other in the common blessing gesture, the *Anjali mudra*. The hands could be opened up to reveal the secret inside: a couple having wild sex under a tree. All these things reflected the deeper meaning of the spring festival during which we had arrived in Khajuraho, by coincidence or destiny.

It was the culmination of the most auspicious of spring rites: *Shivratri*, the great wedding night of lord Shiva and his lady of the mountains, Parvati. On this "Night of Shiva" Indians traditionally stay awake until dawn, participating in offerings to the lingam (phallus of Shiva) resting erect in the yoni of his consort. It is the sign of universal man, *Purusha*, and represents the eternal renewal of life, divine reality, and the springing forth of the creative principle. The lingam is washed repeatedly with milk, yoghurt, ghee and honey water, while *datura* (thorn apple) or *bel* (wood apple) leaves are placed on it as offerings. Throughout the night, hordes of people crowd the temples

---

1 *Pyhiinvaellus*, Salakirjat, 2013.

– sadhus, brahmins, householders, pilgrims, beggars - all devotees of Shiva. In endless repetitions they chant the *Panchakshara*, the "five-syllable" mantra:

ॐ नमः शिवाय

OM NA-MAH SHI-VA-YA

This ancient festival of Shiva and the cult of the phallus still echo throughout the world in similar spring festivals, from Sumeria to ancient Greece, from Tibet to Europe. It still survives in the countless regional traditions, rites, festivities and symbols of mankind. In alchemy it known as *Hieros Gamos*, the sacred marriage. In pre-christian northern Europe, the seat of the cult was located in Uppsala, Sweden, and represented dominantly by a deity with a large phallus, identified as Frikko (commonly known as Frey) by Adam of Bremen. What is so deeply etched into the heart of man cannot be suppressed, and although it sometimes appears in more subtle, hidden forms, it still occupies a most central position in our world.

Close to the main temples of Khajuraho was the Shiv Sagar tank, where devotees came for their ritual bath, especially during this particular night. The tank was surrounded by the hustle and bustle of a fair: camps, tents, street vendors, makeshift shrines and rickety structures with flashy lights scattered throughout the landscape. The streets were crowded with wagons, cars, trucks, rickshas, motorcycles and donkey-carts, cows, dogs and monkeys, cripples, workers, families, schoolchildren, cops, sadhus, beggars, hecklers, tricksters, gawkers, snake-handlers, sellers of everything and nothing, young guys with bleached jeans and cell-phones, ever-present curious bystanders — the usual Indian crowd. It was a sweeping cross between a market, religious gathering and carnival, with chaotic noises, honks and carousel-chimes surreally merging with devotional songs.

We circled the small and more quiet Prem Sagar lake nearby. At the edge of the water was a tiny shrine inside of which a goat was idly chewing on the offerings left therein. An old pipal tree rose through the paved ground with stone images of the gods merging with its roots. In India, the tree itself is a living altar, decorated with bells, colored ribbons, trishuls and murtis. The pipal tree *(Ficus religiosa)*, also known as *bodhi* tree, recognizable by its heart-shaped leafs, is a sacred tree in all of India's native religions. It is under this tree that Shiva sits surrounded by his sages. Another sacred tree, the banyan *(Ficus benghalensis)*, with its thick vines touching the earth, strongly resembles the sadhu holy man with his matted jata locks reaching to the ground. People approach these and other trees for the blessings of their various spirits. The banyan tree is said to embody the blessings of the *Rishis* (the sages of the Vedas). Deriving from *rish*, "to thrust", Rishis embody the spirit of procreation, which is why women tear off pieces from their saris and hang them on the tree so that they might have a child.

I had seen pictures of babas hanging from such trees, their brown and ash-grey limbs merging with the similarly colored trunks and branches. Seeing these striking images, I could not but think of Allfather Odin, the high-god of poetic wisdom, war and magic

One of the Khajuraho temples. (Photo: Justine Cederberg)

in the Nordic tradition. Odin "sacrificed himself to himself", and in a shamanic frenzy hung from the World Tree for nine nights in order to gain knowledge of the runes. The runes were more than mere letters; they were the ever-expansive secrets of the manifest world. I was also reminded of what a baba once told me: that the original temples *were* sacred trees. A temple is something that is built where there is a signature of nature - a spring, a mountaintop, a grove, a tree. Before the edifice of man, these markers of nature were the first temples. This echoed the tradition of my native land as well as most of Europe, where sacred trees still feature prominently in folkways, stories and customs (such as Jul and midsummer), although many people have forgotten their deeper meaning. The trishul of Shiva and the trident-like rune of Odin both mark the same thing: the cosmic World Tree itself, the *axis mundi,* connecting in a tripartite structure the celestial, earthly and chthonic. This structure and principle is seen as existing in everything, not least in man himself (as the phallus), although he may have forgotten it. Certainly there were parallels between these ancient wild gods, who seemed to be drawing me into their realms, toward the great secrets themselves.

Having made our oblations at the tree, we approached the structures of Khajuraho. At the gates we payed the "foreigners only" entrance fee and were frisked by uniformed officers. As we entered the grounds under the brilliant sun, stark silhouettes of ancient monuments stood before us like giants.

Built under the rule of the monarchs of the Chandela dynasty over a span of 200 years, the temples of Khajuraho date back to the 10th century, but are based on a Tantric tradition dating back much farther into prehistory. Occupying twenty-one square kilometers, the temples used to be surrounded by a high wall with eight gates marked by golden palm-trees. As the Chandela dynasty fell, so did the temples fall

Shiva Lingam, Khajuraho. (Photo: Cederberg)

with them. Gradually they were abandoned and forgotten, engulfed by the jungle and eventually covered by the sands of time. Of the original existing eighty temples twenty-two have remained. These remaining temples are now divided into three geographical groups – western, eastern and southern – out of which the western group hosts the largest and most impressive structures. Today, these are perhaps the most unique and famous of all temples in India due to their detailed depictions of divine eroticism.

The sandstone temples are intricately carved with thousands upon thousands of overwhelming, timelessly beautiful and sensual sculptures. Creatures from earth, the heavens and the underworld, gods, men and beasts all populate the edifices of the ancient monuments. Depicted are mythic animals such as Nandi, the bull of Shiva, and a boar incarnation of Vishnu, his surface covered with over six-hundred gods from the Indian pantheon. There are scenes from worldly life: women applying makeup, nursing mothers, musicians, farmers, potters and so on. But the most most dominant and striking among the various motifs present is that of copulation. Voluptuous, big-breasted and heavy-hipped women fill the walls, fully decked out with ornate jewelry and little else. Nude damsels exhibit their well-formed backsides, while casting coy glances over their shoulders. Heavenly maidens seductively pose at every corner. Lovers embrace in ecstasy. Groups of three or more lovers engage in sex, while others watch from the side. Almost every possible sexual act between couples and groups (as well as some animals) is represented and repeated again and again. And of course, as throughout the rest of India, there are Shiva lingams standing erect everywhere.

However, the multitude of portrayals of sex are not merely depictions of perversion run rampant, such as in the decline of ancient Rome. The Khajuraho monuments were built at the height of the culture that gave rise to them. Culture being the expression of the soul of the people who create it, the monuments unveil what was at the core of religion for those people in ancient times: *Maithuna,* sexual union in a ritual context. It seems like all the sculptures, even the ones engaged in more mundane activities, are paused for an eternal moment in witnessing the wedding of Shiva and Parvati – the cosmic union of the male and female. This union not only brings new creatures into life, but is a bridge between worlds of the temporal and of the timeless. It is the sacred marriage of earth and heaven.

Realizing that the experience of union represented by sacred sex is at the core of all life, and that it is an expression of the undivided being variously called god, cosmic being, life force and many number of other things, the ancient people who raised Khajuraho placed this understanding at the center of their worship. The temples pay tribute to the creative forces of the universe which lie at the root of life. The temples are thus a remnant of a time when a more dynamic understanding of the world was still the prevalent norm of the day. They are an ode to purity, a poem set in stone, and represent the confluence of eroticism and religion yet untainted by later ideas of sin and separation. It is in the light of the ecstasy, the passion, the mad abandon, and ultimately the union of the self with the other, which the copulating Shiva-Shakti represents, that other forms of so-called enlightenment pale in comparison. The temples are one of the last remaining bastions of this primeval knowledge, which has survived the destructive onslaught carried out in the name of later ideologies, namely Christianity and Islam. However, degeneration of this knowledge has also happened within modern so-called Hinduism, which has puritanically tried to whitewash the overtly erotic aspects of its mythos, such as Tantra and the worship of Shiva lingam, and reduce them into mere abstract symbols for something wholly different.

If an understanding of sacred sex as embodied in Khajuraho existed in another form in early esoteric Christianity, as has been claimed by various scholars and around which a whole genre of research exists, that understanding has been firmly lost by most modern-day religions and creeds. What was a central sacrament in primordial traditions has become taboo in currently prevailing religions. Instead of a direct experience of the mystery of god, approached through various ecstatic ritual practices such as sex, psychedelic sacraments or ordeals, what we have left are various degenerate priest-classes and written dogmas to act as intermediary forces between us and the sacred we seek. A refined understanding of sexual ecstasy, as carved in the sculptures of Khajuraho, has been displaced. What is essentially joyous, vital and an affirmation of the life principle, has been inverted into something vile, sin-tainted, or abstract and symbolic, or reduced into mere physical action. The various modern-day apologetic interpretations of the supposed "meanings" of the Khajuraho temple art which manage to stand directly in opposition to its apparent nature are forever removed from the direct truths that the art embodies. In such a conflict the concrete and the abstract are forever poised against one another.

It comes as no surprise then that this motif of a celebration of divine union was not well received by the British of the Victorian era. The deserted and overgrown temple complex was rediscovered in the early 1800s by an officer the British Army, who declared their workmanship "beautifully and exquisitely carved", but their

Maidens inside one of the temples of Khajuraho. (Photo: Justine Cederberg)

subject matter "extremely indecent and offensive".

Despite the ever-present tension caused by looming threats at religious festivals in India - terrorist attacks, crowds running amok, violent eruptions - on this night of Shiva something was different. The lines to the main Shiva temple were like throbbing serpents, the crowds large and rowdy, but the spring air was full of revelry. In the mid-day heat, we strolled across the grassy fields from one temple to another, pausing to lay down on the grassy fields outside. In the shades of the ancient seductive statues we took sips of whiskey, embraced and kissed. Doors that were normally closed now seemed to lay open for us. Security guards at the temples welcomed us warmly with loud shouts of "Shiva Parvati!" Possibly, they saw us as an auspicious sign, reminding them of the divine couple of Shiva and his consort Parvati, known to take many, sometimes surprising forms.

Slowly the day turned into twilight, the hour of Shiva, and the temples were being closed for the night. In this liminal hour, we approached the loftiest of the temples, the Kandariya Mahadeva mandir. This temple is built to resemble Mount Kailash in the Himalayas, the abode of Lord Shiva, with its highest peak spire, *sikhara*, rising to thirty one meters, surrounded by eighty-four smaller spires or *urushringas*. Eight hundred sculptures are carved on its interior and exterior walls. The interior of the temple resembles a cave. As we entered the temple grounds, a guard greeted us with the already familiar shout, "Shiva Parvati!" He then led us into the inner chamber, the *Garbha-giha*, where a marble Shiva linga stood in the dark. "Now you sit down and pray", the guard said, and left us to rush all other visitors out from the temple. As we sat in the darkness, the sounds from outside became distant. The ancient stone edifice had darkened with age to the degree that it was hard to even see the ceiling of the cavelike room. Not all places are the same, and this place resonated with the infinite number of invocations conducted here during the course of the ages. I closed my eyes, and thought of Shiva in his form of a column of fire without beginning or end. Instantly, my consciousness expanded like a pillar into space.

Outside the sun was setting. The temple walls, covered with countless couples making love, were gleaming in golden and red.

Leaving the temple grounds, we climbed to the top of a nearby treehouse, and watched the ancient monuments being lit up by colored lights against the darkness. As the lights illuminated the temples, so was this night of Shiva illuminated by the presence of something strong and primal. The celebrations were reaching their peak and there was electricity in the air. We walked through the bustling streets and returned to our guesthouse across a field overlooking the fair.

Incense smoke filled the sweltering air as our shadows moved across the high walls of our room. A typically decrepit guesthouse with cracks in the walls and electric wiring hanging out here and there, we had transformed it into a makeshift temple. A wooden cabinet served as a shrine with candles, flowers and cups filled with to the brim with whisky and a potent aphrodisiac plant. An old, large mirror leaned against the wall, and in the center of the room was our bed. In the distance, we could hear a constant cacophony of clinging bells, wild chanting and shouting.

As echoes of devotion filled the night air, my lover and I worshipped the gods in a more direct way. Rather than seeking effigies of stone, we beheld the divine in each other through the sacrament of sex. It was a rite of spring - violent beauty in a blissful union of opposites. My lover's sweat tasted sweet, as her face blurred and turned into that of some primal goddess. In the mirror we saw our reflection, and here at the flowing confluence of two streams, the sexual and spiritual, we *were* the gods incarnate, the divine couple made flesh.

Finally, exhausted and spent, we drifted into dreams, the night is still resident with Shiva's troupe of ghouls, spirits and beasts – all the wild, untamed forces and personalities of nature.

The next morning, in the afterglow of the night before, we cycled through the quiet countryside, through nearby villages and fields, passing temples and little pastel-hued shacks, dodging calm Hindu cows here and there. Crossing a river, women were doing laundry while carefree children played around a little Shiva lingam on its banks. Eventually we arrived at the eastern group of temples, located slightly outside the Khajuraho center. They were smaller than the ones we had seen the day before, but clearly featured the same motifs. On a field by an Adinath temple (Adinath, the name I was given in initiation, refers to "First Lord" Shiva, and in this case also to the founder of Jainism) hundreds of broken erotic statues lay scattered, fragments embodying a perhaps forgotten knowledge.

At dusk we returned to the center of the town for a final visit to the oldest still functional temple of the Khajuraho structures, dating from circa 900CE, the Matangeshwar mandir. This old temple is revered to the extent that Khajuraho is still sometimes called the "City of Matangeshwar". Entering the temple grounds, we could see it radiating in the distance, its entrance marked by colorful flags.

We followed the winding path leading to the ancient temple. A persistent tout followed us despite our willful ignorance of him, but finally stopped by a large tree growing right by a long staircase ascending to the sacred structure. Finally, we climbed its worn stone stairs and, touching the ground of the threshold and then our foreheads, entered through its gates. Before us stood a giant Shiva lingam, its height and circumference literally enveloping the entire temple. The lingam invoked sublime nobility and awe, its imposing presence a sign of the power that it embodied. And there, on that closing holy night of Shiva, I offered my story, my book, as a gift to the gods. The presiding brahmin priest smiled, and carefully laid the book at the root of the stony colossus.

As we wandered down the stairs and into the night, something had come full circle. The story had returned to its source.

When we would eventually return home some weeks later, it would be Easter. Named after an ancient goddess of dawn, the age-old spring festival filled with hares and eggs marks when the first green would be sprouting forth through the barren winter earth, signifying the eternal return, both in nature and within man himself. In the forest, the snow had finally begun to melt.

Friedrich Hielscher's Vision of the Real Powers

Michael Moynihan

Friedrich Hielscher (1902–1990) is one of the most enigmatic and least-understood Germanic spiritual figures of the twentieth century. This is especially true outside of Germany, where many deceptive myths have been woven about him—most notably in a string of post-WWII exposés of "Nazi occultism," where he appears as a diabolical *éminence noire* who secretly manipulated some of the most powerful personalities in the Third Reich.[1] As lurid as these tall tales may be, the truth about Hielscher's life, ideas, and associations is far more intriguing. And for someone who was already describing himself as a "son of Loki" by the age of sixteen, this should hardly come as a surprise.

Hielscher was born a few years too late to have enlisted as a soldier in the Great War, but he nevertheless shares many qualities with the generation of restless and reckless German WWI veterans who hoped to forge a new nation out of the shattered remnants of their vanquished homeland. Six days after completing his secondary school education in 1919, Hielscher joined a paramilitary *Freikorps* unit that was engaged in border defense against the Poles in Upper Silesia. The unit was soon assimilated into the Reichswehr. When plans arose to take part in the Kapp Putsch, which Hielscher sensed was utterly foolish, he left the military to pursue his university studies. He completed a dual doctorate in legal history and legal philosophy in 1926 with a dissertation titled *Die Selbstherrlichkeit: Versuch einer Darstellung des deutschen Rechtsgrundbegriffs* (Autocracy: An Attempt at a Description of the Foundational Concept of German Law). Hielscher's ideas were heavily indebted to Spengler and Nietzsche, the latter of whom exerted a lasting influence.[2]

Hielscher would also become active within the growing circles of nationalist-revolutionary intellectuals that vied for political influence during the tumultuous

---

1 These yarns are fully unraveled in Peter Bahn, "The Friedrich Hielscher Legend," *TYR: Myth—Culture—Tradition* 2 (2003–2004), 243–62, which is the only reliable overview of Hielscher's life and ideas to yet appear in English. Several in-depth studies of his life and work have been published in German: Peter Bahn, *Friedrich Hielscher 1902–1990: Einführung in Leben und Werk* (Schnellbach: Bublies, 2004); Ina Schmidt, *Der Herr des Feuers: Friedrich Hielscher und sein Kreis zwischen Heidentum, neuem Nationalism und Widerstand gegen den Nationalsozialismus* (Cologne: SH-Verlag, 2004); and, most recently, Kurt M. Lehner's biography *Friedrich Hielscher: Nationalrevolutionär, Widerständler, Heidenpriester* (Paderborn: Schöningh, 2015).

2 On the dissertation, see entry no. 828 in Richard Frank Krummel and Evelyn S. Krummel, *Nietzsche und der deutsche Geist*, vol. 3: *Ausbreitung und Wirkung des Nietzscheanischen Werkes im deutschen Sprachraum bis zum Ende des Zweiten Weltkrieges: Ein Schrifttumsverzeichnis der Jahre 1919–1945* (Berlin: De Gruyter, 1998), 299.

era of the Weimar Republic. His own particular vision was centered on the idea of a mystical Reich as the outward expression of the soul of the German people. The spiritual seeds of this Reich lay not in the medieval Catholic Holy Roman Empire, but in the barbarian era that preceded it. In contrast to his fellow nationalist agitators, who saw things in concrete and materialistic terms, what Hielscher preached was effectively a transcendental political theology.

Not surprisingly, the German Reich that did materialize with Hitler's ascension to power was a far cry from anything that Hielscher had imagined. The fact that Germany was now under the control of the National Socialists—whom Hielscher deemed as "rabble" *(Gesindel)*—could only spell disaster for the nation. By this time Hielscher had attracted a small group of followers, and together they began to formulate a strategy of covert political resistance. This was to be achieved by infiltrating official positions and working behind the scenes. These resistance efforts overlapped with Hielscher's establishment in 1933 of a private "panentheistic heathen church" that called itself the Unabhängige Freikirche (Independent Free Church; UFK). For the remainder of his life Hielscher led this small and secretive group, serving as its theologian, law-giver, and high priest.

Although Hielscher is mostly known for his activities as a Weimar-era nationalist agitator, the personal relationships he cultivated over his life were remarkably varied. Besides the writer Ernst Jünger, with whom he stayed in contact for sixty years, his friends included the liberal politician Theodor Heuss (the first president of the Federal Republic of Germany), the dissident journalist-in-exile Alfred Kantorowicz, and the Jewish philosopher Martin Buber. Unlike many of his fellow nationalists, Hielscher had always rejected biological racism and anti-Semitism. In a 1932 article that he contributed to a monograph on the topic of the "Jewish Question," Hielscher wrote: "One who is superior does not hate. Among the Germans, hatred for the Jews only turns up in places where a secure sense of one's own 'German-ness' *(Deutschtum)* is lacking."[3]

Over the course of the twelve-year Reich, Hielscher and those in his immediate circle managed to achieve a small measure of success in their resistance efforts, mostly by aiding others who were being persecuted by the regime. They were less successful in infiltrating government institutions, although at least one member of the UFK, Wolfram Sievers, held an influential position directing Himmler's SS *Ahnenerbe* office. In the wake of the Stauffenberg plot to assassinate Hitler, Hielscher was arrested and jailed in the fall of 1944. He had not been directly involved with the plot, however, and thanks to the intervention of Sievers he was released after a few months and ordered to fight on the front as probation. By this time Hitler's dictatorship was nearing its doom, and Hielscher managed to survive the end of the war and the collapse of the Third Reich.

After WWII ended, Hielscher began to withdraw from view and focus entirely on his religious work. His last significant public statement was a lengthy memoir published by Rowohlt in 1954, *Fünfzig Jahre unter Deutschen* (Fifty Years among Germans) chronicling the earlier development of his political activities and his religious ideas,

---

3 Hielscher, "Reich und Israel," in Ernst Johannsen, ed., *Klärung: 12 Autoren, Politiker über die Judenfrage* (Berlin: Kolk, 1932), 41.

each of which informed the other. In the book he recounted in detail his interactions with various personalities. Some of these people were members of the UFK, but he avoided any overt mention of his heathen church. And for the rest of his life, Hielscher would keep his spiritual life private. Although he occasionally sought feedback on some of his religious writings from a trusted intellectual confidant such as Ernst Jünger, for the most part he restricted the circulation of his theological and liturgical texts to the UFK's small congregation.[4]

In his younger days, however, Hielscher had not been so guarded with respect to his spiritual revelations. In the early 1930s, just as he was laying the groundwork for his heathen church, he wrote several deeply esoteric explorations that were published in anthologies of fiction. One such text is "Die wirklichen Mächte" (The Real Powers), which I present here in English for the first time. It was originally published in *Mondstein: Magische Geschichten* (Moonstone: Magical Stories), a collection of twenty contemporary novellas edited by Hielscher's friend Franz Schauwecker.[5] The book begins with Ernst Jünger's "Sizilianischer Brief an den Mann im Mond" (Sicilian Letter to the Man in the Moon)[6] and ends with Hielscher's rather startling contribution. It reads less like a fantasy story and more like a war report from the battle-zone of the soul and psyche.

In this short work Hielscher synthesizes a host of formative ideas and influences, distilling them down into a kind of magical revelation. Hielscher was highly erudite with regard to literature, religious history, theology, mythology, mysticism, jurisprudence and philosophy, and these all informed his writing. Here I will briefly comment on a few notable aspects of the text, the depths of which could surely be plumbed much further.

Friedrich Nietzsche's ideas cast a strong spell on the young Hielscher. He would even claim that he had a direct initiatic link to the philosopher through his encounters with Nietzsche's sister, whom he met while conducting research at the Nietzsche Archive in Weimar in the early 1920s. "The Real Powers" owes a great debt to Nietzsche's style, and Hielscher adopts an overtly Nietzschean term, *die Vielzuvielen* (literally "the much-too-many"), to designate the slavish and herdlike masses. In the final part of the text, Hielscher's description of the initiate's struggle to penetrate the mysteries of reality resonates deeply with Nietzsche's joyful antinomianism and welcome embrace of conflict, famously summed up in the aphorism *"was mich nicht umbringt, macht mich stärker."*

Drawing upon diverse thinkers such as Johannes Scotus Eriugena and Goethe, Hielscher developed a syncretic doctrine of panentheism in which polytheistic heathenism is seen as an expression of a single overarching and all-encompassing godhead. This unique theology sets Hielscher and his church apart from other attempts

---

4 Cf. Ina Schmidt and Stefan Breuer, eds., *Ernst Jünger–Friedrich Hielscher: Briefe 1927–1985* (Stuttgart: Klett-Cotta, 2005). The texts written for the UFK have been released posthumously in Friedrich Hielscher, *Die Leitbriefe der Unabhängigen Freikirche,* ed. Peter Bahn (Schwielowsee: Telesma-Verlag, 2009).

5 The book was published in Berlin by the Frundsberg-Verlag in 1930. Schauwecker's foreword to the book seems to have been influenced quite a bit by the tone of Hielscher's contribution. Here I would like to thank Carl Abrahamsson, who kindly sent a copy of *Mondstein* as a gift and thereby enabled my discovery of Hielscher's text.

6 An English version of Jünger's fascinating text can be found as an appendix to his *The Adventurous Heart: Figures and Capriccios,* trans. Thomas Friese (Candor, NY: Telos, 2012), 121–30.

to revive Germanic paganism that had been underway since the end of the nineteenth century and which tended to be based on historical manifestations of folk religion. Hielscher's panentheism comes to the forefront in the last three paragraphs of the text, when the reader is told of the "One Living Being" (*der Eine Lebendige*) who created— but at the same time contains—all known reality, material and metaphysical. Since Hielscher describes this divine entity as masculine, I have done likewise by using male pronouns (He, His, and Him) when referring to it.

Esotericism implies a process of initiation into the mysteries, and Hielscher felt that the latter were not only encoded in religious texts but also in fairy tales and certain works of romantic literature. For example, he makes a specific reference to E. T. A. Hoffmann's *The Golden Pot* and its description of the dreamlike reality that envelops the student Anselmus. For comparison, we may quote the following passage from the "Fourth Vigil" of Hoffmann's tale:

> Let me ask you outright, gentle reader, if there have not been hours, indeed whole days and weeks of your life, during which all your usual activities were painfully repugnant, and everything you believed in and valued seemed foolish and worthless? At such times you did not know what to do or where to turn; your breast was stirred by an obscure feeling that a noble desire for an object surpassing all earthly pleasures must somewhere, sometime be fulfilled, a desire which your mind, like a timid child brought up by severe parents, dared not put into words; this yearning for something unknown obsessed you wherever you went, like a translucent dream whose airy shapes dissolve when looked at too closely, and you lost all interest in your surroundings. You crept to and fro with downcast gaze like a rejected lover, and none of humanity's many and varied activities gave you either joy or pain, as though you had ceased to belong to this world. If you have ever felt such a mood, gentle reader, then you know from your own experience the state in which Anselmus found himself.[7]

Hielscher was not alone in ascribing great spiritual and magical value to such bewildering states of mind. The Surrealists had a similar appreciation for the uncanny facets of human experience and were likewise able to communicate this through the medium of fiction.[8] Many of the Surrealists also shared Hielscher's ideas regarding the esoteric significance of fairy tales.[9]

Some references made by Hielscher remain more obscure. Early on in the essay he speaks of "a wonder, an unknown reality that desires to be discovered" and which lies behind "every image of day-to-day existence." He then explains that the meaning of such a discovery "is shown with immediate clarity by Luther when he speaks of

---

7 E. T. A. Hoffmann, *The Golden Pot and Other Tales*, trans. Ritchie Robertson (Oxford and New York: Oxford University Press, 1992), 20.

8 A good example is André Breton's short novel *Nadja*, first published in French in 1928.

9 See Bernard Roger, *The Initiatory Path in Fairy Tales: The Alchemical Secrets of Mother Goose*, trans. Jon E. Graham (Rochester, Vermont: Inner Traditions, 2015).

the 'knowledge of the woman' *(Erkenntnis des Weibes)*." Although Hielscher makes the remark as if any reader will see the connection, this was probably not the case in 1930 and it is certainly not so today. While it is admittedly no more than a guess, Hielscher is perhaps alluding here to Luther's assertion that Eve, the first woman, "by her very nature was pure and full of the knowledge of God to such a degree that by herself she knew the Word of God and understood it."[10] If this is indeed the allusion he had in mind, then the discovery of the unknown reality and engagement with its mysteries amounts to a divine revelation.

A mystical text like "The Real Powers" throws up a range of terminological hurdles for the translator, who necessarily must work as an interpreter or, perhaps more accurately, as an exegete. Hielscher is concerned here with the real but mysteriously hidden powers that intersect and interact to shape our human experience. At various times he describes these powers (which also manifest in the form of wonders, signs, and images) as arising from a *Fülle*, translated here as "abundance." In its macrocosmic sense, this term reflects an intrinsic quality of the highest godhead, the One Living Being, which Hielscher referred to in later private writings as being marked by *Fülle und Herrlichkeit*, "abundance and magnificence." In its microcosmic sense, an abundance of powers is present in individual people, though to a greater or lesser degree.

Two words that lie at the heart of Hielscher's text are *unheimlich*, "uncanny," and *Geheimnis*, "mystery." The uncanny is everywhere, and its images (*Bilder*) are always ready to "flash up" (*aufleuchten*) in one's internal consciousness as well as in one's external surroundings, demanding active engagement from those who are bold enough to seek them out. The images are masks that hide yet deeper mysteries. Again emphasizing their visual component, Hielscher calls them *Erscheinungen*, which one could translate as "appearances" or maybe "guises," but which I have opted to translate as "apparitions." Since Hielscher himself makes repeated references in the text to witchcraft, magic circles, and enchantments, translating *Erscheinungen* with a term that has supernatural associations seems fitting. However, it should not be taken to mean ghosts or specters of the dead, but something more ambiguous and universal—though no less frightening. This brings us to another matter. Although his text is brimming with magical imagery, it is important to realize that Hielscher rejected the active practice of magic. He saw himself as a mystic first and foremost, as someone who stood in awe and reverence before the holy powers. He believed that attempts by humans to manipulate such forces through magic or sorcery were misguided and futile.[11]

And what is the real nature of the mystery, *das Geheimnis*? It is undoubtedly akin to the *mysterium tremendans et fascinosum*, both terrifying and fascinating, described by the religious scholar Rudolf Otto in his 1914 book *Das Heilige*.[12] There can be no doubt that Hielscher was thoroughly familiar with Otto's book, as this passage from the latter should show:

---

10 Luther, "Lectures on Genesis 1535," from *Luther's Works*, vol. 1, ed. Jaroslav Pelikan; reprinted in *Luther on Women: A Sourcebook*, ed. Susan C. Karant-Nunn and Merry E. Wiesner-Hanks (Cambridge: Cambridge University Press, 2003), 25.

11 Cf. Hielscher, *Fünfzig Jahre unter Deutschen*, 115–17; Bahn, "The Friedrich Hielscher Legend," 252–53.

12 Published in English as *The Idea of the Holy: An Inquiry into the Non-rational Factor in the Idea of the Divine and Its Relation to the Rational*, trans. John W. Harvey (Oxford: Oxford University Press, 1923).

> Taken, indeed, in its purely natural sense, 'mysterium' would first mean
> merely a secret or a mystery in the sense of that which is alien to us,
> uncomprehended and unexplained… Taken in the religious sense, that
> which is 'mysterious' is—to give it perhaps the most striking expression—
> the 'wholly other' (θάτερον, *anyad*, *alienum*), that which is quite beyond
> the sphere of the usual, the intelligible, and the familiar, which therefore
> falls quite outside the limits of the 'canny' and is contrasted with it,
> filling the mind with blank wonder and astonishment.[13]

As a term for "mystery," *Geheimnis* is a relatively modern development, having only
come into use in the fifteenth century. There is, however, a truly ancient Germanic word
and concept that, I would suggest, thoroughly embodies what Hielscher is alluding to
in "The Real Powers." That word is *runa*, "rune." Although this term has long been used
in connection with written signs, its oldest recoverable meaning is much more abstract.
Paradoxically, it meant something whose true meaning was elusive. It is that which
cannot be wholly fathomed, understood, or taken hold of—a whispered secret, just out
of earshot; a treasure that stays tantalizingly buried in plain sight. If it is grasped and
unmasked, this only leads to further riddles.

Christian Greco-Roman civilization came into head-on contact with tribal Germanic
peoples in the fourth century of the Common Era. A long series of conversions took
place, beginning with the eastern Goths, as the new religion slowly and fitfully spread
westward and northward. It would take nearly 800 years for Christianity to reach the
farthest outposts of the Germanic-speaking world. Time and again, foreign Christian
terminology needed to be translated into the vernacular, for one can hardly adopt a
new belief system unless it is, at least on some basic level, understandable. The word
runa (and its dialectal variants) was used to translate the Christian concept of the divine
mysterium, the "Word of God" that is never fully disclosed. For humans this mystery
remains an *allegoria* to be interpreted or an *arcanum* that is inaccessible to all but the very
few, the holy elect. In the Gothic Bible (the earliest translation of the holy scripture into
any Germanic language), the *runos þiudinassaus gþs* are the "secrets of the Kingdom of
God," and *runa* regularly translates the Greek word μυστήριον (*mustérion*) in reference
to the mystery of faith, the mystery of Christ, and the mystery of the resurrection. The
term can also denote deep religious truths and hidden divine purpose—in essence, the
will of God the Father.

In the Germanic Far North, where a pagan theology was able to continue its own
development in relative isolation up until the eleventh century, the word *runa* was
connected with a different high god and "Allfather." According to the lays of the *Poetic
Edda*, it was Odin who first shaped the elements of the universe and later hung himself
on the World Tree, the cosmic axis, in a rite of self-sacrifice. Reaching down, screaming
with insight, he grasped the runes—the mysteries—and brought them up from the
darkness of the underworld and into the light. These runes were also concretized into
starkly angular written signs: the old Germanic "alphabet" of the runic *fuþark*. But
even this set of symbols still bears much of the old underlying mystery. And this is no

---

13 Otto, *The Idea of the Holy*, 26.

wonder. The signs stand for sounds, and it is through combinations of these sounds that we speak and reveal things to one another, not only face to face, but across unbelievably vast stretches of time and space. Encoded back into signs, these words may live on long after we are dead and gone, and speak to those who are yet unborn.

What Friedrich Hielscher puts forth in "The Real Powers" is runic in the deepest sense of the word. He speaks of a magical universe, thoroughly laden with meaning, a divine world that is built of endless mysteries. And for the seekers who are strong enough to take a step from the known into the unknown—the fearless souls who would dare to fathom the unfathomable—there will always be another rune that waits to be read.

I would like to thank Joshua Buckley, Ingrid Fischer, Annabel Moynihan, and especially Matthias Semmler for reading and commenting upon the following translation. – MM

The Real Powers

Friedrich Hielscher

The thoughts and plans of a human being are not what is essential—rather, it is the depths out of which they grow and the abundance of energy that animates them.

Any doctor can explain how a young girl's body is constructed. But the enchantment her beauty holds for us is not an attribute of her bodily form; instead it makes use of her corporeality in the same way a witch makes use of the image in her magic mirror.

An apple tree blossom consists of a calyx, sepals, petals, stamens, ovaries, and pistils. Learned treatises have been written about the veins and coloring of the leaves, the fiber of the bark, and the heartwood of the trunk. But the magic of a blossoming landscape cannot be communicated in the same way. You know nothing of it unless your heart has been touched by it.

Science teaches us that stones are lifeless. Science is unconcerned that its claims are laughable for those to whom the mountains have spoken—such people are few, and they seldom talk about what they have encountered.

It is only amid such encounters, when a living power has effect within a living being, that the secret essence reveals itself. Behind the image of the witch's mirror arises the silent flame of the alien force that had earlier threatened the viewer impalpably and menacingly, but now manifests its divine magic as feminine and sweet and youthful.

We are all living in a world of cryptic images and mysterious signs. As they surface in our field of vision, they herald an alien life whose path intersects with ours.

Every power is encompassed by a magic circle that it suffuses with its essence. Here its desires and dreams hold sway, here its will gives birth to itself, here its thoughts think themselves, here it has its recesses and its avenues to the eternal.

When the paths of two powers intersect, when their magic circles touch one another, sparks fly—and these sparks are the images and signs that we see.

I encounter a new person. He crosses the street. He buys a newspaper. He looks like a bearded vulture. A few weeks later, I meet him face to face. He is a gardener in Aachen; we talk about figwort sawflies. The next day, he goes away on a trip.

An ant moves across the footpath in the park. It is dragging a piece of wood three times its size. At the edge of the path, the rainwater has pooled into a large puddle. Desperate, the ant races to and fro. I have to keep going on my way. I will never hear anything from this ant again.

A shooting star flies past the earth. The blazing streak, which immediately extinguishes itself, is the first and last sign of a faraway being that I do not know.

The powers speak to one another in images and signs. Reality reveals itself in apparitions. There is no apparition that does not have a reality behind it, and no reality that does not conceal itself from other beings as an apparition and a fluctuating form.

A day-to-day existence can really only be had by those who keep calm amid the apparitions. The herdlike masses are overly content. Because they are weak, they dread the alien world since it might do them harm. A gentle encounter in which the apparitions flash up is the most extreme sort of interaction they can handle. If the alien force came closer, if one of the powers that they brush aside were to shed its mask and seize hold of them, they would be unable to bear it. The masses subsist on the shadows of life and they flit over the earth like shadows themselves. The wind drives them whither it wishes.

But he who would give much will also receive much. He penetrates the things of the world, and they come to him, desiring to be taken in by him. Behind every image of day-to-day existence there is a wonder, an unknown reality that desires to be discovered. What this discovery means is shown with immediate clarity by Luther when he speaks of the "knowledge of the woman."

As living things interpenetrate one another, appearances fall away and the essence remains. "I" and "you" merge into one another. A secret agreement permeates the fused magic circles.

Until we reach this secret agreement, the alien force remains: the uncanny.

The uncanny surrounds us at every step. A stout heart is never content with fleeting contact; it never stops seeking. It constantly hungers after new life and sends out the streams of its will when new images and signs arise in its world.

A new form appears? Well then, a new riddle has arrived—a new danger, a new joy has become possible! Even in the shadow of the day-to-day, the hungry soul discovers something wondrous. With this discovery, the ascent begins. At its end, wonder and soul are united.

The abundance of the wondrous is inexhaustible. That is why the abundance of images and signs that entice us is inexhaustible. Thoughts, flowers, dreams, people, questions, stars: the unknown beckons to us in a thousand forms.

When this beckoning can no longer be ignored, then, from out of the unknown, comes the mystery that draws us under its spell. It does not pass us by and it does not disperse. It awaits. At first, our consciousness doesn't notice a thing. It wants to go further, but it cannot advance. The magic of the mystery has begun. The heart stirs restlessly. The unrest ascends from the heart up into the mind, filling its chambers with an aching, blissful anticipation. The anticipation doesn't subside. The eyes gravitate to a hidden place. The will is transformed. It strives forth toward the mystery. The images behind which the mystery conceals itself are already starting to flash up, and the signs come alive. The letters of a name that we've overheard assume an inexplicable power over us, although we know nothing more than the name. A forested valley that we have never before set foot in feels like a long-familiar place. In the confused visions of a dream, a face emerges that will not go away, nor can we retreat from it. We note with increasing horror that the man sitting across from us must be something completely other than he seems. A historical event, about which we know only the barest facts, fills us with certainty of its grand and hidden significance.

None of these images and signs has an apparent precedence over the others. No greater degree of reality resides in one as opposed to the rest. They are all no more than shapes of our consciousness. Nothing is changed in the slightest if we label one of them a fact and the others dreams or notions. We have no basis for entrusting a higher value to the sensory evidence of touch over that of the eye or ear. Indeed, the primacy of an image is never determined by whether people take it as an objective fact or as a dream. This is utterly irrelevant. One is just as unreal as the other. What is real is only the soul in which the images appear—and the powers are real whose approach and whose attraction is signaled by the sudden flashing-up of images that they have activated in us.

This flashing-up is only the beginning of a mutual penetration in which the soul is loosed of its confines in the shuddering of the final surrender to the ecstasies of the highest mastery.

When the images flash up, we are amazed and we become conscious of the mystery. Other perceptions lose their color. The mystery is present. It rushes into the time and space in which our consciousness conceives things, and in which we see ourselves as animate, as human beings.

These are the sort of hours that the student Anselmus is drawn into by the appearance of the Archivist Lindhorst, until he inwardly discovers the salamander prince who is concealed in the Archivist's form.

This is what opens up the mountain for the traveling knight who has sought it out.

Fairy tales are replete with this quest for the mystery, whose form beckons to us incessantly. Those who follow the beckoning call will be crowned, while the unbelievers and the inattentive will perish. Fairy tales tirelessly tell of this quest and discovery, and how it can go astray. Fairy tales know reality and its powers; they give these powers their proper names, which can only be understood by the initiate. There is a secret kingdom that arches over this world of nixies, kobolds, elves, and sorcerers, over the enchanted mountains, constellations, and forests. The unknown wanderer, the real secret king, will win this kingdom—and he is assured of winning the queen along with it.

It is only those with an inborn abundance of power who know strongly enough how to coerce the mystery of the reality that we designate here with names. The rest grope precariously from one apparition to the next, and in the end they hold nothing more than dead forms in their hands. It does them no good to now assert, in absolute earnestness, these are the only facts that exist. Facts are always unreal. Only the forces that become visible in them are real. But there is no point in discussing this with the foolish. The names that are given to these powers offer no help here either, since they cannot be understood unless one already knows what they mean. These names are really nothing more than labels for the incomprehensible. Only those who have been seized by the incomprehensible know its significance—that is to say, they know what it hints at.

Those who are possessed of the mystery imbed streams into these names that link them with the mystery: Humility, Pride, Thankfulness, Passion, Confidence. With the name they give a new sign to the mystery. They say: "Above you—the one who lives in us and in whom we operate—we hang this name as the sign of our brotherhood, that we have become interior to you; as a sign of the inner basis for the images and faces that you have caused to flash up in our thinking, in our time and in our space."

All of our primordial expressions, which cannot be conceptually identified since they are not concepts, are these sorts of names. They are the final signs for the revelations of our hearts. Love, Loyalty, Belief, Will, Interiority, and Might: a mystery that we are incapable of comprehending, and which we need not comprehend because we live within it, is always taken for granted. The only ones who are compelled to announce such mysteries are the afflicted souls, the creative people and artists, who give voice to the invisible fundament of their being through concepts, images, colors, and slaughters.

Such a person is capable of this confession in his work to the degree that he is not merely a seeker of his mystery but one who—in the same moment—finds it.

If it becomes conscious to him, if he sees the form in which it is concealed flashing up in his world, if the great wonder enthralls him, then the first stage of revelation is reached.

The second stage involves battle. The powers of the higher orders take part in this battle, in which the struggling soul and the mystery are entwined. The greater the abundance of power that we possess, the stronger we feel these forces, and the more surely we know to engage with them in friendship or animosity. Whoever is not up to their ranks must fail. Bismarck was entirely right to doubt Caprivi's statesmanship when the latter, after taking office, had the ancient trees cut down in the chancellery garden. A deed like this betrays a lack of reverence for the essential; the person capable of it lacks an inner abundance of power. Such a person is lowly when measured against the creative ones who, conversant with the higher orders, would dare to battle for the mystery.

As this battle unfolds, the question of whether the soul remains steadfast is dependent upon the nature of the mystery. If the mystery is hostile, then the moment nears when the opponents have become so embattled with one another that the mystery has penetrated the soul with its powers, and vice versa. All that remains is victory or defeat. Either the mystery shatters the soul and seizes control of its abandoned powers now drifting about in terror, fear, and dismay—or the soul shatters the mystery and gains the glory, outfitting itself with the powers of the mystery. Here we are at those borderline states of madness where the battle plays out on a razor's edge. The shapes seen in madness are the signs of a dreadful reality: the mystery that would swallow up the soul. The visions of Nietzsche and of Hölderlin, the sheer radiance and brilliance of their final pronouncements, bear testament to the rare and unheard-of victory of a being that was, when confronted with the magnitude of the chosen enemy, incapable of doing enough and so sacrificially, as a victor, gave itself over to the gods. The higher order, to which the soul belongs, overcame that of the mystery.

But if the mystery befriends the soul, then the battle of the second stage becomes a struggle for the mystery against the other, the unknown, with respect to which the soul and the mystery safeguard and actualize the selfsame order. For how can they befriend one another unless they both agree at their deepest core? And how would this agreement be possible unless it is common to both? From the battle, then, a deeper understanding always comes about between soul and mystery. They are open to one another; they penetrate one another. Willingly, the mystery unveils itself in an exhilarating ecstasy of yearning, dissipation, and benevolence.

Thus, following the second stage of battle comes the third, that of ecstasy. The soul becomes ecstatic like someone overwhelmed, or like the vanquisher of an enemy; this is the ecstasy of one who loves and unites with the befriended mystery.

It is no longer alien to us now. It lives inside us. We ourselves have become the mystery. We ascend up into ourselves; and the Self we discover is more than the Self that was seeking. And yet it exists within that same Self. The soul finds itself as the spark of an infinite fire. Its borders disappear in the great flame.

There is no death. Each of the higher orders partakes of immortality. The Living Being, in whom the orders exist, transforms their confines. Their transformation into one another is His breathing.

Thus, the three effects of the revelation—amazement, battle, and ecstasy—finally resolve themselves in absorption. There is no magic that does not end in absorption; no stream between the powers of reality that does not find its ocean here; no being that does not circulate in this ocean. Whether the mystery of an alien force is shattered and conquered in hostility and victory, or it is united with in devotion and mastery, the One Living Being—who thinks His own infinite thoughts in our faces, images, forms, and apparitions—is always active in us, and we in Him.

Ear Horn: Shamanic Perspectives and Multi-Sensory Inversion

Orryelle Defenestrate Bascule

For Nine Days and Nine Nights have I hung from the World Tree
And I with my One eye, I see
The symbols woven in the webs
And in the Well Above their secret's ebb
The wind whispers to me their names
As Yggdrasil's sap runs through my veins
Yes the wind whispers to me their tunes
The Runes, the Runes!

Thus cried I while hanging upside down from one foot (Hanged Man Tarot Arcana XII style) in my ritual theatre piece *Le Pendu* (French name for that Arcana, meaning 'The Pendulum').

It should be noted that the number Nine (cue *White Album* echo here) often seems to have been used by the Ancient Norse to symbolise 'forever' or Eternity, so it is unsurprising this was the traditional 'amount' of time the Norse Magician-God Odin hung from the World Tree Yggdrasil. Indeed, just three or four hours 'real' time – the longest time I have personally assumed this inverted *asana* – seemed like forever. In that particular ritual I was hanging in an old gnarled tree at the edge of a narrow river in the bush in Victoria, Australia, in the height of summer when the water was low in its earthen crevice and unmoving.

The exposed roots of the tree I hung from jutted out over the dramatic undercut of the riverbank and sank into its startlingly still black depths. In these somewhat abysmal waters was reflected the vast panorama of stars above, further increasing my vertiginous perspective as I gradually forgot what was actually 'above' and 'below.' The water was the sky, the sky the water, as in my verse above where the Well of Remembrance at the 'base' of the World Tree is perceived as Above. The primary axiom of Hermes Trismegistus – 'As Above, So Below' – is taken to the extreme of no distinction at all betwixt macrocosm and microcosm as the initiate through ordeal becomes at One with the Uni-verse. The classic Shamanic Tree whose roots are branches and whose branches are roots is experienced, as:

> I sacrifice outer sight, for inner vision
> My view is inverted, I stare within
> Growing new eyes, under the skin

The Well of Remembrance in the roots of the Tree was the dwelling-place of the severed head of the Giant *Mimir,* who represented Memory. Compare also the Hebrew letter MEM which relates to both the symbol of Water and the Tarot Trump of the Hanged Man (also a path on the Qabbalistic Tree from which he sways?), and the Ancient Greek Goddess of memory *Mnemosyne* who births the *Nine* Muses (eternal inspiration?), and it seems there are many multi-cultural morphic resonances rippling out from this Wyrd Well…

In 'Le Pendu' Hugin – the raven of Thought – perches in the branches 'below' the Hanged God, and his cries are echoed by those of Munin, raven of Memory in the Well 'above.' Given their nature according to their names, perhaps the image of the latter is but a reflection in the well of the form of the former?

Odin cast His sundered eye into the Well. This metaphor for altered perceptions seems apt in our culture which is so focused (yet another self-referential example in our language) on sight as primary sense. Indeed we seem to have no words in English relating to metaphysical sound, taste, touch or smell in the way we have 'visionary'. But 'hearing voices' is not uncommon amidst mystics, and even weeks after smoking the intense psychedelic DMT, I (and others I know) have experienced 'olfactory flashbacks'!

My friend and mentor Eldritch Forest tells me the 'Third Ear' is in the back of the head and this makes some kind of (extrasensory) sense to me as it does indeed seem to be a zone of aural prescience. Oddly it is also where I have an eye (in a circular frame as if looking out the attic window or oriel) tattooed; yet perhaps not so odd as I have always been somewhat of a left-handed (literally as well are literarily) 'Contrary' – or even particularly odd but not so even. Given my penchant for physical reification of metaphysical symbols it is I guess fortunate that tattooing is primarily a visual (though also tactile) medium so I won't end up with an image of an ear inscribed on my forehead!

I only read more recently (over a decade since 'Le Pendu' was written) that even as Odin offered up (/down?) His eye to the Well, the God Heimdall offered His 'horn'. While Heimdall did have a musical horn he was required to blow at the end of the world to herald the onset of Ragnarök (final battle of the Gods), it seems unlikely He would have given this up in the sagas or the Vikings would not have had so much faith in the eminence of these end-times (except perhaps as a 'future-memory'?).

Heimdall also had supersensitive hearing – he was said to be able to hear even the grass growing in Midgard (Earth/the land of mortals) from His post guarding the Rainbow Bridge which spans from there to Asgard (Land of the Gods). Could this rainbow twixt mundane and Godly be feasibly related to the chakras, that spectrum of colours and sounds which connect via our spine our base (Muladhara) instincts to the lofty divine (Sahasrara)?

When I read that in the ancient Icelandic tongue the Eddas were composed in, their word for 'horn' also or alternately often referred to the ear, it inspired (like a draught from the Muses birthed in the Well of the Wyrd) this trance verse:

Dropping a horn in the Well
Third Ear in Memory's Swell
Hearing the Wyrd with sight's loss
Plunging the eye and and the ear from the gross
To the fine, And finding the time to shine, to give gleam to the dross
Gleaning the sibilant meanings of the inner ear,
Cleaning the shells of the wax and the rims of the moss;
Giving the drums a thrum-stunted floss
What can you hear in the depths of the well?
Echoes of Memories or Shadows of Shells
What see with inner eye or imbibe with inner smell?

Sheathed in the waters, Memory's daughters
aMused by senses swimming
While on the outer the inward-turned shelter is dimmed
To drain blood from the beasts of the brink
Listening hearing seeing too much information to think
Leading to links in chains of trains of thought
On tracks of pain which derail our intentions and lead our carriages
to nought
Naught but the bliss of Nuit's kiss when our ego's will is sundered
Aught we to blunder and bluster with clusters of blisters on our brains
When we can float in the waters of Muses unfettered by choices by
voices of reason
This is the season to toss in the currents of cravings
We will be saved by the beacons of living unscathed

The spiralling horn of sound's passage
Captivates and amplifies the message
Ear harp strum Ear drum thrum, a sonic massage
A barrage of decibels, a tinkle of tri-bells
The lip of the shell of the ear's throat
Puckers and hearkens, Vibrational ventures
Silence summons Mnemosyne's daughters
Sound slaughters or fosters their growth

The Figure of the Polish Magician:
Czesław Czynski (1858-1932)

Zbigniew Łagosz

Since the dawn of mankind, religion has been providing theoretical foundations for explaining the existence and functioning of the surrounding world, and its cosmogonic and cosmologic solutions have been remaining unquestionable dogmas for thousands of years. However, the growing number of scientific discoveries over the the last centuries, concerning natural science especially (*e.g.*, physics, chemistry, biology, geology, astronomy), caused more decisive questioning of the elaborated, fairly consistent vision of the world, therefore leading a *chaos* into the monolithic, seemingly known and rather friendly *cosmos*. And yet all attempts to substitute the old religious vision of the world with a new logic and coherent concept constructed by scientists in their laboratories were unsuccessful. Rationalist propositions appeared to have failed the test of time.

Various doubts emerging from time to time do not consider solely the matter of sense of the existing world, but rather result from a desire for more perfect answers to substantial existential questions. The helplessness of rationalism in many issues concerning the explanation of life's mysteries caused concerns and anxiety among some intellectual circles; therefore new, more assuring suggestions and solutions were searched for frantically. Various esoteric-occult societies did not neglect this situation, claiming in their programmes that God and Satan are not of a different nature, but in contrast, they are two aspects of one entity. Therefore, by turning to one of these aspects, the other is turned to as well.

The occult thought gained at that time – that is, since the second half of the 19th century – a new and more complex form. An emergence of people presenting broad horizons, who aimed to link new ideas with already existing religious, scientific and philosophical trends, was often observed. However, it is beyond doubt that greater part of this group consisted of various specialists in secret knowledge and "magicians" proclaiming weird syncretic doctrines adopted from different civilisations (*e.g.*, from India), using tangled rhetoric difficult to verify.

One of the personages in the Polish occult tendency at the turn of the 19th and the 20th century was Czesław Czynski. Having analysed his activity, one may venture to say, in a pompous, modernist-esoteric way, that Czynski was searching for a path of God. In his search, Czynski focused on the study of God's "dark side", favouring *ipso facto* the thesis of God's duality. It must be said that Czynski ought to be classified as belonging to a group of the most important representatives of Esotericism in Poland. However, despite the great respect he gained in aforementioned circles, he has never become internationally famous; thus it is difficult to compare his person with a worldwide known figure such as Aleister Crowley[1]

Czesław Norbert Czynski was born in Turzynek near Nieszawa in 1858 to the landlord Józef Czynski and Matylda Czynska. His father made himself unpopular with the authorities of the Prussian sector after helping insurgents during the January Uprising, and had to flee the country with his family. Like many of their contemporaries who faced similar situation, they found shelter in Paris. Young Czesław was attending the well-known Batignolles School together with his brothers. After the amnesty was declared, his father, driven by an illusory hope, decided to return home. Given a land lease, Józef Czynski sent his sons to a *Realschule* in Cracow. News of the father's suicide surprised young Czesław at the time of graduation. Shortly thereafter Czesław started medical studies at University in Cracow, yet he failed to complete the course due to his lack of orderly manner. In order to terminate the studies Czesław moved to Paris. As a student at Sorbonne, he attended clinical studies in the Charité hospital, in professor Luys's unit, where he had received the certificate of completion of courses used for hypnotherapy. One of clinicians hired at professor Luys's unit was Dr. Gerard Encausse[2] (Papus), the great Master of the Martinist Order. Meeting him opened a new chapter in Czynski's life.

As he notes in his memoirs, this encounter was highly intriguing. In the presence of Papus, Czynski hypnotised a female patient with paresis of the left arm. Having introduced her in a deep hypnotic state, he managed to overcome the paresis symptoms. During the trance the patient asked for a quill to write a message: "You shall uncover the face of Isis". Having read the above, Encausse instantly allowed Czynski to study in his Academia, without the lower degrees. Czynski received the pseudonym "Dr. Punar Bhava" (in Sanskrit: a soul seeking liberation) and climbed up the hierarchy of the Martinist Order. After a few years he was appointed a Sovereign and a Member of Supreme Council.

At that time, Czynski was making a living mainly by translating texts and giving

1 It is worth mentioning that on April 21ˢᵗ 1912 Theodor Reuss, the leader of Ordo Templi Orientis (O.T.O.), provided Czynski with 10ᵗʰ degree of initiation in this organisation on Slavic territories. On the same day, in the same lodge, Aleister Crowley gained O.T.O. degrees 33°, 90° and 95°, which concern the Memphis-Misraim rite (33 = the highest degree of the Scottish Rite freemasonry, 90 = the highest degree of the Misraim rite, 95 = the highest degree of the Memphis rite; the degrees above were assigned also by other Masonic Obediences on specified conditions

2 Gerard Encausse was born in La Coruña, Spain on 13ᵗʰ July 1865. At the age of four, his family moved to Paris, where he began his education. As a young man, Encausse dedicated himself to studying the subject of Kabbalah, tarot, magic and alchemy. He adopted his pseudonym 'Papus' ('physician') from Eliphas Lévi's works. Shortly after Helena Blavatsky established the Theosophical Society, Encausse joined in 1884, resigning after a short time as the fascination of the society with the Oriental Occult proved unacceptable for him. In 1888 Encausse formed, together with his friend Lucien Chamuel, a library and begun publishing the monthly review "*L'Initiation*" in 1914. He also formed an organisation, "l'Ordre des Superieurs Inconus", in 1891, known as the Martinist Order, mainly due to Encausse's claims of possessing original documents of Martinez de Pasquallay and gained succession according to the rite of Louisa Claude de Saint-Martin. The Mariavite rite was of highest importance for Papus till the end of his life. In spite of his engagement in matters concerning magic and the occult, Encausse found time for conventional studies at the University of Paris, where he defended his doctoral thesis on "physiologic anatomy" in 1894. He has left numerous valuable books on magic, Kaballah and tarot, and the Martinist Order exists until this day as one of his most lasting legacies.

private language tuition. Gradually he started to form his sense of superiority over the "material world" and gained greater experience, and not only in therapeutic hypnosis.

Not even a trial, which reflected a wide response throughout Europe, did prevent him from receiving further degrees and further exploration of his hypnotic skills; he was accused of trying to seduce baroness von Zedlitz using hypnosis, arranging an illegal marriage ceremony (due to the lack of a divorce with his wife Ludmiła) and appointing a fake pastor (Czynski's friend, Mr. Wartalski). Czynski was sentenced to three years of imprisonment and took the penalty in the famous prison in Moabit[3], where he experienced numerous psychical and physical sufferings. Prevailing conditions caused Czynski depression, which led him to a suicide attempt. He would have succeeded were it not for the quick arrival of a prison doctor.

> Woeful, exhausted with hunger and cold, I begun to lose myself. A mysterious, elusive phantom prevented me from sober thinking, until deprived of any consolation and hope of escape from these unbearable tortures of despair – I laid violent hands on myself. [4]

The drama of the situation changed his character thoroughly, making him a man of great courage, which contributed to the fact that several years after this incident Stanisław Wotowski dedicated his book, *Sekta diabła* ("The Devil's Sect" – Translator's note) to Czynski, depicting him as an unscrupulous hypnotist, a specialist in black magic and a widely known Satanist. Having been designated by Papus to a Sovereign General Delegate of the Martinist Order for Russia and Poland, Czynski moved to Saint Petersburg in 1907, in consequence of this nomination.

At that time a well-known crime case[5] solved by Czynski gained considerable publicity. The case was of great significance as it concerned a dangerous criminal wanted by the police throughout Europe. One day in Saint Petersburg a mutilated corpse was found in a little hotel. Due to the document found near the body and the paper registration, the dead man was an engineer: Andrzej Gilewicz. After a meticulous investigation the police established that the body belonged to someone else, and that Gilewicz was the murderer, who wanted to swindle an insurance policy. International arrest warrants were sent out, but Gilewicz had disappeared without a trace. Then Punar Bhava (Czynski) joined the action, initiating his magical practices. According to himself, having received technical instructions from Papus, he used the phenomenon of

---

3 Czynski defends himself in, as he calls, "a slander game" in his book *Kartka z tajemnic życia – opowiadanie kryminalnego procesu odbytego w Monachium w roku 1894*, published in 1899 by I. Szkaradziński and Co, where he incompetently contests allegations he was submitted by the judicature. Facts that cannot be debunked are covered with a concern for the good name of person he hurt. There is no certainty about the lack of feelings between the two. When the affair was disclosed, the baroness might have suggested to have been seduced during hypnosis, heeding the lack of permission to remain in a relationship with the middle-class Czynski.

4 *Kartka z tajemnic życia – opowiadanie kryminalnego procesu odbytego w Monachium w roku 1894*. Warsaw, 1899.

5 The whole incident was depicted by Czynski in *Magiczeskie poiski Gilewicza Astralni wichod*, published in Saint Petersburg by M.O.Wolf in 1910 along with introduction written by Papus.

out-of-body experience[6]. Information gained in this way provided information for the public. According to Czynski's knowledge, Gilewicz resided in France and headed to Germany in disguise with a partner dresses as a woman. Czynski foretold, that Gilewicz would not return alive to Russia. And indeed, on December 16th 1909 Gilewicz was arrested in Paris, yet on the same night he poisoned himself. Thus, the information given by Czynski proved to be completely true. It is not surprising that the years of working in Saint Petersburg were his best.

The Martinist Order was founded in Poland[7] by Czynski most probably around 1918, on the basis of a power of attorney from the late Grand Master (died in 1916). The Order focused on deep esoteric studies and examined ceremonial magic. However, the death of the Grand Master influenced Czynski, limiting his activity in the Martinist Order, as Czynski considered some of the principles sent from France wrong. Thus, the growing conflict between leaders of the Order and Czynski resulted in the decision of the latter to establish the Ordo Albi Orientis in Warsaw. One of the reasons for the aforementioned struggle, as well as for breaking the statutes of the Martinist Order, was Czynski's integration of sex magic. Most probably he acquired its techniques due to his nomination in the Ordo Templi Orientis[8].

After the formation of Ordo Albi Orientis[9] things began to go wrong. According to his closest friends and relatives, Czynski appeared to have a God Syndrome, claiming that all his decisions influence the fate of the universe. He was additionally thoroughly absorbed by the Satanic cult, which led to a number of suicides among his apprentices. No considerable documents revealing activity of the order have remained. Its name is associated with the Satanists' trial of 1930, although some sources claim that the trial actually never happened. Such information was based in greater part on press articles of that time, published mainly in unreliable tabloids. The overall picture of this case was presented in a rather subjective manner by J. Walicka in her leaflet called *Kult szatana* ("The Cult of Satan" – Translator's note).

---

6 OOBE (Out Of Body Experience) – a state in which consciousness floats separately outside of one's physical body. An etheric body along with higher astral body leaves the physical body to travel in the astral plane (an 'astral journey'). In such a state, time and space have no boundaries. An astral cord connecting the astral body with the physical body enables a safe return.

7 Data on activity of the Martinist Order in Poland shall be discussed in detail in the article *Zakon Martynistów w Polsce – studium przypadku* ("The Martinist Order in Poland – case study" – Translator's note. In the making).

8 Ordo Templi Orientis (*Order of the Temple of the East*, or the *Order of Oriental Templars*) is an esoteric organisation established around 1895 by Carl Kellner and Theodor Reuss. Its formation was exposed in 1903 in Germany, in the pages of a Freemasonry newspaper, *Oriflame*. Initially, the order operated only in German-speaking European countries. Since 1913, after Crowley joined the order, a first branch of O.T.O. outside the Germany was created in London. Performed rites referred to the Western occult tradition and tantric practices. Contrary to other Freemasonry organisations, O.T.O. accepted women as members. According to Kellner, magical rites of a sexual character were allowed to understand secrets of Christian and Freemasonry mysticism.

9 Ordo Albi Orientes still exists in a straight line of succession. Yet, documents concerning its operations are almost unattainable. Currently, the order is headed by a highly charismatic leader specialising in tradition of Paladines (knights-magicians). Membership may be obtained only by personal invitation; an attempt to define this matter in its overall picture can be found in my work titled *Wpływ Aleistera Crowley'a na środowiska magiczne w Polsce XIX w.* ("Aleister Crowley's influence on the magical societies of the 20th century Poland" – Translator's note.)

The first suicide, Eugeniusz Rostowski, was found by the police with his head shot. Beside the body there was a piece of paper with a note, "By the Satan's order. Brothers are waiting. Shot, midnight", and a Hebrew letter *shin*. The number of suicides grew, among which were Bolesław Wójcicki, Lucjan Krzyżewski, Zbigniew Werner and two female students of university of technology, Wanda and Beata. All of them were found with a mysterious note at the side. On September 30th 1930 Czynski's house was searched by the police and a large-scale official action against Satanists was taken three days later by the order of prosecutor Mieczysław Siewierski. The main accused were Bogdan Filipowski and Mikołaj Mikołajewicz Czaplin. The latter, as testified by witnesses, was a host of Satanic mysteries. As cited in the newspaper *Expres Poranny* in September 1930:

> I [the witness – Author's note] have made a week-long preparation for the black mass, as advised by Wójcicki, which consisted of taking drugs and weakening baths. These practices aimed to put me in a state of ecstasy and to weaken my will. When on a given day Wójcicki took me to a mysterious place at Puławska Street, I found there four men wearing coats and masks. The floor was covered with a carpet. There were inverted triangles hanging on the walls, and a picture of Baphomet, that is a goat sitting on a globe. In front of Baphomet two triangles with bowls made of copper were set, each of them filled with narcotic incense. Then, suddenly Wójcicki appeared, dressed in black vestments with red embroidery of a goat, and wearing a red hat on his head. He was followed by three naked women. [...] After the previous silence of concentration, hysterical screams and squeaks of the women filled the room. Narcotics began to work. Three naked women, forming triangle in front of the Baphomet accrued to Wójcicki and a hideous common orgy begun.

Czynski himself, whether due to his old age at that time, or due to the fabrication of the whole trial, was not judged. He died in 1932[10].

Regarded as a great initiate in his society, Czynski left more than 50 publications after his death. Apart from works strongly bound with Esotericism, e.g., *Podręcznik do kartomancyji czyli sztuka wróżenia z kart,* he produced numerous works not necessarily associated with the subject of magic, such as *O sugestji hipnotycznej w pedagogice* ("On hypnotic suggestion in pedagogy" – Translator's note) or *!!1914!! Przepowiednie polityczne* ("!!1914!! Political prophecies" – Translator's note). His writings were published in Russian, French and German. The periodical *Nowy Kurier Łódzki* (no 304 from 1915) published an article titled *Punar Bhava – Narodowi Polskiemu* ("Punar Bhava for the Polish Nation" – Translator's note) ascribing to him even the "re-discovering" of artificial glass. The fact is that he even expatiated on subjects concerning chemistry and physics.

It appears that Czynski found his spiritual master in Gerard Encausse. Additionally,

---

10 Unique studies conducted by R.T. Prinke provided significant information on the subject of 'Satanism' in Czynski's organisations. The article *Doktor Punar Bhava i polscy sataniści,* published in *Biuletyn informacyjny Stowarzyszenia Radiestezyjnego w Bydgoszczy,* 1986, no 4, consists of all theses and data obtained.

his strong connections with the Martinist Order[11] are indisputable. However, is there clear evidence that he has been thoroughly identified with the activity and basic dogmas of this order? The lack of reliable sources makes it impossible to settle this issue. With the current, very incomplete state of knowledge, one may only conclude that Martinism was not the only idea Czynski identified with. His exclusion from this society, even though he was one of the main representatives of the Martinist Order in Slavic territories, puts the path chosen by Punar Bhava at the end of his days in a new light. In all likelihood it was a path of sex magic, practiced in the other secret society, namely Ordo Templi Orientis.

In this case, "a soul seeking liberation" (that is, Czynski), locked in its physical form, could have sought other paths that the strict and fundamentally Christian rites of the Martinist Order. Due to the lack of information, only speculation remains. One could hypothesize: whether the place of the previous teacher, Papus, was taken on by the other, equally great or even the greatest magician of that time, Aleister Crowley?[12] The traces of history like to fade; thus determining if Czynski did in fact meet Crowley in person has so far been impossible.

No record of such fact can be found in publications or their diaries. Analysing

---

11 Martinèz de Pasqually, a Frenchman of Spanish origin, born in 1710 (or, according to other sources, in 1727), established in 1754 *l'Ordre de Chevaliers Maçons Élus Coëns de l'Univers*, known as 'Elus Cohens'. Through this society he proclaimed Gnostic vision of the world as a creation of archetypical man broken into numberless images carrying a reflection of the divine world, yet imperfect in their fragmentation. The order aimed to initiate a process of unification, leading people to the world of the divine transcendent One through strict discipline, ceremonial magic, prayer and commuting with good spirits. A blooming of this organisation was visible during the sixties of the 18th century, when its temples emerged in Bordeaux, Montpellier, Avignon, Foix, La Rochelle, Versailles, Paris, Metz and Lyons. In 1772 Pasquallay emigrated to San Domingo, leaving a notable group of apprentices in France. One of the most known of his students was certain Louis Claude de Saint-Martin (1743-1803), who published his works on mysticism as *le philosophe inconnu*, "the unknown philosopher". His works aroused interest in the philosophy of spiritual renewal and attracted the elite of the European occult of that time, *inter alia*, Eliphas Lévi and Helena Blavatsky. Both Pasqually and Saint-Martin inspired the tradition of the Occult named Martinism in its form of notional Freemasonry characterized by a hint of Gnosticism, cabal, ceremonial magic and, after some time, additionally elements of Christian mysticism.

12 Considered the father of contemporary magic, Aleister Crowley (1875–1947) was one of the first Westerners to smoothen the way of counterculture by experimenting with alternative lifestyle, drugs, sex magic and introducing Buddhism in Europe. No other man has influenced the 20th century's renaissance of magic and the occult to such a great extent as he did. An erudite scholar, a poet, an alpinist, a magician and an esotericist, Crowley was called by his contemporaries "the wickedest man in the world". Indeed, he was an extraordinary character. His interest in theory and practice of magic, Yoga, Kaballah and tarot brought into the world a new religion of Thelema, a "love under will", where individualism, desire for life and creation are prevalent in comparison to herd behaviour and concern about one's identity. As Crowley was a person difficult to define, his message has not found understanding in his environment; however, after several years Crowley's theses gained acceptance, and the personage of Crowley was to be found in art, film and music of his times. He was a prototype for protagonist of William Somerset Maugham's "The Magician" or Dion Fortune's "The Goat Foot God". In the seventies of 20th century Snoo Wilson wrote a play named "The Beast", which was shown in Shaw Theatre by Royal Shakespeare Company, with Richard Pascoe as Crowley. A photo of Crowley appeared on the cover of the Beatles' legendary album "Sgt. Pepper's Lonely Hearts Club Band" among others. His works have been collected by Jimmy Page from Led Zeppelin for many years, and Crowley's old Boleskine House was eventually bought by the enthusiastic artist. Books written by Crowley have been sold all over the world, including - for a few years - also Poland. His greatest work, the True Will religion has gained numerous followers, and orders popularised by Crowley constantly increase their number of neophytes.

rituals concerning providing members with degrees of the O.T.O is all that can be done. The analysis of participation of third parties is of the highest interest, for if the form of the ceremony did not exclude people connected with the order, it might have been an occasion when "the Beast of the Apocalypse whose number is 666" (that is, Crowley) met Punar Bhava. On the other hand, being acquainted with practices used in various esoteric orders, one may allow for the possibility that on that given day no ceremony did actually take place, as Czynski might as well only have received the participation certificate proving he has merited the relevant insignia. A question arises, whether the same day and place of providing Czynski and Crowley with degrees of initiation was a mere coincidence? When analysing some of Crowley's messages one may feel that they correspond to Czynski's path of spiritual development. Thelema, Crowley's religion, says, "there is no God but Man". A man is perceived here as a being who possesses the power of creation – contrary to the rest of the world of nature. Crowley defined magic as "the Science and Art of causing Change to occur in conformity with Will". In other words, he turned it into a subject of study about human intentionality (where the postulate of 'scientific' magic derives from). The name of his religion, *thelema* (from a Greek word meaning 'will'), is evidence that the transcendent "One" was to be the purpose of human cognition, instead of God, and it could have been cognized only by constant accumulation of experiences[13].

Thus, there is a possibility that Czynski may have been one of the first (though most probably unaware) followers of Crowley's religion in the Polish region. Not only the scientific approach to the magic system Czynski worked on, but also his referring to theses of the most significant text for Thelemites, "The Book of the Law", proves this suggestion to be true. As this paper is not an adequate place for detailed analysis of this "Magical Bible of the New Aeon", only a selection of basic thoughts[14] is presented below:

Do what thou wilt shall be the whole of the Law.
Love is the law, love under will.

An obligation to oneself

1. Make yourself the centre of your universe,
2. Explore the nature and powers of your existence,
3. Never allow any other person's thought or will to interfere with your will
4. Do not suppress or limit your true instincts. Dedicate everything to scrve your truc will.

That such thoughts may have been born in Czynski's mind is beyond doubt. Most of all, he indeed implemented the ideas above (or tried to implement). However, stating that Czynski was in fact a Thelemite is as bold as it's impossible to prove. Each person

---

13 Crowley, A. *Księgi Bestii*. Wrocław, 2000. Translated by D. Misiuna.
14 Polish edition: *Magija w teorii i praktyce*. Cracow, 1998.

can employ techniques he or she has never heard of or read about. Some things (as one's own behaviour) come instinctively, independently of others. From a philosophical point of view, Thelema is closest to the thought of Friedrich Nietzsche; not only due to its opposition against Christian order, but most of all because Crowley's vision of self-cognition reflects the nietzschean postulate of "re-writing one's own history", wherein Crowley interprets Will, the final point of the journey to the Self, as a state of transcending one's Ego. In his occult philosophy reaching the True Will is possible through elimination of false desires, therefore it must follow the training of Will[15]. All of the above may be evidence of a relationship between Crowley and Czynski, as well as of a sort of "fraternity of thought", or both, of parallel or independent developments of similar (or identical) ideas.

---

15 Crowley, A. *Op. cit.*

Rejected Knowledge:
A Look At Our Other Way of Knowing

Gary Lachman

The following lecture was delivered at the Marion Institute in Marion, MA, for their "Living in the Real World" conference, 8 November 2015. – Ed.

This evening I'm going to look at a tradition of thought and a body of ideas that the historian of the occult James Webb calls "rejected knowledge." I'm going to see if we can arrive at answers to four questions:

> What is this tradition?
> Why is it "rejected?"
> Why is it important?
> What does it mean for us?

Now before I start I'm going to ask you all to engage in a bit of philosophy. I'm going to ask you to perform a simple but very important philosophical exercise. This is something called "bracketing," and it was developed in the early twentieth century by the German philosopher Edmund Husserl. Husserl is important for founding a philosophical school and discipline called phenomenology. We needn't know a great deal about it and I'm not going to burden you with a lot of history or definitions. Put briefly, Husserl was scandalized by the mess that western philosophy had gotten itself into by the late nineteenth century and as he loved philosophy – he was obsessed by it – he thought the best way to proceed was to start from scratch. Now, I should point out that wiping the slate clean and starting from scratch is a well-tested tradition in philosophy, so Husserl was not doing anything radically new. But then, in another sense he was.

Phenomenology is essentially a method of *describing* phenomena, which means the things that appear to us, whether physical objects in the outer world, or my thoughts, images, feelings and so on that seem to reside in my inner world, my mind. If you look a tree, that is a phenomenon, and if you then close your eyes and imagine the tree, that is a phenomenon too. Both are objects that are presented to consciousness, and Husserl was interested in *how* phenomena present themselves to consciousness, and what role our own minds have in this presentation.

Now what Husserl suggested is that to begin this study, what we need to do is put aside everything we think we know about our object of observation. So if you were in his class and you were given an object to observe – say a book, a flower, or a chair, it doesn't really matter – he would say "Don't tell me what it *is*; tell me what you *see*."

Now for any philosophers in the audience I admit I am simplifying things very much, but for what I am going to ask you to do that is all we need. The method of putting aside everything we think we know about something is what Husserl called "bracketing." Basically it means to put aside your presumed knowledge of whatever you are observing, and place it in brackets. Placing it in brackets means that you don't reject your knowledge, you don't deny it or change your mind about it. You simply put it aside for the duration of your phenomenological work. You take it out of the equation for the time being. You don't throw it away. You simply pick it up as it were and put it over there for a time. It was in this way that Husserl wanted to arrive at what he called a "presuppositionless philosophy," basically a philosophy that begins without any preconceived ideas.

Now what I'd like you all to do is to become phenomenologists for a short while, at least for the duration of this talk. I'd like you to "bracket" everything you think you know about the world, about reality, about the universe and our place in it. Again, I'm not asking you to forget this or to reject it or to deny it. I am simply asking you to put it aside for a short while. In Husserl's case this usually meant putting aside questions about the "reality" of something, about whether it was "true" or not, about its "essence," and any "explanations" that could account for it, whether materialist ones or idealist ones. Phenomenologists don't ask those questions, at least not at the beginning. What they try to do is describe the objects of consciousness and get some idea of what is involved in how they appear to us.

What this exercise is supposed to do is to make whatever you are observing "strange," "unfamiliar," "unknown," "mysterious." One definition of philosophy that I like very much and which can apply to our exercise here in "bracketing" is that it is "the resolute pursuit of the obvious, leading to radical astonishment." Because one outcome of a successful exercise in "bracketing" is that it transforms something you believed you knew very well, into something quite mysterious. Something, perhaps, that surprises you.

So, let's see if we can all be phenomenologists for a short time and temporarily put aside everything we know about the world we live in and our place in it. This means bracketing the Big Bang, Darwin, and all the scientific explanations about the world that we've been offered over the years, about atoms and electrons and Higgs-bosons and selfish genes and DNA and so forth. Take all of that and put it in brackets.

Okay? Have we done that? Good.

The tradition of rejected knowledge that I'm going to talk about is what we can call the Hermetic tradition, or the Western Inner Tradition, or the Esoteric Tradition, or the Occult tradition. I should point out that "Hermetic" comes from the teachings of Hermes Trismegistus, the mythical founder of philosophy and writing. Esoteric means "inner" and occult means "not seen." Each of these names has a very specific sense but in a broad, general application they all refer to the same thing. They refer to a body of ideas and philosophies and spiritual practices that were for many centuries held in very high regard in the west, but which in the last few centuries – since the rise of science in the 17th century – have lost their status and been relegated to the dust bin of history. They are rooted in several what we can call mystical or metaphysical philosophies and religions of the past, Hermeticism, Gnosticism, Kabbalah, neo-Platonism and related belief systems. We needn't know exactly what these are now and we'll try to get some idea of some of them as go along. We now think of these things and the practices associated with them as superstitions, as myths, more or less as nonsense. I'm thinking of things like astrology, alchemy, magic, mysticism, the Tarot, or of experiences like telepathy, precognition, out-of-the-body experiences, of mystical experiences, of feelings of oneness with nature, with the cosmos, of what we can call "cosmic consciousness," of belief in life after death, in consciousness existing outside the body, of astral travel, of visionary experiences, of contact with angels and other spiritual beings, of strange states of mind that lead to sudden, accurate knowledge of and insight into the workings of the universe, and into the mystery of our own being, of dimensions beyond space and time, of the experience of the soul and the spirit.

Experiences of these and similar things and a real knowledge about them were for very many centuries accepted by both men and women of learning and also by the everyday people, the common folk. These people lived in a world in which such things were possible. More than this, they lived in a world in which such things were considered of the highest importance. Much more important than the everyday, physical world they inhabited. That has gained a supreme importance only in the last few centuries, and it has gained this importance through diminishing the importance of what we may call the "spiritual" or "invisible" side of reality. We'll return to this shortly.

To give you an idea of how important this tradition of thought was considered, let me mention a few of the people who believed in it and occupied themselves with it.

Given that he is considered the father of modern science and the modern world in general, it is surprising to know that Isaac Newton, probably the greatest scientific mind in western history, was a passionate devotee of this tradition. Newton wrote more about alchemy than he did about gravity. Gravity itself is an "occult" force. "Occult" simple means hidden, or unseen, and as far as I know, no one has seen gravity. Newton's investigation into the physical laws of the universe – that have allowed us to put men on the moon and probes out into the deepest regions of space - emerged from his life-long interest in alchemy, in understanding the secret meaning of the Bible and, like Stephen Hawking in our own time, knowing the "mind of God."

Thomas Edison, the inventor of the light bulb and much else, was an early member of the Theosophical Society, the most important occult, esoteric or spiritual society in modern times, founded in New York in 1875 by that remarkable Russian emigre, Madame Blavatsky. Along with all the other inventions he is known for, Edison was very interested in "spirit communication," and for a time he worked on developing a way of recording messages from the "other world."

Wolfgang Amadeus Mozart was deeply involved in Freemasonry, a society that in its early years was profoundly informed by Hermetic, esoteric ideas. Mozart's opera *The Magic Flute*, is a kind of initiation ritual in music. Beethoven was also interested in Freemasonry as was Franz Joseph Haydn and several other famous classical composers. I might also mention that the earliest operas were based on alchemical ideas. I should also mention that it is well-known that George Washington and other of America's founding fathers were Masons.

William James, the great American philosopher and psychologist, and one of the great teachers at Harvard, had a powerful interest in mystical experiences – so powerful that he experimented with nitrous oxide in order to have one himself. He was also deeply interested in the paranormal and he investigated several mediums. His friend, the French philosopher Henri Bergson, a Nobel Prize winner and for a time the most famous thinker in the world, shared James' interest and was a president of the Society for Psychical Research.

Many poets and writers and artists were very keen on this tradition of "rejected knowledge." The German poet Goethe practiced alchemy. W. B. Yeats – another Nobel prize winner - was a Theosophist and also a member of the Hermetic Order of the Golden Dawn, one of the most important occult societies of modern times. The Swedish dramatist August Strindberg was an alchemist too and also a great reader of the Swedish mystical thinker Emanuel Swedenborg. I should mention that Johnny Appleseed, the early American ecologist, was also a devotee of Swedenborg, as was the poet William Blake, who saw angels as a child and had conversations with spirits and inhabitants of "other worlds" throughout his life.

The Renaissance, the revival of classical thought that took place in the 15th century and produced some of the most treasured works of art in the western world, works by Michelangelo, Botticelli, and others, was saturated in Hermetic, esoteric thought. The Renaissance is generally seen as a time when the works of Plato and other Greek philosophers were re-discovered after being lost for centuries. But it was even more a time when the ancient teachings of Hermes Trismegistus, thrice-greatest Hermes, the founder of magic and writing, were rediscovered after being obscured for a millennia.

Some of the early church fathers were followers of some aspects of this tradition and before them Plato, the greatest philosophical mind of the west, was, if not a devotee, certainly a fellow traveller, and we have reason to believe that much of Plato's philosophy was informed with ideas and insights gathered from this tradition.

This list could go on. I mention these names here just to show that, although this tradition is "rejected" by modern thinking, some of the most important figures in science and the arts embraced it whole-heartedly. This, of course, doesn't prove anything, but it does suggest that if world-renowned scientists, Nobel Prize winners, influential poets, musicians, and philosophers – and again, this is just a fraction of the important people with an interest in this tradition – had the time for it and devoted much energy and thought to it, it must have *something* going for it. Or should we accept that Newton and Mozart and Goethe and the others were simply "superstitious," weak-minded, gullible characters who were simply not as smart as modern sceptics ,who consider the tradition these men of genius felt themselves to be a part of sheer nonsense?

I don't know about you, but I hesitate to call Newton or Goethe or Mozart weak-minded and gullible. So if they weren't, why were they interested in something we in the modern world reject?

This leads me to my second question: why was this tradition rejected? And who, exactly, rejected it?

The short answer is that it was rejected because of the rise of science, which began its road to dominance in the 17th century. The story is actually more complicated than that and involves the church and the rise of humanism, an outgrowth of the Renaissance, but for our purposes it is sufficient to contrast the way science sees the world with the way the rejected tradition sees it. Or, I should I say, the way in which science *knows* the world and the way in which the rejected tradition knows it. Because fundamentally, this is the issue. All of the different philosophies and teachings that are rooted in the rejected tradition – magic, alchemy, astrology, mysticism and so on – all share in common a particular way of *knowing* the world. And it was this "way of knowing" that science, or what became what we call "science," rejected, along with the knowledge accumulated through that knowing.

Now as "knowing" is something we do with our minds, it is something directly related to our consciousness. Knowing is an activity performed by a consciousness, whether yours, mine, an alien's, or, perhaps, an intelligent machine's.

One of the things that Husserl and other phenomenological philosophers discovered is that different kinds of consciousness, or different modes of the same consciousness, can "know" things in different ways. Conversely, they also discovered that they can also know different "things." We can see this from our own experience. I know, say, my name, what the product of 2x2 is, and also how to ride a bicycle. But I know these in different ways. I know my name because at some point someone told me what it was, and by now I have accumulated boxes of documents confirming this. I know that 2x2=4 because logic and reason tell me it does. Try as I may to "know" that 2x2=5, I can't because it doesn't. Of course, I can be coerced into *agreeing* that 2x2=5, as the people in Orwell's *1984* are, but this isn't really knowing. And I know how to ride a bicycle because, after many failed attempts I finally "got the knack" of doing it. But if you try to *tell* someone how it is done, as if in a step-by-step manual, you will find that it is not so easy to do. I can *show* someone how to do it, but to give *a clear and adequate account* of how I do it is actually quite difficult.

Another example. I mentioned Mozart, Beethoven and other composers. I *know* that Beethoven's late string quartets are about something deeply moving and profound, but I would find it just as difficult to *say* what they are about as I would if I tried to tell someone how to ride a bike. I can't say exactly what the music is about, but I would also reject any account that said it was just vibrations of air, which, physically, *is* what the music is. It's about something more than that, about something deep, profound, even mystical, but exactly *what*, I can't say.

Or say you have a hunch or an intuition about something and are very certain it is important. A friend asks "But *how* do you know?" All you can say is "I don't know, but I *do!*"

This other kind of "knowing," the kind that recognizes something deep in music, or in poetry, or in works of art, or accepts intuitions and hunches, that knows with the gut, as it were, is, it seems to me, related to our rejected tradition.

Now what differentiated science – and again, let me say I know this is a huge generalisation, and let me make clear that I am no enemy of science, but of what we can call "scientism," which is a kind of "fundamentalist science" in the way that we have "fundamentalist Christianity" or "fundamentalist Islam" – what made it different from earlier modes of knowledge and methods of acquiring it is that it focused solely on observing physical phenomena and, in a way, did its own kind of bracketing by forgetting any ideas about what might be behind the phenomena, making them happen. Roughly this meant jettisoning God, or the angels, or spirits, or soul, or any kind of purpose or mind at work in nature. It puts aside any theories or traditional ideas and just watched and saw what happened. This approach to understanding the world had its roots in the philosopher Aristotle, who was Plato's pupil. But where Plato was interested in understanding what we can call the invisible higher realities behind or above the physical world – what he called the Ideas or Forms, a kind of metaphysical blueprint for reality perceived through the mind, not the senses – Aristotle did just the opposite. He devoted himself to observing the natural world.

Aristotle's theories dominated the west for centuries but eventually were discarded. But between the two – he and Plato – we can see the different ways of knowing. Aristotle is the first "research scientist, " collecting data and devising theories to account for why things are the way they are. Plato is much more interested in the higher reality of which the physical world is just a shadow. He often uses myth in his accounts and started life as a poet. Aristotle started the tradition of the unreadable philosopher. He also started systematic logic, in which A can only be A and never Not A and so on. For Aristotle, something is or it isn't. There's no middle ground. He sees an "either/or" kind of world rather than a "both/and" sort of one.

But along with paying attention to the physical world, which people had been doing all along, science brought to its investigation a powerful tool: measurement. It discovered that the forces at work in the physical world could be measured. Speed, mass, weight, acceleration, space, extension, and so on could be *quantified*. And what was remarkable about this is that with enough knowledge of these quantities, events could be accurately predicted. It is this predictive power of measurement that enabled men to get to the moon and space probes to shoot past Pluto. Needless to say this was truly an achievement and it has enriched our lives and the lives of our ancestors immeasurably – if you can forgive an atrocious pun. But one result of this is that it split the world in two, basically between the kinds of things that could be measured in this way, and the kinds of things that can't.

The person who made this split official was Galileo. What Galileo said was that all the things that could be measured were *primary* phenomena. They were "really real," and existed in their own right. They were *objective*. The other things were less real. They were *subjective*, which meant that they only existed in our minds, our psyches. So the brilliant, moving colors of a sunset are our subjective experience of the objective reality, which is wavelengths of electromagnetic radiation. Color, scent, texture, taste, are all subjective. They don't exist on their own. We *add* them to our experience. But they don't "really" exist, at least not in the way that the primary things, that can be measured, do. We can't measure the awe and wonder we feel looking at the sunset, but we can measure the electromagnetic radiations we are being dazzled by.

This worked well for science. It gave it something hard and solid to hold on to. But this was at a cost. Because what we value in experience are precisely those things that science has told us for some centuries now are not real. The things that science can measure accurately and make effective predictions from are things that no one except scientists get excited about. And the kinds of things that thrill all of us, science has explained to us are only in our head. The world really isn't beautiful. We see it that way. But it itself isn't. Not really.

The other thing the new way of knowing did was to break things up into smaller and smaller bits and pieces, which were subject to cause and effect. There was no pattern holding things together, no "great chain of being," no "web of life" or "whole" into which everything found its place. A world of atoms subject to physical forces could account for everything. The world really was a huge machine, a mechanical cosmos that needed no mind or intelligence or spirit or anything else to run, merely blind physical forces.

Now, what does all this have to do with our "rejected tradition?"

Well, the kind of knowing associated with that tradition is the polar opposite of the kind that made science so successful. And I should point out that science is successful because it is immensely helpful in our attempt to control the world. It has immense utilitarian and practical benefits. It gets results. It makes things happen. The kind of knowing associated with the other tradition isn't like this. It isn't practical or utilitarian in that sense. It isn't a "know how," more a "know why." It's a knowing that isn't about controlling the world – which, in itself, is not bad, and absolutely necessary for our survival – but of *participating* with it, even of communicating and, as we say today, interacting with it.

Probably the most fundamental way in which these two kinds of knowing differ is that in the new, scientific mode, we stand *apart* from the world. We keep it at a distance, at arm's length. It becomes an object of observation; we become spectators, separated from what we are observing. With this separation the world is *objectified*, made into an object. What this means is that it loses, or is seen not to have, an *inside*. It is a machine, soul-less, inanimate, dead. We object to this when it happens to us, when we feel that someone is not taking into account our inner world, our self, and is seeing us as an object, as something without freedom, will, completely determined. But it is through this mode that we can get to grips with the world and arrange it according to our needs.

Whether we are scientists or not, this is the way in which we experience the world now, at least most of the time. There is the world: solid, mute, oblivious, and firmly "out there." And "inside here" is a mind, a little puddle of consciousness in an otherwise unconscious universe.

The mode of knowing of the rejected tradition is the opposite of this. It does recognize the "inside" of things. It does not stand apart from the world and observe it from behind a plate glass window. It participates with the world. It sees the world as alive, as animate, as a living, even a conscious being. And it sees connections, links among everything in this world. Where the new mode worked best by breaking the world down into easily handled bits and pieces that were best understood as subject to physical laws of cause of effect, the kind of knowing of the rejected tradition saw connections, correspondences among everything in the world, it saw everything as part of a total living whole. We can say that where the scientific mode works through analysis, the other mode works through analogy and synthesis. Elements of the world are linked for it not by mechanical cause and effect, but by similarity, by resemblance, by a kind of poetry, by what we can call living metaphors. Plants, colors, sounds, scents, shapes, patterns, the position of the stars, the times of day, different gods and goddesses, angels and spirits were woven together into subtle webs of relations, where each echoed the other in some mysterious way. In ancient times, this was known as "the sympathy of all things," the *anima mundi*, or "soul of the world." We can say that instead of wanting to take things apart in order to see what makes them tick – and the machine analogy here is telling – the rejected tradition wants to link them together to see how they live. And where the new way of knowing worked with facts and formulae, the other way worked with images and symbols.

The most concise expression of this other way of knowing is the ancient Hermetic dictum, "as above, so below." This comes from the fabled *Emerald Tablet of Hermes Trismegistus*, a work of alchemy attributed to Hermes but which makes its appearance round about the eight century AD. This means that there is a correspondence between the things in heaven and the things on earth. In one sense, this is understood as a correspondence between the position and movements of the stars and human destiny. This is astrology. But in a broader, more fundamental sense it means that man, human beings are a kind of microcosm, a little universe, and that we contain within ourselves vast inner spaces, that mirror the vast outer spaces in which our physical world exists. In the rejected tradition, the whole universe exists within each of us, and it is our task to bring these dormant cosmic forces and realities to life. If in the new, scientific tradition we have begun to explore outer space, in the rejected tradition we turn our attention inward and explore inner space. And just as they do on *Star Trek*, we find inside ourselves "strange new worlds."

This is a very different picture of humankind than what we get with the scientific mode of knowing. There we are just another collection of bits and pieces pushed and pulled by a variety of forces, with no special role to play or purpose to serve. Physical forces, biological forces, social forces, economic forces have us at their beck and call. There is no universe inside us. Our minds are a product of purely material forces and are driven by physical needs and appetites.

The rejected tradition sees humankind as very different, as central to the universe, as the answer to the riddle of existence. And this is why it is important to understand its place in our history.

One of the consequences of the scientific mode of knowing is that it ultimately arrives at a meaningless, mechanical universe. This is why the astrophysicist Steven Weinberg can say that "the more the universe seems comprehensible the more it also seems pointless." He is not alone in thinking this. With the rise of science and the decline of religion, the idea that there is any *meaning* to existence also declined. Science did not set out to arrive at a meaningless universe, but it was driven to do so by the force of its own logic. If the only "really real" things are the sorts of things that are amenable to measurement – basically, physical bits and pieces - then things like "meaning" or "purpose" and other "spiritual" kinds of things are not really real. And if the universe is pointless, then human existence must be too. There is no reason for our existence. Like everything else, we just happened.

This is pretty much what the accepted picture is in the modern world. For the past few centuries we've slowly become accustomed to the idea that life is ultimately meaningless. Science presents one version of this insight, and much of the literature and art and philosophy of modern times does too. A great deal of this sentiment is summed up in the existential philosopher Jean-Paul-Sartre's remark, "man is a useless passion." "It is meaningless that we live," Sartre said, "and it is meaningless that we die." Martin Heidegger says we are "thrown into existence." Albert Camus talks of the "absurd." These thinkers from the last century were at least troubled by these reflections and sought to arrive at some stoic endurance of fate, some meaningful response to meaninglessness. But today, in the postmodern world, we're not fussed. Life's meaningless? Okay. We're lost in the cosmos? No biggie. We've been there and done that and got the tee-shirt. We have accepted as a given what the writer and philosopher Colin Wilson called "the fallacy of insignificance," the unquestioned belief that each of us individually and humanity in general is of no significance whatsoever.

The problem with this is that such a bland acceptance leads to a cynical, shallow view of life. It reduces it to a bad joke. It makes it small, trivial, and shrinks everything to an anonymous, uniform, "whatever." I don't think it takes a great deal of observation to see that we have become addicted to trivia and are up to our ears in methods and techniques of distraction. We have become used to nihilism, to the idea that "nothing matters." In many ways we like it, because it lets us off the hook. We no longer have to think about serious things or take ourselves seriously. And in a world in which there are no "spiritual" values, the only thing worth pursuing is material gain. Needless to say there's quite a lot of that going on. But even that can only go so far. My own feeling is that soon even it will be seen to be pointless. What we will do after that to entertain ourselves is unclear, but I shudder to consider the possibilities.

I would also say that our pressing ecological, environmental, economic, social and other crises have their roots, ultimately, in this "fallacy of insignificance" in the lack of belief in any values other than material ones.

Now this rather bleak spiritual landscape is a result, I believe, of our overvaluing one way of knowing at the expense of the other. It is a result of our understandable over-appreciation of the new way of knowing. And I should make clear that I am not saying the new way of knowing is bad, or evil, or that we should get rid of it and return to the older way. Developing the scientific way of knowing was a true breakthrough and a necessary and indispensable part of the evolution of consciousness. But as I've tried to point out, it has its drawbacks. While a return to a pre-scientific time is neither possible nor desirable, what we can do is see if the rejected tradition can offer anything to even out the imbalance. Can we learn something from it to help us move through this rather uninspiring time? Can we salvage some of our "rejected knowledge" and see if it can inform us and help us make creative, positive decisions about ourselves and the world? Can we accept some of this knowledge so that it is no longer rejected?
Let's take a look at it.

We've already seen that it sees the cosmos as living, even conscious, rather than as a dead, empty mechanism.

We've seen that it sees connections running throughout the elements of this cosmos, patterns, correspondences, analogies, sympathies, echoes, communication. Blake, a student of the Neo-Platonic tradition, wrote that "A robin redbreast in a cage puts all Nature in a rage." There is the sense that everything is connected in some way with everything else, is in a way *integrated*. This would mean that the other mode of knowing sees the world as "dis-integrated," as broken up, fragmented, as things jumbled up in a box rather than a whole.

It also recognizes realities that the other way of knowing does not. Invisible forces and energies, subtle influences, spirits and souls, but also values like beauty, truth, the good, the values that make up what the psychologist Abraham Maslow called the "higher reaches of human nature" and which we associate with a spiritual orientation to life, rather than a material one.

We have also seen that the other way of knowing *enters into* the world, rather than remaining detached from it. And this I think is the key thing to grasp. Because it is this through this kind of "participatory consciousness" that everything else follows. And it is something that we can experience for ourselves.

Probably the most difficult part of the rejected tradition that someone firmly convinced of the accuracy of the scientific picture of reality will have accepting, is its attitude toward consciousness. To put it simply, in the scientific, modern view, consciousness is a product of the material world. Whether it is neurons, electrochemical exchanges, or elementary particles, in some way consciousness is *explained* via some physical agent, and it is something that takes place exclusively inside our heads. I address this belief – for this is what it is – in my book *A Secret History of Consciousness*, where I look at several philosophies of consciousness which take a very different view. This other view is the polar opposite of the scientific one. In this view, consciousness is primary, and the physical world, the world "out there," the world we are all inhabiting is in some way produced by consciousness. This means that you and I, right here and now, are in some way creating the world around us, are responsible for it. This is why the nineteenth century French Hermetic philosopher Louis Claude de Saint-Martin said that we should not explain man by the world, as material science tries to do, but the world by man, as the Hermetic, esoteric tradition does. This is also what is meant by the Hermetic belief that man, the human being, contains an entire universe within him, is a microcosm. Within his mind, his spirit, there are infinite worlds. The world we see here and now is only one of them. If you change consciousness, you change the world.

Perhaps you can see why at the beginning I asked you to perform an act of "bracketing." *Everything* we have been taught throughout our lives has in one way or another told us the complete opposite of what I just said. We have grown up within what Husserl called "the natural standpoint." I should point out that by "natural standpoint," Husserl was not thinking of "nature," or a "natural" way of living. He simply meant the accepted, the usual, the ordinary, the everyday, the unquestioned. When we open our eyes in the morning we see a world "out there" and we assume quite *naturally* that all our perception is doing is reflecting it, as a mirror would. We, ourselves, our consciousness, has nothing to do with forming or shaping or providing that world. It is "there" and we simply "see" it. Husserl believed that the first step in philosophy, in understanding ourselves and in achieving self-knowledge is to challenge this. He believed we needed to *step out* of the "natural standpoint," which in effect means to *make the world strange*. Not by distorting it as, say, surrealism does, or altering it as, say, what happens when we ingest a mind-altering substance, or seeing it as threatening, as happens in certain abnormal mental states. But simply by withholding assent to what we have hitherto never questioned, by bracketing what we "know" about the world and trying to see it from a different perspective. This is the "resolute pursuit of the obvious" which leads, if done correctly, to "radical astonishment." The most obvious thing in the world is the world itself and it is also obvious that we are just a part of it, like everything else. Husserl and, in its own way, the Western Inner Tradition, asks us to put this belief aside and to try to see things differently.

I should point out that Husserl was not a devotee of this tradition. He was a genuine Herr Professor working all his life in the academy on questions of logic, mathematics, and epistemology. What is fascinating to me is that the sort of shift in our focus of consciousness that he asks for is in many ways the same as required in the Hermetic, inner tradition. Both ask us to put aside certain habits of thought, for this is all that the "natural standpoint" and the most rigorous expression of it, the modern, scientific mode of knowing, are. They are ways of perceiving, of knowing, and of thinking that have been built up, arrived at, over time. This is not to devalue them in any way, merely to show that they have *evolved*. They are not simply "given" as natural. This suggests that other ways of perceiving, knowing, and thinking can also evolve. And this is where we come in.

One of the first effects of "making the world strange" in the way that Husserl suggests is that it makes "you" strange too. The consciousness that has stepped out of the "natural standpoint" and taken an active stance toward "the world" rather than a passive acceptance of it, becomes aware of itself in a way that it never does when remaining in the "natural standpoint." It becomes aware of itself as an *activity*, as a source of action. It feels more lively, more alive, more present, and becomes aware that what it had believed up till then to be absolute fact may not be as absolute as it had thought. Most important, it becomes aware of itself as a willed activity. Not wilful, in the egotistic sense – along with everything else, the everyday self that is associated with "wilfulness" is bracketed too – but in the sense of feeling its own "participation" in the "world" – it, after all, is doing the bracketing. Up till then it had simply accepted "the world" as something "there," with which it had nothing to do aside from passive reflecting it. It becomes more aware of "I" as a living, vital, experience. It understands what Buckminster Fuller said when he remarked that "I seem to be a verb." It overcomes its "forgetfulness of being," in Heidegger's phrase, and "remembers itself" as the esoteric teacher Gurdjieff believed we all needed to do. (In light of what we said about a "dis-integrated" consciousness, "re-membering" seems particularly apt.)

There are moments when we already feel this kind of "participation," although we mostly are not explicitly aware of it and don't speak of it in this way. But the effect of great art, poetry, music, literature, natural beauty, love, religious and spiritual practices all tend toward making us more aware of our inner life. They *widen* us, expand our interior, give us glimpses of that inner universe the rejected tradition tells us resides within us all. They are the "peak experiences" that Maslow believed came to all psychologically healthy people, and what he meant by "psychologically healthy people," were people who rejected the "fallacy of insignificance" and who strove to actualize the "higher reaches" of their nature, the aspects of human being that are the central concern of our rejected tradition. And I should point out that as we actualise these "higher reaches," the world around us is actualized too. We no longer see it as something solely to exploit or to abuse, as a dead, oblivious, mechanism, but as something living with which we can develop a relation. We develop an attitude of care toward it, we become, as the title of one of my books has it, "caretakers of the cosmos," rather than insignificant accidents produced randomly within it.

And just as our present consciousness has evolved out of earlier forms, a new consciousness, more aware of the kind of knowledge and knowing that informs our rejected tradition, can also evolve. I am of the opinion that this is happening already and has been happening for some time and that we, now, are in a very good position to help it along. We are the inheritors of both traditions, both kinds of knowing, and we can see where and how the two need to be balanced and integrated. This is precisely the theme of my latest book, *The Secret Teachers of the Western World*, a historical-evolutionary overview of the place of the rejected tradition within western culture. It is my sincere hope that our other tradition no longer remains rejected and that its teachers and what they have to teach remains a secret no longer.

Intuition as a State of Grace

Carl Abrahamsson

This text was originally delivered as a lecture at the the Overgaden Institute for Contemporary Art, Copenhagen, Denmark on June 25th, 2015. – Ed.

Imagine a person fiercely focused on the creation of an object. He or she is undisturbed and the surroundings are optimized for this specific creation. The vision is clear, sketches or preparatory fragments have helped the gearing up for the moment of execution, amplified by suitable music and perhaps even special clothes for the occasion. The tension increases, the work is begun and when it's over, a great sense of well-being and release becomes overwhelming.

Did I just describe an artist or a magician at work? Did I just describe someone externalizing inner creative concepts or someone programming the cosmos? Well, both of course, as they're essentially the same in method and approach. This little talk today will focus on the conceptual similarities of the creative process involved in art and magic. As we'll see, there are considerably more aspects that unite them than set them apart.

This is not implying that the one always perfectly corresponds to the other. But there is more than enough common ground to see that the creative process involved is highly similar. What makes the two areas differ is usually one of purpose and potential-in-extension.

The common ground is not surprising. At one point in time, art and magic were basically the same. Intertwined and necessary for tribal well-being. Cave paintings, ritual dances, evocative music, programmatic poetry, talismanic jewelry, charged weapons were all part of a creative process with a distinct purpose: to make something desired happen and to make something undesired not happen.

As with many things in human cultural development, major existential shifts took place and things became specialized and compartmentalized – a process still going on today, for good or bad. The mystically spiritual and ecstatic became organized in religions with professional proxy-priesthoods. The previously so integrated artistic expressions as agents of willed change instead became particular professions for individuals with a specific talent. But where did this talent originally come from?

In our human progress, evolution and development, we contain everything that's passed before us in our DNA. We are like cosmic tape recorders in an ever-evolving process of refinement and adaptation. Special qualities needed for survival are passed on in tradition, myth and genetic mass. This is still being conceptualized and expressed by artistically creative people in many fields. That's their function, so to speak. To move everything onwards and bring the good stuff along.

As mentioned before, this creative strain was divided into specialized skills and professions. Some became scientists, some historians, and some continued manifesting their own personal visions in externalized artistic forms. These have been some of the main sanctioned expressions and professions within human culture. But there have also been those who've retained a traditional yet highly experimental labor in working with the unseen and immeasurable. Sometimes these have been more or less integrated in society, but most often not. The magicians have most often worked on their own or in small groups of like-minded souls. Dealing with basically the same behavioral methods and questions but usually with an added ingredient: personal will. Meaning that what is created also carries a charge that helps change things in unseen, immeasurable and presently unknown ways.

When art as such became integrated as a more or less necessary but commodified field of work, it was still an expression of this same human need. We need art and culture as reflective surfaces, personal catharsis and release, as something to initiate existential conversations and thought fodder. Essential fuel for progress and development. Everyone knows that, and it's always there. The amount of people actively dealing with art (as opposed to dealing *in* art) is minimal today compared to the totality of human beings, and yet the status is still high. That is, if the artist in question is successful. Even in the most totalitarian of societies, there is art to amplify the condoned, allowed, and encouraged agenda.

One should perhaps also enter the very sensitive question here: what exactly is art? There have been so many definitions over the centuries that one gets tired by the mere overview: Berenson's life enhancement angle, Tolstoy's egalitarian, almost anti-beatific angle, Goethe's and later Steiner's spiritual ditto, Beuys' Social Sculpture ditto, Gurdjieff's objective ditto, Duchamp's sardonically detached ditto… It's all one big mess or mesh of contradicting yet eloquent theories and postulates. It's really no wonder that contemporary art theory is so ephemeral and illusive. Basically, the definitions seem to go intimately hand in hand with whatever tradition or school that will soon be obsolete. The only common denominator that really seems to permeate is art's original function: a magical one. But that aspect is seldom looked upon with admiring eyes by our civilization's defining minds.

What then of magic? It's almost as chaotic there but more muddled and often quite vile. Aleister Crowley I think came up with the best one so far with his "Magick is the science and art of causing change to occur in conformity with will." All other attempts seem quite futile compared to that.

Even in the most well-ordered and confined expressions, the artist often feels a need to go beyond the formal norms and normal forms. Art history is packed with individual examples that have led themselves straight into Draconian measures because they felt some kind of need to. As is the history of science. The pioneers are seldom praised until the masses catch up. And then it's usually too late to enjoy it. The deviators, rebels, iconoclasts have always been able to sneak at least some degree of seed-sowing into works of art otherwise condoned and integrated in a wholesome totality of a "greater good." This can vary from a new stylistic touch to an unseen piece of content, as in hidden symbols, or even conscious subversions of content or form, etc.

Basic psychology tells us that the artist needs to express him- or herself, almost compulsively. Feelings, desires, skill, excellence or even self-doubt in a form that touches people enough to react. The reaction becomes a validation not only of the process involved but also of course of the person and mind behind it all. When that's not there, the frustration of invisibility and poverty abounds. When it's there, on the other hand, a deep-rooted sense of bliss and meaning takes hold. This vulnerability of the individual supports a strong system of market and moral control, which is something artists have far too often adapted to and also something magicians have fought against throughout the millennia.

For reasons having to do with traditional stigma or ostracism, the magician has up until recently been quite content with working in silence or in a hidden sphere. Let's not forget that the word "Occult" means "hidden" in Latin. That, however, doesn't mean that magicians and occultists have been less susceptible to personal sensitivity, weakness and ego compensation. Quite often on the contrary. But there's one thing that usually sets their work apart from that of the artists. It's the concept of defined will. A magician has a sense of distinct purpose, a (hopingly) well-thought-through plan and a goal for the work in question. If it's a matter of a ceremony, it's to uphold a balance and atmosphere. If it's an active ritual, it's to change something specific in the small or grand scale of life. The creative process then acts as a means and not an end in itself.

It's interesting to note that magicians usually avoid the limelight, as the work itself holds precedence. The artist on the other hand can use both negative and positive visibility to his or her own benefit. That's simply because our society needs scandalous individuals and outsiders in general to relieve collective tension. A successful and media-conscious artist works equally well as a movie star. At times, some magicians appear who take on celebrity or notoriety status, but they can only expect flack or negative exposure. Aleister Crowley and Anton LaVey are two well-known examples from the 20th century.

So, what unites these two proto-human endeavors that were once wholly intertwined? Some principal ties are:

—∞— Irrationality as key or necessary agent. The rational mind-frame hampers genuine creativity.

—∞— Imagination and visionary ability. You trust what you perceive and not what others tell you to perceive.

—∞— Heavy emotional engagement in the creative process (as opposed to purely causal, detached labor). If you don't feel and believe in what's going on, everything will be a barren and soulless endeavor.

—⁓— Externalization of inner processes. As mentioned above, new life comes from within and moves outside.

—⁓— Creation as an umbrella for a supra-ecstatic flow: more than mere "joy" in working. Elevated states of mind, ideas and epiphanies as results of the mind being in "neutral gear", so to speak.

—⁓— Manifestation as building block or aggregate of experience. "A life's work." One thing leads to another, and if one is conscious of and grateful about it, many life-enhancing synchronicities will follow.

—⁓— Integration of the symbolic. Naturalism is not possible and only pleases the rational mind. Where schooling in one tradition is often necessary, the development of one's own language or code is crucial for maximum impact. In magic, this means for instance being schooled in one specific tradition like Western Ceremonial Magic and then drifting off into your own devices and methods. In art it could be schooling or being inspired within, for instance, surrealism, and then moving on in personal integrations of, for instance, scientific symbols and codes.

—⁓— An integrated breach of the previous stage: tradition is transcended, not seldom aggressively. Rebels rebel in both instances. Hiccups and revolutions are necessary for overall health because the most radical and extreme occurrences always end up as rigid and conservative environments. Iconoclastic bowel movements.

There is also another common key ingredient in this magical art-soup: Intuition. That lovely non-rational flow of existence so cherished by Taoists and all-round creative people. What exactly is it? It's a temporary freedom from causal bonds and rational thinking that sets inner creativity and happiness free. It's a well-known but pretty undefined positive state of mind that helps us in decision-making and creation. What would art be if intuition wasn't there? A mere outer construction work of ideas or concepts. What would magic be without intuition? A mere reading of a cosmic user's manual. Trusting one's intuition may be the most important ingredient there is. Especially so in an overall culture that is increasingly binary and dualistic in both outlook and method.

An artist in our sphere of the world usually works in a much more causal and commodified structure than a magician. In your studio, you create. That's highly satisfying, but you also know that you have to get by by going through many motions to secure sustenance and exposure of your creations. That's because our culture as such only really allows "approved" entrepreneurs and manufacturers of acceptable influx through complex systems of exhibition, appraisal, validation, criticism and financial compensation. If you play the game by the rules you're more than welcome to compete for your place in the sun of recognition and appreciation.

This is of course a generalized view of the situation. But no less true. Most artists unnecessarily restrain themselves by adapting to a very clearly defined set of rules. You fight and get bitter and disillusioned if you don't succeed, or fight and get happy if you do. In a way, the outer circumstances dictate the inner feelings because there's an outer arbiter or commander commenting and judging whether or not what you make has any value or merit as such.

But the direction should be from the inside outwards. Yes, a filtering of external influx is inevitable and perhaps even essential. But it needs to be filtered on the inside, in the alchemical oven, in the fire, in the womb. Seed come from the outside in, but the new life comes from the inside outwards. That sexual or procreative analogy is a central one in both art and magic. Or should be. We should remember these kinds of very basic wisdoms from many bright minds within philosophy and magic, but perhaps specifically Buckminster Fuller when he declared: "Mimic nature and you can't go wrong!"

Let's zoom back to earlier phases when art was still ingrained with magic and vice versa. That is, when it had the power to change and not only entertain. When the power of the artwork, object or performance wasn't measured by transactions validating the creator in question but rather by if the outcome of its charge was successful. The worth of the artist then lay in the ability to systematize and charge chosen artistic expressions, like a sculpture, dance, song, painting, etc. Success in that sphere guaranteed an elevated status within the tribe or commune.

In my experience, however, it's as if contemporary magic and its practitioners are lost in a maze of conservative content and very rigid traditional approaches to form when it comes to applying this ancient, primordial science and art to a modern world. In the same way as art-as-such has been pushed back to being an estheticized, commodified world of forms filtered through desperate and petty egos and their external commanders. Too much content and energy on the one hand and too much form and intellectual nervousness on the other... It seems both areas have become victims of our binary times, with rigidity and lack of courage as banners. The result being that positions become heavier and heavier in the choking illusion of safety. With occasional volcanic, psychic outbursts when the respective intellectual decompression chambers aren't working as they should.

It seems I can't deliver a lecture without returning to one of the most potent and beautiful metaphorical scenes ever in movie history: Mickey Mouse as the sorcerer's apprentice in Disney's *Fantasia*. In youthful enthusiasm yet ample laziness, Mickey uses magical tricks to make cleaning house simpler. This to catastrophic results. But he learns his lesson well from the returning and very angry magician: one needs to know not only the tools of one's trade but also to be very clear in what one wants to achieve with these tools.

I don't need to state what I've already implied... But I'll do it anyway. "What if...?" And this is potentially a very dangerous question: What if...? What if a young generation consciously connected the currently separated ends of the power cable of meta-programmatic content and alluringly suitable form? And what if they not only joined forces but actually joined the very life force itself? It's a very challenging thought and, again, a potentially dangerous one.

During the past decade, a keen interest in esoteric protagonists, movements and artists has seeped into the art world. We have, for instance, seen a revitalized appraisal of masters like Swedish painter Hilma af Klint. The exhibition that was on at Louisiana last year has been seen by over a million people all over Europe. That hardly sounds like an "esoteric" exhibition. In 2008, the Centre Pompidou in Paris housed an enormous exhibition called "Traces de Sacré" (traces of the sacred), which was an overwhelming celebration of art and the occult. The Venice Biennale of 2013 was packed with works of an occult nature, ranging from Lady Frieda Harris, the woman who painted Crowley's *Thoth* Tarot deck, Carl Jung's "Red Book", Borges' imaginary beings to Xul Solar's collages. There are nowadays academic symposia focusing on the intersection between art and occult history. The term "occulture" is now almost mainstream and indicates previously esoteric themes as having been accepted and "exotericized." Also, new generations of artists are re-expressing and integrating occult, religious or spiritual themes in their own way, both in form and content. This could vary from using Goethe's color schemes, listening to inner voices, experimenting with higher states of consciousness, allowing experiences in nature to shape one's expressions with inclusion of distinctly occult iconography in images and other kinds of works. Quite simply, the colorful grey area between art and the occult is established and ever growing.

To a greater extent than ever before, young artists tend not to separate the process from the product, so to speak. The process can be magical, and the art object then becomes something that carries a charge beyond the merely esthetic or personally cathartic. In fact, in these times, an increasing number of artworks become talismans. They are the results of a consciously willed yet intuitive process, and they contain remnants not only of that process as a "result" but also energy that has been set in motion in a desired direction. Whether the partakers realize or know this is irrelevant. But that artists work with this kind of thinking and making is in fact highly relevant.

Where art for so long has touched upon "attribute" rather than on "essence", there seems to be a shift going on in which the positions are being diametrically changed. The essential meaning becomes more important than the "attributal" esthetics and commercial value. This of course brings us back to primordial times when it was indeed more important that the artwork contained power than an attractive surface. When language gradually took over, rationality and structure followed suit. Yet the need for the primordial, magical expression has always been there all along and now seems to finally resurface within its own perimeters.

This is without a doubt an effect of a rational culture gone wrong. In our desperation to survive as a species, let alone as individuals, different remedies are needed than the ones prescribed by a *status quo* complacency. This is an all-permeating and anxious movement in our present times. So it's hardly surprising that art shrugs off some superficiality and assumes the responsibility it once had. Art should not only inspire us to live more fully and think free thoughts and feel free emotions. It should also present solutions and alternatives beyond the many rationalistic, materialistic, binary fallacies we have already experienced or committed. But the beauty of it all is that this is not going to happen in dogmatic, intellectual ways or through an abstract, post-modernist discourse. It's going to be more direct, vibrant, alive, poetic, emotional, violent and expressive. Although perhaps shaped in entirely new languages and codes, it won't be hard to interpret at all. It's going to be guided by intuition and survival instinct and not by faint references to previous -isms or demagogic simplifications to alleviate bad Western consciences. Individual intuition may be that original state of Grace so brutally shoved aside by monotheistic religion to pave the way for hubristic self-destruction. The art that catches this drift and integrates proto-human desire and behavior will become the talismanic art that will literally help save the world as we know it and love it.

The Golden Thread:
Soteriological Aspects of the Gnostic Catholicism in E.G.C.

Bishop T Omphalos

> Salvation? But – from what? Every man and every woman is a star. And that's that. There is no imperfection in the "star"; it only appears as such when examining its phase of experience at the moment.[1]

As indicated in the above quote, the Gnostic Catholicism[2] of Aleister Crowley harbored a downright hostile attitude towards the notion that man was in need of redemption. The reason for this is indicated by his reference to the doctrine of the starry nature of every man and woman expressed in *Liber AL vel Legis* I:3.

Crowley would note concerning the implication of this doctrine, that although 'each star has its own number, each number is equal and supreme. Every man and every woman is not only a part of God, but the Ultimate God.'[3] This doctrine abrogated the old mystical notion of man being an imperfect and fallen spark, which was in need of being reunited with God in order to attain perfection:

> I think that we are warned against the idea of a Pleroma, a flame of which we are Sparks, and to which we return when we "attain". That would indeed be to make the whole curse of separate existence ridiculous, a senseless and inexcusable folly. It would throw us back on the dilemma of Manichaeism.[4]

Crowley's argument concerning the mystery of incarnation, rests on the assumption that man does not attain perfection by incarnation, but instead develops his being by expanding his sphere of consciousness to know and encompass more of his environment.

---

1 Aleister Crowley, OTO *Archives Film #5*, O.T.O., 2002, June 21st, 1944.

2 Gnostic Catholicism is defined in this essay as the doctrine of the Gnostic Catholic Church that is expressed in the writings on the Law of Thelema by Aleister Crowley. The Gnostic Mass, as we shall see, is an expression of these doctrines in the form of a dramatic invocation.

3 Aleister Crowley, *The Law is for All* , p. 27, New Falcon Publications, 1998, p. 27.

4 Aleister Crowley, *The Law is for All*, New Falcon Publications, 1998, pp. 32-33. For more on Crowley's thoughts on what he called the heresy of Manicheism, cf. *Liber Aleph vel CXI*, 1991, 93 Publishing Limited, in particular chapter 200 on p. 200.

SALVATION FROM WHAT?

In his letter to W.B. Crow, Crowley did however beg the question about what it was that we needed to be saved from? Did not *Liber Porta Lucis* announce the coming of the Messiah, V.V.V.V.V., and promise a certain type of salvation?

> First, there are many and diverse conditions of life upon this earth. In all of these is some seed of sorrow. Who can escape from sickness and from old age and from death? We are come to save our fellows from these things. For there is a life intense with knowledge and extreme bliss which is untouched by any of them. To this life we attain even here and now. The adepts, the servants of V.V.V.V.V., have attained thereunto.[5]

The false promises of the slave-gods of the Old Aeon can't help us, as we are unable to escape the conditions of life upon this earth. All of us, without exception, partakes in the mystery of incarnation, and must endure sickness, old age, and death. It is however possible to change our point of view from the terrestrial to the solar, coming to the realization that we are fiery globes of consciousness, a specific and localized expression of the play of love between Hadit and Nuit.

That chilled spark from the Sun is in other words no longer the divine part of us that must return to God. Rather, it is now revealed to embrace the capability of setting us on fire with *energized enthusiasm*. Our minds thus destroyed, it allows for us to partake in the *Covenant of Resurrection* as Priests of this Royal Mystery. A covenant where we proudly proclaim with burning hearts in the *Gnostic Mass*, that 'there is no part of me that is not of the Gods.'[6]

The Gnostic Mass is a dramatic invocation of this process. Moreover, the Gnostic Mass grants adherents[7] to the Law of Thelema a brief access to this Royal Mystery through the ecstasy[8] it bestows upon its celebrants. It reinforces this solar point of view in the core of their being, through the regular attendance and organizing of one's life around the sacraments and calendar of the Gnostic Catholic Church. This is accomplished by bearing witness to the word of V.V.V.V.V. and expressing his magical doctrine of salvation.[9] As such, the Gnostic Mass enables everyone to take part in the

---

5 Aleister Crowley, Liber Porta Lucis sub figura X in *The Equinox III:9 - The Holy Books of Thelema*, 93 Publishing Limited, 1989, p. 40.

6 Aleister Crowley, The Gnostic Mass in *Magick: Liber ABA, book 4, parts I-IV*, Samuel Weiser Inc., 2000, pp. 584-597.

7 The Book of the Law differentiates between three types of grades in the Order of Thelema. The Man of Earth, the Lover, and the Hermit. Whereas the other two give their Life and Light to the Law of Thelema, the Man of Earth is simply an adherent who having accepted the Law of Thelema as the Letter and Word of Truth, seeks to adhere to it as well as he can. For more on this doctrine cf. Aleister Crowley, The Vision and the Voice in *The Equinox IV:2*, Samuel Weiser Inc., 1998, pp. 1-256, and Aleister Crowley, *The Law is for All*, New Falcon Publications, 1998.

8 For more on this doctrine cf. Aleister Crowley, Energized Enthusiasm in *The Equinox I:10*, privately published by the A.'.A.'., 1913, pp. 17-46.

9 Though Crowley was quite open about this (see footnote 10), the fact that he considered V.V.V.V.V. as the origin of all the various Class A writings of Thelema, including Liber AL vel Legis, will probably surprise more than a few of my readers. As will be demonstrated later, an understanding of this, will clarify the often

Communion with the Saints of the true church of old times, whose head is V.V.V.V.V.

THE SAVIOUR OF THE WORLD

Though Crowley clearly differentiates between the Book of the Law and the other Class A writings of Thelema, at least twice he makes an admission that they all are examples of utterances of V.V.V.V.V.[10] In *Liber Porta Lucis*, the coming of this Messiah and those who are to make his word known among the men and women of the Earth is declared:[11]

> I behold a small dark orb, wheeling in an abyss of infinite space. It is minute among a myriad vast ones, dark amid a myriad bright ones. I who comprehend in myself all the vast and the minute, all the bright and the dark, have mitigated the brilliance of mine unutterable splendour, sending forth V.V.V.V.V. as a ray of my light, as a messenger unto that small dark orb. Then V.V.V.V.V. taketh up the word, and sayeth: Men and women of the Earth, to you am I come from the Ages beyond the Ages, from the Space beyond your vision; and I bring to you these words. But they heard him not, for they were not ready to receive them. But certain men heard and understood, and through them shall this Knowledge be made known. The least therefore of them, the servant of them all, writeth this book. He writeth for them that are ready.[12]

This mirrors the pageant in the *Gnostic Mass* where the Priest, upon being awakened from the tomb in order to administrate the virtues to the brethren, declares that he is a Man among Men.[13] The priestess then consecrates him and makes him fervent in body and mind. Mind being another word for psyche or soul, this is a clear reference the Master of the Temple, Crowley writes in *The Temple of Solomon the King I:X*:

> And in relation to his true life, it is mixed with the blood of all his fellows in the Cup of BABALON. And in relation to his body and mind he is but a vehicle of the forces that are beyond the Abyss. He will therefore speak, but as a man among men, of that which he has seen and heard.[14]

confusing doctrines of salvation in Crowley's writings. That Crowley vocally dismissed certain types of salvation that our soteriology was opposed to, has further confused an already complex doctrine that is easily misunderstood.

10 Cf. the admission of Liber Legis being the word of V.V.V.V.V. in Aleister Crowley, Liber LXI in *The Equinox III:9 - The Holy Books of Thelema*, 93 Publishing Limited, 1989, p. xlv and Aleister Crowley, The Equinox of the Gods in *Magick, Liber ABA, book 4, parts I-IV*, Samuel Weiser Inc., p. 421, for a discussion on the provenance of the Book of the Law.

11 That is the adherent or Man of Earth. See footnote 7 for a brief discussion of the three types of grades of Thelemites.

12 Aleister Crowley, Liber Porta Lucis sub figura X in *The Equinox III:9 - The Holy Books of Thelema*, 93 Publishing Limited, 1989, p. 39.

13 Aleister Crowley, The Gnostic Mass in *Magick: Liber ABA, book 4, parts I-IV*, Samuel Weiser Inc., 2000, pp. 584-597.

14 Aleister Crowley, The Temple of the Solomon the King in *The Equinox I:X*, privately printed by the A.'.A.'., 1913, p. 123.

This awakening of the sleeper from the dreamless sleep, is the foundation of the Great-er Great Work, that of declaring the Word unto the men and women of the earth. Through this, the dark star might be brought to realize its starry nature and make that which is dark, shine and become bright, as a beacon of blazing light that bids others to come under the Aegis of the Law of Thelema. As such they form a link back to the true Church of old time.

THE TRUE CHURCH OF OLD TIME

This interior community of light that heard the word of V.V.V.V.V. and made it known is identified in *An Account of A.'.A.'.*[15] , as being identical to the Great White Brother-hood. It is the single impetus behind all true expressions of religious community:

> This interior community of light is the reunion of all those capable of receiving light, and it is known as the Communion of Saints, the primi-tive receptacle for all strength and truth, confided to it from all time.[16]

The same document declares V.V.V.V.V. to be the head of this community of light[17] and he is declared to be *the Way, the Light and the Truth*, a description that many will note was reserved for another Messiah: Jesus Christ. This astonishing similarity is readily explained by the fact that this document openly declares itself to be a rewritten version of parts of *The Cloud Upon the Sanctuary* by Karl von Eckartshausen[18], which describes the Great White Brotherhood as the interior Church that gave the impetus to all true Christian groups and whose head is Jesus Christ.

But it also hides a deeper truth, which is contained in the assertion that Satan is worshipped on Earth as Jesus Christ.[19] For Satan as Pan, the feminine aspect of Ma,

---

15 Aleister Crowley, An Account of the A.'.A.'. in T*he Equinox I:1*, privately published by the A.'.A.'., 1909, pp. 5-13. As demonstrated in Robert A. Gilbert, Baphomet & Son: a little known chapter in the life of 666 in *Nuit Isis 1*, Mandrake of Oxford, 1993, pp. 10—21, after receiving a charter from Theodor Reuss, Crowley secured additional authority to found the British Section of the O.T.O. from the Secret Chiefs whose Head is V.V.V.V.V. The conditions given him was that within his jurisdiction the *Volume of the Sacred Law*, would be *Liber Al vel Legis*. An acknowledgement of the sense of duplexity, detailing the harmony existing between the O.T.O. and the A.'.A.'. and how the former depended upon the latter, was first published in Franz Hart-mann, Mysteria Mystica Maxima: First Instruction in *The Equinox I:10*, privately published by the A.'.A.'., pp. v-xv. This duplexity was later that year reaffirmed in Aleister Crowley, *Manifesto of the M.'.M.'.M.'.*, privately published by the O.T.O., 1913, and republished as Aleister Crowley, Manifesto of the O.T.O. in *The Equinox III:1*, privately published by the O.T.O. and A.'.A.'., pp. 195-206. This became later a source of contention between Theodor Reuss and Aleister Crowley, and led to their ceasing communication. Upon seizing control of the O.T.O. after the death of Reuss, starting with the Weida Conference, Crowley secured this duplexity beyond his own jurisdiction in Great Britain (cf. Kjetil Fjell, *Turmoil in Weida: The Secret Confence* revisited, forthcoming).
16 *Ibid*, p. 10.
17 *Ibid*, p. 7.
18 Karl von Eckartshausen, *The Cloud upon the Sanctuary: An announcement to those capable of Light*, Kes-singer Publishing LLC, 2010.
19 Aleister Crowley, The Vision and the Voice with Commentary in *The Equinox IV:2 - The Vision and the Voice with Commentary and other papers*, Samuel Weiser Inc., 1998, pp. 213.

is the Savior[20] from what is called the *Wrong in the Beginning.*[21] But the path to him is through the Heart of Blood of V.V.V.V.V. as expressed in the Voice of the Pelican:

> I A O : all that liveth is blood of the Heart of the Master: all stars are at Feast on that Pasture, abiding in Light.[22]

THE HEART OF BLOOD

Contained in the name of V.V.V.V.V., there is hidden a certain tenfold[23] key to this Covenant of Resurrection. This key takes the form of an averse triangle, the Heart of Blood, which is hidden deep within the groves of Eleusis.[24] The Heart of Blood is one of the most sacred symbols in the system of Thelema. It was given to Crowley by Aiwaz himself in 1904 and is mentioned openly for the first time in connection with Θελημα in a letter to J. F. C. Fuller dated November 19, 1909:

> The Red [averse triangle] is a Thelema symbol, but the colours of these robes are on A.'.A.'. lines.[25]

His first explanation of this symbol is to be found in chapter 69 of *The Book of Lies*, where he describes the interlocking two triangles of the Thelemic hexagram:

> This is the Holy Hexagram. Plunge from the height, O God, and interlock with Man! Plunge from the height, O Man, and interlock with Beast! The Red Triangle is the desceding tongue of grace; the Blue Triangle is the ascending tongue of prayer.[26]

His commentary on this chapter, notes this magical hexagram and explains it as the two methods of attainment:

> In the magical hexagram this is reversed; the descending red triangle is that of Horus, a sign specially revealed by him personally, at the Equinox of the Gods. (It is the flame descending upon the altar, and licking up the burnt offering.) The blue triangle represents the aspiration, since

---

20 Aleister Crowley, The Paris Working in *The Equinox IV:2 - The Vision and the Voice with Commentary and other papers*, Samuel Weiser Inc., 1998, p. 362.

21 (Crowley, 1989c, p. 28)

22 Aleister Crowley, *The Heart of the Master*, New Falcon Publications, 1992, p. 39.

23 Tenfold because that is his name as given in *The Vision and the Voice*, five names for the Upright Pentagram and Five names for the Averse Pentagram. A pantacle showing the golden thread back to the Heart of Blood of V.V.V.V.V. in the Groves of Eleusis can be found in figure 1. For a more thorough discussion on this doctrine of the tenfold nature of V.V.V.V.V., cf. J. Daniel Gunther, Initiation in the *Aeon of the Child: The Angel & the Abyss*, Ibis Books, 2014.

24 Cf. the Class A writings Tzaddi, LXV and VII in Aleister Crowley, *The Equinox III:9 - The Holy Books of Thelema*, 93 Publishing Limited, 1989, for more on the Groves of Eleusis.

25 Aleister Crowley, *Correspondence* with J. F. C. Fuller, King's College, London School of Economics, unpublished.

26 Aleister Crowley, *The Book of Lies*, Samuel Weiser Inc., 1991, p. 148.

blue is the colour of devotion, and the triangle, kinetically considered, is
the symbol of directed force.[27]

From this we see, that the red triangle represents the plunging of Man to become in-
terlocked with the Beast. It is a very special symbol of Horus and represents the gnostic
teachings and soteriology of Thelema. Consequently, we see in *Liber VII*, V:41-43, the
following comment and the titling of the red triangle as the Heart of Blood:

> He leads us into the Inverted Palace. There is the Heart of Blood, a pyra-
> mid reaching its apex down beyond the Wrong of the Beginning. Bury
> me unto Thy Glory, O beloved, O princely lover of this harlot maiden,
> within the Secretest Chamber of the Palace![28]

Of this Heart of Blood, it's written further in *Liber LXV*, III:28, noting the inherent
blasphemy of the White School of Magick:

> The red three-angled heart hath been set up in Thy shrine; for the priests
> despised equally the shrine and the god.[29]

Deep within this doctrine is hidden the mystery of the fourfold name of the Lord. The
four letters of ADNI are the four gates that leads into the Inverted Palace.[30] The *harlot-
maiden* that awaits us within "the Secretest Chamber of the Palace" is H, making the
secret name of the Lord, ADHNI, which transforms the Lord from 65 to 70, *Ayin*, the
Devil or the Eye.

We see in the identification of the *harlot-maiden* with the Mother and the Daughter, how the Daughter as *virgin* is set upon the throne of the Mother as *harlot*. Closely
associated with this is the mystery of Aquarius or the Star, the fish-hook (*Tzaddi*) that
is the only thing that may rise us up from the pool of the Heart. J. Daniel Gunther
wrote in his first book, *Initiation in the Aeon of the Child*, concerning the identity of
this redeemer:

> This Christ is the Guardian of the Abyss, He who is like a Woman that
> jetteth out the milk of the stars from her paps.[31]

Gunther writes further in the same book, concerning this Heart of Blood as the *guard
of Water* mentioned in *Liber Trigrammaton*:

> A 'guard of Water' [Averse Triangle] (also called the "Heart of Blood")

---

27 *Ibid*, p. 149.
28 Aleister Crowley, Liber Liberi vel Lapidus Lazuli Adumbratio Kabbalæ Ægyptiorum sub figura VII in *The
Equinox III:9 - The Holy Books of Thelema*, 93 Publishing Limited, 1989, p. 28.
29 Aleister Crowley, Liber Cordis Cincti Serpente sub figura LXV in *The Equinox III:9 - The Holy Books of
Thelema (editor Grady L. McMurtry)*, 93 Publishing Limited, 1989, pp. 66-67.
30 For further discussion on the doctrine of the four gates, cf. J. Daniel Gunther, *Initiation in the Aeon of the
Child. The Inward Journey*, Ibis Books, 2009, pp. 148-157.
31 J. Daniel Gunther, *Initiation in the Aeon of the Child: The Inwards Journey*, Ibis Books, 1999, p. 122.

placed in each [of the five paths intersected by the Abyss, that link the Supernals with the lower Sephiroth,] conceals and reveals the Name [of V.V.V.V.V.][32]

THE WRONG OF THE BEGINNING

The wording *down beyond the Wrong of the Beginning* in Liber *VII*[33] is curious, but we see an elucidation on this being put forth in the Class AB paper, *The Paris Working*. Here Crowley notes during a vision concerning the *Wrong in the Beginning*:

> Every drop of semen which Hermes sheds is a world. The technical term for this semen is KRATOS. Those worlds are held in chains, but invisibly. People upon the worlds are like maggots upon an apple - all forms of life bred by the worlds are in the nature of parasites. Pure worlds are flaming globes, each a conscious being. Number of worlds ejected, 7,482,135.
>
> The name of this Phallus is Thoth, Hermes or Ma. Ma is the god who seduced the Phallus away from the Yoni; hence the physical Universe. All worlds are excreta; they represent wasted semen. Therefore all is blasphemy. This explains why man made god in his own image.[34]

It is interesting to note here that we can see here the contours of a true Gnostic soteriology of Thelema, one that I will touch on further below. As of now I want to mention that these maggots represent our thoughts. As Crowley wrote in *The Book of Lies*, 'Mind is a disease of semen.'[35] When these thoughts are quenched, all that is left is the pure Will; then our woes and seeds of sorrow have left us, and we have regained the fountain of youth and become redeemed from the *dis-ease* of life.

THE MESSIAH AND THE SERPENT

These chains that binds together the pure flaming globes of consciousness is a reference to the chain of systems mentioned in verse 34 to 40, that preface the introduction of the inverted palace in *Liber VII*, chapter V:

> Then, O my God, the breath of the Garden of Spices. All these have a savour averse. The cone is cut with an infinite ray; the curve of hyperbolic life springs into being. Farther and farther we float; yet we are still. It is the chain of systems that is falling away from us. First falls the silly world; the world of the old grey land. Falls it unthinkably far, with its sorrowful bearded face presiding over it; it fades to silence and woe. We

---

32 J. Daniel Gunther, *Initiation in the Aeon of the Child: The Inwards Journey*, Ibis Books, 1999, p. 121.
33 Cf. footnote 28.
34 Aleister Crowley, The Paris Working in *The Equinox IV:2 - The Vision and the Voice with Commentary and other papers*, Samuel Weiser Inc., 1998, p. 362.
35 Aleister Crowley, *The Book of Lies*, Samuel Weiser Inc., 1991, p. 26

to silence and bliss, and the face is the laughing face of Eros. Smiling we greet him with the secret signs.[36]

The chain of systems are falling away from us because we are introduced to a new chain, a chain of aspirants going back to V.V.V.V.V., who has the double nature of both a Messiah and a Serpent. The Serpent tempted Man, which resulted in the expulsion from paradise, or the Garden of Eden referenced in the writings of Thelema, as the Groves of Eleusis.

Both the Messiah and the Serpent in Hebrew give the number 358. They express in other words the same number as that of the interlocking of two other triangles, that of *IAO* (the Father, the Holy Spirit and the Son) and that of *ShMA* (the Blood, the Water and the Breath). The latter trinity was that of Jesus Christ, giving up himself as he died upon the Cross, symbolizes the Greater Mysteries of Redemption.

These six, representing the three fathers *(IAO)* and the three mothers *(ShMA)*, showcase the two modes of attainment, that of becoming still as water and making one's mind as a living flame.[37] Interestingly enough, Crowley received a similar formula by Aiwaz in 1904 where the triangle revealed is given the following conceptualization in his diary of the Cairo Working:

> The officers are always Ankh-f-n-khonsu (m) = RHK. Bes-n-maut (m) = H. Ta-nech (f) = N. The red [averse triangle]. A. only touches candidate. B. + T. may be present or not: they are the force behind A. B. is the force of matter in ether. T. the force of Generation & Light. Their union produces A. The force of Magick Union , occult power = [scorpio] the force of the key of Nun, + reflected light, the Moon.[38]

Concerning the identity of this Savior with that of Satan, indicates the 'feminine side of Ma is Pan, which explains why Pan is a devil. The only way to be really born is by annihilation - to be born into Chaos, where Pan is the Savior.'[39]

THE FORMULA OF THE ROSY CROSS

This gives an expression of the Formula of the Rosy Cross, a cross inside of a circle, also known as the Brand 666. This formula contains within itself the true secret of Magick in the New Aeon and is a universal formula. The Heart of Blood is the Heart Girt with a Serpent. The serpent being Hadit or the blood in the Heart, and the Heart being Nuit. Their union is the complete symbol, being of Ra Hoor Khuit. This being made conscious is Heru-Ra-Ha, the Great Work completed and expressed as lust

---

36 Aleister Crowley, Liber Liberi vel Lapidus Lazuli Adumbratio Kabbalæ Ægyptiorum sub figura VII in *The Equinox III·9 - The Holy Books of Thelema*, 93 Publishing Limited, 1989, p. 28.

37 Aleister Crowley, Liber HHH in *The Equinox I:V*, privately published by the A.'.A.'., 1911, p. 7.

38 Aleister Crowley, Diary, Warburg Institute, unpublished, 1904, without date but probably written between March 20th and April 9th.

39 Aleister Crowley, The Paris Working in *The Equinox IV:2 - The Vision and the Voice with Commentary and other papers*, Samuel Weiser Inc., 1998, p. 362.

without result and the Day-of-be-with-us.

The true secret of Magick then is not a mere physical thing or a single process, but rather as evolutionary science, an organizational principle, wherein ecstasy (Hadit) unites with the body (Nuit) and is given direction and movement. That is, it is made into an awakened child (Heru-Ra-Ha). This principle underlies all phenomena, including that of the developing child whose mother and father create in their union. As the child grows he attains self-awareness and in time his own volition as a sentient star or conscious globe.

The whole of the universe is then concerned with the creation of consciousness through this process, by the right order of the union of matter with energy. No wonder Crowley wrote to Charles S. Jones[40] and remarked that Magick is a way to activate kundalini, that is in this instance magical energy, presumably by giving this direction after fusing it to some object that becomes an eidolon or child of one's will.

It readily expresses the process of everything from development to evolution, scientific inquiry, and all kinds of Magick. It is none of all these things, yet it is all of those things as it is its unifying principle. Universal in application due to its elasticity and specific enough to become focused as an engine of pure will when applied for practical or mystical results. It finds its most perfect manifestation in the Miracle of the Mass, where the eucharist represents the union between ecstasy (wine) of mind or soul, and body (wafer), the magical hexagram.[41]

The High Priestess

The Priestess in the Gnostic Mass is in many ways the single most important officer of the ritual. Being referred to at first as Virgin and then the Priestess, she brings to mind another representation of this devil, the *harlot-maiden* mentioned in *Liber VII*.[42]

Jesus Christ himself is often represented in a feminine form as the Rose of Sharon. Moreover, he is the Rose that hangs upon the Phallus, which was pierced by a lance so that blood, water, and breath issued forth and was collected into a Cup. Having emptied his life into her Cup of Fornication, the Virgin has become the Harlot, ready to express the Light of the Supernal Triad, calling upon new Lovers or Priests of this Royal Mystery wherein God is perceived as being Love, and to Love him is more than enough, the oath of a Knight of the Royal Mystery.[43]

Those who have emptied their life, no longer have a functioning ego in the sense that having become No Man (of Earth), their personality is no more. That is, they are ready

---

40 Aleister Crowley, Correspondence with C. S. Jones in *OTO Archives Film #5*, O.T.O., 2002, undated but probably written in 1915.

41 For more on this formula cf. chapter 83-89 of Aleister Crowley, *Liber Aleph vel CXI*, 93 Publishing Limited, 1991, pp. 83-89.

42 Aleister Crowley, Liber Liberi vel Lapidus Lazuli Adumbratio Kabbalæ Ægyptiorum sub figura VII in *The Equinox III:9 - The Holy Books of Thelema*, 93 Publishing Limited, 1989, p. 28.

43 Cf. the tragedy in three acts that befell the Grand Master of the Order of the Temple and the subsequent institution of the degree Knight of the Royal Mystery and their oath in Aleister Crowley, The Scorpion in *The Equinox I:VI*, privately published by the A.'.A.'., 1911, pp. 67-107. Knight of the Royal Mystery was the Antient and Primitive Rite's equivalent to the degree Prince of the Royal Secret in the Ancient and Accepted Rite and the O.T.O..

to express the pure light of the interior church to the rest of mankind, creating a chain back to V.V.V.V.V., as 'the Priestess shall seek another altar, and perform my ceremonies thereon' after having completed this ritual herself.[44]

Having purged themselves of a soul or ego, the aspirant no longer becomes an aspirant or brother of the A.'.A.'., but a member or sister of the A.'.A.'. Essentially the Virgin has become a Harlot that is ready to receive and transmit unto Mankind the Communion of the Saints[45] and through that, regardless of their original gender, a Scarlet Woman.[46]

As this ritual, given in *Liber Stellæ Rubeæ*, is for the few and secret, the same ritual also declares that V.V.V.V.V. 'will give thee another ceremony whereby many shall rejoice.' The only ceremony Crowley 'received' which were for the celebration of the general population was the Gnostic Mass.[47] The identity between V.V.V.V.V. and the Priestess of the Gnostic Mass is then made perfect when we realize that the name V.V.V.V.V. itself is the five footprints of a Camel, being Gimel, and attributed to the High Priestess of the Silver Star.

GREETINGS FROM EARTH AND HEAVEN

This would give us a formula of the Gnostic Mass where the Virgin awakens the occult puberty of the Man among Men who bears witness of the Word of V.V.V.V.V. through administering the virtues to the brethren, consecrating, robing, and crowning him as a Priest. This longing or call to attain,[48] which in turn sets him in motion, ends with the throning of the Virgin, or our Soul, as the Harlot, or No Man, as Priestess upon the summit of the Earth within the Chapel of Abominations, the secret chamber of the Palace. This crowns the Man of Earth, a Lover who is ready to be received in the Chapel of Abomination.

The summit of the Earth would be a Mountain, Mons Abiegnus, or mountain of initiation. Another name of that mountain is ZION, which enumerates to 156, the number of BABALON, the Scarlet Woman, the Great Mother whom we seek to return to and become. Our soul having entered the Palace of Hell (our unconscious), and become worthy of the Groves of Eleusis by the Covenant of Resurrection, the next step is to redeem itself by pouring our life and blood into that Cup. A triangle of pure flame, whose tongues eat up our devotion.

This Mystery of Redemption, essentially aids us to return to the Groves of Eleusis *beyond the Wrong of the Beginning*. That is the creation of duality, which needs to be destroyed in or-

---

44 Aleister Crowley, Liber Stellæ Rubeæ in *The Equinox III:9 - The Holy Books of Thelema*, 93 Publishing Limited, 1989, p.89. In his commentary to this verse published in Aleister Crowley, Commentary on the Holy Books and other papers, Samuel Weiser Inc., 1998, p. 348, Crowley notes that the meaning of this verse is that one «Initiate passes it on to the next in a chain.»
45 Identified by Crowley as equalling the religious value of copulating with your magical partner, in Norman Mudd, Conversations with Crowley in *The Magical Link I·10*, privately published by the O.T.O., 1988, p 84.
46 For more on this occult doctrine concerning the soul as relating to the Master of the Temple and gender, cf. Aleister Crowley, *The Book of Lies*, Samuel Weiser Inc., 1991, Aleister Crowley, *Liber Aleph*, 93 Publishing Limited, 1991, Aleister Crowley, *The Law is for All*, New Falcon Publications, 1996, (Crowley, 1996) and J. Daniel Gunther, *Initiation in the Aeon of the Child: The Inwards Journey*, Ibis Books, 1999.
47 Aleister Crowley, *The Law is for All*, New Falcon Publications, 1996, p. 84.
48 Cf. the Infernal adorations of OAI in Aleister Crowley, Liber Stellæ Rubeæ in *The Equinox III.9 - The Holy Books of Thelema*, 93 Publishing Limited, 1989, p. 87-88 and the Song of the Sphinx in Aleister Crowley, The Vision and the Voice in *The Equinox IV·2 - The Vision and the Voice with Commentary and other papers*, Samuel Weiser Inc., 1998, pp. 239-241.

der for us to overcome the seeds of sorrow. As it is written, only 'if ye are sorrowful, or weary, or angry, or discomforted; then ye may know that ye have lost the golden thread, the thread wherewith I guide you to the heart of the groves of Eleusis.'[49]

*Figure 1. The Golden Thread that leads to the
Heart of the Master in the Groves of Eleusis.*

---

49 Aleister Crowley, Liber Tzaddi vel Hamus Hermeticus in *The Equinox III:9 - The Holy Books of Thelema*, 93 Publishing, 1989, p. 96.

iMagus

Kendell Geers

"So, you mock my blindness? Let me tell you this. You with your precious eyes, you're blind to the corruption of your life."
— Oedipus, The King

"In order to move others deeply we must deliberately allow ourselves to be carried away beyond the bounds of our normal sensibility."
— Joseph Conrad

"For my thoughts are not your thoughts, neither are your ways my ways, saith the Lord. For as the heavens are higher than the earth, so are my ways higher than your ways, and my thoughts than your thoughts."
— Isaiah 55: 8-9

We are living in an age of confusion, an age of technological acceleration compounded by an incomprehensible digital velocity. Generations are now separated by a few years only, marked by seasons of mobile phone updates and the ebb and flow of social media. An iPhone 5 or 6 marks time the way a decade once did. Time is marked by the image, marked by the representation of events, catastrophes, lifestyles and of the image itself. Where the image was once the strict domain of artists, designers or photographers, it is now within the reach of everybody with a telephone, smartpad or computer.

On the 25 October 1917 Leon Trotsky declared, "You are pitiful, isolated individuals! You are bankrupts. Your role is played out. Go where you belong from now on – into the dustbin of history!" A year short of an entire century later, I wonder what might be thrown out as the garbage of today, what will be remembered and what shall define the epicentre of this image saturated era?

Looking further back through history, we amuse ourselves with the image of an illiterate Medieval era. We chuckle about the ignorance of an age in which the word, written and spoken, was used as a weapon of mass distraction by the Medieval church to subjugate the masses. The literate priestly classes used their education and knowledge to terrify the illiterate, who, unable to read the Bible themselves, flocked faithfully to believe in everything they were told, mediated by images. With monastic zeal, the priests, clergy and monks propagated an image of Hell filled with terror and torture, a place where sinners were condemned for all eternity.

With the help of artists, the church offered the illiterate the consolation of knowledge and understanding mediated through images. The artists gave form to the Papal propaganda, fleshing out the descriptions of the Devil, and of his domain of Hell, terrorising the faithful with imagery that was not inspired by anything other than conjured fear. The image was used, in paintings, stained glass windows, manuscripts, frescoes, icons and illustrations to instil fear and terror, an opiate and weapon in maintaining political control.

The priests spoke of the Devil as a vile and venomous serpent with hooked tail and burning demonic eyes. They carefully obscured and equivocated upon the scriptural description of the shining beautiful morning star of Isaiah 14:12 and the wilful fallen angel of Ezekiel 28:11-17, "full of wisdom and perfect in beauty" covered with every precious stone "the sardius, topaz, and the diamond, the beryl, the onyx, and the jasper, the sapphire, the emerald, and the carbuncle, and gold." Instead of being the seal of perfection, God's own most perfect creation, the exquisitely crafted arch angel, instead of being a fallen angel, the Devil was represented as everything we might imagine we could be terrified of.

Satan was not the *Shayṭ*ān (Arabic: الشيطان) or *Shaitan* of the Quran, the first created Djinn who refused to bow before Adam.

> "It is We Who created you and gave you shape; then We bade the angels prostrate to Adam, and they prostrate; not so Iblis; He refused to be of those who prostrate. (Allah) said: 'What prevented thee from prostrating when I commanded thee?' He said: 'I am better than he: Thou didst create me from fire, and him from clay.'" – Quran, sura 7 (Al-A'raf) ayat 11-12

The Devil was not *Iblis*, a proud Djinn that the Quran says considered himself superior to Adam and whose name translates from the Ancient Greek *Diábolos* (διάβολος) a word that later evolved into the French *Diable* and finally the English *Devil*.

For a thousand years, fear and ideological terror held a continent in the dark, under the cloak of images stitched together by artists, commissioned by an educated elite few who had elevated themselves to positions of uncontested power and unquestionable authority.

How is it any different today? How is our contemporary experience any different from that of the Dark Ages? How is the contemporary image of our world any less Medieval as we believe what we see, a world we know through images rather than first hand?

We might have access to the world's entire library of knowledge in the palms of our hands, just a click of the thumb away on our smart phone, but too many have abdicated the skill of reading and the right of understanding in favour of seeing to believe. Knowledge is conflated with information on the assumption that being able to look up any fact, date or detail, makes for intelligence. Dinner discussions are punctuated with grand slams through Google to check the date of a film or the name of an actress, the forgotten details of a world unremembered.

As our ancestors lost the skill of remembering once the written word subjugated the oral tradition, so too has the smart phone replaced the skill of first-hand experience of learning. The palms of our hands are encrusted, not with William Blake's "World in a Grain of Sand and a Heaven in a Wild Flower" of "Eternity in an hour," but with uploads and status checks as every waking moment gets hash tagged against the theatre curtain of a mediatised world swimming in an ocean of images.

We read newspapers online and watch news flashes on our phones, trusting that the information being transmitted is correct and authentic, with the same trust our Medieval forefathers had in their clergy. Images of tornadoes, charts and graphs of heatwaves, death tolls, financial values, rankings and percentages of bee populations in decline are interspersed with images of extremist beheadings, race riots, invading shiploads of refugees drowning on the waves of discontent. Shocking images of terror and tyranny keep us on the very edge of social fear and paranoia. The vast majority of people on the planet prefer to experience their world pre-digested and mediated by images. The need to touch the fire to learn the lesson has lost its magick as most people are more than content to watch endless loops of Jackasses burning their hands on YouTube as substitute.

Free time is no longer ours, as the beach, the airplane, the train station, subway and café, have all been tied into the web. Free time, that lonely domain that used to be the offset of boredom kicking off curiosity, play, seduction and the hedonistic pleasures of excess, is now a moment to status check and upload more selfies. The critical mass of free time that once signaled the offset of unproductive pleasure has been hijacked as trophy. People are captured with images, then tagged as proof of friendship. We prove our worth by capturing experience on our smartphone, caught in and on the act. Everybody is now both paparazzi and celebrity, famous for a second online. We are all the prey of our own image and hunters of each other's.

The image has accumulated spectacle status and becomes the ultimate trophy of experience. It's not just any trophy but the hollow and stuffed trophy of an emptied out experience. Instagram does not permit the image to be enlarged, saved, edited or in any way changed. Content is reduced to hashtags, random semi-literate or ironic phrases that fix the image like the wood used to attach the skull and horns of a deer to the wall of the colonial trophy room.

What you see is what you get and that's all there is. There is no room for detail, error or content, no room for reading, no possibility to inspire emotional response or aesthetic confusion. Simply put, the image is reduced to the shadow of a dried out corpse.

The world's oldest profession, the artists, have always been the traditional custodians of the image, sustaining it since the Neolithic time of the cave paintings. Artists wrestle the image to its limits, from representation to abstraction and back, from iconoclasm and protest to celebration. Artists live on the knife's edge of the image, cutting themselves to the core, twisting and turning the lines of logic and illogic to tie the image down to something meaningful or meaningless.

But the image is no longer theirs to create, much less have any control over. The image is now the domain of everybody with a phone pre-programmed for zero defect.

Every photograph is guaranteed to look good and the possibility of human error taken out from our hands.

The filters and settings automatically adjust the focus, aperture, exposure and control every variable to ensure that the image is always perfect. Even then, once the photo has been taken, the software to edit and upload the photograph are jammed with their own filters and pre-sets, ensuring that the image is always perfectly tailored to the standards of our expectations. Our choices are limited to colour, or black and white, more or less exposed, old school or hip. The pre-programmed filters make a photographer and artist out of everybody, with the guarantee that the image will always look good, no matter what. The filters permit a degree of freedom, but not enough to make a mistake.

The rustic darkroom, dank with human error, experiment and creativity has been abandoned in favour of the Photoshop plugin and filter. I recall the story of the mouse that ran over Lee Miller's foot in Man Ray's darkroom. She screamed and panicked, turning the lights on, then realising her error, quickly turned them off again, an accident that created the "Solarisation" technique. Whilst Photoshop now provides the perfect filter to solarise your digital photographs, the "mistake" that led to its invention would be impossible today.

> "The worst is not death but being blind, blind to the fact that everything about life is in the nature of the miraculous. The language of society is conformity; the language of the creative individual is freedom. Life will continue to be a hell as long as people who make up the world shut their eyes to reality." – Henry Miller

More than half the world's population live in Medieval conditions of poverty and disease. A privileged few live out lifestyles of luxury and have grown lazy with comfort, demanding perfect delivery of everything with the least effort. All knowledge and information is available with the press of a button, the entire history of everything ever thought, ever said, ever invented or imagined, delivered at the push of a button directly to the palm of our hands. Clothes, food, cars, furniture, cosmetics and lifestyle are available without effort delivered without delay or any effort at all in perfect shape and form.

Everything is possible and available and therefore nothing has consequence or meaning. The image of our daily lives is reduced to a thumbnail, in form, as well as content. Unselfconscious social habits ensure the survival of the social media as the pressure to be "liked" escalates and we are judged by the number of followers and nothing else. We would rather lie to ourselves than offend strangers by expressing unlikeable truths.

> "She lacks confidence; she craves admiration insatiably. She lives on the reflections of herself in the eyes of others. She does not dare to be herself." – Anaïs Nin

"We become sphinxes, though fake, up to the point we no longer know who we are." – Fernando Pessoa

Resistance is futile because every protest or subversion is drowned out in the noise of empty, hollowed out images. Read MTV as Empty V. The nature of social media precludes the possibility of any counter culture or underground movement because content is not tolerated. If you want to destroy anything subversive or revolutionary, make it fashionable so that it gets lost in the crowd.

Behind the scenes, bots are busy scanning, flagging and eliminating anything inappropriate, determined by the fears of the consensual classes. Machines read us, read between our lines, mapping out our desires to sell our data to other machines that will in turn manipulate our perceptions online, to sell our own habits back to us as lifestyle. There is nothing sensual about consensual censure as flesh and blood are wiped from the screens of digital reality.

ENTER TAINT HEM ASSES!

This mass meltdown of critical content is symptomatic of our species, for as soon as a crowd gathers, we lose our sense of individual and the group takes over. Online social media embody and emulate the exact same social relations of any crowd, anywhere. The alpha males and better females will lead and the rest will follow. We love to hate Marina Abramovic because we hate to love the people who love their image of her. This is neither a conscious process, nor simple, but it cannot be disregarded. It would even appear that thoughts are viral and spread across a group, from person to person without verbal encouragement or conscious directive. In a crowd of drunk people, the strictest of Alcoholics Anonymous Teetotallers will find themselves acting and feeling as if they are drunk, without having had anything at all to drink. Yawn in a crowded room and observe the yawn being passed around from person to person without anybody noticing.

Fans seated in a football stadium will find themselves in one mind, as the virus of a common interest leads their chanting, waving and anticipation. They will rise and fall together in their seats, exclaiming shrieks of disappointment and whoops of joy as if they were a single person with twenty thousand mouths. The entire stadium of fans from two opposing teams behave with the same ecstatic force as two lovers "in flagrante delicto."

This is also the reason why an entire continent of people once believed the world to be flat and happy to stand by, watching anybody who dared to challenge that habit, burn at the stake. It is our natural condition to seek the path of least resistance, to fall into line, doing exactly what we imagine we are told. We fall into places of habit and call them "normal" or "common sense," believing absolutely anything, following absolutely any fashion, trend or dogma that stands upon the horizon of our perceptions.

Nature has been offset as alien and external to our reality, something invasive and dangerous that needs to be contained, an unwelcome intruder to our perfectly tailored and wonderfully serviced world of culture. Nature is our enemy because it is out of control. Nature is dirty, chaotic, it stinks, bites, stings and itches. So we genetically modified seeds to germinate only unreproductive symmetrical crops. Imagine the confusion if tomatoes were all shades of red and grew in different sizes and shapes, from the same plant, and just sprouted wild in our parks and traffic islands right next to the banal public art?

Our own natures' stink and grow out of order as we sweat and decay with age, so we made enemies of ourselves. Our hair is out of control as men lose their hair from all the wrong places and women sprout hair from all the wrong places, if it's not the wrong colour, or too grey. The skin wrinkles and is either too pale or too dark. We stink from work and itch with age so we hate everything that links us to our individual natures.

We gaze upon our individual selves through the prism of the image, saturated with perfection, filtered through the media. The virus of consensus assails our senses until we believe that it is normal common sense to destroy everything that makes us human in favour of the perfectly photoshopped image of what makes us human. In his 1972 classic, "Ways of Seeing" John Berger sums up the process of how women adapted their perception of themselves to fit male perception: "Men look at women. Women watch themselves being looked at. This determines not only most relations between men and women but also the relation of women to themselves."

Laura Mulvey followed on with an even more radical Feminist analysis of how women perceive their individual selves through the eyes of male others:

> "In a world ordered by sexual imbalance, pleasure in looking has been split between active/male and passive/female. The determining male gaze projects its phantasy on to the female form which is styled accordingly. In their traditional exhibitionist role women are simultaneously looked at and displayed, with their appearance coded for strong visual and erotic impact so that they can be said to connote to-be-looked-at-ness."

> "To be the object of desire is to be defined in the passive case. To exist in the passive case is to die in the passive case – that is, to be killed. This is the moral of the fairy tale about the perfect woman" – Angela Carter

It's not just women who perform the exhibitionist phantasy, blind to their own being, living in the mirror of the virus that we might mistakenly call normal. We have all fallen prey to the edited image of perfection and might even say, it makes us feel better, more beautiful to be hairless, scentless, colourless bipeds of high cultural, socially mediated understanding. Every man and woman, child and churl, sees themselves through the eyes of everybody else looking through the image of what we are supposed to look like. As the image has lost its complexity so too has our nature.

The seasons of Summer, Autumn, Winter and Spring have been rebranded as Fashion Weeks.

The simplification of our nature and of experience into simplistic one dimensional harmony is the by-product of a monopolised culture that is monotheistic and monogamous. In the first Medieval age, the Catholic church needed to simplify our habits into a monotheistic cult that was centred around the white European male. They invented the fear of the infadel and the infidel to maintain their order. Capitalism, the progenitor of the second Medieval age, inherited this single-minded habit and built its own towers of conformity upon the same foundations as though they were God's will.

As the church needed artists to supply the terrifying imagery necessary to maintain the hierarchies of its dogma, the captains of monopoly interest and capitalist culture need artists to do the same. This is where things went wrong and we imagined the world should naturally be Monogamous, Monotheistic and Monopolised.

Artists have traditionally crossed every social, moral, political and spiritual boundary, revelling in contradiction and ambiguity, saying one thing to their patrons and another to those who take the time to see. Instead of crossing boundaries and living between borders, too many artists today have taken leave of their senses and began to illustrate the culture industry's will. The craft of creation was adapted to illustrating the desire for total control over all nature.

"The Devil is truly the artist's best patron." – Barry William Hale

Consider the representation of Liberty in Eugène Delacroix's 1830 painting *Liberty Leading the People*. The Goddess of freedom, the embodied figure of liberty, walks barefoot over the debris and corpses of civilisation, barefoot across the noble divide between indentured royal culture and human nature. Her yellow dress of cultivated refinement is ripped open from battle and falls from her shoulders to reveal her breasts. She is proud of her sexuality and her freedom, does not care that her upper body is exposed. Her nudity is her weapon because she is complete, as a woman, as she is, refusing to accept the moral codes of encultured masculine fear. Her desire for freedom is greater than the male fear of desire. When Delacroix first exhibited the Goddess, shock and scandal followed her because it was considered bad taste to represent the Goddess with hair in her armpits. The Goddess of Liberty was represented as nature, unshaved, bare breasted and bare foot. Naturally she was unconstrained by the habits of fashionable convention.

"Nature is the difference between the soul and God… Not pleasure, not glory, not power: freedom, only freedom." – Fernando Pessoa

The image of liberty and nature is dead to the contemporary art gallery as much as upon the Instagram timeline for the same reason. At two separate Human Rights Watch charity auctions in Brussels, the legendary auctioneer Simon de Pury tried to raise the prices of Anthony Gormley and Anish Kapoor, in two consecutive years, by referring to them as brands. Each year, as the bidding began to wane, he explained that Gormley and Kapoor were not artists, but brands, and therefore worth more than artists who were not branded. It did not matter what was being auctioned, nor what the works of art meant, or whether the artist had even touched the work because the name of the artist has the same social status as Coca Cola, Apple or BMW.

In May 2015 Richard Prince closed the circle between Instagram and contemporary art with a photographic series called "New Portraits," exhibited at the Madison Avenue branch of Gagosian Gallery. The images were culled straight off the timeline and selling for $90,000. In protest, one of his subjects, Suicide Girls founder Selena Mooney, began selling her own photograph of the exact same Instagram post for $90. The two photographs are indistinguishable in every way, except that Prince's brand sells for more than the Suicide Girl's. Both images are dead, regardless of their price.

Being branded was once the curse of cattle, a red hot poker burnt into their skin signifying ownership. It also represents the subjugation of savage nature by the domesticating habits of man. The artists, whose work can be read as branded, no longer belong to themselves, for their branding, burned deep into their flesh, makes them nothing more than one more possession in the trophy rooms of their collector. Branding cannot be too complex, otherwise the flesh burns over into an uncontrollable scar with bleeding edges. The brand has to be simple to be understood at a glance and avoid any confusion about who the artist or cow belongs to. Art has to look like the idea of art, otherwise confusion corrupts the image like woodworms devouring a trophy. Branded art has to be no more demanding, nor any more complex than any other corporate logo.

The only excess or contradiction permitted are the number of assistants in the assembly lines of production on the factory flaw manufacturing the designer dissent of luxury merchandise mistakenly referred to as art.

Alfred Jarry prophesized this condition more than a century ago when he warned that "The work of art is a stuffed crocodile." Little did he know that his absurd irony would become our tragic reality.

The effort of understanding, of reading, or even of experience, is not necessary to acquire value or meaning in contemporary art. If Wittgenstein is correct that the meaning is the use, then the meaning of Prince, Kapoor or Gormley is to be collected as expensive lifestyle brands, acquired from charity auctions, trying to raise money in defence of defend Human Rights. Somewhere in the back of the collector's mind, they might whisper to themselves that Kapoor is "about spirituality" and Prince is a Marlboro Man, but it does not really matter what, how or why.

"Just add Happiness" – "It's the Real Thing!"

The white cube gallery grew out of this branded conception of art, a sacred space that excludes everything but itself. Natural light, dirt, dust, warmth, water, air, movement, colour, anything that might distract from the painting, photograph or sculpture, is excluded. Every life force is denied and chaos is subjugated in favour of manufacturing branded singular meaning.

The work of art is no longer defined as a spirit, nor an energy, not even technique or form. It is not even the expression of the artist's will, but a bra(i)n-dead image.

Life drawing classes and nature studies are no longer on the art school curriculum. Nature is neither observed, respected nor experienced. As compensation, artists study artists copying artists. The system devolved into a self-devouring social beast that digests itself in order to replicate itself. Art about art about the market of art about art.

Where the artist was once the life force of the art system, that honour now befalls the system itself. The viral nature of the art mob of galleries, collectors, curators, consultants, critics and life-stylists are now the collective life force sustaining the system. The condition might have been created by humans, spawned by artists, but it has since taken possession of itself, just like the machines in the *Terminator* series of films. We are all suffering a mass collective case of Stockholm Syndrome, having been kidnapped by Big Brother playing hideous seek.

"Je t'aime... moi non plus..." – Serge Gainsbourg

The gathering of social forces at openings, biennials, art fairs and auctions is now the function of art. The artist, the last surviving element of nature, out of control, has been excluded from a system defined by socioeconomic exchange rates. The old school of artists; drunk, bipolar, stoned, licentious, untoward and anti-social, has been purged in favour of those who doubled up their art school education with an MBA degree and finishing school etiquette.

> "You have a right to do that... but you have no right to judge me. It's impossible for words to describe what is necessary to those who do not know what horror means. Horror... Horror has a face... and you must make a friend of horror." – *Apocalypse Now*

In the flow of content to consensus, theory is hammered out from the moral high ground and flows down the hill from the Capital towards the consumer. On the extreme to the one side, the self-appointed politically correct elite have taken it upon themselves to protect everybody and everything from behind the watchtowers of their social media machines. They watch, listen, wait in check of every word and syllable, the self-appointed neighbourhood thought police defending everything except human nature. Theirs is a one-dimensional world of cliché in which human beings are reduced to simplified bots with hashtags for brains. Their weapon, with which they bludgeon the world into submission is the threat of being outcast as sexist, racist, homophobic, anti-Semitic, Zionist, alcoholic, addict, intellectual, privileged, colonial, male, neo-liberal, anti-social, reactionary, radical, vulgar, anti-social, old school, avant garde, romantic, unsold or bought in at auction and any other number of social scars that rumour will use to destroy anybody's reputation.

We fear to be extreme, to be too left or too right, to be left out or right on. We live in fear of not being normal, of not being part of the flow, of not fitting in with the consensus. An empty contentless one liner on Facebook accusing somebody of being out of political step is all that is required to destroy a reputation. There is no space for contradiction or complexity, much less content or context. Both Gauguin and Egon Schiele's careers would have been instantly destroyed today with accusations of being paedophiles and pornographers. Caravaggio would have been ostracised as a violent homicidal maniac.

The rise of the materialist twentieth century, underpinned by the rigor of a Marxist-Feminist critique, found moral reason to devalue the concept of "Genius." From such a perspective, the long list of historical genii had all been male, just as from a colonial perspective, they had all been White, if not European, a prejudice that favours the race, sex and class of the ruling class. In her seminal 1971 essay, "Why have there been no great women artists", Linda Nochlin explained that:

> "... in the arts as in a hundred other areas, things remain stultifying, oppressive, and discouraging to all those – women included – who did not have the good fortune to be born white, preferably middle class and, above all, male. The fault lies not in our stars, our hormones, our menstrual cycles, or our empty internal spaces, but in our institutions and our education – education understood to include everything that happens to us from the moment we enter, head first, into this world of meaningful symbols, signs, and signals. The miracle is, in fact, that given the overwhelming odds against women, or blacks, so many of both have managed to achieve so much excellence – if not towering grandeur – in those bailiwicks of white masculine prerogative like science, politics, or the arts."

The prejudice was certainly flawed and success or recognition were undeniably in favour of white heterosexual men, but the flaw had nothing to do with the concept of genius. Discrediting genius on account of it having been abused by a social class would be akin to blaming sailors for the tides.

The term genius derives from the concept of the genie, the magical creature that grants wishes to the man or woman who rubs the magic lamp or casts their magickal circle. The word is inherited from Latin and means "the guardian spirit of a person" or literally "inborn nature." Genius was understood to be something the artist "possessed," a guardian spirit assigned to each person at birth and does not refer to any latent talent for making pretty pictures.

The word was derived from the Persian and Arabic concept of the Djinn, an invisible race of divine beings that inhabit the space between humans and angels. In Islamic Theology, Djinn are said to be creatures with free will, made from smokeless fire by Allah, as humans were made of clay. They are usually invisible to humans, but we have the power to control them. They in turn have the power to possess and influence us, to guide and protect us, creating the impression that our wishes are coming true. This spiritual interaction across multiple dimensions is the mythical origin of the true story of Aladdin's lamp. King Solomon is said to have built his temple with the help of the Djinn, controlling them with "a small, golden ring, inset with a stone set in the form of an eight-rayed star. On it was engraved the hexagon seal, and within that the four letters of the ineffable name of God."

Djinn also have their own sense of humour and might prefer to humiliate their host than submit to wanton will. Recall that Iblis was proud and considered himself superior to Adam and preferred to be cast out from heaven than worship a human being. In order to converse with the unseen, inviting genius to take its possession, demands leaving behind the comfort zone of three dimensions of socially determined habit. Conjuring other ways of seeing demands entry into other ways of being, none of which are pleasant or polite by ordinary social measure.

Conjuring the Djinn, manifesting genius, is not as easy as rubbing an oil lamp and the process can be as painful as it is difficult. This is where the cliché of sex, drugs and rock and roll lifestyles has helped artists trance-form their worlds into creation. In *Diary of Drug Fiend*, Aleister Crowley observed that "In ninety-nine cases out of a hundred, any stimulant of whatever nature operates by destroying temporarily the inhibitions of education. The ordinary drunken man loses the veneer of civilisation. But if you get the right man, the administration of a drug is quite likely to suppress his mental faculties, with the result that his genius is set free."

> "The Artist is a creative genius; that is, he is of the nature of Godhead which devised the Soul as a medium for self-realization. Also, as History assures us, the Artist is of the caste of the initiated rulers of Mankind; he understands the theory of the Universe, he is an Epopt of the Mysteries of Nature, and an Hierophant of the Inviolable Sanctuary." – Aleister Crowley

The history of art is littered with the shadows and scars of artists wrestling their demons with the help of alcohol, drugs, sex, violence, suicide, schizophrenia, belligerence and more passion than patience. The habit that grinds us into obedience can only be offset through excess and force fields of disruptive bliss or pain.

It was fortuitous for the materialists of the last century, both Marxist and Capitalist, thought fit to dispossess the artist of their genius or Djinn, because that is the only condition under which art could be reduced to its material form alone. The dislocation of form and content, the divorce between spirit and matter degenerated into the space between the thumb and forefinger swiping their way across the telephone screen.

Two days after last year's April Fool, artist and critic Walter Robinson coined the term "Zombie Formalism" to describe "art that obeys all the codes of Clement Greenburg's Formalism, but is lacking any form of content." Unlike the generation of Prince, Kapoor or Gormley who, once upon a time, made the effort to think about art and its discourse, positioning themselves accordingly, the youngest generation of Zombie Formalists are entering the world of art as simply branded. Their work is remarkable not for its genius, but for their name and some sleight of hand trick. They are the market's stage magicians inviting viewers to "get-it" by not looking too closely.

Works of art are made with fire extinguishers, the drop cloth of an engineering workshop, inkjet printer errors, an artist's name scribbled and scrawled over and over again, rain splattered, windblown, skids marks, folded stains and glass boxes send by Fedex to crack on route. Every process or manner of production is valid and quickly marks the branding of one artist against another. Once branded, the artist repeats ad nauseum ad infinitum the process, copy pasting pasting pasting pasting their pastiche. The vapid nature of such work plays into the hands of an exclusively materialist market, driven by investors who would rather not be challenged as they play off their investments. The results are short lived but nobody cares as long as you are not the last in line caught out trying to flog a stain or sell a crack.

"With their simple and direct manufacture, these artworks are elegant and elemental, and can be said to say something basic about what painting is – about its ontology, if you think of abstraction as a philosophical venture. Like a figure of speech or, perhaps, like a joke, this kind of painting is easy to understand, yet suggestive of multiple meanings… These pictures all have certain qualities – a chic strangeness, a mysterious drama, a meditative calm – that function well in the realm of high-end, hyper-contemporary interior design… Another important element of Zombie Formalism is what I like to think of as a simulacrum of originality. Looking back at art history, aesthetic importance is measured by novelty, by the artist doing something that had never been done before." – Walter Robinson

In 1969 Sol Lewitt warned that "Banal ideas cannot be rescued by beautiful execution."

Contemporary artists are no longer judged by content, nor even by historical contribution or relevance, but by their market position. Starting with Picasso's "Women of Algiers" which sold at auction for $179,000,000, works of art and artists are ranked by sales down to the dollar. Art has grown into a multi-billion Dollar religion dedicated to the new age Gods of Capital. Where once people went to church to renew their faith, today they go to museums, galleries and auction houses, walking slowly through the chapels of galleries and talking with hushed whispers in the cathedral museums.

The deification of economy and beatification of the art market might best be illustrated through the shift in practice of metropolitan urban design. With respect to nature, to the rising and setting sun, cities like Paris, London and Washington were historically planned according to a talismanic logic. The mapping of a city like London was linked to the cycles of nature - the two great cathedrals of Saint Paul's and Westminster Abbey, were placed in the East and West accordingly, to symbolise either the rising or the setting sun. Lady Diana was married to Prince Charles in the East, with the rising sun at Saint Paul's – her funeral followed the setting sun, to the West, in Westminster Abbey.

In the year 2000, that symbolic logic of natural cycles found an altogether different spin. Standing on the Millennium Bridge, looking North, you face Saint Paul's, now dwarfed by the skyscrapers of the financiers and bankers around it. Looking South, across the Thames that once protected the Roman city of Londinium from heathen invaders, you gaze directly into the new cathedral of power, the rising sun of the new faith, the Tate Museum. The old East/West natural cycle of life and death has been replaced by the North/South of Capital and Global Investment symbolised by the banks and museums of art. The new cathedrals of power are the Tate, Moma, Guggenheim, Pompidou with icons of Capital Faith authenticated by the Popes of Christie's, Sotheby's and the likes of Gagosian Gallery. The world's richest and most powerful men and women stand in long lines to buy their icons of devotion, paying billions for the contemporary art of their new faith.

The problem is not these new cathedrals, nor the new faith, but that artists have yet to figure out how to fill them with symbols befitting this new age. Artists have yet to figure out how to speak in tongues and materialise the spirits and demons of an age that is accelerating faster than our senses could comprehend. How do we kick back from this moment of corporate confusion, this condition of art tethered to the yoke of a bull market? The world has changed and so too must our understanding of art. Extreme times call for even more extreme measures.

In a letter to Georges Izambard penned on the 13th of May 1871, the poet Rimbaud explained:

> "Right now I am debauching myself as much as possible. Why? I want to be a poet, and I am working to make myself a visionary: you will not understand this at all, and I don't know how to explain it to you. It is a question of arriving at the unknown by an immense, long, deliberate derangement of all the senses. The sufferings are enormous, but one must be strong, to be a poet. It's not all my fault. It's wrong to say; I think. One should say; I am 'thought up'...."

Two days later he rephrased his thoughts in a letter to Paul Demeny:

> "The poet makes himself a visionary by a long, prodigious, and rational disordering of all the senses. Every form of love, of suffering, of madness; he searches himself, he consumes all the poisons in him, and keeps only their quintessences. This is an unspeakable torture during which he needs all his faith and superhuman strength, and during which he becomes the great patient, the great criminal, the great accursed – and the great learned one! – among men. – For he arrives at the unknown! Because he has cultivated his own soul – which was rich to begin with – more than any other man! He reaches the unknown; and even if, crazed, he ends up by losing the understanding of his visions, at least he has seen them! Let him die charging through those unutterable, unnameable things: other horrible workers will come; they will begin from the horizons where he has succumbed."

Jackson Pollock was one hell of a debauched drunk, creating through an immense, long, deliberate derangement of all the senses: a trickster and a shaman. This image does not neatly fit that of an artist whose painting "Number 5, 1948" sold for $163,800,000 at Sotheby's in 2006.

The record prices for Basquiat, Bacon or Pollock are neither measure of their genius, nor in any way a distraction. The current market rankings have no relation to their art, positive or negative. Money, like art, is an electrical force that cannot be possessed. The coins in your pocket belong to you for only as long as you have them in your pocket until they move along, like electrons, down the copper wire of exchange when you buy a glass of wine or cup of coffee. They flow along from bank to pocket through wallet via transfer, flowing like water and electricity. The same process protects art, for long after the market, long after this era, long after Capitalism has collapsed, the great works of art will still be there, still flowing and inspiring and trance-forming reality with experience.

Money is not the problem any more than bullets are dangerous without people pulling the trigger. At its symbolic origin, the Dollar symbol has two different possible readings. The vertical lines with the serpentine S through them, may either refer to the caduceus and serpent of Hermes, the patron saint of artists, or else symbolise the crossing of European explorers into the New World, passing through and beyond the straits of Gibraltar, that ancient maritime limit of territory known. Either way, the Dollar sign symbolically represents trickster freedom and the liberty of the boundary rider explorer from the worlds of perceived limits. This freedom is why Governments are so afraid of "cash" which flows freely and cannot be controlled or taxed in the same way as credit or digital money.

"Charon's obol" refers to the practice of placing a coin placed in or on the mouth (or eyes) of the deceased, awaiting burial, in the ancient pagan tradition. Greek and Latin literary sources specify the coin was an obol, the payment or bribe for Charon, the ferryman who conveyed souls across the river that divided the world of the living from the world of the dead. Charon was a psychopomp, a guide like Hermes, Hecate, Mercury, Orpheus and Anubis whose primary function is to escort souls to the afterlife. The coinage could obviously not be taken into the afterlife, but functioned symbolically as a precious metal that was at the same time a conductor of electricity. Gold, copper, iron, silver, tin and lead were not only used to make coins, but also the symbolic metal attributes of alchemy representing Apollo, Venus, Mars, Artemisia, Zeus and Saturn. The movement of money, or currency, flows coin by coin like an electrical circuit from the underworld of pocket through the sweaty palm of hand to the bank vault and back to pocket, obeying the same principles of exchange as any electrical force. In metal it is the exchange of electrons that generates electrical current.

The electro-spiritual properties of coinage are a symbolic detail that those who think art should have no relation to money might consider. Besides artists, like prostitutes, have never been far from the moneyed class, never far from power, never far from the cash, biting the hand that feeds with sharp teeth that challenge power by inverting authority in a disregard of habit.

The Nkisi Nkondi nail fetish figures of the Congo stand out against all other cultural artefacts as being perceived to be uniquely African, often cited and reproduced for their ethnic difference as evidence of an authentic culture untouched by European influence. These nail fetishes have terrified European explorers and missionaries for generations on account of their violent iconography with countless nails driven into the wooden figure. The European viewer can only stand back to gaze upon these figures in terror because they have grown blind to their own cultural history.

In his *Naturalis Historia*, written between 77 and 79 AD, Pliny the Elder declared "ex africa semper aliquid novi" which translates as [there is] "always something new out of Africa" in praise of the complexity and diversity of the continent that spreads out from the South and to the West of Ancient Egypt. Africa was never a lost continent and always an active participant in exchange of ideas and goods, to and fro, across the Mediterranean basin.

As ideas spread through the trade networks, so too did cultural traditions adapt to the embrace new ideas based on different religious practices. The Kingdom of Kongo was the first in Africa to convert to Christianity, as a state religion. In 1483, the Portuguese explorer Diogo Cão sailed up the then uncharted Congo River, becoming the first European to encounter the Kongo Kingdom. Following his visit, many Kongo nobles, including King Nzinga a Nkuwu returned with Cão to Portugal where they converted to Christianity. King Nzinga a Nkuwu was baptised in 1491, changing his name to João I. He later reverted to his traditional beliefs, but his son Afonso I, established Christianity as the state religion of the Kongo Kingdom.

It is only with extreme European prejudice that the Nkisi Nkondi nail fetish is not read through the iconography of Christian symbolism after 600 years of being a Christian Kingdom. The nail, made from iron, a conductive precious metal of high import and value, is driven into the living wood, with exactly the same intention and manner as Christ being nailed to the wooden cross. The Nkisi Nkondi fetish figure is the psychopomp and intercessor between the worlds of flesh and that of spirit. The stomach area of the Nkisi Nkondi figure is often constructed with a mirror or glass that reveals behind it the world of spirit and to which the faithful may address their prayers. The wooden Nkisi Nkondi figure is pierced with nails, each nail a prayer to the world of spirit for guidance and protection in the world of flesh.

The form of the fetish figure seems to be fundamentally different from that of the crucifix at first glance, but it does in fact embody exactly the same symbolic attributes. To the Western eye, the difference is startling only because the eye has grown lazy in search of pre-digested content and easily decoded form. The effort required to read the nails, lance and wood through the prism of ancient symbolic code is too much for even the historian of African art. There are colonial reasons seeped in cultural prejudice that would prefer to read the Nkisi figure as "primitive" and the crucifix as sophisticated.

The figure holds an arm up high, in the position of the Tarot card of The Magician as well as the Roman God Mars, holding up a lance no less. The Nkisi Nkondi figure is in every detail the iconographic and alchemical equivalent of the crucified Christ, a syncretic Christian interpretation of a European pagan God.

The contemporary representation of Christ nailed to the cross is on the other hand very different from the popular European medieval depiction that was current at the end of the fifteenth century when the Kongo people first embraced Christianity. The Arma Christi or Weapons of Christ refer to the tools and instruments of the passion, most significantly the wooden cross, nails, crown of thorns, whip, lance, sponge and veil. The depictions and representations of these objects are every bit as violent and bloody as any Kongo fetish. The outstretched arm of the Nkisi holds a lance above whilst around the figure twine is used to attach and bind small pouches of symbolic liquids like blood, saliva, sperm or sweat. From this perspective the Nkisi Nkondi embodies exactly the same symbolism as any popular European depiction of the Arma Christi from the late fifteenth and sixteenth century.

Jesus Christ was born into the constellation of Aries, the pagan God of war and guardian of agriculture. Jesus then selected 12 fishermen as disciples to rule over the 12 constellations, marking the 2000 year long age of Pisces with Ichthys symbolism. Jesus was unequivocal in Matthew 10.34 "Think not that I am come to send peace on earth: I came not to send peace, but a sword," a declaration that marks his colonisation of and assimilation of the symbolic code of the pagan deity of war. To further embody the symbolic code, he baptised himself as the sacrificial lamb and the shepherd of his flock of followers.

The alchemical symbol of Aries and Mars is iron, a fitting symbolic reason why Jesus had to be nailed to the wooden cross, just as his side had to be pierced by the iron lance of Longinus. The consequence of the iron age was blood spilled by weapons forged in iron and used by nations at war defending the territories of land colonised by the sedentary farmers. The God of War and guardian of agriculture, the sworn enemy of nomadic invaders, is symbolised by iron that rusts the colour of blood and it is not without symbolic coincidence that blood tastes like rusted iron.

At exactly the same time that King Nzinga a Nkuwu was being baptised, changing his name to João and declaring Christianity State Religion of the Kongo Kingdom, the Renaissance artist Sandro Botticelli was working on his "Birth of Venus," the icon of Renaissance sophisticated proportion and symbolic beauty. The sea out of which Venus is born, the background from which her scallop shell emerges, is painted in a delicate turquoise green. At that time, the artist would have had to mix his paints himself so he would have been very aware of its mineral, material as well as symbolic properties. The green pigment would have been ground from Verdigris which is literally the rust of copper. As the metal of the God of war rusts blood red, so the metal of the Goddess of love and nature rusts bright green. In the Birth of Venus, Botticelli painted his Goddess with the very pigment that she is symbolised by, the form and content, mineral and symbol all being the same thing. As above so below.

For Botticelli, as with the syncretic artists of the Kongo Kingdom, the form and material, the spirit and the flesh, the symbol and its attributes, the image and its code are all the one single mirror of every interconnected other and cannot be unravelled into the individual parts. They created from a holistic concept of art that did not make a distinction between inner space or outer space, the world of the image or the world of the imagination.

Modern and contemporary artists like Basquiat and Pollock are confusing to the Zombie Formalists because their work looks so easy, dripping paint here and there, painting like a child without a thought to composition or content. Their conception of art however is not unlike that of the sculptors of the Kongo Kingdom in which the artist is more of a midwife to creation than the authoritarian author. It is not about the materials, nor the process, neither the form nor the content that makes the work of art, but a holistic conception in which the artist and every detail of his or her creation is interconnected with every other detail, above, below, without and within. When asked if he painted from nature, Jackson Pollock replied "I am Nature" and all he needed to do to create was open his senses.

> "My painting does not come from the easel. I hardly ever stretch my canvas before painting. I prefer to tack the unstretched canvas to the hard wall or the floor. I need the resistance of a hard surface. On the floor I am more at ease. I feel nearer, more a part of the painting, since

this way I can walk around it, work from the four sides and literally be in the painting. This is akin to the method of the Indian sand painters of the West." – Jackson Pollock

Pollock worked horizontally, in tune with nature, in harmony with gravity and the laws of nature and not against them. Deeply influenced by the nomadic shamans of the American plains, he channelled his spirits onto the canvas, manifesting energy and higher forces that he respected without the need to domesticate them.

"When I am in my painting, I am not aware of what I'm doing. It is only after a sort of 'get acquainted' period that I see what I have been about. I have no fears about making changes, destroying the image, etc., because the painting has a life of its own. I try to let it come through. It is only when I lose contact with the painting that the result is a mess. Otherwise there is pure harmony, an easy give and take, and the painting comes out well. . . ['Shewolf'] came into existence because I had to paint it. Any attempt on my part to say something about it, to attempt explanation of the inexplicable, could only destroy it…The modern artist, it seems to me, is working and expressing an inner world – in other words – expressing the energy, the motion and the other inner forces. Painting is a state of being… Painting is self-discovery. Every good artist paints what he is. My concern is with the rhythms of nature... I work inside out, like nature." – Jackson Pollock

Francis Bacon described the very same collaboration with nature (chance) in different words:

"I believe in deeply ordered chaos. In my case all painting is an accident. I foresee it and yet I hardly ever carry it out as I foresee it. It transforms itself by the actual paint. I don't in fact know very often what the paint will do, and it does many things which are very much better than I could make it do."

"I began in absolute chaos and darkness, in a bog or swamp of ideas and emotions and experiences. Even now I do not consider myself a writer, in the ordinary sense of the word. I am a man telling the story of his life, a process which appears more and more inexhaustible as I go on. Like the world-evolution, It Is endless. It is a turning inside out, a voyaging through X dimensions, with the result that somewhere along the way one discovers that what one has to tell is not nearly so important as the telling itself. It is this quality about all art which gives it a metaphysical hue, which lifts it out of time and space and centres or integrates it to the whole cosmic process." – Henry Miller

If I had to be perfectly honest I would love to hate the work of artists like Jackson Pollock (not to mention Basquiat and Bacon). I hate everything about his work and about his machismo, the virile masculinity that spills its seed across the canvas, the brute force of the anti-intellectual casting his shadow of chance upon the floor of synchronicity. I might wish to say that it's all just too easy and that any living dead Zombie can do it, but I cannot.

Pollock practiced like any shaman, walking the razor edge that separates the multi-dimensional abyss of infinite creation from three dimensional rational understanding. He never touched the canvas, but hovered above it like an incubus, dancing back and forth, like a reed possessed by the wind. He gives birth to the creation, but cannot claim to be the sole creator.

The splash, drip, dribble, the memory of an energy cast through the air and left to find its own memory of form upon the canvas might just be the perfect embodiment of the contradiction between nature and culture. Nature provides the impetus, creates the resistance, generates the limits and obscures the process with chaos, but the artist dances upon those limits, dancing naked through the air, hovering with his will tuned in like an x-ray apparatus to the mysteries of creation. The artist, with his education, his language, literature, poetry and desire flow through the mists of intent but the final decision is nature's own to make, as the mark explodes with its own rhythm upon the canvas surface.

This splash of chance can be read, by a seer, in the very same way as they read tea leaves in China and coffee grinds in Istanbul, manifesting and embodying destiny much as the tarot cards, I Ching or the lines on the palm of your hand. The splash of paint obeys the laws of nature, follows the call of gravity and finds form in accordance with divine will.

Picabia's *La Sainte Vierge*, a splash of indian ink on a sheet of paper is not at all heretical, nor absurd Dada provocation, but was as sacred as any Black Madonna, an unmediated way to re-member sacred spirits. To the divinatory illiterate it remains nothing but a splash of black ink.

Our inability to read destiny in the splash, much less decide or understand how the laws of destiny play out through chance, does not make it random or meaningless. The alphabet would read as meaningless lines of abstraction to an illiterate and hieroglyphics exotic to the uninitiated. Destiny is playing her games and writing our dimensions, regardless of our feeble witness or perceptual insecurities.

"The roll of the dice will never abolish chance." – Stephane Mallarmé

Standing in front of a Jackson Pollock (or Francis Bacon or Basquiat) painting, I fall to my knees in submission. I am drawn, against my will, to his masculinity like a moth into the flame, bound by his virile charms, locked into a vision of worlds I cannot comprehend. His visceral drips and ejaculatory splashes, the wounds of colour and scars of tone are cast from the perfect storm, that spark of creation that first lit the dark skies before the dawn of our three human dimensions. He paints infinity with a feather and gives form to the crushing brutality of human nature, raw and untamed.

Pollock continues to disturb our sensibilities because he was filthy nature, because he grasped his untamed nature without shame or guilt. We are still terrified because he continues to masturbate his spiritual nature in full force, right there in front of us, daring us to enjoy watching. Instead of embracing his visionary liberty we blindfold our senses and look through pinholes at the paint only. We blind ourselves to see his energy, his vital forces, his sexuality, his nature, the genius that he was channelling. We squint and half close our eyes because we are afraid that we might be fatally attracted to what we perceive, that we might find ourselves turned on by fear and excited beyond control. We feel the terror of experience sirening our names from beyond the borders of our domesticated habits, so we pluck out our eyes to blind our ears and call it self-control.

We are terrified because he re-minds us that very few amongst us today could answer the question "What is your Nature?" and even less could find the courage to live by it. We accept the reduction of perception to 30 degrees of vision and even then disregard the 70 blurred degrees, on either side, that would save our lives in the jungle or on the battlefield. We see only in straight lines and limit our perception to that which pleases us.

Our natures are in truth contradictory, violent, virile, carnal, tactile, nomadic, curious, playful, destructive and creative, but most of all our nature is blind to itself. This innate blindness might be the very reason why Oedipus had to gouge out his eyes with his mother's golden pins in order to see what he truly is. The flow of consensus into habit might be the darkest trait of our nature, the blind ability to accept anything as normal if sufficiently repeated.

What of our other senses, wider angles and a depth of field?

> "There are more than seventy octaves of electromagnetic radiation, and the human being acknowledges the visibility of less than one octave, our sight being cramped, as it were, between the red and the violet; the colour of our arterial and intravenous blood." – Peter Redgrove

> "For I am the size of what I see, not my height's size." – Fernando Pessoa

If we do not recognise, much less respect the natural scent of our own body, how could we possibly begin to understand the natural laws that are playing out in our bodies, day and night. How many readers could perceive the difference between their own pheromones and the reverse engineered perfume that has taken possession of our nature's? The creature said to have been created in the image of God with all its scents, sweats, sperm, menses, tears, saliva, mucus, urine, pheromones, chemicals, enzymes and bacteria has taken leave of its divine nature and been hijacked into the deadly hollows of domestic complicity. It's become common sense that we should all smell like Chanel, Old Spice and Dove, because otherwise we would stink. It's common sense that hygiene is not scent, but consensus compels us into submitting to the flow. Opium and Revolution are no longer the subversive domain of counter culture idealists, but perfume brands in the culture of counter kids. It's difficult to know whether this limitation of the senses is a habit acquired after nine thousand years of sedentary living, or whether it has always been hard-wired into our being.

In his book *The Spirit Molecule*, Rick Strassman explained that the shamanic entheogenic brew Ayahuasca is made of two vines, the leaves of the Chacruna or Chagropanga plant, rich in dimethyltryptamine (DMT) and Banisteriopsis Caapi, a vine that functions as a Monoamine Oxidase Inhibitor (MAOI). The DMT is inactive if taken without the MAO inhibitor, which functions like a perceptual border patrol guard within our brains, controlling normal and altered states of consciousness.

Strassman goes further to suggest that our pineal glands are actually producing DMT all the time, and we only experience its hallucinatory effects and altered states of consciousness when the body secretes a MAO inhibitor at moments of life threatening stress, such as during a car crash, or as we are being born and pass away into death. This is the tunnel of bright lights, the flashing of images and appearance of angels frequently witnessed by people who have survived near death experiences.

Might this MAO Inhibitor also lie at the root of our entire pre/sub/un/conscious being? In researching Sami shamans, the anthropologist Michael Harner travelled through snow and across very difficult terrain to Alta, a very small village in the northernmost part of Norway. He walked for many days deep within the Arctic circle to meet the last known Sami shaman who knew how to perform healing rituals, using the erroneously named Witches' Drum. When he finally arrived at the shaman's abode, he knocked on the door many times without a response. He waited more than half an hour before pushing upon the unlocked door, opening it with a cinematic creak. He entered the dark empty room and made his way to a second door which he tried to open. Suddenly and without any warning, a very large man appeared from the shadows and violently threw Harner to the ground, aggressively shouting in an unknown language. As quickly as he had appeared, the assailant disappeared, leaving the Anthropologist lying in dazed terror upon the floor. Finally the shaman entered the room and asked "Do you believe in the power of the Sun?"

Before the healing could begin, the subject, Harner, needed to be shocked clean of habit and his senses opened up to other ways of seeing.

This process of disrupting the quotidian and breaking open the sensory numbing effects of habit lies at the heart of all shamanic practice and what Mircea Eliade referred to as "Ecstasy," taking his cue from the Greek etymology, a word that breaks down into "Ex" and "Stasis" or "out of the static". It is only by breaking free from the straightjacket of the consensus that flows into habit, that we are able surrender our senses to accept the responsibility of change.

For Georges Bataille, this ecstasy of experience supersedes all knowledge and demands constant renewal. The danger is that every new experience repeated, degenerates into habit. "We reach ecstasy by a contestation of knowledge. Were I to stop at ecstasy and grasp it, in the end I would define it. I remain in intolerable non-knowledge, which has no other way out than ecstasy itself."

Daniel Pinchbeck calls it "Breaking open the Head," the mind altering process of smashing to bits the numbing habits of quotidian comfort. The expression originates with the Bwiti tribe of Gabon who use the highly hallucinatory Iboga plant to induce the panic states of being necessary to trance-form.

"His greatest desire is to burn with ecstasy, to commerge his little flame with the central fire of the universe. If he accords the angels' wings, so that they may come to him with messages of peace, harmony and radiance from worlds beyond, it is only to nourish his own dreams of flight, to sustain his own belief that he will one day reach beyond himself, and on wings of gold. One creation matches another; in essence they are all alike. The brotherhood of man consists not in thinking alike, nor in acting alike, but in aspiring to praise creation. The song of creation springs from the ruins of earthly endeavor. The outer man dies away in order to reveal the golden bird which is winging its way toward divinity." – Henry Miller

In Plato's *Republic*, the artists, poets and musicians were relegated to the outskirts of society. It was believed that they were dangerous and therefore should be excluded. Today we know that is not at all true, for artists, poets and musicians are living comfortably at the very centre of society. Celine Dion, Britney Spears, Jeff Koons, Steven Spielberg or E. L. James are anything but subversive, much less anti-social. Perhaps the exclusion of the artist from the Republic was as much in protection of the artist as it was of the Republic? Having since spent way too much time downtown in the financial district, with the captains of industry, the kings of deceit and queens of corruption, once great artists get entrapped by the money and take leave of their senses to betray their craft.

Too many artists, across too many generations, have eventually grown accustomed to the luxury habit of being treated like any other celebrity or franchise. It is very difficult for artists to not get suckered in by their own success and lose touch with their vision through the repetition that degenerates into the habits that eventually destroy experience.

The critical engagement with history and the languages of art has been washed out by market demands and the artist is inevitably branded with their own earlier conceptual success. The artist may not even be aware of the ways in which the market blade cuts through practice and decimates intention. If Picasso were a young artist today, he would be stuck forever in his Blue Period with an army of assistants mixing shades in carefully prepared and labelled pots.

How does the contemporary artist begin to save their craft, to embody the creation spirit and experience of Rimbaud's "immense, long, deliberate derangement of all the senses," accessing the inner shamanic experience that precedes thought? Pollock said: "If you want to do the unconscious, you do primitive."

In a rarely quoted 1937 interview between Andre Malraux and Pablo Picasso, the Cubist artist said:

"When I went to the Trocadéro it was disgusting. The flea market. The smell. I was all alone. I wanted to get away. But I didn't leave. I stayed. I stayed. I understood something very important: something was happening to me, wasn't it?"

"The masks weren't like other kinds of sculpture. Not at all. They were magical things. And why weren't the Egyptian or the Chaldean pieces? We hadn't realized it. Those were archaic, not magical things. The Negroes' (sic) sculptures were intercessors, I've known the French word ever since. Against everything; against unknown, threatening spirits. I kept looking at the fetishes. I understood: I too am against everything. I too think that everything is unknown, is the enemy! Everything! Not just the details – women, children, animals, tobacco, playing – but everything! I understood what the purpose of the sculpture was for the Negroes (sic). Why sculpt like that and not some other way?"

"But all the fetishes were used for the same thing. They were weapons to help people stop being dominated by spirits, to become independent tools. If we give form to the spirits, we become independent of them. The spirits, the unconscious (which wasn't yet much spoken of then), emotion, it's the same thing. I understood why I was a painter. All alone in that awful museum, the masks, the Red Indian dolls, the dusty mannequins. *Les Demoiselles d'Avignon* must have come to me that day, but not at all because of the forms: but because it was my first canvas of exorcism – yes, absolutely!"

"That's also what separated me from Braque. He loved the Negro (sic) pieces, but as I've said: because they were good sculptures. He wasn't ever afraid of them. Exorcism didn't interest him. Because he didn't feel what I called everything, life, or I don't know what, the Earth? Everything that surrounds us, everything that isn't us, he didn't find at all hostile. Not even – imagine! – not even strange! He always felt at home. And still does. He doesn't understand these things at all: he isn't superstitious!"

This difference between spiritual exorcism and aesthetic formalism is what separates the faux craft of *50 Shades of Grey* from the bloodline of *120 Days of Sodom*.

Picasso spoke of the African sculptures as "intercessors" between the world of human and that of spirit, his craft as an exorcism. From this perspective we might even think of the work of art as a medium, no less. The blind sight of looking at art only as its material elements, only its medium in a physical sense, has left us with a handicap of perception that overlooks the spiritual and mediumistic role of art. It is only by reducing reality to three dimensions and experience to five crippled senses that we can be capable of believing that what we see is what we get. It was by ennobling his sense of smell to permit the synaesthesia of seeing beyond perception, that permitted Picasso to perform his exorcism of reading.

For Christian mystic Meister Eckhart, we all possess an external set of eyes with which to see the world of three dimensions and an inner set of eyes with which we may perceive the world of spirit.

We know less today about our inner space than the Medievalists knew about outer space. By inner space, I am not referring to any anatomy lesson or x-ray scan, but the inner space of our thoughts, emotions, fears, desires, dreams, hallucinations, hypnagogic phenomenon, the imagination. We know precious little about the relation between emotions and illness, or how perception influences reality. Sit still for one minute and the inner world of your senses will begin to make your ear itch for no reason at all. Sit still for ten minutes and your muscles will begin to ache. Sit still for an hour and your physical body will be tortured by the excruciating pains of an inner world manifesting itself upon your flesh. All you have to do to feel the presence of this inner world is to do nothing at all.

Even then, we know precious little about the inner experience of three anatomical dimensions because everything that we know about our bodies has been through the study of corpses, lab rats and guinea pigs. Scientists have simply assumed that living flesh is no different than dead flesh (or rodents) and generated an entire medical industry based on cutting open dead flesh. Is it any wonder that when you visit a hospital you are treated like a piece of rodent meat in need of curing?

> "What are the butcherly delights of meat? These are not sensual but analytical. The satisfaction of scientific curiosity in dissection. A clinical pleasure in the precision with which the process of reducing the living, moving, vivid object to the dead status of thing is accomplished. The pleasure of watching the spectacle of the slaughter that derives from the knowledge one is disassociated from the spectacle; the bloody excitation of the audience in the abattoir, who watch the dramatic transformation act, from living flesh to dead meat, derives from the knowledge they are safe from the knife themselves. There is the technical pleasure of carving and the anticipatory pleasure of the prospect of eating the meat, of the assimilation of the dead stuff, after which it will be humanly transformed into flesh." – Angela Carter

What if we are not the sum of our parts and our bodies are not three-dimensional containers of flesh, blood and bone? What if our bodies, our brains, our thoughts, emotions and senses are really more like transmitter-receivers communicating with multi-dimensional versions of ourselves? Does the toe understand that it does not decide where the leg walks? Or the leg conceive that the eye leads without knowing? Could the pointing finger begin to imagine the eye seeing the path, upside down, unconsciously inverted, directed by the desire that has been translated deep within our animal need for the stomach to be sated by tastes remembered on the palate? We are so much more complex than we permit ourselves to accept.

Might this be what Peter Redgrove means when he speaks about "the physical enhancement of atmosphere in a church at the height of a ceremony, at the theatre or concert hall, at a football match, in a room where people have been making love, or during the mutations of a storm... In creating a ritual atmosphere, we are also creating a charged gas that is sensitive not only to ourselves, but to outside atmospheric and cosmic influences: a kind of radio set or radiation detector."

Novalis has the key when he asks "Who has divined the high meaning of the earthly body?" Only very recently, as technological advances permit us tiny peeks into living tissue, have researchers begun to suggest that the fascias, that network of inter-connective tissue, might be the very same energetic network of Acupoints and Meridians that Chinese medicine is based on. These very real fascia channels dry up shortly after we die and have therefore been overlooked by western research, just as the Chinese Meridians have been dismissed as superstition.

It is only because we live with our heads stuck up our own backsides that we think the world revolves around our five senses of three dimensions. We would have a very different perception if we gouged out our three-dimensional eyes to gaze deeper into the bowels of what we are, taking time and giving space to respect our nature without the prejudice of rational understanding.

William Blake summed it up by saying:

> "Man cannot naturally perceive but through his natural or bodily organs. Man by his reasoning power can only compare and judge of what he has already perceived. From a perception of only three senses or three elements none could deduce a fourth or fifth. None could have other than natural or organic thoughts if he had none but organic perceptions. Man's desires are limited by his perceptions; none can desire what he has not perceived. The desires and perceptions of man, untaught by anything but organs of sense, must be limited to objects of sense."

Our inner world of thoughts, dreams, fears, desires, intuitions, emotions and imagination is every bit as real and consequent as the world of this text and the paper it's printed upon. Bataille called this the world of "inner experience", a world that "is not easily accessible and, viewed from the outside by intelligence, it would even be necessary to see in it a sum of distinct operations, some intellectual, others aesthetic, yet others moral… It is only from within, lived to the point of terror, that it appears to unify that which discursive thought must separate."

I prefer to call this "Radical Subjectivity", the poetic militarisation of the senses in the war against cynical materialist objectivity.

The pain of love lost or the lonely trauma of separation by death is every much as real as breaking a leg. The beads of cold sweat churned out from a nightmare are no less real than the hot sweat of labour or the steam jets of sex. The mind racking pain of depression can be as deadly and just as fatal as a bullet with your name on it.

This is the world of the artist and the bucking spirits they ride into creation. This interzone between the inner worlds of experience, of emotion, intuition, instinct, imagination and the outer worlds of the image. The task of the Radical Subjective artist is to turn themselves inside out, in an upside down world with an exorcism of spirit, to spiritualise matter and materialise spirit. It is most often neither pleasant, nor easy, but it's never about aesthetics, beauty or form.

According to Joséphin Péladan, "Art is man's effort to realise the Ideal, to form and represent the supreme idea, the idea par excellence, the abstract idea, and great artists are religious, because to materialize the idea of God, the idea of an angel, the idea of the Virgin Mother, requires an incomparable psychic effort and procedure. Making the invisible visible; that is the true purpose of art and its only reason for existence."

Carl Jung described the relation between the two worlds as "the phenomenology of an 'objective' spirit, a true matrix of psychic experience, the most appropriate symbol for which is matter. Nowhere and never has man controlled matter without closely observing its behaviours and paying heed to its laws. The same is true of that objective spirit which today we call the unconscious: it is refractory like matter, mysterious and elusive, and obeys laws which are... non-human or superhuman."

The trance-formation of inner experience and Radical Subjectivity into the image demands "Breaking Open the Head," using whatever means available to experience the inside-out turn. Terence McKenna says that the task of the artist is "to break through the machinery of cultural conditioning, in the same way that the shaman does, and to attempt to discover something authentic – something authentic outside the self-generated language cloud... It is not shining from behind you; it is shining ahead of you. It is actually that the same organizational principles which called us forth into self-reflection has called forth self-reflection out of the planet itself. And the problem then is for us to suspect this, act on our suspicion, and be good detectives and track down the spirit in its lair. And this is what shamans are doing. They are hunters of spirit."

The process begins with understanding that the i-mage cannot be separated from the i-magus who conjured it out from the multi-dimensional domain of the i-magination, into these three poor dimensions we mistakenly call reality. The image is the embodied three-dimensional re-presentation of the multi-dimensional spirit of the i-mage. The artist or i-magus is the midwife of creation, opening the way to channel manifestation. The Quantum physicist might prefer to call these inner dimensions Dark Matter or "spooky action at a distance" (Albert Einstein).

"Reality exists in the human mind, and nowhere else." – George Orwell

"By conviction an atheist perhaps, he is taken by surprise with moments of extraordinary exaltation. Nothing exists outside us except a state of mind, he thinks; a desire for solace, for relief, for something outside these miserable pygmies, these feeble, these ugly, these craven men and women." – Virginia Woolf

"Every day things happen in the world that cannot be explained by any law of things we know. Every day they're mentioned and forgotten, and the same mystery that brought them takes them away, transforming their secret into oblivion. Such is the law by which things that can't be explained must be forgotten. The visible world goes on as usual in the broad daylight. Otherness watches us from the shadows." – Fernando Pessoa

The i-mage is not separate from the artist who delivers it, nor from the subject who reads it or ultimately from the embodied object. The interior experience of contradiction, the dark domain of the imagination, of the underworld of non-ordinary consciousness is the block of irrational reality from which the artist must conjure the i-mage that ultimately gives rise to the image on the material planes. The creation begins deep within the domain of Hades, the underworld of Persephone, and slowly emerges, like Orpheus, into dimensions that we may read, see, hear and perceive within the domains of our five limited senses. The i-mage is created by the magus and embodied by the artist.

Reading the image through the i-mage re-members the process whereby spirit and matter can be read through each other, as above and below. The wood of the African fetish is every bit as alive as the tree that once rooted it, both conditions suggesting the other. The i-mage can be understood in exactly the same terms as Goethe's reading of nature, re-presented and re-membered:

> "Nature speaks upward to the known senses of man, downward to unknown senses of his... every process in nature, rightly observed, wakens in us a new organ or cognition... creating in the wake of an ever creative nature… Each phenomenon in nature, rightly observed, wakens in us a new organ of inner understanding."

Our process of creating, through the experience of perceiving, is ultimately responsible for nature, just as nature unfolds into manifesting the i-mage. We are not made in the i-mage of God, so much as create the image of God to give form to that which defies and resists every definition of form. We are limited by our imagination only, by our contradictory ability to conjure the i-mage through our limited senses of perception.

> "How difficult it is to refrain from replacing the thing with its sign, to keep the object alive before us instead of killing it with the word. If we cannot understand a particular phenomenon, we must learn to make fuller use of our senses and to bring our intellect into line with what they tell… There may be a difference, between seeing and seeing... The eyes of the spirit have to work in perpetual living connexion with those of the body, for one otherwise risks seeing yet seeing past a thing. [Images] should be sought and investigated as they are and not to suit observers, but respectfully as if they were divine beings." – Goethe

The stock and trade of the Avant Garde artist has always been shock, and it would do us well to re-member that today. Through violence, shock, the terror of the sublime, the artist challenges socially conditioned perceptions.

> "In the very space of suffering and obsession, you introduce such exaltation, such magnificent violence, welded to the hammering of words, that the evil is progressively dissolved, replaced by an airy demonic sphere – a marvellous state!" – Henry Michaux

That is one of the primary reasons for being outcast by Plato as subversive and dangerous. The shock that I refer to however should not be confused with the shock doctrine of contemporary artists instrumentalizing reactionary tastes into seasonal scandals, with which to kick-start their careers. By shock I am not referring to the manipulation of mediatised controversy by killing animals with a hammer or going to jail as a means of acquiring brand, but something closer to shock therapy. The shock that I speak of should be understood in the very same terms as the Sami shaman who threw Harner to the floor and asked him "Do you believe in the power of the Sun?" The shock of unbinding habits using the intensity of experience as catalyst. The ecstatic process re-presents the image in electrically shocking ways that restore their magick.

In "The Soul of the Ape," South African Naturist Eugene Marais wrote about his research in hypnotising a young woman into forgetting everything that she had been taught. In this way he discovered that her sense of smell, sight, memory and sensitivity exceeded that of the Chacma Baboons that he spent three years living with.

We don't need to be hypnotised to know, in our flesh and bones, that we are capable of so much more than we give ourselves permission for. Anyone who has taken mind altering substances, be they chemically engineered drugs or natural entheogens, knows very well that we can see, think, understand and conceive of things beyond our perceived limits once the cerebral censor board and inner perception police have been silenced.

A new designer drug called Flakka gives its subject superhuman strength. After enough wine or MDMA our morality slides and permits us pleasures that would otherwise be taboo.

It's not just through inebriation that we might find re-lease, but by taking the time to listen to the Radical Subjectivity of our senses, to shock ourselves into wakeful consciousness. Ask any athlete about the adrenaline rush and second wind that follows total exhaustion. Tibetan Buddhists speak of the exact same hallucinatory shift of perception as the Ayahuasca shaman, but after decades of strict meditation. Using Holotropic Breathwork alone, Stanislav Grof is able to induce states of consciousness comparable to his own 1960s experiments using L.S.D. The San Bushmen danced themselves into trance through 24 hours of exhaustion and the Sami shaman used nothing more than the beat of a Witch's Drum.

In an emergency, through trauma, or under shocking circumstances, people have been known find the strength to lift motor cars, leap across ravines or even fight off a hungry shark; feats that under normal states of consciousness would be impossible to even consider, let alone achieve. Many a Nobel prize-winning scientist found the keys to their research on L.S.D. or by mindlessly relaxing in a hot bath. Archimedes was so taken by his ecstatic understanding of volume and displacement in the warm bath, that he ran naked through the streets of Syracuse screaming "Eureka!" It is by now common knowledge that a sugar coated placebo will induce the same results on the subject as the drug it pretends to be, if the subject believes it to be true.

These non-ordinary abilities and shifts of perception are not induced, nor enhanced by the mind altering substances, but inherent to our beings, and the drugs, alcohol, hypnosis, shock or trauma merely turn off the mechanisms of control.

Already in 1938, Antonin Artaud understood the tragedy of our perceptual condition when he said:

"How hard is it, when everything encourages us to sleep, though we may
look about us with conscious, clinging eyes, to wake and yet look about
us as in a dream, with eyes that no longer know their function and whose
gaze is turned inward. If our life lacks a constant magic it is because we
choose to observe our acts and lose ourselves in consideration of their
imagined form and meaning, instead of being impelled by their force."

Consider the possibility that our bodies might be nothing more or less than transmitter
receivers and that the Radical Subjectivity of lived experience generates the waves of
change with which we may tune ourselves. The most powerful and easily accessible
quotidian mind altering experience we are capable of, but choose to ignore, is that of
sexuality. It opens every channel, in every dimension, of every pore, nerve ending and
hair follicle, literally creating life. During sex, our senses open up to the slightest touch,
the most subtle of scents, the hardest thrust, the pain of pleasure, the deafening sound
of breathing and a heart beating with savage re-lease. A mind-blowing, body-racking
orgasm, is the equivalent of a hundred hours at the psychologist.

"There are so many minor senses, all running like tributaries into the
mainstream of sex, nourishing it. Only the united beat of sex and heart
together can create ecstasy." – Anaïs Nin

Sex is not unlike art in its process of using a fragile balance of fear and desire to create
something living. Both are perfect mediums with which to bind together the Radically
Subjective worlds within to these three dimensions without. Both demand total
surrender of the five senses and an abdication of rational processes to access the little
death of orgasm and ecstatic re-lease.

Sex has an intimate relationship with fear. We fear that which we desire and desire
that which we fear. The disciples of cliché love to quote from Frank Herbert's *Dune:*

"I must not fear. Fear is the mind-killer. Fear is the little-death that brings
total obliteration. I will face my fear. I will permit it to pass over me and
through me. And when it has gone past I will turn the inner eye to see its
path. Where the fear has gone there will be nothing. Only I will remain."

The truth is far more complex and mysterious, for fear is not a mind-killer at all, but a
mind-sharpener. With fear, our subjective senses open up to experience every tiny fragile
detail, heightened to the point of terror, if not panic. Comfort and our dependency on
habit are the real mind-killers that fear devours like a hungry wolf in the acid bath of
chaos.

In his film *The Sacrifice,* filmmaker Andrei Tarkovsky suggest that the ritualisation
of habit, the excessive repetition of quotidian rites like a mantra, might be the way of
breaking them down into something spiritual: "You know, sometimes I say to myself,
if every single day, at exactly the same stroke of the clock one were to perform the same
act, like a ritual, unchanging, systematic, every day at the same time, the world would

be changed. Yes, something would change, it would have to." The word ritual can only be removed from the word spiritual by semantic exorcism.

> "Every situation means dependency, hundreds of dependencies. It would be unheard of if this state of affairs were perfectly satisfying or if a man – however active he might be – could really fight against all these dependencies effectively. One of the things you can do: exorcism." – Henri Michaux

We fear the experience of fear because it cannot be controlled, but mistake that for a bad thing. Fear is indeed the "little death that brings total obliteration," but in English we call the "little death" an orgasm. We speak about getting turned on by sex and electrified or shocked by fear, words we use loosely, but which speak volumes about the potential of their transformative electrical nature.

The Medieval church used the proximity of sex to fear as vehicle for demonising sexuality into taboo, limiting the experience of the body to prayer and procreation. They needed to do so in order to emasculate the pagan traditions of believing in the body as a sacred temple of nine holes. Julius Caesar already tried to destroy the Celtic tribes, citing the fact that women fought alongside men in battle, as equals, to be barbaric and reason enough to commit genocide.

The nature based traditions of the Celts, and other European pagans, celebrated sexuality as a sacred key to the divine mysteries, integrating it into their rites and rituals. Women were not only equal to men in battle, but in every detail of the social matrix. In initiatory rites of passage, they were considered superior to men. Given the close natural relation between the female menstrual cycle and its celestial mirror, the moon cycle, women were worshipped as priestess and initiatrix, channeling the spiritual mysteries into sacred embodiment.

It was believed that women are either the descendants of Eve or of Lilith. The Talmud explains that God created Adam and Lilith, at the same time, from the same clay making them equals in every way. Before long the macho Adam grew tired of this equality and protested that Lilith refused to obey him, refused to lie beneath him during intercourse and refused to be anything but his equal. He begged God to create a more subservient and obedient woman as replacement.

Taking pity on his pathetic creation, God created Eve, from Adam's rib, that she may forever be an acquiescent part of his flesh. God took Lilith as own consort when his Shekinah was away, but still she refused to be domesticated and eventually flew off through the night skies, screaming with pleasure.

Where Eve represents the seeded, functional, fecund, moment of the menstrual cycle, Lilith represents the contrary, that moment of menstrual infertility when any bloody sexual contact can only be for reasons of pleasure. Eve's sexuality is defined by its service to men, whereas Lilith's is entirely her own as she takes possession of her pleasure. She terrified insecure macho men, like Adam, into believing she was "the night-demoness, the succubus-incubus, the left-hand wife-husband who consorts with those who sleep alone and who blesses or curses them with nocturnal orgasms and erotic dreams. She was the child-killing witch of the menstrual period, when the womb fills with blood instead of offspring." (Peter Redgove)

The rise of male-centred Christianity had no space for an independent sexually emancipated Goddess, the erotic consort of God himself, so they imprisoned her in the image of a woman of sin and offered mankind the image of the Virgin as consolation.

Eve was the original unsoiled, untouched Virgin, eventually reincarnated as the mother of God. She represents "man's" image of fertility and fecundity, the unsullied mother who carries the unsoiled egg, waiting to be fertilized by her man's sperm. Eve embodies the idea of sexuality without pleasure, sex for purely procreative function. In every way she is the domesticated lady in waiting, at the service of Adam, quickly transforming from innocent virgin to naïve mother. Once the man has sown his seed, the virgin woman is defiled and in the process 'completed' by man, her hole filled. Her function and destiny being to make more virgins for more men to desecrate with procreating further male phantasy.

> "Mother is in herself a concrete denial of the idea of sexual pleasure since her sexuality has been placed at the service of reproductive function alone. She is the perpetually violated passive principle; her autonomy has been sufficiently eroded by the presence within her of the embryo she brought to term. Her unthinking ability to reproduce, which is her pride, is, since it is beyond choice, not a specific virtue of her own." – Angela Carter

Just as men are attracted to virgins that they might deflower sexually and subjugate through childbirth, so too are they distracted by whores with whom they can be their animal selves. Nomadic whores, wandering the dark streets, inviting men to fuck without thinking, to lose their culture in exchange for a brief moment of animal frenzy. Men are terrified of strong women who are not afraid of their sexuality, not afraid of their nature, but cannot stop themselves from coming for more.

When Édouard Manet first exhibited his "Olympia" at the 1865 Paris Salon, it unleashed unprecedented scandal because the artist had decided to depict his reclining nude, his Venus as a prostitute rather than the coy Eve with downcast eyes. Not only was she a Lady of the Darkest Hour, but she was not ashamed, nor embarrassed, gazing out at male viewer, looking his masculine fears straight in the eye. The painting was condemned "immoral" and "vulgar." Émile Zola said, "You wanted a nude, and you chose Olympia, the first that came along. When our artists give us Venuses, they correct nature, they lie. Édouard Manet asked himself why lie, why not tell the truth; he introduced us to Olympia, this lady of our time, whom you meet on the sidewalks."

> "Thou Who didst lend the eyes and hearts of whores. Their love of tatters and their cult of sores, Satan, O pity my long wretchedness !
> Thou, sage's lamp and exile's staff, serene. Guide to those kneeling by the guillotine, Satan, O pity my long wretchedness !
> Father to those whom God the Father's vice Of vengeance drove from earthly paradise, Satan, O pity my long wretchedness!

Envoi
Glory and praise to Thee, Satan, on high, Where Thou didst reign, in
Hell where Thou dost lie, Vanquished, silent, dreaming eternally.
Grant that my soul some day rest close to Thee Under the Tree of
Knowledge which shall spread Its branches like a Temple overhead."
– Baudelaire, *Litanies of Satan*

The Egyptians worshipped Lilith as Isis, just as the Sumerians worshipped her as Inanna
and the Akkadian, Assyrian and Babylonians called her Ishtar. The ancient pagans served
their Goddess in their temples as sacred prostitutes. Secret sexual rites were considered a
sacred service and if a child was conceived, the woman was still considered a virgin and
the child none other than God's own. Even St Helena, the mother of the first Christian
Emperor Constantine, served as a temple prostitute.

These women, these unashamed worshippers of Lilith, were known as Horae in
Greece and Houri in Persian, a word that later evolved into the modern term whore.
The Egyptians referred to them as "Ladies of the Hour" for the nightly pagan ceremonies
were marked by the passing of the solar vessel of Ra, much as the Christian monks
would later keep the hours of the day with calls to prayer. The Horae laid hands upon
their devotees in a tantric rite known as horasis that would culminate in a whole-body
orgasm and re-lease their consort into the visionary knowledgeable continuum, a rite
of crossing, from which he would return transformed. The body secretions of these
Temple Prostitutes were said to be so sacred that they could even heal the blind.

> "No longer was she merely the dancing-girl who extorts a cry of lust
> and concupiscence from an old man by the lascivious contortions of her
> body; who breaks the will, masters the mind of a King by the spectacle
> of her quivering bosoms, heaving belly and tossing thighs; she was now
> revealed in a sense as the symbolic incarnation of world-old Vice, the
> goddess of immortal Hysteria, the Curse of Beauty supreme above all
> other beauties by the cataleptic spasm that stirs her flesh and steels her
> muscles – a monstrous Beast of the Apocalypse, indifferent, irresponsible,
> insensible, poisoning." – Joris-Karl Huysmans

In French, the orgasm is referred to as the "little death," an apt description of that brief
moment when the senses take leave, and we lose consciousness, which is not unlike
death. No scientist, doctor or psychologist can explain where our minds slip off to,
nor can that experience be mechanically measured, but anybody that has been ripped
apart by an orgasm can testify to the earth-shattering, mind-blowing experience. The
initiate can learn to postpone the re-lease, slowly building up the intensity, wave after
wave, loading the little death, like a time bomb aching to explode in the liberation of
every sense.

As we die in orgasm for a split second, so too is life created. We lose our rational
senses and dive into the unknown unconscious darkness and return, like Orpheus,
from the underworld having created life, no less. Under these circumstances, it's very

possible, that the initiatrix might be able to hold her subject deep within the darkness just long enough for him/her to re-member and re-turn trance-formed. Chaos Magick initiates and artists dive through these layers of consciousness into the little death of infinity, using their fears of the unknown as the red rope to bind the efforts of their will. The process has to remain electrifying, otherwise the terror loses its charm and habit binds them instead to the dead end of routine. The Tantric sects of India forbid the initiatory practice between married couples because the offset of fear, terror and erotic uncertainty necessary to kick off the ecstatic chain reaction is impossible between a couple bound by domestic social habit.

> "Dear Collector: We hate you. Sex loses all its power and magic when it becomes explicit, mechanical, overdone, when it becomes a mechanistic obsession. It becomes a bore. You have taught us more than anyone I know how wrong it is not to mix it with emotion, hunger, desire, lust, whims, caprices, personal ties, deeper relationships that change its colour, flavour, rhythms, intensities. You do not know what you are missing by your microscopic examination of sexual activity to the exclusion of aspects which are the fuel that ignites it. Intellectual, imaginative, romantic, emotional. This is what gives sex its surprising textures, its subtle transformations, its aphrodisiac elements. You are shrinking your world of sensations. You are withering it, starving it, draining its blood. The source of sexual power is curiosity, passion. You are watching its little flame die of asphyxiation. Sex does not thrive on monotony. Without feeling, inventions, moods, no surprises in bed. Sex must be mixed with tears, laughter, words, promises, scenes, jealousy, envy, all the spices of fear, foreign travel, new faces, novels, stories, dreams, fantasies, music, dancing, opium, wine." – Anaïs Nin

Plutarch described horasis as "'a clean light together with warmth. This warmth brings to pass a marvellous and fruitful opening out like pores, which open to give forth persuasion and affection; but little time is needed to pass beyond the body of the loved one to pass inwards to the roots of the being, and to attach oneself to the soul, now perceptible to the cleansed vision."

The word Horasis has been mistranslated in *Acts 2:17* as "visions."

> "In the last days, God says, I will pour out my Spirit on all people. Your sons and daughters will prophesy, your young men will see 'VISIONS,' your old men will dream dreams."

This chapter of *Acts* describes the ecstatic events of Pentecost, the exorcism of the three dimensions when the faithful suddenly began speaking languages they neither understood, nor had ever learned. This Speaking in Tongues, or Glossolalia, was described as "a sound like the blowing of a violent wind came from heaven and filled the whole house where they were sitting. They saw what seemed to be tongues of fire that separated and came to rest on each of them. All of them were filled with the Holy Spirit and began to speak in other tongues as the Spirit enabled them."

Not surprisingly the events of Pentecost were said to have been the work of the Holy Spirit, that female aspect of God that is referred to as Shekinah.

This is the "Third Mind" that Burroughs and Gysin conjured with the words:

> "Why am I here? I am here because you are here… and let me quote to you young officers this phrase: 'No two minds ever come together without, thereby, creating a third, invisible, intangible force which may be likened to a third mind.' Who is the third that walks beside you?"

> "For where two or three gather in my name, there am I with them." – *Matthew 18:20*

This Third Mind is the mystical interzone of the Holy Spirit taking possession of a libidinal force, the holy trinity of creation using the forces of art and sexuality to conjure and embody the Gods. The Shekinah, that female aspect of the virile male God of the Old Testament, is the key to understanding the artist's creative process.

> "When you have proved that God is merely a name for the sex instinct, it appears to me not far to the perception that the sex instinct is God." – Aleister Crowley

> "Whether or not they exist, we're slaves to the gods." – Fernando Pessoa

The Shek(h)inah is the English transliteration of a Hebrew and Arabic noun (Hebrew: שְׁכִינָה; Arabic: السكينة), meaning dwelling or settling, implying the dwelling or settling of the divine presence of God and His Glory. The root word is often used to refer to birds' nesting and nests, a connection that might provide a key to understanding what the mystical "Language of the Birds" might have been. The word, with its connotation of the dwelling place of divine presence also seeded the word for Tabernacle (mishkan).

The Shekinah belongs to the world of spirit, the holy ghost of Malkuth, but her name means both a temple and a divine presence. We cannot enter her domain with our flesh and blood, for her realm is the meta-physical world of our imagination. As God took Lilith as his own consort in the absence of Shekinah, he offers our dimensions the same alternative, the divine Tantric "Temple of nine Holes." Lilith belongs to this world of flesh and blood, the world created in his image, but she is no less divine than any other consort of God that we may actually touch with our bodies through trance-formative lust, penetrating the inner subjective experience of the trance-physical Shekinah.

In 1919 Marcel Duchamp shocked the Parisian art world with a small, enigmatic work of art, launching Dada as a historical force. Using a lead pencil, he added a small goatee and moustache to a postcard reproduction of the Mona Lisa and the letters L.H.O.O.Q. below. These letters, pronounced in French, sound like "Elle a chaud au cul" which means "She is hot in the arse." Whilst the work is dated 1919, the very first time it was ever publically presented was in issue number 12 of Francis Picabia's magazine *391* in March 1920. It has been noted that Marcel Duchamp was not even in town at the time and might not have been consulted on the matter. The L.H.O.O.Q. is reproduced opposite Picabia's own "La Sainte Vierge," a simple drop of indian ink that was his Holy Virgin.

Earlier, in 1919, Picabia made a painting called "Le Double Monde" (The Double World) an often overlooked painting depicting a black figure eight upon an ochre background. The word letters M'AMENEZ'Y mark the centre, letters that might mean "amnesie" (amnesia) emmenez-moi (take me there) or perhaps even a wink to AMEN (so be it). Just below that it reads "que les maladies dieu n'a jamais gueri" (the diseases god could never heal). The word "bas" (bottom) is written upside down at the top of the painting and "haut" (above) is written at the bottom.

As Above So Below.

Most significantly the letters L.H.O.O.Q. are written vertically down through the centre of the tableau. History can never prove whether the letters on this painting preceded the Duchamp postcard or not, so the historians prefer to forget the detail with amnesiac dis-ease.

The expression "as above so below," that recurring mantra of the alchemists, is often associated with Malkuth on the Kabbalistic Tree of Life, the tenth sephiroth at the bottom of the tree. Although Malkuth is seen as the "lowest" sephiroth, it also contains within it the potential to reach the highest and "Kether is in Malkuth, and Malkuth is in Kether."

Malkuth is the home of the Shekinah and is symbolised by the Bride just as Tiphereth is symbolized by the Bridegroom. Unlike the other nine sephiroth, Malkuth is an attribute of God which does not emanate from God directly. Rather it emanates from God's creation when that creation reflects or mirrors God's glory from within itself. It is also associated with the feet and anus of the human body, the feet connecting the body to Earth, and the anus being the body's "filter" through which waste is excreted. Might this be a better reading of the "hot arse" than Dada non-sense?

The two worlds of the manifest and unmanifest, the physical anus of divine creation below mirroring by the divine splendour of the materially inconceivable. These two worlds, mirroring, above and below, within and without, are the two domains and double worlds of Marcel Duchamp's "BRIDE Stripped Bare by Her Bachelors, Even" the 2.75 metres tall panel of glass, divided into two parts that the artist worked on from 1915 to 1923. His final work, made between 1946 and 1966 maintains the same symbolic dualistic division of worlds mirrored: "Étant donnés: 1° la chute d'eau / 2° le gaz d'éclairage" (Given: 1. The Waterfall, 2. The Illuminating Gas)

The visitor to the Philadelphia Museum where the work is on permanent display encounters a wooden door at the end of a darkened room and must peer through two small holes to behold the three dimensional relief of a headless woman with her legs erotically spread wide. Her pose mirrors that of Courbet's *L'Origin Du Monde* or "origin of the world". Here both Courbet and Duchamp, through the key provided by Picabia, suggest the deep connection between the creation of art and creation of life, both being tantric forces that bring together the two worlds of spirit and flesh. Like the copper plated Statue of Liberty, Duchamp's Venus holds up the gas lamp of Mithras, that other solar deity who was born on the 25 December from a virgin mother, to die and be resurrected again. As Christ marked the transition from Aries into Pisces with his shepherded flock guided by fishermen disciples, Mithras was most commonly depicted sacrificing the bull of Taurus, signalling the transition into Aries.

Aleister Crowley proposed that the name Baphomet might actually have been derived from "Father Mithras":

"I had taken the name Baphomet as my motto in the O.T.O. For six years and more I had tried to discover the proper way to spell this name. I knew that it must have eight letters, and also that the numerical and literal correspondences must be such as to express the meaning of the name in such a ways as to confirm what scholarship had found out about it, and also to clear up those problems which archaeologists had so far failed to solve ... One theory of the name is that it represents the words βαφὴ μήτεος, the baptism of wisdom; another, that it is a corruption of a title meaning "Father Mithras." Needless to say, the suffix R supported the latter theory. I added up the word as spelt by the Wizard. It totalled 729. This number had never appeared in my Cabbalistic working and therefore meant nothing to me. It however justified itself as being the cube of nine. The word κηφας, the mystic title given by Christ to Peter as the cornerstone of the Church, has this same value. So far, the Wizard had shown great qualities! He had cleared up the etymological problem and shown why the Templars should have given the name Baphomet to their so-called idol. Baphomet was Father Mithras, the cubical stone which was the corner of the Temple."

The androgyne that Duchamp created out of the Mona Lisa with her "hot arse" and male goatee and moustache is Baphomet, no less. Baphomet, like Aries and the Nkisi Nkondi nail fetish figures of the Kongo Kingdom, holds his arm aloft, the other pointing down, the two worlds mirrored.

Consider the description Saint Teresa of Avila gave of her encounter with an angel:

"I saw in his hand a long spear of gold, and at the iron's point there seemed to be a little fire. He appeared to me to be thrusting it at times into my heart, and to pierce my very entrails; when he drew it out, he seemed to draw them out also, and to leave me all on fire with a great love of God. The pain was so great, that it made me moan; and yet so surpassing was the sweetness of this excessive pain, that I could not wish to be rid of it. The soul is satisfied now with nothing less than God. The pain is not bodily, but spiritual; though the body has its share in it. It is a caressing of love so sweet which now takes place between the soul and God, that I pray God of His goodness to make him experience it who may think that I am lying."

Consider now Octavio Paz's introduction to *Miserable Miracle*, the book that Henry Michaux published in 1967 about his Mescaline experiences.

> "It all begins with a vibration. An imperceptible movement that accelerates minute by minute. Wind, a long screeching whistle, a lashing hurricane, a torrent of faces, forms, lines. Everything falling, rushing forward, ascending, disappearing, reappearing. A dizzying evaporation and condensation. Bubbles, more bubbles, pebbles, little stones. Rocky cliffs of gas. Lines that cross, rivers meeting, endless bifurcations, meanders, deltas, deserts that walk, deserts that fly. Disintegrations, agglutinations, fragmentations, reconstitutions. Shattered words, the copulation of syllables, the fornication of meanings. Destruction of language. Mescaline reigns through silence – and it screams! A return to vibrations, a plunge into undulations. Repetitions: mescaline is an 'infinity-machine.' Nothing is fixed. Avalanches, the kingdom of uncountable numbers, accursed proliferation. Gangrenous space, cancerous time."

The full body orgasmic wind of experience of Michaux, the glowing Pentecostal disciples and the full body hallucinatory experience of St. Teresa, lie beyond the limits of our quotidian experience, outside the walls of our domestic habits, beyond that which we pretend to think of as real. St. Teresa understood the disturbingly uncanny nature of her confession and admitted that the uninitiated would console themselves with believing it to be a lie.

In this instance, seeing is not believing because the experience can only be synesthetic. Georges Bataille explains the experience can only be reached "through an intimate cessation of all intellectual operations that the mind is laid bare. If not, discourse maintains it in its little complacency. The difference between inner experience and philosophy resides principally in this: that in experience, what counts is no longer the statement of wind, but the wind."

This "intimate cessation of all intellectual operations" is also the "debauch" that Rimbaud was seeking, "the disordering of all the senses" by "an immense, long, deliberate derangement of all the senses", the very same "caressing of love so sweet which now takes place between the soul and God" – the whole body orgasm that re-leases creation. It is not an intellectual process, nor can it be contained within five senses or three dimensions. It is what Pollock means when he says "If you want to do the unconscious, you do primitive" or what Picasso and Michaux mean by "exorcism," the artist speaking in the tongues of languages they don't know, giving form to something they neither learned nor understand, the latent liberty that might be unleashed through unlocking the doors of perception to our Radical Subjectivity.

Entering into this state of being demands letting go of everything you think you know in favour of everything you already know but do not yet know. This unlearned knowledge demands leaving behind the comfort of the Republic by abandoning all forms of knowledge through ordinary learning. Bataille defined it by "the states of ecstasy, of rapture, at least of meditated emotion. But I am thinking less of confessional experience, to which one has had to adhere up to now, that of an experience laid bare, free of ties, even of an origin, of any confession whatever."

The difference between the domesticated "sofatic" safety of the Republic and the savagery that lies beyond its walls is as old as humanity itself and as ancient as the oldest testament of the Bible. The story of Cain and Abel, the two sons of Adam and Eve, tells of the conflict between the two irreconcilable ways of life of our ancestors. Cain, the domesticated sedentary farmer was threatened by the nomadic freedom of his shepherd brother Abel. So one day in a fit of jealousy, the agriculturist, with his fixed domestic abode, private property, paranoia, fences and borders, murders his unconstrained nomadic brother. This myth embodies the transition from the pagan hunter gatherer tribes into the sedentary farmer, a habit that evolved into the cities which became states and eventually countries. The psychological conflict between the domestic and the wild, between cultivated culture and untamed nature continues to be played out century after century in different guises.

> "A mind of a certain size can feel only exasperation toward a city. Nothing can drive me more fully into despair. The walls first of all, and even then all the rest is only so many horrid images of selfishness, mistrust, stupidity, and narrow-mindedness. Cities, architectures, how I loathe you! Great surfaces of vaults, vaults cemented into the earth, vaults set out in compartments, forming vaults to eat in, vaults for sex, vaults on the watch, ready to open fire. How sad, sad..." – Henri Michaux

Every time we pass through an airport today, that duty-free zone of nomadic transition, we are treated as terrorists and smugglers. Our private space is scanned and checked, our bodies treated as suspect, our belts, shoes, toothpaste and deodorants clothing as weapons, our thoughts dangerous. We are interrogated by fools with stupid questions like whether we packed our bags ourselves, or might be carrying any lethal weapons. Even something as innocent and pure as crystal clear water acquires the status of lethal weapon. Dare play, joke or tease and even think the word "bomb" or suggest that your bare hands or tongue might be weapons and you shall be whisked off for further interrogation.

We have all been turned into suspects of the Republics of Big Brother and willingly concede to be searched and invaded, probed and prodded as if it were normal. Of course no bombs have ever been found because no terrorist would be stupid enough to walk up to the airport gates and introduce themselves with a bomb under their arms. We have all been programmed into the habit of believing that our neighbours might be dangerous if they use water in ways that differ from our own habits. We suspect anybody who crosses the street with a different timing and suspect any sexual, social, religious, moral or aesthetic practice that does not fit nice and snugly into our own box of comfortable habit.

Government pseudo-propaganda is used to terrify us with the shock doctrine images of invading extremists, terrorists, immigrants and the criminally insane.

The threat is always nomadic, originating from outside the Republic's borders of domesticated nature with its cosy walls and deep rooted habits. The threat is mobile, an invading force that will destroy the very fabric of society if not eliminated. The nomadic invading threat can be viral like Ebola, Sars and the Bird Flu, or can even be the threat of abnormal weather patterns, or Locust and Bees from another continent. As with the Middle ages, the threat is inevitably Terrorists in the guise of Muslims, Arabs, illegals, immigrants or refugees.

When the terrifying image of nomadic foreign invasion fails, we are shocked into submission with the image of all manner of domestic nomads, from anti-social militia without any fixed address and who don't pay taxes, to Communists, Hippies and Indigenous people who do not believe in the idea of private property and who practice polygamy. We fill every room of our alarmed home with panic buttons for fear of escaped convicts, schizophrenics, gypsies, vagrants, homeless, carnies, drug addicts or anybody else who does not live in one domesticated place.

This nomadic zone of Abel, Lilith, the drunken Dionysus and trickster Hermes is the delirious and mythical playground of the artist, the shaman and witch. The ancient crossroads were marked by a Herm, a tall stone column, with the face of Hermes above and a proud erection half way down. Hermes was the trickster brother of the rational Apollo who stole his sibling's domesticated cattle by making them walk backwards into the wild fields, out from the walled safety of the cave. For this reason, Hermes was considered the patron saint of thieves to whom travellers made their prayers for protection, by leaving behind their gifts at the foot of the Herm altar marking every crossroads. Like Jesus, Dionysus, Bacchus and Osiris, Hermes was born on the 25 December, in the dead cold of the Northern Hemisphere's Winter Solstice. Like Jesus, Dionysus, Bacchus and Osiris he dies and is res-erected as the seasons change, symbolised by the proud erection of the virile God who conquers death.

This is the domain of the artist, the dangerous crossroads between the known and the virile unknown, the transgression between inner experience of Radical Subjectivity and outer objective reality. The artist works by surrendering to the extreme, by entering mental states of terror that channel into the physical, the stolen creations we will eventually call works of art. The artist must die the little death to this world of five senses to be res-erected through their creation, seeding change through trance-formation. In an unfragmented holistic world, there should be no difference between the artist, magician, shaman, sorcerer or witch. Alan Moore says that:

> "Magic in its earliest form is often referred to as 'the art.' I believe this is completely literal. I believe that magic is art and that art, whether it be writing, music, sculpture, or any other form is literally magic. Art is, like magic, the science of manipulating symbols, words, or images, to achieve changes in consciousness… It's not the job of the artist to give the audience what the audience wants. If the audience knew what they needed, then they wouldn't be the audience. They would be the artists. It

is the job of artists to give the audience what they need."

"The smaller the Artist, the narrower his view, the more vulgar his vocabulary, the more familiar his figures, the more readily is he recognized as a guide. To be accepted and admired, he must say what we all know, but have not told each other till it is tedious, and say it in simple and clear language, a little more emphatically and eloquently than we have been accustomed to hear; and he must please and flatter us in the telling by soothing our fears and stimulating our hopes and our self-esteem. When an Artist selects a set of facts too large, too recondite, or too "regrettable" to receive instant as-sent from everybody; when he presents conclusions which conflict with popular credence or prejudice; when he employs a language which is not generally intelligible to all; in such cases he must be content to appeal to the few. He must wait for the world to awake to the value of his work. The greater he is, the more individual and the less intelligible he will appear to be, although in reality he is more universal and more simple than anybody. He must be indifferent to anything but his own integrity in the realization and imagination of himself." – Aleister Crowley

"Something is always born of excess: great art was born of great terror, great loneliness, great inhibitions, instabilities, and it always balances them." – Anaïs Nin

"The creative process is a cocktail of instinct, skill, culture and a highly creative feverishness. It is not like a drug; it is a particular state when everything happens very quickly, a mixture of consciousness and unconsciousness, of fear and pleasure; it's a little like making love, the physical act of love." – Francis Bacon

Octavio Paz said of Michaux:

"The vision of chaos is a sort of ritual bath, a regeneration through immersion in the original fountain, a return to the 'life before'. Primitive tribes, the early Greeks, the Chinese, Taoists, and other peoples have had no fear of this awesome contact. The western attitude is unwholesome. It is moral. Morality, the great isolator, the great separator, divides man in half. To return to the unity of the vision is to reconcile body, soul, and the world. At the end of the experiment, Michaux recalls a fragment of a Tantric poem:

Inaccessible to impregnations,
Enjoying all joys,
Touching everything like the wind,

Everything penetrating it like ether,
The ever-pure yogi
Bathes in the ever-flowing river.
He enjoys all joys and nothing defiles him."

Sexuality can be the unlocking key. But so can fear, depression, rage or Artaud's Theatre of Cruelty: "theatre difficult and cruel for myself first of all. And, on the level of performance, it is not the cruelty we can exercise upon each other by hacking at each other's bodies, carving up our personal anatomies, or, like Assyrian emperors, sending parcels of human ears, noses, or neatly detached nostrils through the mail, but the much more terrible and necessary cruelty which things can exercise against us. We are not free. And the sky can still fall on our heads. And the theatre has been created to teach us that first of all."

Our natures are lazy and we learn only in crisis, with pain, through violence, excess or Artaud's cruelty. Comfort and consolation take us into the cul-de-sac of habit, the blind acceptance of domestic stasis. We fix our borders closer and closer to our skin until we lose contact with our sensual selves.

"I feel ever so strongly that an artist must be nourished by his passions and his despairs. These things alter an artist whether for the good or the better or the worse. It must alter him. The feelings of desperation and unhappiness are more useful to an artist than the feeling of contentment, because desperation and unhappiness stretch your whole sensibility." – Francis Bacon

Artists cannot be fixed by limits of any form, cannot be contained in habit, class, sexuality, medium, tradition or consensus. As state terror has been used to change our perceptions of social reality, it befalls artists to use the weapon of sublime terror to change perceptions of states that trance-form every reality. Each habit that degenerates into the cancer of consensus is like a scab that dries up as a crusty hard shell that numbs experience. Habit destroys creativity and comfort prevents the artist from materialising spirit that flows only when our entire being is opened by the debauchery of "an immense, long, deliberate derangement of all the senses."
Freud would have called this "uncanny" for lack of a better word. He said:

"The subject of the 'unheimlich' is a province of this kind. It is undoubtedly related to what is frightening to what arouses dread and horror; equally certainly, too, the word is not always used in a clearly definable sense, so that it tends to coincide with what excites fear in general. Yet we may expect that a special core of feeling is present which justifies the use of a special conceptual term. One is curious to know what this common core is which allows us to distinguish as 'unheimlich';

certain things which lie within the field of what is frightening."

"The German word 'unheimlich' is obviously the opposite of 'heimlich' ['homely'], 'heimisch' ['native'] the opposite of what is familiar; and we are tempted to conclude that what is 'uncanny' is frightening precisely because it is not known and familiar. Naturally not everything that is new and unfamiliar is frightening, however; the relation is not capable of inversion."

"We can only say that what is novel can easily become frightening but not by any means all. Something has to be added to what is novel and unfamiliar in order to make it uncanny."

It falls upon artists to re-possess their craft, re-claiming the gallery, taking time to feel, stepping back from habit, giving space to fear, turning on our flesh, tuning in our senses and dropping out of the timelines of social media, breaking open the head of habits, re-fusing as normal the complete detachment from our natures. Protest, resist and re-claim the i-mage, breathing the fire of life back into creation. It's time for artists to fuck their brains out, to stop thinking in boxes and kickstart that pendulum back towards the rhythms of nature, back towards Hermes and Lilith. Strip naked your fears and ride them like a banshee, transcending obedience like a shooting star through the caves of ignorance. It's time to admit that our age is darker than Medieval, that we have so lost touch with our selves that we cannot see the image for what it truly is. Magick.

Following on from *Genesis 1:27* that "God created man in his own image, in the image of God created he him; male and female created he them," let us reinvent the image of the artist as i-Magus. The magus ultimately responsible for the conjuring of the image of reality, applying "the Science and Art of causing Change to occur in conformity with Will… a creative genius; that is, he is of the nature of Godhead which devised the Soul as a medium for self-realization. Also, as History assures us, the Artist is of the caste of the initiated rulers of Mankind; he understands the theory of the Universe, he is an Epopt of the Mysteries of Nature, and an Hierophant of the Inviolable Sanctuary." (Aleister Crowley)

Readers with a materialistic bias will try to discredit my musings by pulling the words out from under my tongue, calling me Romantic. To them I concede and quote Novalis:

"The world must be romanticized. In this way the originary meaning may be found again. To romanticize the world is to make us aware of the magic, mystery and wonder of the world; it is to educate the senses to see the ordinary as extraordinary, the familiar as strange, the mundane as sacred, the finite as infinite."

Imagine a world without art, the cold and tragic culture of living without paintings, poetry, sculptures, drawings and music to mediate the space between three cold dimensions and the fiery tempest of the imagination. Imagine a world without images and without the magickal visions that can only be conjured by artists.

Now look around you and imagine a world with art, a world of exception, ecstasy and beautiful sublime terror, a world trance-formed. Now re-claim the gallery by re-leasing the craft.

"Today I awoke from a sound sleep with curses of joy on my lips, with gibberish on my tongue, repeating to myself like a litany – "Fay ce que vouldras!… fay ce que vouldras!"; Do anything, but let it produce joy. Do anything, but let it yield ecstasy. So much crowds into my head when I say this to myself: images, gay ones, terrible ones, maddening ones, the wolf and the goat, the spider, the crab, syphilis with her wings outstretched and the door of the womb always on the latch, always open, ready like the tomb. Lust, crime, holiness: the lives of my adored ones, the failures of my adored ones, the words they left behind them, the words they left unfinished; the good they dragged after them and the evil, the sorrow, the discord, the rancour, the strife they created. But above all, the ecstasy!" – Henry Miller

04:47 28 September 2015

Defending Paper Gods
– Aleister Crowley and the Reception of Daoism in Early 20th Century Esotericism

Johan Nilsson

In 1906 English occultist Aleister Crowley traveled on horseback through the distant Chinese province of Yunnan. The regions he visited were poor, and home to malaria and opium, but the journey was to be the beginning of a lifelong fascination with Daoism. This paper explores Crowley as an example of the early 20th century fascination with Chinese religion within Western esotericism and tries to make sense of his ambivalent relationship towards dominant representations of Chinese culture in the intellectual climate of his times. – JN

The Esoteric Reception of Chinese Religion

In studies of the historical relationship between China and the West there is broad agreement that Western representations of Chinese culture and society underwent a radical change over a period ranging from the 1500s to the colonial expansion of the 19th century. Descriptions of the country brought home by early travelers like Marco Polo had a utopian flavor and the Jesuit missionaries who were active in the country from the 16th century had a relatively tolerant attitude towards Chinese culture and religion. They spread the image of a society that was admirable in many ways and in some respects even superior to Europe.

The idealizing of the Chinese culture reached its peak during the 18th century and then transformed radically. In line with the expansion of European imperialism in Asia, and the changing values of the West after the Enlightenment, the Chinese empire came to be perceived as a stagnant and superstitious competitor.[1]

Nevertheless, studies of Western representations of China conducted by sinologists and historians like Colin MacKerras or Jonathan Spence disregard the fact that by the end of the 19th century and the beginning of the 20th there were religious movements in Western societies whose attitudes to Chinese culture and religion differed significantly from those that were most influential at this time. Within movements related to

---

1 See for example Colin Mackerras, *Western Images of China* (Oxford. Oxford University Press, 1989). Ulrike Hillemann, *Asian Empire and British Knowledge* (Basingstoke: Palgrave Macmillan, 2009).

esotericism, like Theosophy or Guénonian traditionalism, there was an interest in Chinese religion. The image of East Asia in the journals and books published by people linked to such movements had more in common with the idealized China of the Jesuits than with the contemporary image of an empire in decline, left hopelessly behind the Western nations that embodied the very idea of progress and modernity.

It would be a mistake to interpret these dissenting voices as irrelevant or obscure. In recent decades, research on Western Esotericism has shown that esoteric movements at the time helped to shape the Western image of Asian religions.[2] Movements such as the Theosophical Society played a significant role not only in terms of shaping the widespread Western perceptions of India and Tibet; the theosophists also contributed, albeit in their own way and with their own goals and motives, to the political developments in India leading up to independence.[3]

Within the study of Western Esotericism, the influence of Asian religions has become perceived as important to the esotericism around the turn of the last century. Wouter Hanegraaff discusses the issue in the context of the theory of secularization of esotericism which he presents in his influential work *New Age religion and Western Culture*. However, even though several examples of the Indian influence on esotericism have been explored,[4] very little has yet been done with regard to the relationship with East Asian religions.

Although the topic is almost completely uncharted, there was clearly an interest in Chinese religion, especially Daoism, in the esoteric environment around the turn of the last century. For example, it is easy to find articles on Daoism in esoteric journals from the period. Journals like *Lucifer* (Theosophical), *Le Voile d'Isis* (Martinist), or more general occult periodicals like *The Occult Review*, published essays on the subject of Chinese religion. Such an interest was shared by many of the movements associated with the esoteric environment of the period. Within the Teosophical Society the interest in Indian and Tibetan religion was more pronounced but subjects related to Daoism and

---

2 See Hammer, Ola & Rothstein, Mikael, *Handbook of the theosophical current.* (Leiden: Brill, 2013); Åsa Piltz, *Seger åt Tibet! Den tibetanska diasporan och den religiösa nationen* (Lund: Dept. of History and Anthropology of Religions, Lund University, 2005). Pasi, Marco, "Oriental Kabbalah and the parting of East and West in the early Theosophical Society". in Marco Pasi, Boaz Huss & Kocku von Stuckrad, *Kabbalah and Modernity Interpretations, Transformations, Adaptations* (Leiden: Brill, 2010).

3 On the Teosophical influence on Indian Women's Suffrage See Joy Dixon, *Devine Feminine: Theosophy and Feminism in England,* (Baltimore: Johns Hopkins University Press, 2001) 208. On Theosophy and the building of Buddhist schools in India and Ceylon, as well as on connections with the Indian Home Rule Movement see Lubelsky, Isaac, *Celestial india: Madame Blavatsky and the birth of Indian Nationalism.* (Sheffield: Equinox, 2012); Fjällsby, Per-Olof, *Indien som utopi och verklighet: Om den teosofiska rörelsens bidrag till indisk utbildning och politik 1879-1930.* (Doktorsavhandling, Karlstad universitet, 2012); Bevir, Mark. "Theosophy and the Origins of the Indian National Congress". *International Journal of Hindu Studies 7* (2003), 1-3: 99-115. The western occultism of the 19th and early 20th century was in fact deeply entangled with several Indian religious movements of the same period in ways that we have only begun to discover. Some examples of this phenomenon include Bogdan, Henrik. "Reception of occultism in India: the case of the holy order of Krishna". in Henrik Bogdan & Gordan Djurdjevic (red.) *Occultism in a global perspective* (Acumen: Durham, 2013); Brown, Mackenzie. "Three Historical Probes: The Western roots of avataric evolutionism in colonial India". *Zygon*, vol. 42, no. 2. (2007); Heehs, Peter. "The Kabbalah, the Philosophie Cosmique, and the Integral Yoga. A Study in Cross-Cultural Influence". *Aries* 11.2 (2011): 219-247.

4 Se for example Hugh B. Urban's books on Aleister Crowley and Tantra.

Chinese Buddhism was a recurring theme in publications related to the organization.

René Guénon and the French traditionalists were influenced by the Daoist-enthusiasm and former member of the French Foreign Legion Albert de Pouvourville, and interest in Chinese culture is a recurring feature of Guénon's writings. The same goes for the journal Études traditionnelles that was closely linked to Guénon.

Much the same is true for the so called Thelemic movement founded by Aleister Crowley. The trend in this direction that can be seen in later Thelemites like Kenneth Grant and C F Russell originated in Crowley himself. Crowley placed Daoism in such a high regard that he believed himself to be a reincarnation of mystic Ge Xuan[5] and wrote paraphrases of Daoist writings. He also frequently and aggressively criticized Christian missionaries for their views on Chinese religion and their methods in spreading Christianity in Asia. Even though his attempt to spread Daoist teachings in the West at a time when the general intellectual climate was hostile to Chinese religion should be of a broad interest even outside the study of western esotericism, his writings on the subject have remained unexamined by historians of religion.

This paper will give an overview of the influence of Daoism on the worldview of Aleister Crowley and explore the representations of Chinese religion that appear in his writings. It will also discuss the cultural context constituted by mainstream images of Chinese religion based on the works of British protestant missionaries and contrast these with the views of Crowley. Finally, it will explore the idea that although Crowley was an outspoken critic of dominant representations of China in the West he was ultimately unable to completely free himself from the underlying logic of these representations. In this he reflects important tendencies within the esotericism of his time.

The paper will begin by an account of Crowley's journey through China in the winter and spring of 1905-6; a journey that proved to be an influential event in his life, the beginning of his sympathy with Daoism and Chinese culture. The second half will discuss Crowley's understanding of Daoism and its intellectual context.

The Walk Across China

Crowley arrived in China during turbulent times. In the 19th century the Chinese empire had been the center of a series of severe conflicts involving the expanding colonial powers of the West as well as internal turmoil based on regional, political, religious and ethnic animosities; from the Opium Wars to the Taiping Rebellion[6], which, although almost unknown in the West, was one of the bloodiest conflicts in world history. A few years before Crowley's journey through Yunnan the Boxer Rebellion had erupted and a few years later the Qing dynasty collapsed and was replaced by the Chinese republic under Sun Yat-sen.

At the beginning of the 20th century there had been a British presence in China for about two centuries. Before the time of the first opium war the British activity in

---

5 See Stephen R. Bokenkamp "Ge Xuan," in *The Encyclopedia of Taoism*, ed. Fabrizio Pregadio (London: Routledge, 2008).
6 The conflict was partly connected to the spread of Christianity in China (as was the better known but less deadly Boxer Rebellion).

the empire was almost exclusively related to trade. In Canton, the only harbor that was open to the British, the East India Company and a small number of independent merchants had been operating since the early 1700s. By the end of the 18th and early 19th century the British made a series of more or less failed attempts to establish closer diplomatic ties with the court in Beijing as well as to convince the Chinese government to lift restrictions on trade.[7]

Yunnan, the focus of Crowley's accounts of his journey, was however by no means a representative province of the Chinese Empire; located as it is outside of the major centers of Han Chinese population it was perceived as exotic and distant to the inhabitants of the political and economic centers of the kingdom. Yunnan was known for its difficult, mountainous terrain and for its malaria that was said to affect Han Chinese and other non-indigenous groups especially hard; a fact that the Qing bureaucracy viewed as an obstacle to the governing of the province. Perhaps the best example of how Yunnan was viewed by its rulers was the fact that criminals or deserters within the imperial army could be sentenced to exile in the province; a punishment known as "military exile for life to an insalubrious region".[8] In addition, Yunnan was at this time one of the world's major producers of opium. What was widely held to be the premier Chinese variety of opium, *mafen*, was cultivated here. Opium from the district was highly regarded in Europe where it was celebrated in the French literary subculture that was centered around opium smoking at the turn of the last century, and that exerted a certain influence on Crowley's views on drugs. Crowley's interest in opium is one of the major themes in the narrative of his Chinese journey.[9]

Some decades before Crowley's arrival the province had been the scene of ethnic and religious violence.

To this ravaged land Crowley arrived in December of 1905. With him were his wife and child, an unknown number of porters, a nurse and his personal servant Salama Tantra. Crowley was used to this way of traveling from his two attempts at ascending major peaks of the Himalayas, which had been organized as expeditions comprising several hundreds of porters. They traveled in the only way possible on foot and on horseback, or more accurately riding ponies and donkeys. Sometimes they camped outdoors, sometimes in temples and inns.[10]

The journey from the Burmese border in the west, through what is today Tengchong, Baoshan, Dali, Kunming, Menzi and Hekou,[11] to the border of Tonkin in the south took about three and a half months. In March they reached Hanoi and from there Crowley traveled to Shanghai where he arrived on the sixth of April 1906.

The account of the journey comprises chapters 56 and 57 in Crowley's autobiography.

---

7 Ulrike Hillemann ,"At the China Coast", in Ulrike Hillemann, *Asian Empire and British Knowledge* (Basingstoke: Palgrave Macmillan, 2009)

8 David A. Bello, "To Go Where No Han Could Go for Long: Malaria and the Qing Construction of Ethnic Administrative Space in Frontier Yunnan," *Modern China* vol. 31, no. 3 (2005): 283-317

9 Regarding the cultivation of opium in Yunnan and Chinese opium culture in general see Frank Dikötter, *Narcotic Culture: A History of Drugs in China*, (London: C Hurst, 2004). Yangwen Zheng, The Social Life of Opium in China, (Cambridge: Cambridge University Press, 2005).

10 The narrative reconstructed here is based on the one published in Aleister Crowley, *The Confessions of Aleister Crowley* (London: Penguin Books, 1989).

11 Modern names in pinyin have been given as a rule for Chinese place names mentioned by Crowley.

All in all the narrative is relatively brief. Another even shorter description of the journey was published in "The Temple of Solomon the King" in *The Equinox*[12] but its focus is almost exclusively on the spiritual exercises Crowley performed during the period, and are of no interest to the subject of this essay.

'The walk across China', as it has become known in Thelemic texts, has as a rule been neglected in biographies on Crowley. This is probably due in the first place to the laconic nature of the sources; another reason perhaps being that the journey coincides with a period in Crowley's religious development that was considered to be of major importance by him and which therefore has tended to be portrayed in detail in connection with the narrative of the journey. Because the subject of Crowley's religious experiences and the interpretations made of them had very little to do with the physical and cultural environment of the journey, this focus on Crowley's inner life has tended to distract from the external events, and from his reflections on the experiences of the journey itself.

British Victorian and Edwardian travelogues are often more than the picturesque adventure stories, balancing between romanticizing naïveté and bigoted condescension in their representations of Chinese society, that they may seem to be at first glance. They reveal just as much about their authors and the worldviews of these authors as they say about the alien manners and customs of the foreign land they purport to describe. In the case of Crowley and other travelers they represent excellent examples of how representations of Chinese society and culture were created and contrasted with English identity.

Although it contains no detailed reflections on the religious life of Yunnan Crowley made some scattered remarks on things he saw during his journey. Among other things he mentions religious art. The aspect of religious life that most interested Crowley, however, was the presence and activity of foreign missionaries in the province. It is easy to dismiss the recurrent attacks on missionaries in *Confessions* as just an expression of Crowley's antagonism towards Christianity, but his assertions on the subject are linked to attitudes and ideas connected with the Western reception of Chinese religion. They are also the beginning of a growing fascination with Daoism that would always retain an element of hostility towards the influential missionary narrative of Chinese religion as decadent and ready to be replaced by a vibrant and modern Christianity.[13]

As has been stated above, during the 16th to 18th century discourse on Chinese culture in the West was dominated by Jesuits, and during the 19th and early 20th century representations of China was shaped by mainly British, protestant missionaries. The differences between these two groups can be schematically summarized in the following way. While the Jesuits regarded Chinese culture as admirable, considered parts of as Chinese religion compatible with Christianity and aimed their missionary efforts at nobility and the elite in order to create acceptance for their own religion, the protestant missionaries viewed Chinese culture as stagnant and decadent, held that

---

12 The relevant part is in *The Equinox* vol 1 no 8 (1912).

13 Almost forty years later in the last years of his life he would still publish comparisons between Christianity and "Chinese Thought" where the former is severely criticized. See for example the paragraph on the "Prince of disks" in The Book of Thoth. See Aleister Crowley, *The Book of Thoth*, (Stamford: U.S. Games Systems, 2002)

the Chinese religions of their time had to be replaced in their entirety by Christianity and focused their attention on the masses.[14] The protestant missionary movement moreover often had connections to European merchants and to the colonial projects of their home countries. Even if British missionaries sometimes were in disagreement with their countrymen, for example on the subject of the opium trade, they were often sympathetic towards Britain's colonial and economic expansion and, for example, often regarded the spread of Christianity as the only way to convince the Chinese of the value of free trade.[15]

The first protestant missionary arrived in Canton in April 1807. During the early 19th century it was still hard for foreign preachers to proselytize in the empire and the restrictions would not begin to ease until further into the century when the colonial powers had gained new advantages in their diplomatic relations with the Qing Dynasty, among other things as a result of the opium war.[16]

It would be unfair however to characterize the accounts of Chinese religion by protestant missionaries as entirely polemic and hostile. There was of course a certain amount of diversity of opinion among missionaries even during the 19th century and there was debate and disagreements within the missionary societies. Several pioneering western sinologists and students of Chinese languages were missionaries, among them the famous James Legge. Missionary sinologists made some of the first translations to European languages of historical texts relating to Confucianism, Daoism and Chinese Buddhism.[17] Despite this it cannot be denied that the principal attitude towards the religion of the people the missionaries wanted to convert was hostile. Daoism and Buddhism were seen as problematic expressions of superstition and idolatry hindering the modernization of Chinese society. When the Taiping rebels destroyed Daoist and Buddhist temples in the 1850-60s many Western missionaries expressed their support.[18]

The missionary view of Chinese culture was to a large extent shaped by their understanding of the Christian reformation as well as by common 19th century tropes of degeneration. Eric Reinders states that: "Protestant narrative of Christian history was superimposed onto Chinese history: a degeneration from an original pure community to institutional idolatry, followed by (at least the possibility of) a Reformation. Protestant history pictured Christianity as having fallen from a bright early moment into centuries of ritualism until it had been purified in the reformation."[19]

As a contrast to the protestant self-image as a faith characterized by active and virile simplicity, with a religious practice aimed at moral and worldly improvement, Chinese religion was perceived as superstitious and unworldly, built on empty ritual and more interested in sensual mysticism than human progress. It shared many traits associated with the Catholic Church in Protestant discourse.

It is worth pointing out that Crowley never was such an obvious opponent of

---

14 Eric Reinders, *Borrowed Gods and Foreign Bodies: Christian Missionaries Imagine Chinese Religion*, (Berkeley: University of California Press, 2004)
15 Hillemann, *Asian Empire and British Knowledge*, 66.
16 Hillemann, *Asian Empire and British Knowledge*, 91ff.
17 Reinders, *Borrowed Gods and Foreign Bodies*, 98.
18 Reinders, *Borrowed Gods and Foreign Bodies*, 28.
19 Reinders, *Borrowed Gods and Foreign Bodies*, 25.

missionary ideology as one might imagine. Although the religious ideas he would develop obviously in many ways stood in opposition to Victorian evangelicalism there were also deep similarities. There has for some time existed a suspicion among several of Crowley's biographers about the possible similarities between some areas of Thelema and the Plymouth Brethren ideology that shaped Crowley's upbringing.[20] With the recent tendency in the academic study of religion to treat Crowley and other expressions of early 20th century esotericism as serious objects of research, a certain influence from protestant theology on Crowley's writings has been recognized.[21] In this context it could be said that Crowley shared many of the values inherent in the Victorian work ethic that permeated much of missionary ideology.

The missionary condemnation of Chinese religion often had these values as its point of departure. Frequently it attacked Buddhism for being apathetic, feminizing and unworldly. It is not impossible that Crowley, if circumstances were different, would have shared this criticism. That passivity and inactivity was problematic concepts for him is clear.

Having said this, Crowleys encounter with western missionaries in China was characterized by violent dislike. Almost, it seems, by actual violence. In *Confessions* he describes a confrontation between a missionary and a group of locals participating in a religious procession. According to Crowley the missionary had reacted violently when he saw the image of some unidentified deity being carried through the village as a part of a Chinese new year's celebration.

> "…instead of attending to his own affairs [he] took it upon himself to insult (in wretchedly and comically illiterate Chinese) some villagers who happened to be carrying an idol in procession as part of the festivities of New Year's Day (January 25th). He might as well have spoiled a children's party on the ground that the fairy stories which amused them were not strictly true. The action was morally indistinguishable from brawling in church. I may not believe in the liquefaction of the blood of St. Januarius, but I see no reason for inflicting my incredulity on the people of Naples. The villagers naturally resented the ill manners of this brainless boor and told him to shut up. He immediately began to scream that he was being martyred for Christ's sake. I told him that if I could have brought myself to touch him, I would have thrashed him within an inch of his life."[22]

Crowleys main point of criticism of missionaries in China, however, was that they were uninformed and misled by an irrational belief in the superiority of their own particular version of Christianity. How, he asks in *Confessions*, could these people expect to convert

---

20 See for example see Richard Kaczynski, *Perdurabo: The Life of Aleister Crowley*, (Tempe: New Falcon Publications, 2002) 101.

21 See Henrik Bogdan "Envisioning the Birth of a New Aeon· Dispensionalism and Millenarianism in the Thelemic Tradition," in *Aleister Crowley and Western Esotericism*, ed. Henrik Bogdan and Martin P. Starr (New York: Oxford University Press, 2012)

22 Aleister Crowley, *The Confessions of Aleister Crowley*, 483.

Buddhists and Muslims when they were completely ignorant of the beliefs and practices of these religions. Apparently he brought up the subjects with missionaries he met on his journey. In *Confessions* the following resigned statement can be found:

> "Dr. Clark, the medical missionary of Talifu, received us with great courtesy and hospitality. I found him a sincere and earnest man; more, even an enlightened man, so far as it is possible for a missionary to be so; but that is not very far. I found him totally ignorant both of canonical Buddhism and of local beliefs. I tried to point out to him that he could hardly hope to show the natives the errors of their way of thinking, unless he knew what that was. But he declined to see the point."[23]

SIMON IFF AND THE DAODEJING

At the time of his journey Crowley had hardly yet developed any clear views on the Chinese religions. It would be a while before he tried to formulate his own opinion as anything other than a negation of the attitudes formulated by the missionaries he encountered on his journey. During the following decades his interest in Daoism would become a growing component in his esoteric system. In the preface to his own edition of *Daodejing* he states: "The philosophy of Lao-tzu communicated itself to me … . This process, having thus taking root in my innermost intuition during those tremendous months of wandering across Yunnan, grew continually throughout succeeding years."[24]

References to Chinese religion are relatively rare in Crowley's works from the first years after the journey through China. Daoist texts like the Daodejing and "the Writings of Kwang Tzu"[25] became required reading in his new magical order of the AA but other than that, Daoist religious figures, usually Laozi, are mentioned mostly in the context of lists of examples of religious traditions that also include Buddhist, Hindu, Muslim and Cabbalist texts, figures and concepts. In *The Equinox* vol 1 no 2 appears an advertisement for the then recently published *777* where it is stated that: "For the first time Western and Qabalistic symbols have been harmonized with those of Hinduism, Buddhism, Mohammedanism, Taoism, &c." The example is typical and suggests that although Crowley was aware of Daoism (not banishing it to the nebulous category of "&c"[26]) he viewed it as a not very differentiated part of what he considered to be humanity's great expressions of religious truth.

It is also interesting to note that references to Chinese religion are rare in what Crowley considered to be the most important "magical workings" of the period. Chinese imagery is conspicuously absent from the visions recorded in *The Vision and the Voice* and *The Paris Working*, as is Chinese terminology and Chinese concepts (more

---

23 Aleister Crowley, *The Confessions of Aleister Crowley*, 488.

24 Aleister Crowley, introduction to *Tao te ching, Liber CLVII* (York Beach: Samuel Weiser, 1995).

25 The citation can be found in Aleister Crowley ed., *The Equinox vol 1 no 8* (1912) and refers to Legges edition of The Writings of Kwang Ze, published in The Sacred Books of the East series. Kwang Ze (pinyin: Zuangzi).

26 Presumably left for Scandinavian pre-Christian religion and the likes, if we consider the actual content of the *777*.

or less) from the interpretations of those visions. There are some exceptions to be sure; a handful of more enthusiastic endorsements of Laozi and Daoist writings as well as Crowley's interest in divination inspired by the Yi Jing.[27] The overall impression up until the end of the First World War however is one of a somewhat vague and lukewarm interest. If it is true, as he later stated, that Crowley studied the *Daodejing* during the whole of this period his study left few marks on his writings.[28]

At the end of the First World War Crowley's interest in Daoism seems to have deepened. From 1918 it became more visible in his writing. During this year he authored a paraphrase of James Legge's translation of the *Daodejing* and the *Qingjing jing*,[29] a result of an attempt to explore the texts using esoteric visionary techniques. According to Crowley a spiritual entity called Amalantrah showed him Laozi's "original" version of the *Daodejing* and made it possible for him to see mistakes in Legge's translation. Apparently unhindered by the fact that Crowley didn't speak a word of Chinese, in any dialect. In addition to the visionary element Crowley simply brought the text more in line with what he perceived to be the universal essence of mysticism as well as with his own religious system of Thelema. To Crowley, universal mysticism, although theoretically found in every culture, was in practice a mixture of late 19th century occultist cabbala in the tradition of the Hermetic Order of the Golden Dawn and a version of yoga more or less close to the system presented in the yoga sutras of Patanjali, interpreted by people such as Ponnambalam Ramanathan, Vivekananda, Sabapati Swami, and, no doubt, Allan Bennett.

From this period it's possible to find more references to Daoism in Crowley's works, and he also identified more strongly with this religion. Some of the more interesting examples of this are his belief that he was in fact a reincarnation of the Three Kingdoms period Daoist figure Ge Xuan[30] and his creation of the fictional character of Simon Iff.

Simon Iff was the protagonist of a series of detective stories Crowley started writing in the winter of 1916-7. For some years he continued to write about the character that, correctly in my view, has often been regarded as an idealized self-portrait of Crowley in old age.[31] All in all he created more than twenty short stories portraying the adventures of Iff most of which were never published in his lifetime.[32] Simon Iff also makes an appearance in Crowley's novel *Moonchild* (published in 1929 but written in 1917). Considering that the character is an idealized mouthpiece of Crowley himself the Daoist leaning of the esoteric detective are particularly noteworthy. Iff is said to have spent ten years in China. "I was ten years in China. I've smoked opium as hard as anybody", as he puts it in "Outside the bank's routine" (1917). His years in China gave Iff a taste for the Daoist scriptures. About his enthusiasm for the

---

27 Crowley mostly used the transliteration "Yi King", following Legge as usual.

28 He makes the claim in Aleister Crowley, introduction to *Tao te ching, Liber CLVII* (York Beach: Samuel Weiser, 1995).

29 Transliterated "Khing Kang King" by Crowley.

30 See Stephen R. Bokenkamp "Ge Xuan," in *The Encyclopedia of Taoism*, ed. Fabrizio Pregadio (London: Routledge, 2008).

31 See Richard Kaczynski, *Perdurabo: The Life of Aleister Crowley*, 248. William Breeze, introduction to *The Simon Iff Stories & Other Works*, ed. David Stuart Davies and William Breeze, (London: Wordsworth, 2012).

32 The first stories were published in the periodical The International from 1917-8. Recently a collection of all surviving stories has been published as Aleister Crowley, *The Simon Iff Stories & Other Works*, ed. David Stuart Davies and William Breeze, (Ware: Wordsworth, 2012).

Daodejing it is said that "he had read it every morning for forty years without once failing to find something new in it".[33] He refers to the text in several of the stories and often talks of "the Tao". His distaste for missionaries becomes apparent in "Desert Justice".[34] In *Moonchild*, Iff's discourse on Daoist non-action comprises a large part of chapter five.

<h2 style="text-align:center">CHALLENGING THE MISSIONARY DAO</h2>

On a superficial level it is clear that Crowley's estimation of Daoism differs from the influential protestant understanding of Chinese culture. This is seen when Crowley's understanding of Chinese religion is compared with important themes in the representations of the subject in the broader culture of Victorian and Edwardian Britain, especially such as was expressed in the dominant discourse represented by protestant missionaries and missionary sinologists. Perhaps it would not be too much of an exaggeration to say that these views were each other's opposites on some levels; however, as we shall see this did not exclude important similarities on others. Crowley did not regard Chinese religion as stagnant in relation to any of the common 19th century concepts of the evolutionary classification of religions or less systematic notions of degeneration common in missionary writings. This line of thinking was common in writings on Asian culture whether stated explicitly or implicitly in the idea that other religions should learn from Christianity.[35] In Crowley's syncretic thinking Daoism instead was represented as one of several "traditions" that could offer something to Western students of esotericism. There are several indications that the Daoism had a particularly strong position in this system. Discussing the subject of founders of religion and their presumed mystical experiences in *Book Four* Crowley writes:

> "Lao Tze is one of our best examples of a man who went away and had a mysterious experience; perhaps the best of all examples, as his system is the best of all systems. We have full details of his method of training in the *Khang Kang King*, and elsewhere. But it is so little known that we shall omit consideration of it in this popular account."[36]

Even though there are several examples of the same kind, too much should not be read into them. After all Daoism could never compete with yoga or occult ritual magic in the style of The Golden Dawn when it comes to influence on Crowley.

The obvious syncretism of Crowley's religious views and the apparent ease with which he incorporated influences from very different religious traditions and esoteric systems into his own worldview was at least partly based on his belief in universal

---

33 Aleister Crowley "The Monkey and the Buzz-Saw" in Aleister Crowley, The Simon Iff Stories & Other Works, ed. David Stuart Davies and William Breeze, (Ware: Wordsworth, 2012).

34 Aleister Crowley "Desert Justice" in Aleister Crowley, The Simon Iff Stories & Other Works, ed. David Stuart Davies and William Breeze, (Ware: Wordsworth, 2012).

35 Reinders, *Borrowed Gods and Foreign Bodies,* 41.

36 See Aleister Crowley "Mysticism", in Aleister Crowley, *Book 4 I-IV*, (Samuel Weiser, York Beach, 1994), 10n.

mysticism. This belief, in turn, was a reflection of an attitude that was commonly shared by esoteric thinkers long before Crowley, what Faivre called the praxis of concordance (one of the two secondary components in his definition of esotericism)[37] and viewed as the will to see a common core in diverse religious traditions.

Earlier expressions of this kind of thinking often rested on some version of perennialism that explained the common core of the world's religions by postulating a *philosophia perennis*, the teachings of which constituted the essence of all, or some, of the now existing religions.[38] Crowley never embraced this kind of historical explanation; instead he argued and implied that the essence of religion is systematized knowledge based on mystical experiences; experiences that constitute a way of gaining empirical knowledge of a transcendent reality.

The idea of the foundation of religion as uniform and shared implies that it can be revealed by comparative studies, hermeneutical interpretation of sacred texts and through spiritual practices, which of course was the means favored by Crowley.[39] This view of the essence of religion as mystical experiences created a certain ambivalence in Crowley's writings because it could be understood both in terms of biological reductionism[40] and supernaturalism. To sum up, it is not the historical background that makes mystical traditions or experiences appear a certain way (though it might be the nature of the brain), instead it is the mystical experiences that shape the historical religions. One of the clearest articulations of this position in Crowley's writings can be found in the rather obscure semi-pornographic *The Scented Garden of Abdullah the Satirist of Shiraz* (1910). It deserves to be quoted in full.

> Now the revealing of one is the revealing of all : for from Fez to Nikko, there is one mysticism and not two. The fanatic followers of el Senussi can suck the pious honey from the obscene Aphorisms of Kwaw, and the twelve Buddhist sects of Japan would perfectly understand the inarticulate yells of the fire-eaters of el Maghraby. Not that there is or has ever been a common religious tradition; but for the very much simpler reason that all the traditions are based on the same set of facts. Just as the festivals of Spring all the world round more or less suggest the story of the Crucifixion [sic] and Resurrection, simply because the actual phenomena which every man is bound to observe in Nature are essentially the same in every clime: so also is Mysticism One, because the

---

37 See for example Antoine Faivre, *Access to Western Esotericism*, (Albany: State University of New York Press) 14.

38 See Faivre, *Access to Western Esotericism*. For some further examples see Mark Sedgwick, *Against the Modern World*, (Oxford: Oxford University Press, 2004)

39 See for example the subordination of ethical considerations to mystical experience in his discussion of yama and niyama in Aleister Crowley "Mysticism", in Aleister Crowley, *Book 4 I-IV*, (Samuel Weiser, York Beach, 1994). Crowley's position on the value of intellectual interpretation summed up nicely in the expression "experience and some knowledge of comparative religion" from the chapter on "Dhyana" in the above mentioned source.

40 In connection with this Marco Pasi's remarks on Crowley's interest in scientific naturalism are particularly interesting. See Marco Pasi, "Varieties of Magical Experience," in *Aleister Crowley and Western Esotericism*, ed. Henrik Bogdan and Martin P. Starr (New York: Oxford University Press, 2012)

physiological constitution of mankind is practically identical the wide world over [...] We have then the right to buy our pigs in the cheapest market...[41]

Contrary to what the context or the tone might suggest the views expressed here were meant to be taken seriously and the argument would reappear in several of Crowley's books. It did so in the context of Daoism too. In his preface to the *Daodejing* Crowley claims to have studied "all varieties of Asiatic philosophy" and remarks that: "The physiological and psychological uniformity of mankind guaranteed that the diversity of expressions concealed a unity of significance."[42]

Crowley didn't just place a higher value on Daoism because he saw it as a part of a universal expression of religious truth. His understanding of Chinese religion deviates from that of the missionaries in other ways too. This becomes obvious if we ask the question of what he meant by the term itself. To begin with it should be noted that Chinese religion ("Chinese philosophy", "Chinese Thought" or any of the other expressions used by Crowley) almost exclusively meant Daoism. After the Buddhist period which Crowley passed through around the turn of the century he almost completely lost interest in the religion.[43] Chinese Buddhism was no exception. Predictably enough the same goes for Confucianism. Master Kong and his disciples are rarely mentioned by Crowley. The list of saints in the Crowley's Gnostic Mass begins with Laozi but never even mentions Kongzi. Nor did he ever show any interest in Chinese Islamic or Christian movements.

In this way Crowley turned the hierarchy of religions often implicit in missionary and sinological writings of his day upside down. Christian missionaries, beginning with the Jesuits, had traditionally viewed Confucianism as the most developed (or least reprehensible) form of Chinese religion.[44] Crowley and other writers in early 20th century esotericism were early examples of the growing esteem of Daoism (or parts of it) during the second half of the 20th century.

At this point however, we would do well to stop and ask what Crowley meant by Daoism. Interestingly enough, in defending the religion, Crowley made no real effort to deny missionary charges of idolatry or polytheism. Instead he chose to ignore those aspects of Chinese religious culture that hostile critics labeled in this way. Even if these religious expressions hardly bothered him the way they did members of the China Inland Mission or The London Missionary Society, they did not fit his views of the simplicity of Chinese religion; nor did Daoist monasticism or, apparently, the Chinese pantheon, in any of its forms. There are almost no references at all to Chinese deities in Crowleys writings, not even the xian seems to have interested him that much, even though the idea of immortal spiritual masters would have fit nicely with his belief in the secret chiefs. Ignorance is not a very good explanation even though a lack of

---

41 Aleister Crowley, Introduction to Aleister Crowley, *The Scented Garden of Abdullah the Satirist of Shiraz*, (Chicago: The Teitan Press), 13.
42 Aleister Crowley, introduction to *Tao te ching, Liber CLVII* (York Beach: Samuel Weiser, 1995) 3f.
43 He even developed a distaste for it.
44 See for example Eric Reinders, *Borrowed Gods and Foreign Bodies: Christian Missionaries Imagine Chinese Religion*, 23f.

information[45] probably played a part. Crowley after all had visited Chinese temples, he would have known that there were Daoist monks and cults around specific deities even if he didn't know the finer points of, say, Daoist alchemy.

If we are to explain why Crowley ignored many of the elements of Daoism as the religion was actually practiced by the majority of its adherents we must look closer at an aspect of the Western reception of Asian religions that is interesting because it so clearly reflects and exemplifies broader trends in the development of Western esotericism in Crowley's time; namely the focus on written expressions. It will then be clear that even though Crowley deviated from the dominant representations of Chinese religion in his time in terms of his high regard for Daoism, he was in some ways dependent on the logic implicit in these representations.

A distinct tendency in Western interpretations of Asian religions well into the 20th century was the fact that the archaic was valued higher than the contemporary, and written expression of philosophy or theology was valued higher than practice. If the contemporary religious practice deviated from the archaic theory, it was a sign of decadence.

"The study of what was worthy in Chinese religion was for many years almost entirely a textual matter. Disparities between the ideas of the classical texts and observed practices in Chinese temples were explained as degeneration," Reinders argues.[46] This tendency was not only visible in the interpretation of Chinese religion. It was also apparent in Western writings on Buddhism in the same period. Philip C. Almond, who has studied interpretations of Buddhism during the 19th century, writes concerning this religion that:

> "It was to become progressively less a living religion of the present to be found in China, Nepal, Mongolia, etc. and more a religion of the past bound by its own textuality. Defined, classified, and understood as a textual object, its contemporary manifestations were seen in the light of this, as more or less adequate representations, reflections, images of it, but no longer the thing itself."[47]

Crowley was heavily influenced by Orientalist writings in his understanding of Buddhism.[48] His inclination to privilege textual expressions of religion was less pronounced in the context of Daoism but it is also obvious that it was a constitutive pattern of Crowley's understanding of the religion. After all, if James Legge hadn't chosen the specific handful of texts he chose from the vast Daoist canon, Crowley's understanding of what constituted Daoism could have been very different. And that choice was hardly random. Nor was Crowley a completely passive or completely unconscious recipient of other people's ideology. He embraced the basic pattern valuing

---

45 After all, if we were to add up the sources on Chinese religion mentioned by Crowley himself his real knowledge of the subject would have been somewhat slim.
46 Eric Reinders, *Borrowed Gods and Foreign Bodies: Christian Missionaries Imagine Chinese Religion*, 33.
47 Philip C. Almond, *The British Discovery of Buddhism*, (Cambridge: Cambridge University Press 1998) 25.
48 His interpretation of this religion was influenced by concepts such as the canonical-popular dichotomy underlying many early studies of Buddhism.

the ancient and textual above the contemporary and practical.[49] [50] If he hadn't, he would perhaps not have gone so far as to follow in the footsteps of Allan Bennett, ending up as a convert and monk, but he would probably have shown a greater interest in the temple cult, monasticism, magic, alchemy etc that constituted Daoist religious practices.

PAPER GODS

Crowley's dependence on tendencies within the sinology of his time is a very interesting example of secularization in one of the senses explored by Hanegraaff in *New Age religion and Western Culture*, that is, in the sense of esotericism implicitly making the secular, academic study of religion a spiritual authority.

As has been stated above, the belief in a shared essence of the world's religions has been common within esotericism since early modern times. It has been noticed several times however, by Faivre, Godwin and Hanegraaff[51] among others, that this perennialist perspective was both vitalized and transformed in the 19th century as a result of the rise of the scientific and comparative study of religions and the growing amount of information that was made available by this enterprise. (It reappeared in "triumphant form" in the 19th century, as Faivre puts it.) One of the results was the rising interest in Asian religions exemplified by the Theosophical Society or by Crowley's interest in Indian or Chinese religions. Another consequence however, in line with what Hanegraaff calls the second process of secularization of esotericism, was the rise of the academic study of religion as a religious authority in itself, through its position as a mediator of the wisdom of geographically or temporally distant cultures.

The fact that much can be said about a religious movement based on its views on what constitutes authoritative knowledge can be illustrated by an example from a similar religious landscape as the one that was inhabited by Crowley. It is often argued that the difference between spiritism/spiritualism and fin de siècle occult movements like Theosophy, Martinism or Rosicrucianism lay in the fact that while spiritualists placed authority in messages of the spirits of the dead, the authoritative sources of spiritual knowledge for Theosophists and Martinists were primarily the writings and handed down wisdom of an alleged tradition of adepts.[52] In this case the distinction may not really be that clear cut, but it can hardly be denied that the choice of sources of authoritative knowledge has profound consequences for a religious movement. One of the consequences in the case of individuals like Crowley being that the perspective and values of scholars and translators like Max Müller, Thomas Rhys Davids or James Legge came to color the views of those like him who used their works as a way to access the sacred texts of Buddhism, Hinduism or Daoism. In that way, although engaging

---

49 Paradoxically perhaps, since it didn't fit that well with the almost sacralized modernism of *The Book of the Law*. But Crowley seems to have treated non-Western religious traditions differently in this regard.

50 The one notable exception was his practice of divinatory techniques inspired by the Yi Jing.

51 See for example Joscelyn Godwin (1994), *The Teosophical Enlightenment*, (Albany: State of New York Press, 1994). Antoine Faivre, *Access to Western Esotericism*, (Albany: State University of New York Press)

52 See for example Harvey, David Allen *Beyond enlightenment: occultism and politics in modern France* (London: Northern Illinois University Press, 2005) s 97.

in aggressive anti-missionary polemics, Crowley was actually locked in a position of simultaneous rejection and dependence with missionary sinology, a dependence deeply intertwined with trends of modernity and secularization in early 20th century western esotericism.

THE BIRTH OF THE NEW AEON:
MAGICK AND MYSTICISM OF THELEMA FROM THE PERSPECTIVE OF POSTMODERN A/THEOLOGY

Gordan Djurdjevic

[Aleister Crowley] reflects some of the central sexual and cultural issues of the early twentieth century, even as he foreshadows the crisis of modernity after the Second World War and many trends in recent postmodern thought as well.

– Urban (2006, 17)

Historically and ideologically, Western esoteric tradition was for the most part involved in an uneasy and complex relationship with Abrahamic religions of Judaism, Christianity, and to a lesser extent Islam.[1] In 1904, British poet and occultist Aleister Crowley (1875- 1947)[2] claimed to have received a short prophetic text of *The Book of the Law*,[3] announcing the birth of the New Aeon symbolized by the 'Crowned and Conquering Child,' an aspect of the god Horus. The philosophical and religious worldview of the book was designated as Thelema, a Greek word for will. Crowley interpreted the central message of the book, encapsulated in the phrase "Do what thou wilt shall be the whole of the Law" (AL I: 40), as a decree to search for and carry out one's true purpose in life, in other words, to do one's Will. The best method to accomplish this task, Crowley maintained, was a pursuit of what he termed Magick. In Crowley's reinterpretation, Magick is a form of theory and practice, which embraces both Eastern and Western esoteric traditions, infused by the dominant ideological orientation anchored in the message of *The Book of the Law* and the Law of Thelema.

I suggest that the Thelemic ideological position shares consanguinity with the

---

1 The influence of Islam has been the strongest among the loosely organized movement of Traditionalism, which was mostly a 20th century phenomenon. On traditionalism, see, *inter alia*, Sedgwick (2004). For the overview of major trends and principles of Western Esotericism, see Faivre (1994), Stuckrad (2005), and, more popular in approach, Godwin (2007).

2 The only major scholarly monograph about Crowley is Pasi (1999); German translation is Pasi (2006). For a biographical account see, among a dozen others, Kaczynski (2002).

3 The manuscript of *The Book of the Law* or *Liber AL vel Legis* (hereafter cited as AL with Roman and Arabic numerals referring to the chapters and verses respectively) was initially published in Crowley (1912) and the printed text in Crowley (1913), after which it had numerous publications. It has been included in the posthumous collection with other received or 'holy books' in Crowley (1983).

general orientation of postmodernism in assigning the principal value to the relative (individual) experience of the world and point of view, and in assuming a plurality of truths about the nature of reality. Thelema distances itself from Western monotheistic traditions in its syncretism, an attribute that is congenial to the worldview of esotericism and shares parallels with the postmodern notions of pastiche and intertextuality. Hermeneutically, Thelemic perspective is consonant with the conjectures about the death of author and with the reader-response theories of literary criticism, for its central scripture, *The Book of the Law*, is denied an official commentary and the meaning of the text is left to be decided 'each for himself.' In addition, Thelema abounds in aporias to such an extent that the play of contradictions and reversals provides 'the key' to *The Book of the Law*.[4] By claiming that "existence is pure joy" (AL II: 9) this ideology seems to incarnate what Nietzsche,[5] a major influence on both Crowley and postmodernism, calls *la gaya scienza*; the other links to Nietzsche include notions such as will to power, glorification of individualism, martial rhetoric, and a critique of Christianity. My main argument is that Thelema may be conceptualized as a postmodern, post-monotheistic, esoteric religion.[6]

This paper explores theoretical principles and implications of Thelema with reference to the problems of postmodern a/theology as put forward by Mark C. Taylor (1984): the death of God, the disappearance of the self, the end of history, and the closure of the book. It warrants immediate observation that the horizon of these problems is circumscribed by the ideological framework of the Judeo-Christian worldview[7] and its secular philosophical counterpart, while Thelema, in Crowley's interpretation, offers a new point of departure and a different religio-philosophical perspective. It announces the birth of the new Gods, the appearance of the ever-changing self, the beginning of the New Aeon, and the opening of the new book. In what follows I will elaborate on these four themes, basing my exposition primarily on Crowley's writings.

The Death of God and the Birth
of the Crowned and Conquering Child

Theism is *obscurum per obscurius.*
    (Crowley 1996 b, 26)

The old definition of God takes new meaning for us. Each one of us is
the One God.
    (Crowley 1996 b, 27)

There are three major deities in *The Book of the Law*, each one of them represented (or, given voice) by a respective chapter of the text. Their names – Nuit, Hadit, and Ra-

---

4 See Jones (1998).
5 Nietzsche's influence on Crowley's thought has been substantial and deserves a study of its own.
6 This is not meant to imply that there are no alternative possibilities of conceptualizing Thelema.
7 These four theoretical / theological 'problems' are, for example, of no consequence within the context of the Buddhist view of the world.

Hoor-Khuit – appear Egyptian[8] but this is not the case of the revival of the Egyptian religion, for these are new gods. Nuit is the Goddess of space and infinite potentiality of existence. Hadit is the atomic principle of consciousness, her counterpart. "Our central Truth – beyond other philosophies – is that these two infinities cannot exist apart" (Crowley 1996 b, 23). It is however Ra-Hoor-Khuit that is principally related to the New Aeon, the beginning of which was signaled by the 'Cairo revelation,'[9] for he is its Lord.[10] The nature of Ra-Hoor-Khuit (and other Thelemic deities), however, is such that it allows for a great freedom of interpretation, and it leaves open the possibility of non-theistic approach and understanding. From a certain point of view, the birth of the 'Crowned and Conquering Child,' as Ra-Hoor-Khuit is designated in *Liber AL*, does indeed coincide with 'the death of God.' Let me elaborate on this idea.

Ra-Hoor-Khuit relates to the concept of the death of God by the fact that he is not necessarily an external deity[11]: every marriage between Nuit (object) and Hadit (subject) represents their 'child' – i.e. Ra-Hoor-Khuit. It follows that every human being is in a sense Ra-Hoor-Khuit,[12] just as *The Book of the Law* declares that "[e]very man and every woman is a star" (AL I: 3). Everyone is the central unit of the Universe, the focal point of a mandala, which is coterminous with one's experience and perception of the world. "Therefore," writes Crowley, "you have an infinite number of gods, *individual and equal and yet diverse*, each one supreme and utterly indestructible" (1996 b, 26; emphasis added). Plurality of equal but diverse gods is on the one hand an interesting example of the Thelemic henotheism while at the same time and on the other hand it represents, by this very fact, a particular form of atheism, for god (the sacred, the numinous) is here emphatically *not* the 'wholly other' – as one of the classical definitions[13] would have it. The alterity of the numinous is thus erased, and the sacred is understood as coincidental with the personal point of view[14] and individual will. As a consequence, it may be argued that the concept of god is unstable – in other words, god as the *absolute* is 'dead' and made *relative* – to the extent that Thelema implies the possibility of coexistent monotheism, polytheism, and atheism.[15] This attitude also suggests that the notions of morality, justice, beauty, and truth (among others) are relative and individual, and from this the precept of "Do what thou wilt shall be the whole of the Law" (AL I: 40)

---

8 For an overview of the role and influence that the *idea* of Egypt had on the Western Esotericism, see Hornung (2001).

9 The Cairo Revelation is Crowley's term for the reception of the *Liber AL*, which took place in that city on April 8th, 9th, and 10th 1904.

10 "All leads up to the Crowned Child, Horus, the Lord of the New Aeon" (Crowley 1998 b, 34).

11 "I think that we are warned against the idea of a *pleroma*, a flame of which we are Sparks, and to which we return when we 'attain'" (Crowley 1996 b, 32).

12 "We may then take it that this Solar-Phallic Heru-ra-ha [i.e. Horus] is Each Man Himself. ... Each man's 'Child'-consciousness is a Star in the Cosmos of the Sun, as the Sun is a Star in the Cosmos of Nuit" (Crowley 1996 b, 168).

13 See Otto (1958). Similarly, Taylor states that "the divine Other is eternally *beyond*, always *elsewhere*,and absolutely *transcendent*" (1984, 72; emphasis in the original).

14 Crowley calls the point-of-view "the only philosophically tenable conception of Reality" (1944, 115) and "the Quintessence of Individuality" (1998, 69, n. 6).

15 Monotheism: "Each one of us is *the One God*" (Crowley 1996 b, 27; emphasis added). Polytheism:"*Each one of us* is the One God" (ibid.; emphasis added). And, since the identity is based on difference, if everyone is God then, in a sense, nobody is. See also AL II: 23, where Hadit states: "I am alone: there is no God where I am."

follows by necessity.[16] God as the wholly other and as the external lawgiver is dead. What remains is the play of the androgynous child whose nature lies in the constant act of going, i.e. change.[17]

Ra-Hoor-Khuit is also a child that rebels against the patriarchal society and its scale of values. This rebellion is particularly vocal in certain parts of the third chapter of the *Liber AL*, where we find the following verses: "I am in a secret fourfold word, the blasphemy against all gods of men. Curse them! Curse them! Curse them!" (AL III: 49-50). "Bahlasti! Ompehda! I spit on your crapulous creeds" (AL III: 54). The sacrilegious and anti-metaphysical tenor of these and similar proclamations is especially interesting and relevant when Ra-Hoor-Khuit is understood as a metaphor for the contemporary Zeitgeist. Taylor is not the only one to claim and realize that the contemporary critical trend in scholarship, which is perhaps most typically exemplified by the deconstruction of authority and metaphysical assumptions of Western culture, represents just another aspect of the death of God. "Deconstructive criticism unravels the very fabric of most Western theology and philosophy. ... *[D]econstruction is the 'hermeneutic' of the death of God*" (Taylor 1984, 10, 6; emphasis in the original). Thus we have an important alignment of analogous metaphors (rhetorical choices): the spirit of the times, the death of God, anti-authoritarianism, deconstruction, and Ra-Hoor-Khuit. In other words, if Ra- Hoor-Khuit is the sign of the contemporary Zeitgeist, then one of his expressions consists in the deconstruction of the religious authority: the birth of the Crowned and Conquering Child is equivalent to the death of God.

THE DISAPPEARANCE OF THE SELF
AND THE EMERGENCE OF THE IMPERSONAL IDENTITY

Know Thyself through Thy Way
(Crowley 1944, 254)

The notion of the self is intertwined with a number of traditional presuppositions of Western metaphysics. In Taylor's assertion, "knowledge of self is mediated by knowledge of God" (1984, 14), while the postmodern perspective, suspicious of all metanarratives,[18] including those about self and God, disrupts the certainty of and reliance upon these anchors of identity. The self is at present habitually seen as a construct, a contingent

---

16 Thus "each human being is an Element of the Cosmos, self determined and supreme, co-equal with all other Gods. From this the Law 'Do what thou wilt shall be the whole of the Law' *follows logically*" (1996 b, 25; emphasis added).

17 Statements such as "Every man and every woman is a star" (AL I. 3) and similar verses from *The Book of the Law* reinforce the notion that Thelema accommodates the death of God by recognizing the divinity of humankind. Crowley will eventually adopt as the motto of his magical fraternity Ordo Templi Orientis the phrase "There is no God but Man." (See "Liber OZ" in Crowley 1986, 144). The Latin variant of the motto could be read in two ways, as either "Deus est Homo," which brings down the divinity to the human level, or as "Homo est Deus," which raises the status of humanity to the level of Gods. But the major implication of this proclamation consists in the erasure of difference between the human and the divine whereby the binary opposition between the two dissolves. In that sense, God is dead.

18 In Lyotard's phrase.

product of social, psychological, and historical factors, devoid of permanent substance and reality. The master narrative of a unified self, which is governed by rational decisions of the free agent, is shown to be fiction. In the final instance, the person is overcome by temporality, and subjection to the condition of impermanence and change "subverts the identity, propriety, presence, and property of selfhood. This subversion effectively dispossesses the subject" (Taylor 1984, 14).

Crowley is keenly aware of the contingent nature of selfhood, as it is non-critically understood by what he customarily designates as 'uninitiated.' "The uninitiated is a 'Dark Star' and the Great Work for him is to make his veils transparent by 'purifying them" (Crowley 1996 b, 32).[19] By this process, it is supposed that the person eventually becomes aware of her inner stellar nature, and as a star that has its source of light within she is free to follow her own course. This inmost star is designated as Hadit, the essential identity of each man and woman.[20] Crowley however, and here lies a paradox, interprets Hadit as being *impersonal*. Hadit's principal function is to go, in other words, to change.[21] Temporality and continuous transformation, which otherwise seem to jeopardize the solidity of selfhood, paradoxically turn out to be the signatures of impersonal identity. "The death of the individual is his awakening to the impersonal immortality of Hadit," writes Crowley (1996 b, 92).[22] " In other words, Hadit is "the Impersonal Identity within the Individuality of 'every man and every woman'" (87).

In the final analysis, the ultimate selfhood appears to consist of the function of knowing, of being a conscious witness that undergoes experiences, which constitute one's life (or many lives). The self is thus a verb rather than a noun; becoming, rather than being.[23] The horizon of this becoming is open and endless, since there is no goal or purpose that might bring it to a closure. An important implication of this position lies in the recognition that there is no fixed essence to one's being and that there is, strictly speaking, no discovery of what one is but rather *creation* of what one may will to be. This coincides with Foucault's assertion that it is futile to search for the 'truth' of one's being, and that it is much more interesting to *fashion* than to 'discover' one's self. "From the idea that the self is not given to us, I think that there is only one practical consequence: we have to create ourselves as a work of art" (Foucault 1984, 351).[24] As a

---

19 Similarly and as a further example, Crowley asserts that a person "may attain to be aware that one is but a particular 'child' of the Play of Hadit and Nuit; one's personality is then perceived as being a disguise. It is ... a mere symbol without a substance ... The conscious and sensible 'man' is to his Self just what the printed letters on this page are to me who have caused them to manifest in colour and form. They are arbitrary devices for conveying my thought; I could use French or Greek just as well" (1996 b, 92).

20 "Hadit is the 'core of every star.'" writes Crowley (1996 b, 87).

21 "We may here say briefly that Hadit is Motion, that is, Change or 'Love'" (Crowley 1996 b, 93).

22 "The Aspirant must well understand that it is no paradox to say that the Annihilation of the Ego in the Abyss is the condition of emancipating the true Self, and exalting it to unimaginable heights" (Crowley 1996 b, 95).

23 "True Self is the meaning of the True Will: *I know Thyself through Thy Way*" (Crowley 1944, 254; emphasis added).

24 In Crowley's case, the creation of one's self as a work of art resulted, *inter alia*, in his adoption of many personas and a number of literary pseudonyms. Similarly, in a practice laid out in "Liber Jugorum" Crowley (1997, 659) suggests to students the following: "By some device, such as the changing of thy ring from one finger to another, create in thyself two personalities, the thoughts of one being within entirely different limits from that of the other, the common ground being the necessities of life." In the note he elaborates: "For instance, let A be the man of strong passions, skilled in the Holy Qabalah, a vegetarian, and a keen 'reaction-

result, "life becomes serpentine wandering" (Taylor 1984, 15), for to have an end or an aim would ultimately be a limiting condition. In Crowley's formulation, "the True Will has no goal; its nature being To Go" (1997, 581). Instead of a purpose, action results in play. Similarly, instead of "the unhappy consciousness of the historical agent" (Taylor 1984, 15), the joy of aimless wandering is experienced by the subject that has outgrown the limitations of rational purpose[25] and of personal identity. The true self is no self[26] and thus the binary opposition between the two dissolves.

THE END OF HISTORY AND THE BEGINNING OF THE NEW AEON

… the world *was* destroyed by fire on 21 March, 1904 …
(Crowley 1944, 24)

Ideas about progression of time in cycles are widespread. Among the best known are the Greek conception of the ages of the world as given in Hesiod's *Works and Days* and the Hindu teaching about the four *yugas*. In the 20th century, the most popular notion on the subject is expressed in speculations about the entry into the astrological Age of Aquarius. Crowley has on his part expounded the theory about the succession of Aeons, the names and major characteristics of which are associated with the Egyptian deities. Roughly speaking, each Aeon consists of 2000-year period. The earliest remembered Aeon was that of Isis, during which the conception of the divine was related to the nature, approached and worshipped as the Mother. The Aeon of Osiris was the age of the masculine, monotheistic, dying-and-resurrecting God.[27] It was the period of patriarchal authority and it projected suffering as the condition of the world and as an avenue towards approaching the divine. The Aeon of Horus commenced in 1904, the year of the reception of *The Book of the Law*.

Taylor suggests that, "[i]f God, self, and history are so closely bound, then the death of God and the disappearance of the self would seem to spell the end of history" (1984, 54). This is so because "History, as well as self, is a theological notion" (1984, 52). The postmodern deconstruction of the traditional Western ideas about history centers on the recognition that history is fiction, influenced and shaped by ideological agendas,

---

ary' politician; let B be a bloodless and ascetic thinker, occupied with business and family cares, an eater of meat, and a keen progressive politician. Let no thought proper to 'A' arise when the ring is on the 'B' finger; and vice versa."

25 "The free exercise of one's faculties is pure joy: if I felt the need of achieving some object thereby, it would imply the pain of desire, the strain of effort, and the fear of failure" (Crowley 1996a, 106-7).

26 In the conclusion of her study of the concept of the formless self in Zen Buddhism and related philosophical traditions, Joan Stambaugh (1999) makes the following statements, which provide an interesting correspondence with the idea of Hadit as one's impersonal identity: "With regard to the question in what sense a Formless Self can be a self, we would in conclusion be able to reply that if selfhood is not to be conceived egotistically as a separate self opposed and hostile to everything other than itself, formlessness offers an eminent possibility of rethinking selfhood. Overcoming and abandoning its anxious sense of itself as an encapsulated separate 'I,' the self gains the wondrous freedom and openness to emerge in joyous compassion from the shackles of its self-imposed boundaries" (165).

27 Crowley's ideas about the dying God were to a significant degree influenced by the studies in comparative religion of James George Frazer.

and constructed as a narrative discourse in such a manner that the distinction between it and the literary texts is blurred. Hayden White, in particular, has explored this idea in a series of studies. In the spirit of Nietzsche's proclamation that there are no facts, only interpretations, White argues that important question is not "What are the facts? but rather, how are the facts to be described in order to sanction one mode of explaining rather than another" (1978, 134). Crowley himself has expressed doubts about the possibility of arriving at certain knowledge of past events. In his 'banned lecture' on Gilles de Rais, he claims (in the context of conjectures about Napoleon's lost battle at Waterloo):

> Now all these things are merely *matters of opinion*. There may be a little truth in some of them. But we have practically no means of finding out exactly how much, even if our documentary support is valid to establish any of these theories. It is, also, almost impossible to estimate the causes of any given event, if only because those causes are infinite, and each one of them is to a certain extent an efficient determining cause (Crowley 1998 a, 196; emphasis added).

From the perspective of the contingent and interpretative nature of our conceptualizations about history, Crowley draws a major conclusion and interprets to his advantage the traditional Christian teaching about the end of days and coming of the Anti-Christ.

Simply stated, his main argument is that the author of the Revelation was correct in envisioning the end of the reign of Christianity but wrong in interpreting this event as the end of the world and as morally abhorrent. In describing the Tarot card "Lust," which in the Crowley-Harris 'Thoth deck' depicts the Scarlet Woman riding upon the Beast, he writes: "The seers in the early days of the Aeon of Osiris foresaw the Manifestation of this coming Aeon in which we now live, and they regarded it with intense horror and fear, not understanding the precession of the Aeons, and regarding every change as catastrophe" (1944, 93-4). On several occasions, Crowley maintains that the old world was indeed 'destroyed by fire' in 1904. The same relativity and terminality applies to the current Aeon, which will be replaced by the Aeon of Justice, "presumably in about 2,000 years" (1944, 116).

Taylor inquires: "since time 'clearly' continues, what can it possibly mean to say that history is over?" (1984, 54). The inherent weakness of the question lies in its assumption that history (or God, or self) is one. In Crowley's terminology, the 'end of history' merely signals the beginning of the Aeon of Horus. The character of this new Aeon at its birth has been vividly described in a visionary text, what might be considered a Thelemic apocalypse, called *The Heart of the Master* (Crowley, 1992). Included within this text is the "Mediterranean Manifesto," a document wherein Crowley, in rather Biblical language, describes his mission as the Prophet of Thelema by stating:

> My Term of Office upon the Earth being come in the year of the foundation of Theosophical Society, I took upon myself, in my turn, the sin of the whole World, that the Prophecies might be fulfilled, so that

Mankind may take the Next Step from the Magical Formula of Osiris to
that of Horus (1992, 117).

On an esoteric level, Crowley understands the notion of the 'end of the world' as a
symbolic reference to the destruction of one's limited personality in the mystical trance
of self-overcoming. This event Crowley often glyphs through the metaphor of the
'opening of the eye of Shiva.' "In Hindu philosophy," he writes, "it is said that Shiva, the
Destroyer, is asleep, and that when he opens his eye the universe is destroyed – another
synonym, therefore, for the accomplishment of the Great Work" (1981, 133). This
mode of interpretation reinforces the gesturing away from uncritical understanding of
the world events. But the most important implication, in the present context, is that
Crowley's distancing from traditional modes of perceiving the world and the 'spirit of
the times' is at home with the postmodern relativism applied to the meaning and scope
of history. History thus ends in the sense that it ceases to be the instrument of divine
providence, "plotted along a single line, which extends from a definite beginning,
through an identifiable middle, to an expected end" (Taylor 1984, 54). It becomes
instead the playground of manifold *personal narratives*[28] without the external and
universal reference point of meaning and determination.

The Closure of the Book
and the Opening of The Book of the Law

God is the Author of authors who dictates the Book of books. For this
reason, God is the Author to whom all authors finally defer, and His
Book is the Book to which all books ultimately refer.
(Taylor 1984, 81).

The closure of the book is a necessary correlate of the death of God, the disappearance
of the self, and the end of history. By deconstructing the notion of the book as an
independent and completely original creation of an author who is the ultimate arbiter
of its meaning, one is led towards the mutually related concepts such as intertextuality,
pastiche, and the death of author. Roland Barthes suggests that the reader, not the
author, determines the meaning of the text. This idea is fundamental to the so-called
reader-response theories of literary criticism. The final consequence of the death of
author is, by extension, the death of God, understood as the ultimate author / creator,
whose 'book' is the world. Emphasizing the role of the reader takes away the supremacy
of the author; "refusing to assign a 'secret,' an ultimate meaning to the text (and to the
world as text), liberates what may be called an anti-theological activity, an activity that
is truly revolutionary since to refuse to fix meaning is, in the end, to refuse God and his
hypostases – reason, science, law" (Barthes 1977, 147).

The Book of the Law, the central scripture of the New Aeon, to a certain degree

---

28 "Treat time and all conditions of Event as Servants / of thy Will, appointed to present the Universe to /
thee in the form of thy Plan" (Crowley 1944, 260).

deconstructs itself explicitly, while the play of contradictions, or the refusal to ascertain veracity to any truth claim, constitutes an important epistemological principle of Thelema and its associated form of spiritual practice, magick. *The Book of the Law* resists interpretation on several levels but its central aporia is that it proclaims the *law*, which generally refers to a restrictive force, the message of which is *freedom*, expressed through a precept "Do what thou wilt" (AL I:40), while "The word of Sin is Restriction" (AL I: 41). The 'key' to the book, similarly, consists of the interplay between concepts AL, meaning God, and LA, meaning Not: the one negates the other, while both simultaneously coexist in the state of *coincidentia oppositorum*.

On the subject of fixed meanings and contradictions, Crowley offers important insights by stating: "One must constantly keep in mind the bivalence of every symbol. Insistence upon either one or other of the contrary attributions inherent in a symbol is simply a mark of spiritual incapacity ... It is characteristic of all spiritual vision that the formulation of any idea is immediately destroyed or cancelled out by the arising of the contradictory" (Crowley 1944, 63). These statements call to the mind the general principle of deconstruction: truth claims are made through language based on binary oppositions, while the suppressed or marginalized opposite of any assertion disrupts (deconstructs) its claim to self-sufficiency or universality. In Crowley's formulation, "there could be nothing true except by virtue of the contradiction that is contained in itself" (1998 b, 205).

Hermeneutically, *The Book of the Law* deconstructs the interpretative authority of any other agent besides the reader. Its 'official' or 'inspired' Comment in fact calls for the destruction of the book itself and discourages not only the discussion about but also even the study of the text. "The study of this Book is forbidden. It is wise to destroy this copy after the first reading... Those who discuss the contents of this Book are to be shunned by all, as centres of pestilence. All questions of the Law are to be decided only by appeal to my writings, each for himself. There is no law beyond Do what thou wilt" (Crowley 1983, 196). By investing the reader with the ultimate authority to decide about its meaning, *The Book of the Law* in effect actualizes the death of the author.

Both Taylor and Barthes suggest that the contemporary (postmodern) condition implies a transition from the (closed, finished, absolute) Book to the (open and continuously written) text. The "infinite interrelationship of interpretations cannot be captured in a closed book; it must be written in an open text" (Taylor 1984, 16). This observation relates to the general perception that postmodernism is primarily concerned with the philosophy of language. In an important sense, magic shares this same concern. In his study of Agrippa's occult philosophy, Christopher Lehrich (2003) advances the thesis that magic is parallel or analogous to writing. Just as Derrida (1976) has shown that writing is a necessary supplement of speech, often thought of as less valuable because it is an indicator of absence, magic turns out to be a necessary supplement of religion and science.[29] This is a significant conclusion and it is consonant with some of Crowley's ideas on the subject.

---

29 Lehrich also observes that Derrida, in discussing a pertinent myth, overlooks the fact that Thoth is the inventor of both writing *and* magic. Thus Derrida marginalizes magic in the same text where he accuses traditional Western philosophy of logocentrism (the philosophy of presence), which in its turn marginalizes writing. For the relationship between magic and philosophy of language, see also Lehrich (2007).

In his essay on "The Revival of Magick" (1998 a), Crowley draws attention to the fact that Thoth is equally the God of magick as of writing. He adds that the "word used by Sir Walter Scott for Magick is 'gramarye,' and a ritual of magick is a 'grimoire,' 'grimorium,' or grammar; all from *gramma,* a letter" (1998 a, 13). Magick is then, just as writing, an activity of signification and communication.[30] The correspondence between Crowley's and postmodern attitude lies in the suggestion that there are no external absolute measures of standard, meaning, beauty, or truth. The difference is that the Thelemic orientation is not secular but, in the final analysis, religious. The Book is closed; the meaning of *Liber AL* does not rest in the intention of its author; instead, the book invokes the reader to do her will and *that in itself* is the act of signification: "Know thyself through Thy way" (Crowley 1944, 254).

The way of Thelema, its mode of 'writing,' is basically twofold. It consists of the dynamic (one could also say, erotic) interrelationship between Hadit and Nuit, manifested through the person (incarnation) of the Crowned and Conquering Child. The full name of this Child is Heru-Ra-Ha, which again represents a particular union of opposites. The active form is Ra-Hoor-Khuit, God of 'force and fire'; its passive twin is the God of Silence, Hoor-Paar-Kraath. These two forms symbolize, among other possibilities, the 'will to live" or Magick, and the 'will to die' or Mysticism. It is highly significant that Crowley maintains that these two methods of achievement, although apparently opposite, ultimately amount to the same.[31] In a manner that is typical of postmodern deconstruction, or of postmodern a/theology, the boundary line that separates this and other binary oppositions is erased.

BIBLIOGRAPHY

—∞— Barthes, Roland, 1977, 'The Death of the Author,' in *Image, Music, Text,* trans. Stephen Heath, Hill and Wang, New York.

—∞—Crowley, Aleister, 1912, *The Equinox: The Review of Scientific Illuminism,* Vol. I, no. 7.

- - - -, 1913, *The Equinox: The Review of Scientific Illuminism,* Vol. I, no. 10.

- - - -, 1944, *The Book of Thoth: A Short Essay on the Tarot of the Egyptians,* Ordo Templi Orientis, London.

- - - -, 1981, *The Book of Lies,* Samuel Weiser, York Beach, ME.

- - - -, 1983, *The Holy Books of Thelema,* Samuel Weiser, York Beach, ME.

- - - -, 1986, *The Equinox: The Review of Scientific Illuminism,* Vol. III, no. 10.

---

30 "Magick then may be defined for our present purpose as the art of communicating without obvious means" (Crowley 1998 a, 13).

31 See Crowley (1991)

- - - -, 1991, *Magick Without Tears*, ed. Israel Regardie, New Falcon, Scottsdale, AZ.

- - - -, 1992, *The Heart of the Master: And Other Papers,* Ordo Templi Orientis and New Falcon, Tempe, AZ.

- - - -, 1996 a, *Commentaries on the Holy Books and Other Papers*, Samuel Weiser, York Beach, ME.

- - - -, 1996 b, *The Law is for All: The Authorized Popular Commentary on Liber AL vel Legis sub figura CCXX The Book of the Law*, eds. Louis Wilkinson and Hymenaeus Beta, New Falcon, Tempe, AZ.

- - - -, 1997, *Magick: Liber ABA, Book Four: Parts I-IV*, 2nd ed., ed. Hymenaeus Beta, Samuel Weiser, York Beach, ME.

- - - -, 1998 a, *The Revival of Magick: And Other Essays*, eds. Hymenaeus Beta and Richard Kaczynski, Ordo Templi Orientis and New Falcon, Tempe, AZ.

- - - -, 1998 b, *The Vision and the Voice: With Commentary and Other Papers*, Samuel Weiser, York Beach, ME.

—⚛— Derrida, Jacques, 1976, *Of Grammatology*, trans. Gayatri Chakravorty Spivak, Johns Hopkins University Press, Baltimore and London.

—⚛— Faivre, Antoine, 1994, *Access to Western Esotericism*, SUNY Press, Albany.

—⚛— Foucault, Michel, 1984, 'On the Genealogy of Ethics: An Overview of Work in Progress,' in Paul Rabinow, ed., *The Foucault Reader,* Pantheon, New York, 340- 72.

—⚛— Godwin, Joscelyn, 2007, *The Golden Thread: The Ageless Wisdom of the Western Mystery Traditions*, Quest Books, Wheaton, IL.

—⚛— Hornung, Erik, 2001, *The Secret Lore of Egypt: Its Impact on the West*, trans. David Lorton, Cornell University Press, Ithaca and London.

—⚛— Jones, C[harles] S[tansfeld], 1998, *Liber Thirty-One*, ed. Allen Greenfield, Luxor Press, Marietta, GA.

—⚛— Kaczynski, Richard, 2002, *Perdurabo: The Life of Aleister Crowley*, New Falcon, Tempe, AZ.

—⚛— Lehrich, Christopher, 2003, *The Language of Demons and Angels: Cornelius Agrippa's Occult Philosophy*, Brill, Leiden and Boston.

- - - -, 2007, *The Occult Mind: Magic in Theory and Practice*, Cornell University Press, Ithaca.

—⚛— Otto, Rudolph, 1958 [1917], *The Idea of the Holy: An Inquiry into the Non-rational Factor in the Idea of the Divine and Its Relation to the Rational*, Galaxy, New York.

—⚛— Pasi, Marco, 1999, *Aleister Crowley e la Tentazione della Politica*, FrancoAngeli, Mailand.

- - - -, 2006, *Aleister Crowley und die Versuchung der Politik*, trans. Ferdinand Leopold, Ares, Graz.

—⚛— Sedgwick, Mark, 2004, *Against the Modern World: Traditionalism and the Secret Intellectual History of the Twentieth Century*, Oxford University Press, Oxford.

—⚛— Stambaugh, Joan, 1999, *The Formless Self*, SUNY Press, Albany.

—⚛— Stuckrad, Kocku von, 2005, *Western Esotericism: A Brief History of Secret Knowledge*, trans. Nicholas Goodrick-Clarke, Equinox, London and Oakville, CT.

—⚛— Urban, Hugh, 2006, *Magia Sexualis: Sex, Magic, and Liberation in Modern Western Esotericism*, University of California Press, Berkeley.

—∞— Taylor, Mark. C, 1984, *Erring: A Postmodern A/Theology*, University of Chicago Press, Chicago and London.
—∞— White, Hayden, 1978, *Tropics of Discourse: Essays in Cultural Criticism*, Johns Hopkins University Press, Baltimore.

The Derleth Error

A Problem and Promise in Formatting Chaos Magick

Timothy O'Neill

The critical role that Wisconsin writer August Derleth played in perserving the works of H.P. Lovecraft is well known and needs no amplification. At issue here is Derleth's ill-advised attempt to construct a consistent theory of magic that would fit Lovecraft's unruly aliens and monsters. Why would he do this in the first place? Well, not everyone is an H.P.Lovecraft, and Derleth felt that other writers working under his influence needed a clear and consistent structure to give these creaures a clear place and purpose in the Universe. This would thereby give himself and the other writers in the Lovecraft Circle something to go by in their own handling of what Derleth called "The Cthulhu Mythos." Lovecraft wrote much more poetically, not always maintaining consistency with his creatures or any clear "Mythos." His writing, is still the much more powerful and memorable than his erstwhile correspondent, Derleth.

This is the schemata that Derleth came up with to control the Lovecraftian entities into a recognizable pattern:

Derleth's elemental classifications

Air	Earth	Fire	Water
Hastur	Cyäegha	Aphoom-Zhah	Cthulhu
Ithaqua*	Nyogtha	Cthugha*	Dagon
Nyarlathotep	Shub-Niggurath		Ghatanothoa
Zhar and Lloigor*	Tsathoggua		Mother Hydra
			Zoth-Ommog

* Deity created by Derleth

Derleth not only linked the whole structure of the Western tradition of Magical correspondences, he also proposed that the Great Ancient Ones were evil monsters who had been put under control by the victorious Elder Gods. This created a war in heaven not unlike that found in classic Western Religion and Literature. In point of fact, Derleth was a devout Catholic and he simply reduced the Lovecraftian Mystery down to the old story of demons and angels. Add to this the fact that other authors in Lovecraft's tradition picked up on this scheme and added onto it and you have a serious deviation from Lovecrafts original intent to portray alien creatures who display an absolute disdain and indifference toward Humanity in the Cosmic vastness.[1]

The problem with this whole attempt to link traditional magical correspondences and the war of light and dark to Lovecraft is that this is the exact inverse of the world-view that H.P.L consistently stated for his fundamental premise:

> "Now all my tales are based on the fundamental premise that common human laws and interests and emotions have no validity or significance in the vast cosmos-at-large. To me there is nothing but puerility in a tale in which the human form—and the local human passions and conditions and standards—are depicted as native to other worlds or other universes. To achieve the essence of real externality, whether of time or space or dimension, one must forget that such things as organic life, good and evil, love and hate, and all such local attributes of a negligible and temporary race called mankind, have any existence at all. Only the human scenes and characters must have human qualities. These must be handled with unsparing realism (not catch-penny romanticism), but when we cross the line to the boundless and hideous unknown—the shadow-haunted Outside—we must remember to leave our humanity and terrestrialism at the threshold."

Lovecraft's entire conception of what he called "Cosmicism"[2] is the basic idea that humanity finds itself in a vast and uncaring Universe. I am going to quote from the Wikipedia entries on Cosmicism and Cosmic indifferentism since they express this perfectly.

PRINCIPLES OF COSMICISM

The philosophy of cosmicism states that there is no recognizable divine presence, such as a god, in the universe, and that humans are particularly insignificant in the larger scheme of intergalactic existence, and perhaps are just a small species projecting their own mental idolatries onto the vast cosmos, ever susceptible to being wiped from existence at any moment. This also suggested that the majority of undiscerning humanity are creatures with the same significance as insects and plants, who, in their small, visionless and unimportant nature, do not recognize a much greater struggle between greater forces.

Perhaps the most prominent theme in cosmicism is the utter insignificance of humanity. Lovecraft believed that "the human race will disappear. Other races will appear and disappear in turn. The sky will become icy and void, pierced by the feeble light of half-dead stars. Which will also disappear. Everything will disappear. And what human beings do is just as free of sense as the free motion of elementary

---

1 http://www.yog sothoth.com/wiki/index.php/Cthulhu_Mythos
2 https://en.wikipedia.org/wiki/Cosmicism

particles. Good, evil, morality, feelings? Pure 'Victorian fictions'. Only egotism exists." Cosmicism shares many characteristics with nihilism, though one important difference is that cosmicism tends to emphasize the inconsequentiality of humanity and its doings, rather than summarily rejecting the possible existence of some higher purpose (or purposes). For example, in Lovecraft's Cthulhu stories, it is not so much the absence of meaning that causes terror for the protagonists as it is their discovery that they have absolutely no power to effect any change in the vast, indifferent, and ultimately incomprehensible universe that surrounds them. Whatever meaning or purpose may or may not be invested in the actions of the cosmic beings in Lovecraft's stories is completely inaccessible to the human characters, in the way an amoeba (for example) is completely unequipped to grasp the concepts that drive human behavior.

Lovecraft's cosmicism was a result of his complete disdain for all things religious, his feeling of humanity's existential helplessness in the face of what he called the "infinite spaces" opened up by scientific thought, and his belief that humanity was fundamentally at the mercy of the vastness and emptiness of the cosmos. In his fictional works, these ideas are often explored humorously (*Herbert West–Reanimator*, 1922), through fantastic dreamlike narratives (*The Dream Quest of Unknown Kadath*, 1927), or through his well-known Cthulhu Mythos *(The Call of Cthulhu*, 1928, and others). Common themes related to cosmicism in Lovecraft's fiction are the insignificance of humanity in the universe and the search for knowledge ending in disaster.

COSMIC INDIFFERENTISM

Though cosmicism appears deeply pessimistic, H.P. Lovecraft thought of himself as neither a pessimist nor an optimist but rather a "scientific" or "cosmic" indifferentist; a theme expressed in his fiction. In Lovecraft's work, human beings are often subject to powerful beings and other cosmic forces, but these forces are not so much malevolent as they are indifferent toward humanity.

This clearly militates against any idea that the aliens and monsters in Lovecraft's works have any sort of understanding of or appreciation for human perspective and catregories. They emerge from the Multiverse in mysterious ways through higher dimensional geometry and fantastic powers of penetration through time and space. They are by definition complete anomalies in the orderly and scientific structure of the Universe. They are Outsiders who accessed our World and took it by brute force. What appears to us as sadistic brutality and evil is actually, to them, their natural way of being and indifference to our struggle or fate.

So, the biggest hole in the stories is the question of why and how these fearsome creatures were constrained and controlled during fierce cosmic battles with the Elder Gods millions of years ago. The mechanism of this magic of entrapment is never really explained. This left enough room for interpretation that various versions of the infamous imaginary magical book, the *Necronomicon*, which Lovecraft created on the model of Robert Chambers' *The King in Yellow* could be created to fill the void.

The "Simon Necronomicon" was one of the first of these attempts to create a real grimoire to give life to Lovecraft's fictional book. Using Sumerian and Babylonian ideas, the Hero Marduk from the Gilgamesh becomes the hero that traps the Great Ancient Ones, much like he trapped and skinned the Tiamat Dragon. Hence, the fifty names of Marduk offer powerful protection against these vast cosmic entities. Simon also explores the evocation of these entities which is more to our purpose.

Following that lead, Donald Tyson develops a tremendously elaborate and lengthy series of books, including a grimoire, which are intended to raise the Great Ancient Ones again, although within oneself. There is also a grain of usefulness there.

Phil Hine's *Pseudonomicon* takes a personal approach to the idea of experiencing the madness that Lovecraft posits as the price of seeing these unearthly entities which should not exist in our world. There are many other such attempts to either experience or invoke the Great Ancient Ones as described by Lovecraft and filtered through Derleth

What I think though is that most of these attempts to create a magical structure for Lovecraft's literary creations focus on Cthulhu and the least human of those entities. I think it would make more sense to focus on the three of them that have some actual visual similarities with Humanity and some sort of interest in at least using us for their mysterious purposes.

Nyarlathotep is the great trickster and Pied Piper of the Lovecraft mythos, luring humanity to decimation through sleight of hand and circus sideshow tricks of science.

"I had never heard the name NYARLATHOTEP before, but seemed to understand the allusion. Nyarlathotep was a kind of itinerant showman or lecturer who held forth in public halls and aroused widespread fear and discussion with his exhibitions. These exhibitions consisted of two parts — first, a horrible — possibly prophetic — cinema reel; and later some extraordinary experiments with scientific and electrical apparatus. As I received the letter, I seemed to recall that Nyarlathotep was already in Providence.... I seemed to remember that persons had whispered to me in awe of his horrors, and warned me not to go near him. But Loveman's dream letter decided me.... As I left the house I saw throngs of men plodding through the night, all whispering affrightedly and bound in one direction. I fell in with them, afraid yet eager to see and hear the great, the obscure, the unutterable Nyarlathotep." – HPL

Y'golonac is the strange obese god, humanlike in form, except headless, having mouths in each hand. Y'golonac is actually similar in some ways to the "Headless One" of late Hellenistic-gnostic magic, who is considered to be a very powerful demon. Y'golonac has nothing of the demon and is not constrained within the Xtian vision of the Universe. He is the god of perversion and obsession, capturing his followers and inspiring them to emulate his own form. They become blind ants, crawling over his real body, which is vast yet enclosed in a brick and mortar tower. They lose all sense of what they are and simply crawl eternally in obsessive pain, lust and suffering.

> "Beyond a gulf in the subterranean night a passage leads to a wall of massive bricks, and beyond the wall rises Y'golonac to be served by the tattered eyeless figures of the dark. Long has he slept beyond the wall, and those which crawl over the bricks scuttle across his body never knowing it to be Y'golonac; but when his name is spoken or read he comes forth to be worshipped or to feed and take on the shape and soul of those he feeds upon. For those who read of evil and search for its form within their minds call forth evil, and so may Y'golonac return to walk among men…" – *Revelations of Glaaki*, Volume 12

Finally, we have Hastur, the un-nameable. Lovecraft opined toward the end of his life that Robert W. Chambers had been the real central inspiration in his writing and that what he called his "Arkham Cycle" or "yogsothothery" should actually be called the Hastur Mythos. Hastur is the mysterious and un-nameable god who inhabits the City of Carcosa; the City that infects the Universe with its corruption, decay and madness.

> "Hastur (*The Unspeakable One, Him Who Is Not to be Named, Assatur, Xastur, H'aaztre*, or *Kaiwan*) is an entity of the Cthulhu Mythos. Hastur first appeared in Ambrose Bierce's short story "Haïta the Shepherd" (1893) as a benign god of shepherds. Hastur is briefly mentioned in H.P. Lovecraft's *The Whisperer in Darkness*; previously, Robert W. Chambers had used the name in his own stories to represent both a person and a place associated with the names of several stars, including Aldebaran."

With the figure of Hastur, we come very close to the heart of Lovecraft's vision of magic. These are entities who lure, trap and corrupt humanity at every turn and treat them with the ultimate indifference and contempt. So why would we want to evoke them into our minds and bodies? I think Lovecraft supplies the answer: because humankind always wants to know the ultimate truths and is willing to give up everything to reach them.

The method to reach that Dark Gnosis of the Great Ancient Ones is a vast problem. We cannot use any of the traditional methods of either evocation or invocation. These entities cannot be called, dismissed, protected against or banished. Our sole useful guide here is what I am going to call an "Inverse Gnosis" that seeks their signs and traces that reach back to the Voidness. My previous articles have discussed the Voidness, which has as one of its aspects, the Quantum flux that lies at the core of our Universe. The Voidness has no characteristics though; no qualities that are discernible to the human mind. In this way, it resembles the Great Ancient Ones and I would have to intuitively opine that they share one and the same sort of reality, whatever that might be, which is beyond our ken. How can we learn anything about these three fearsome entities then? The answer must lie in the Voidness, which is its own conundrum. We *can* experience and mentally "map" the Voidness, though, by the usual methods of the Death Posture, breath control, trance, lucid dreaming and potentially even such Nyarlathotep type scientific devices as the Dream Machine of Brion Gysin. Like all other entities, these three have specific geometries and mathematical signatures. They are vastly more complicated and indecipherable than most, but that does not mean they cannot be discerned with intuitive work. What we are looking for is not any sense of their purpose or way of being, since those are indescernible and indescribable. What we can get is a flavor on the tip of our tongues that gives us the essence of the truly alien experience. Since these are the most anthropoid yet bizarre of the Lovecraftian school's literary creations (Lovecraft created Nyarlathotep; Hastur was created by Chambers and Ambrose Bierce, and Y'Golonac is the creation of Ramsey Campbell), they are the closest approach we can have to the experience of being in the presence of these entities and that is as close as we will ever get.

Greek Mysteries

A Primer

Antti P. Balk

A version of this essay was published as Chapter 2 of Saints & Sinners: An Account of Western Civilization *(Helsinki: Thelema Publications, 2008).* – Ed.

Greek traders and colonists had wandered about the whole Mediterranean basin by the late seventh century BCE, and were spreading northward to the Black Sea; southward to North Africa in the areas left unclaimed by the Phoenicians; eastward to Asia Minor; and westward to southern Italy, Sicily, France, and Spain. Trade with the colonies enabled many of the *poleis* in Hellas to turn themselves into manufacturing centres or to focus on developing specialized crops such as the olive and the grape, produce that could be traded for grain, minerals, and fur.

Wealth and seafaring had generated broad-mindedness and sophistication that often formed a potent contrast to the blood orgies of legends and myth. The early geographer, Hecatæus of Miletus, made a discovery on his extensive travels that shook the foundations of the belief in the pre-eminence of the Greek aristocracy. The Greek aristocrats traced their pedigree six or seven generations back to a god or perhaps rather to the promiscuity of a god. But when Hecatæus journeyed through Egypt, the priests took him to see the graves of the kings, showing him the mummies of Egyptian families dating back 20 or 30 generations. That was when he saw the truth, that is to say the falsity of the claims that the Greek aristocrats descended from the gods, and as soon as he returned, he would spread the word of his discovery to everyone he met.

Around 600 BCE, just when the Gods of Olympus were losing touch with reality, fading and succumbing to their own sumptuous perfection, there came a fresh religious impulse into Greece: the Thracian Bacchos, arrived as *theos xenikos*, a "foreign deity," among the Greeks, who were to call him Dionysos.

Long before his arrival, the Greeks had nature-gods: Demeter was the goddess of the corn; Poseidon, the god of the growth of plants; and Charites were the givers of all increase. But each of these and many other nature-gods had now passed into a state of complete anthropomorphism, representing human rather than merely physical relations, hopelessly cut off from their plant and animal ancestry. Demeter was now much more mother than corn; Hermes, in spite of his herm-shape and phallic worship, was all but forgotten as a spirit of generation in flocks and plants, being now perceived as a young man in all his human grace. In art, Hermes and Dionysos still appeared as they were worshipped – as herms. The symbol of both as fertility-gods was, of course, the phallos. It was impossible to distinguish the young Dionysos from Hermes.

Pan was a solitary god, who wandered among the heaths and woods, and dwelt on mountains and in caves. To a people of goat-herds, like the Arcadians, the goat was the personification of life and generation – to a people of cowherds, the ox was a more suitable vehicle. Dionysos the bull-god was god of all growing things, of every tree and plant and product of nature – only later exclusively of the vine.

Plutarch, discussing the identity of Dionysos and Osiris, says that the Greeks regarded the former as not only the lord and originator of wine, but of the whole *hugra phusis*, the "moist principle" – representing not only the liquid fire of the grapes, but also the sap rushing in young trees, the blood throbbing in the veins of young animals, all the mysterious and unchecked tides that ebb and flow in the Natural Kingdom. Both appeared in ritual as slain and dismembered, and in both cases, there was clearly some form of resurrection of the god, or a new birth as a little child.

Honouring Dionysos was the appropriate task of the women of every Greek city. Every spring, those who ordinarily could not leave the house, abandoned their babies and met together on the barren mountain tops, where they sang and danced to awaken the infant Dionysos from his sleep. They not only nursed and mothered the young god, but young plants and animals as well. As mothers, they had the power to make the earth bloom and the wild animals come to them.

The affiliation of the worship of the wine-god to that of the corn-goddess is eminently important. The winnowing-fan, a simple agricultural instrument figured in the mystic rites of Dionysos, is intrinsically and inevitably an instrument of Demeter. According to tradition and affirmed by art, Dionysos was placed at birth in a winnowing-fan as in a cradle, and from this, he derived the epithet of *Liknites*, "He of the Winnowing-Fan."

The wind is, of course, the natural winnower, but man can assist the wind by throwing the cob up against the wind, which blows away the chaff, while the heavier grain falls to the ground. Two tools – dissimilar in shape and made of different materials – were used in ancient times for winnowing: the *ptuon*, the "chaff-consumer" of Homer, was an oar-like pole with a long handle, made of wood and later of iron, broadened at the end to work as a shovel; the *liknon*, a *vannus* in Vergil, was made of wicker-work and shaped like an old-fashioned scuttle.

The latter was not as convenient as the former, since the labourer had to squat to scoop up the grain and then stand up again to toss it against the wind. It could hold more grain, however, and double as a basket – to hold grain or fruit or sacred relics – and as a cradle for a child. The worship of Dionysos, and later the Orphic mysteries, would adopt the *liknon*, the winnowing-curb, and leave the *ptuon*, the winnowing-shovel, to Demeter.

The shift from winnowing-fan to fruit-basket represents the transition from agriculture to viticulture, from Demeter to Dionysos. The vine-growers have turned their winnowing-fans into fruit-baskets, taken over from the winnowing-fan its proper symbolism and applied it to the fruit-basket. Both the *liknon* and the *vannus* begin as winnowing-fans and end as baskets for fruit or corn. The child rises out of the *cornucopia*, a symbol of fertility; he is the fruits of the earth. The beautiful archaic symbolism that refuses to discriminate between the human and the natural sees in earth the mother, in marriage the plough, in man the sower, and in the fruits of the earth the new-born child.

The worship by women of Liknites, the child in the cradle, reflects the primitive, matriarchal stage of society, an age when the principal conceived function of a woman was motherhood, while the more advanced, patriarchal function of wedded wife was hardly speculated. The closest relationship of parent and child mirrored in mythology is surely not that of the mother and the daughter, but that of the mother and the son. That he is the son of his mother is both the main point and chief note in the mythology of Dionysos. The relationship of the father and the son, Zeus and Apollo, Yahweh and Yeshua, reflects yet a further advance in civilization.

The cult of Dionysos, based on the worship of Mother and Son, gave women a freedom and a rank possible only among the primitive peoples of the north. In a matriarchal civilization, the Son is still naturally only the attribute of motherhood. As long as the worship is primarily in the hands of women, they tend to keep the male divinity in the one shape they can keep him – as a babe. But were their cult to advance with civilization, were their god to have male worshippers, he must grow to a man.

At Athens, Dionysos is a bridegroom, not a new-born child. His development from child to man was probably precipitated by his appropriation of the vine, for a god of intoxication will be worshipped by males at least as much as by females. Dionysos is then a primitive nature-god possessed by an intoxicating spirit, the male correlative as it were of Kore, transfigured by this new element of intoxication and revel.

Though the primary note of the religion of Dionysos was always the cult of an intoxicant, wine is not the only intoxicant, and certainly not the most primitive. Man has never been without the rudimentary means of intoxication: long before he had advanced to agriculture, he had a drink made of naturally fermented honey, a drink now known as mead; he offered to the Chthonian divinities libations of honey – this was the ancient Nectar of the Gods.

Greece acquired beer from its neighbours, notably from the northern barbarians. War and drink, Ares and Dionysos, have always been the preferred divinities in the north.[1] The drinks that the Thracians made of fermented grain, their various beers and crude malt spirits, gave to Bacchos the names of Bromios, Braites, and Sabazios. What the countless number of primitive beers have in common is that they are all alcoholic beverages made of fermented grain, appear with the introduction of agriculture, supersede mead, and are in turn superseded by wine. When "He of the Cereal-Intoxicant" became "He of the Grape-Wine", the implement that had been a winnowing-fan was transformed into a grape-basket.

The Thracians never conquered Greece, so there was no historical reason for their god to impose himself. He no doubt owed his supremacy to the introduction and rapid spread of vine; his characteristic gift, by which he won hearts and minds of men,

---

1 Herodotus asserts that the thirst of the northerners was often their undoing: lured to a rival's camp, their chieftains drank themselves senseless and were easily slain.

was wine – wine made not out of barley, but out of the juice of the grape. A newly-imported plant will attach itself to the local divinity, whoever he or she be. The olive attached itself to Athena, who was there before its arrival, and increased the prestige of the goddess. In all the southern European countries, olive oil took the place of butter, which was hard to keep fresh in a warm climate. Still, the supersession of butter by oil was a quiet and inconspicuous advance, not a triumphant step forward like the advent of the vine.

Not that the Greeks were a nation of drunkards; on the contrary, their way of life was modest, almost ascetic. A couple of elegant clay pots and finely cut wooden rinks satisfied their need for luxury; few fishes and salt cakes, figs and olives, formed their regular meals; mixing two thirds of wine with one third of water was considered excessive. When they came in contact with northern peoples like the Thracians, who drank in earnest, they were both amazed and disgusted. There is no question that with respect to wine and food as to everything else, the Greeks were true to their motto: *mêden agan*, "nothing to excess."

In all of this predominated the same, not moral, but aesthetic economy, which also manifested itself in the Greek architectural forms and in the subjects, concepts, and imagery of their poetry. This strange sobriety is perhaps the central phenomenon of Greek culture and such that has never been encountered since. The Greek simplicity, misconstrued in the 18th century as austerity, dignity, and purity of the soul, was in reality nothing but the lesser refinement of life and the surer limitation of scope that produced the firm, clear, unbending contours of the Greek way of life. Their much praised temperance, self-discipline, and love of moderation is confined to the fact that in everything they were characterized by the comfortable medium size, a reasonable and "due proportion."

Large drinking cups were characteristic to the northern barbarians. Originally made of the huge horns of the large breed of cattle common to the north, these were later set in silver and gold, and sometimes actually made of precious metals. When the savage tastes an intoxicant for the first time, a great delight overwhelms him; he is sure that he is possessed by a spirit, not figuratively, but literally; he is mad, but with a divine madness. Not only did the Greeks dilute their wine with several parts of water, tempering the madness of the god, but they saw in Dionysos the god of spiritual as well as physical intoxication. The wine-drinker tends to treat the beer-drinker as an inferior person. Wine in itself is finer, rarer beverage, and Sabazios, god of the cheap cereal drink, brings sleep rather than inspiration.

According to the legend as related by Euripides, Dionysos, as a thank-you for being greeted as god everywhere he went, taught men the cultivation of vine. After establishing his cult across the known world, he returned to Greece, bringing his Thracian rites with him, and demanding to be worshipped as a god. Pentheus, King of Thebes, had him arrested, tried, scourged, and thrown into prison. For this, Dionysos drove all the women of Thebes mad, including Agaue, mother of Pentheus. They became Mænads, going out into the mountains to conduct the Dionysian orgies – the word *orgia* (from *erga*, "works") originally connoted a divine service. Pentheus imprudently followed Agaue and her companions, who fell upon him, inflamed by wine and religious ecstasy, tearing him to pieces. Thus was the length and breadth of Hellas converted to the religion of Dionysos, and he moved on.

A Mænad means simply a "mad woman", and the Mænads are the female worshippers of Dionysos of whatever stock, maddened, or as the ancients would say, inspired by his spirit. The Mænad is, however, only one, if the most common, of the many names applied to the worshipping women. In Thrace, they were called Bacchæ, in Athens, Lenai, in Delphi, Thyiades, in Lydia, Bassarids, in Macedon, Clodones and Mimallones, etc. The terms *Mænad* and *Bacchæ* were themselves adjectival, and thus could be applied not only to the female worshippers of Dionysos, but to those of any orgiastic deity.

Homeric theology was wholly untouched by Orphism: the human divinities of Olympus, being as they are distinctive and departmental, share no kinship with the partless and passionless Protogonos. The Olympians claim neither omnipotence nor omniscience; in no sense are they creators, sources of life. Homer has no cosmogony, only a marvellous, ready-made human society. His gods are immortal simply because death would shade and spoil their splendour, not because they should be the perennial sources of life or its ultimate purpose. Concerning themselves as little with the before as with the hereafter, the Olympians are, in the strictest sense, human.

Anthropomorphism may provide lovely motifs for art, but the spirit which makes Eros a boy rolling a hoop, Apollo a youth aiming a stone at a lizard, and Nike a woman fastening her sandal, is hardly religious. And while the art of painting was as important as sculpture in ancient Greece, no examples of it other than vase-paintings have been preserved.[2] The visual arts were not at the centre of Hellenic life; music was.

What we usually define as music is actually a quite limited concept. In normal usage, it means for us the Western music that has developed in Europe during the last two and a half millennia. This definition excludes a large number of older and extra-European phenomena, such as the playing and singing practised in ancient high cultures. The history of Western music is usually begun with Greece, though the Greeks themselves gave a much broader significance to the word *mousikê*, the Art of the Muses, than the derived word "music" has today; in fact, they associated all artistic presentations with it, including the literary ones. The singer was thought to be directly inspired by god, even as every prayer was a song. There can be no doubt that music, the most intimate and moving of arts, has done much to create as well as to express the religious feelings, thus modifying more or less deeply the fabric of belief for which alone it at first sight seems to cater.

The importance of the ancient Greek music to posterity is evident from the fact that many modern musical terms are Greek loans; including the words "melody," "rhythm," and "harmony," "orchestra" and "chorus," "lyre," "zither," and "guitar," and many, many another. Music had such an effect on the Greek soul that it could be used to heal the sick. Even the military rested on music, considered as it was the most efficient means to tactical cohesion: the flutist was as the most important man in both infantry and galley. The announcements of the herms, who made the way known to the traveller, were

---

2 The Greek vase-painters were considered artisans, not artists, and at Athens, they lived and worked in the same district as the city's prostitutes.

all written in hexameter, and all the poets were primarily composers. The new lyricist was, above all, the inventor of a new melody, the word taken out of its literal meaning. Tyrtæus and Pindar, Alcæus and Sappho had been singers, while the epics themselves were originally sung, and later at the very least melodramatically recited.

The step from the *epos*, the narrative, to the *drama*, the enactment, is a monumental one, not taken in Greece until after centuries of epic achievement, and then taken suddenly, almost inadvertently, and quite irrevocably. Most primitive religions do have ritual or *dromena*, "things done," but in the religion of Dionysos was fathered the *drama*, a "thing acted" in the stage sense. Clear as the analogy between the two seems today, no other Greek divinities have drama, only *dromena*. The transition came about in the cult of Dionysos and in his alone; his nurses are not only Mænads, but also Muses; from him alone comes the beauty and enchantment of their song, "Hail, thou child of beautiful Semele, none that is mindless of thee can fashion sweet minstrelsy."

In the early Athenian form of drama, the *chorus*, the band of dancing and singing men, was always dressed up as Satyrs, and Aristotle claimed that tragedy had developed from these Satyr-plays; according to him, the word *tragodia* itself means a "goat-song" (tragos = goat). Yet the real impulse to the drama lay in no sacrificial goat-song, but in the principal, and in its essence, dramatic conviction of the Dionysian religion, that the worshipper can not only worship but become his god. Neither Zeus nor Athena have drama, because no worshipper of theirs, even for one passionate moment, ever believed he could become, or be, his god.

Only in the orgiastic religions can the rapturous moments of energized enthusiasm come about, and only in orgiastic religion did the Greek drama arise. Early worshippers of Dionysos apparently re-enacted the gruesome fate of Pentheus by whipping themselves into a frenzy and tearing a live bull to pieces with their teeth. These terrifying rites, accompanied by loud music and the clashing of cymbals, were intended to thrust the revellers into a state of ecstasy. They hoped thereby to transcend their earthly bonds, to allow the soul to temporary free itself from the body – the Greek word *ekstasis* means literally "to be placed outside." Only by standing outside itself, by giving up its individual identity, could the soul achieve a condition of *enthousiasmos*, the state of being "inside the god," believed by the worshippers to be a taste of what they would one day enjoy in eternity.

Tragedy was a kind of a composite work of art, formed by the scene, text, mime, song, and dance, and held together by music. The instrumentations were, according our own standards, simple, almost deficient. The Greek music knew no hair instruments, used horns only in signalling purposes, and was, by and large, merely vocal, employing instruments almost exclusively in accompaniment and only rarely and very scantily in solo performances – the whole tragedy orchestra was formed by a guitarist and one or two flutists. Above all, It rejected polyphony: Greek vocal music was sung either solo or in chorus, but always monophonic. The primary accompanying instruments were the *aulos*, a reed instrument, and the *kithara*, a stringed one.[3] The performance of the principal vocalist shifted between rhapsodies, duets, and monological arias.

To be called "lyric," a poem had to be sung with a lyre accompanying. These types of

---

3 Associated with Dionysos and Apollo, respectively

performances were evidently ancient, though this form of poetry was perfected before all on the island of Lesbos, where in the late seventh century BCE, there lived perhaps the greatest Greek lyric poet, Sappho. She was renowned for her charming and graceful yet passionate love poetry, addressed, as it happens, to women – hence our modern term "lesbian." She was a well-respected noblewoman, the idol of the daughters of the aristocracy, whom she seems to have given expert tutoring in music and etiquette. When they subsequently married, she wrote the wedding songs that were instrumental in her rise to renown. Sappho, like most ancient literary giants, became the subject of fables; in fact, the Greeks held her in so great a respect that they referred to her as the "Tenth Muse."

The musician has played as great a part as the prophet and the thinker in the founding of religion. Every faith has its appropriate music, the differences between the creeds being expressed to a significant degree in their respective musical notations.[4] Orpheus, the quintessential bard, whose masterful singing and music upon the lyre could tame wild beasts and even move rocks and trees, came, of course, from the home of music, the north. As Conon the Mythographer attests, "the stock of the Thracians and Macedonians is music-loving."

Orpheus, whom Diodorus places two generations later than Dionysos, apparently won the hearts of the men of Thrace and Macedon by his music, but refused to reveal his mysteries to women, whom he since the loss of his wife had hated indiscriminately. The men were wont to assemble on certain fixed days in Libethra, at a large building suitable for the celebration of their orgiastic rites, and before going in, they always laid down their arms in front of the entrance. Realizing their opportunity, the women seized the arms, slew the men, and tore Orpheus to pieces, throwing his limbs to the monsters of the sea to devour.[5]

The above details, supplied by Conon in his *Narrations*, are no doubt aetiological. Still, we can discern behind them a basis of historical fact, an outrage of the Thracian women against a real immigrant prophet, whose reforms they perceived as blasphemy of their own rites. Instead of revering Dionysos, he accounted Apollo the greatest of the gods: each morning, he climbed Mount Pangæus to watch Apollo bring up the Sun and to greet him. The Mænads tore Orpheus to pieces, not because he was an incarnation of their god, but because he despised them and they hated him. There is always about him a touch of the reformers' smugness, and it is impossible not to feel sympathy for the determined women who went to put a stop to all this sun-watching and lyre-playing.

The modern reader thinks of Orpheus as two things: as a magical musician, which he was; and as a passionate lover, which he originally was not. The myth of Eurydice is very interesting indeed, but not as a love story. It is a piece of theology taken over from Dionysos that had initially nothing to do with Orpheus. A priest of Dionysos, Orpheus took on his resurrection as well as his death; this is the germ from which sprang the sentimental love story. *Semelê*, the green earth, comes up from below, year by year, and with her comes her son Dionysos, who was thought to have gone to fetch her. *Eurydice,*

---

4 Æschylus asserts that Orpheus preferred the calm and soothing sound of the Greek lyre over the harsh Phrygian flutes and cymbals used in Bacchos' frenzied rites.

5 According to legend, Orpheus' singing head and playing lyre drifted down the River Hebrus, out to sea, and onto the shores of Lesbos, where the Muses buried it, making the Lesbians adept at music.

finally, is the "Wide-Ruless," one of those universal, adjectival names appropriate to any and every goddess.

Orpheus was a Thracian, and yet it is primarily through his influence at Athens that we know him: there he took a primitive superstition, rooted deeply in the savage rite of Dionysos, and gave it new spiritual significance. In the Dionysian orgies, live animals were not only torn to pieces, but devoured raw – it was believed that the god entered the worshippers and possessed them through this eucharist of living flesh. But Orpheus sought to obtain that godhead by wholly different means: he replaced the old Dionysian *omophagia*, the ritual devouring of the raw flesh of a sacrificial animal, with the offering and consumption of cakes of meal and honey in commemoration of the slain Son of God.

Though Dionysos as Bromios, Braites, Sabazios, as god of intoxication, was much, Dionysos as Zagreus, Nyktelios, Isodaites, he who is "a meal shared by all" was infinitely more. In the breaking of bread, and even more in the drinking of wine, both physical and spiritual life is renewed, equanimity and magnanimity are restored, reason and morality rule again. We will not share a meal with a man we hate – it is regarded as a sacrilege that leaves the body and soul sick. The first breaking of bread and drinking of wine together is the seal of a new friendship; the last eaten in silence at parting speaks louder than any words. The sacrament of bread and wine is spread for the newly married, as it is for the newly dead.[6]

The Orphics turned the most barbarous element of their own religion not just into a vague monotheism, but into a sacrament of spiritual purification, the ritual consumption of the body of god. To the Orphics, man was a child of Earth and starry Heaven; his body of the earth, but his soul "rooted in the celestial element." The Orphic way of atonement is to stop the repetition of behaviour that reduces human life to a circle of repetitiousness in parody of the cyclic rhythms of nature, binding us eternally to a wheel of false catharsis prepared by our distant forebears, the earth-born Titans.

Entirely Orphic, rather than Dionysian, are also the regulations as to the peace and order to be observed: "Within the place of sacrifice no one is to make a noise, or clap his hands, or sing, but each man is to say his part and do it in all quietness and order as the priest and the Archibacchos direct."[7] Still more striking is the rule that if any member should act riotously, an officer appointed by the priest shall set against him the thyrsus of the god; the phallic staff, in a truly Orphic fashion, has transformed from the symbol of revel and license, into the sign of an orderly conducted worship.

The coming of Dionysos brought to the Greek religion a new spiritual impulse, central to which was the ascetic notion that the body is the tomb of the soul, that this world is but preparation to a higher life, and that man, by mystically uniting with the divinity, can be redeemed. In the EleusinianMysteries, generally regarded as the high point of Greek religion, all that was not a part of primitive harvest festival was borrowed from the cult of Dionysos.

Unlike the Egyptians, the Greeks had not developed a doctrine of immortality out

---

6 The making of wine involved symbolism reminiscent of the tending of the dead and the hope for resurrection: the blood of the grape was fermented in subterranean, tomb-like containers, which, when opened, released the god, who returned from the grave to celebrate his new birth.

7 From the inscription on a temple column at the Baccheion of Athens.

of the symbolism of the corn, but when that doctrine came to them from without, the symbolism of the seed was ready at hand. The worship of Dionysos in its Orphic form, arriving at Eleusis, modified the simple rites of the Mother and the Maid: at Eleusis, the god was known by the title of Iacchos, and worshipped amidst not only the goddesses Demeter and Kore, but also the gods Pluto and Zeus, the god of the underworld and the god of the sky respectively – in this conjunction linked to the vegetative power of the earth, and the fertilizing showers of the sky.

In a far-off time, Eleusis was an independent city-state, before the stately procession of the mysteries had defiled over the low chain of barren hills, which divides the flat Eleusinian corn plain from the more spacious olive field of the Athenian plain. Though Athens ultimately emerged to political supremacy, it was Eleusis to which the Thracian migrant, Eumolpus, first brought his rites, and she maintained her religious hegemony to the end. Athens did what she could: she built herself an Eleusinion and instituted Lesser Mysteries; the *hiera* or "sacred objects" were brought from Eleusis, and Iacchos, who had his sanctuary at Athens, made a return visit – but the final initiation still took place at Eleusis and the *hierophant* is always and forever a Thracian Eumolpid, a member of the hereditary priesthood.

The festival of the mysteries was held on two separate occasions during the Athenian year (each city-state had its own calendar), and each and every candidate was twice initiated. The Lesser Mysteries were celebrated in the spring, at Athens, to welcome the return of vegetation; the Greater at harvest time, in Eleusis. Iacchos was a god made by the Athenians in their own image: as they were guests at Eleusis, so was their god. Large crowds of worshippers from all over Greece – later from all over the Roman Empire – would gather to make the sacred pilgrimage between the two cities and participate in the secret rites. Each new initiate, known as a *mystes*, would receive preliminary guidance from an experienced sponsor, a *mystagogos*, who would usually be from one of the leading families of Eleusis. A *mystes* who returned a second time to Eleusis was referred to as an *epoptes*.

The Lesser Mysteries were a sort of a preliminary purification for the Greater, being founded, according to tradition, in order that Herakles, tainted though he was with the blood of the Centaurs, might be initiated. In the Greater Mysteries, those of Demeter, Dionysos was to the end only a visitor; in the Lesser, a later foundation, he shared the honours with her daughter Kore. Iacchos at Eleusis is not the beer-god, nor the wine-god, but the son-god, the "Child of Semele" – the same as Liknites, "He of the Cradle," whom the Thyiades year by year wakened to new life on Mount Parnassus. Pursuant to the sacred dogma, "A virgin shall conceive and bear a son," this mystic child was born of a maiden.

The union of the sky-god Zeus with the virgin-goddess Kore was ritually represented by the union of the *hierophant* with the priestess, who acted the parts of the god and goddess. The torches having been extinguished, the couple descended into a murky place, while the *mystai* awaited in anxious suspense the result of the *hieros gamos*, on which they believed their salvation to depend. After a while, the *hierophant* reappeared, and in a blaze of light, exhibited to the congregation the supreme revelation of a "green ear of corn reaped," declaring the birth of a sacred child: "Unto us a Child is born, unto us a Son is given."

In the wake of political and economic strength came a blossoming of Hellenic culture, particularly in Ionia, where a tradition of Greek philosophy began with the speculations of Thales, Anaximander, and Anaximenes. Uniting all of ancient Greece was the Homeric religion; the sanctuary of Delphi, with its famous oracle, became the greatest national shrine; the Eleusinian rites became a state religion, politically and socially sacred. The Orphics were dissenters, living in small communities, and following an ascetic lifestyle – intended to symbolize the renunciation of the Titanic side of human nature, and to ultimately liberate the spirit from the "tomb of the body" and the "sorrowful wheel of generation."

The earliest Greek we can link to Orphism is the 6th-century BCE thinker, Pherecydes. Through Heraclitus and Empedocles to Plato and Plotinus, the Orphic wisdom followed the Greek thought like a dark shadow. Orphism influenced the works of the tragics Æschylus and Sophocles, those of the most favoured of Greek poets, Pindar, and of the greatest poet of Rome, Vergil; Pythagoras was an Orphic initiate.

A pupil of Pherecydes, Pythagoras was forced to flee his birthplace on the island of Sámos because of Polycrates, the tyrant of Syracuse. He settled at Croton, in southern Italy, where he established the famous Pythagorean school of philosophy, mathematics, and natural science. People from all classes of society came to his school to hear his lectures, among them women, even though the law in those days forbade the participation of women in public meetings. Indeed, these Orphic Pythagoreans tended to revive religious ideas that were matriarchal rather than patriarchal, the house of Pythagoras being even known to the people of Metapontum as "the temple of Demeter."

Pythagoras became the first famous exponent of Orphism and was the individual most responsible for disseminating it throughout ancient Greece. He gathered together his more talented disciples, male and female, founding around 530 BCE an order that preached modesty, rigorous self-discipline, patience, and self-control. Discipline has always been a part of religious practice, mental and otherwise. Long ago, all intellectual acts, anything that did not involve working with the hands, was prayer, or something much like it. To read a book, to study a mental discipline, was to pray – a categorization still common in the East. Pythagoras believed that all relations could be reduced to number relations, a generalization that stemmed from his observations in mathematics, astronomy, and music.

Some mathematicians still relate their art to their religion as an attempt to behold the perfection of the created universe. From the deductive regularity of the propositions of geometry, we may discern a model for the laws which govern the universe, both physical and moral. "The first and noblest of Sciences," geometry may have been man's first exercise in abstraction outside of language. The word means to "measure the earth," and this was no doubt its first application. In time, it became sacred as well as practical, for the ancients reckoned all its figures to be of religious significance.

Being the first to observe that natural phenomena, especially those of the astronomical world, may be expressed in mathematical formulas, Pythagoras maintained that numbers were not only the symbols of reality, but the very substance of things. Through numbers a divine order was imposed on the world, invisible to the eye, but discernible by the mind. The Heavens, Pythagoras taught, are the realm of pure number, where objects move in perfect circles, a realm that is best perceived through pure reason; the Earth, realm of sense and appearances, is where human souls are condemned.

It was not any of these particular doctrines of the school so much as the prevalent notion among the Pythagoreans concerning the scope and aim of philosophy, that influenced the subsequent course of speculation among the Greeks. The "philosophers" of the day called themselves by the noun *sophos*, a "wise man" or a "sage" – Pythagoras was the first to use instead the title *philosophos*, a "lover of wisdom." His school was devoted to the cultivation of not only philosophy in the modern sense, but also of mathematics, music, and even gymnastics, the aim of the organization being primarily ethical; the oath ascribed to Hippocrates may have originally been drawn up for a Pythagorean sect.

The most important scientific discovery of the Pythagorean school was the fact that the diagonal of a square is not a rational multiple of its side, a result which revealed the existence of irrational numbers. This upset not only Greek mathematics, but also the Pythagoreans' own belief that integers and their ratios could alone account for geometrical properties. They never ceased to study this subject, adopting as their emblem the pentagram, a five-pointed star that has for its centre a regular pentagon; this figure contains within itself an unusual amount of irrational variables, and became, in time, a magical symbol for Faust and the other mediaeval wizards.

Besides the above-mentioned geometric theorem, the Pythagoreans, who had to make do without either algebra or the Arabic numerals, are also credited with the discovery of the numerical ratios that determine the concordant scale. They noticed that vibrating strings produce harmonious tones when the ratios of the lengths of the strings are whole numbers, and that these ratios can be extended to other instruments – it is from this discovery that all Western music derives.

All in all, the Pythagorean school made an outstanding contribution to science: its members invented the Multiplication Table, knew that the Earth is round and that it rotates on its axis, and raised important scientific problems which would not be solved until a millennium and a half later. In a sense, they invented the whole Western science: by associating measurements of length with musical tones, they made the first known reduction of a quality (sound) into a quantity (length and ratio).

The time-honoured tradition that Pythagoras forbade his disciples to eat beans, for which various reasons, more or less fabulous, were invented by ancient and mediaeval writers, has been refuted by modern scholars, who understand the phrase, *Kyamon apechete*, "Abstain from beans," to refer not so much to an obscure dietary prescription, as to a principle of practical prudence. Beans, black and white, were the means of voting in Magna Græcia, and abstaining from beans would, therefore, refer only to avoiding politics – a warning well warranted by the troubles which the school was involved in due to the active part it took during the lifetime of its founder in the struggles of the popular with the aristocratic party in southern Italy.

You see, the early Pythagorean order was a notable political factor, gaining ground in many southern Italian communities. Croton enjoyed for some time a great prosperity under the Pythagorean rule, but eventually a revolt broke out, led by a Crotonian called Kylon. The rebels took the Pythagoreans by surprise at a symposium, killed many, and banished the rest. Most of the brethren died during the uprising, presumably also Pythagoras. Those who lived settled at Thebes and Phlius, where they revived the order. Within its ranks rose two divergent groups, dedicated to religion and science respectively – it was the latter group which would come under the leadership of Archytas of Tarentum.

The theoretical doctrines first taught by Pythagoras were strictly adhered to, so much so that the Pythagoreans were known for their constant citation of the *ipse dixit* of their founder. As soon as the legends began to grow around his name, he was ascribed many tenets which were only introduced by later Pythagoreans, such as Archytas, Philolaus, and Aristoxenus.

Before the year 300 BCE, the Pythagorean school vanished from view once again, only to be revived by the neo-Pythagoreans at Rome and Alexandria in the 1st century BCE. Unlike the Ionians, who related philosophy to knowledge only,[8] the Pythagoreans, being religiously and ethically inclined, aspired to bring philosophy into relation with life as well as with knowledge. Aristotelianism, which reduced philosophy to knowledge, never could challenge Christianity, as neo-Pythagoreanism did, by claiming that the teachings of its founder offered a way of life preferable to its Christian counterpart.

REFERENCES

—∽— Æschylus. *Eumenides*, trans. by Herbert Weir Smyth (Cambridge, MA: Harvard University Press, 1926)

—∽— Aristotle. *Theory of Poetry and Fine Art*, 3rd ed., ed. & trans. by Samuel Henry Butcher (London: Macmillan, 1902)

—∽— Athenæus of Naucratis. *The Deipnosophists*, 7 vols, trans. by Charles Burton Gulick (London: Heinemann, 1937)

—∽— Augustine. "De Civitate Dei," trans. by Marcus Dods, in *Nicene and Post-Nicene Fathers*, Series I, Vol. II, ed. by Philip Schaff (Edinburgh: T & T Clark, 1887)

—∽— Bronowski, Jacob. *The Ascent of Man* (Boston: Little, Brown, 1973)

—∽— Burkert, Walter. *Greek Religion: Archaic and Classical*, trans. by John Raffan (Oxford: Basil Blackwell, 1985)

—∽— Burnet, John. *Early Greek Philosophy* (London: A & C Black, 1892)

—∽— *The Catholic Encyclopedia*, 15 vols, ed. by Charles G. Herbermann et al. (New York: Robert Appleton, 1907–12)

—∽— Diodorus Siculus. *Bibliotheca Historica*, 2 vols, trans. by John Skelton, ed. by F. M. Salter & H. L. R. Edwards (London: Early English Text Society, 1956–57)

—∽— Diogenes Laërtius. *The Lives and Opinions of Eminent Philosophers*, trans. by C. D. Yonge (London: H. G. Bohn, 1853)

—∽— Eliade, Mircea. *A History of Religious Ideas*, 3 vols, trans. by Willard R. Trask (Chicago: University of Chicago Press, 1978–85)

---

8 The most important achievement of the early Ionian thinkers was the development of "logic," the view that it is necessary to give reasons for one's conclusions and to persuade others by arguments based on evidence.

_____. *Patterns in Comparative Religion*, trans. by Rosemary Sheed (London: Sheed & Ward, 1958)

—ᴡ— Euripides. "Bacchae," trans. by Philip Vellacott, in *The Bacchae and Other Plays* (London: Penguin, 1954)

—ᴡ— Frazer, Sir James George. *The Golden Bough*, 3rd ed. in 12 vols (London: Macmillan, 1911–15)

—ᴡ— Guthrie, W. K. C. *The Greeks and Their Gods* (London: Methuen, 1950)

_____. *A History of Greek Philosophy*, 6 vols (Cambridge: Cambridge University Press, 1962–81)

—ᴡ— Harrison, Jane. *Ancient Art & Ritual* (London: Williams & Norgate, 1913)

_____. *Prolegomena to the study of Greek Religion*, 3rd ed. (London: Cambridge University Press, 1921)

—ᴡ— Herodotus. *The History of Herodotus*, 2 vols, trans. by G. C. Macauley (London: Macmillan, 1890)

—ᴡ— Hesiod. "Theogony" & "Works and Days," trans. by Hugh G. Evelyn-White, in *Hesiod, the Homeric Hymns, and Homerica* (London: Heinemann, 1914)

—ᴡ— Hippolytus. "Refutation of All Heresies," trans. by J. H. MacMahon, in *The Ante-Nicene Fathers*, Vol. V, ed. by Alexander Roberts & James Donaldson (Edinburgh: T & T Clark, 1868)

—ᴡ— Homer. *Odyssey*, ed. by Karl Friedrich Ameis, rev. by Carl Hentze (Leipzig: Teubner, 1895)

—ᴡ— *The Homeric Hymns*, trans. Andrew Lang (London: George Allen, 1899)

—ᴡ— Iamblichus. *Life of Pythagoras, or, Pythagoric Life*, trans. by Thomas Taylor (London: Watkins, 1818)

—ᴡ— Murray, Gilbert. *Five Stages of Greek Religion*, 3rd ed. (Boston: Beacon Press, 1951)

—ᴡ— Pausanias. *Description of Greece*, 6 vols, trans. by Sir James George Frazer (London: Macmillan, 1898)

—ᴡ— Plato. *The Dialogues of Plato*, 4 vols, trans. by Benjamin Jowett (Oxford: Clarendon Press, 1871)

—ᴡ— Plotinus. *The Six Enneads*, 6 vols, trans. by Stephen MacKenna & B. S. Page (London: Encyclopædia Britannica, 1952)

—ᴡ— Plutarch. "On Isis and Osiris," trans. Frank Cole Babbitt, in *Plutarch's Moralia*, Vol. V (London: Heinemann, 1927)

—ᴡ— Vergil. *Georgics*, trans. L. P. Wilkinson (Harmondsworth: Penguin, 1982)

The Economy of Magic

Carl Abrahamsson

The following text was originally delivered as a lecture at Nekropolis in Copenhagen, Denmark, on February 12th, 2015. – Ed.

In several sequences of the TV-series *Carnivale* we can see the protagonist Ben Hawkins heal wounds and even bring people back from the dead. It looks impressive, but the process takes a toll on the young, almost unwilling magician. It's because he knows there's a price to pay. Around him, the vital energy needed for the operation at hand is always sucked from someone or something else. Human beings, birds and fields of crops perish when he transfers that energy into the dead and the injured.

The equation is obvious and brings us to the quintessential magical dilemma. You get, you give. You give, you get. It's there in that classic Faustian deal, and it's there as a basis for all kinds of sacrificial rituals, from the smallest of cults to the greatest of the world religions. We can look at it from the smallest level of personal need or greed and up to global or even cosmic interrelationships.

Although this is essentially a well-known axiom or equation all through various myths and teachings, I still notice that many young occultists within a Western sphere school themselves, or are schooled, in a kind of smash-and-grab mentality. This undoubtedly ties in with a general Occidental mind-frame, in which it's apparently possible to just get and get and get. But we all know that somewhere in a third world country, or at sea, rests the toxic debris and waste of that attitude. Which in turn is or will be eventually impossible to escape for *anyone* residing on this planet.

For the Occidental occultist mind, quite often with no ties to larger moral or religious clusters, it seems possible to command spirits, demons or other kinds of forces merely because it's his or her will. An endless series of demands, in which the mere opening of the door and greeting should bring success and manifestation. It should be made clear though, that this is not how things work. Not on the smallest of small levels, and not on the grandest of grand scales.

Whether looking at outer or inner process, there's a balance that needs to be set. The equation of supply, demand and cost is all-permeating. Everything requires something to be able to produce the force or item that's desired. The complicated web of outer productivity seems banal, but serves as a good example: Someone spends time and energy to make something that is then sold to a buyer, who pays for it with the magical energy of money, that in turn has been procured somehow in other generative circles.

This is the most basic example of a relationship that permeates everything around us and in us. It's almost as if it's a general fundament, a prerequisite of civilized life. The mere demanding without willingness to give anything back is then a suggestion of massive potential or actual failure.

If we begin on the grand scale, which is no less magical than the incense-clouded personal temples, we can see that in the major myths, there has always been some kind of existential sacrifice involved. Two main examples: The human being Jesus became a christic force by sacrificing his life with determination and free will. This created a phantasmagoric residue, a psychopomp, that was then integrated by the Christian power structure as myth. The focus was on the deed itself and its implications. "Jesus died for *your* sins," implying a transference of sacrificial magical energy beyond the realm of the personal human being Jesus. This, handled by a clever organization, can apparently work wonders too.

The second example: The Buddha reached enlightenment by realizing the necessity of balance, where neither death-related ascetic behavior nor sensual debauchery was favored. In Samsara, the world of the senses, it was necessary to renounce these extremes and also important to embrace the concept of Karma, meaning in this context *not* "you will get good things and possible release from Samsara if you do good things" but rather "If you do good things, you will get good things and possible release from Samsara." Although logically the same, morally they're not. This has to do with the relationship with the concepts of Self and Will.

Long before this, a similar concept was in use in Egyptian mythology. The heart of a person deceased would be weighed on scales against the feather of Maat, the goddess of truth, by Anubis, god of the afterlife. If it was pure, everything was fine and the deceased could move on to afterlife. If not, the heart would be devoured by the demon Ammit. The heart's purity was defined by the moral standards of the day and the tool used a central one in economy and trade: the scales.

As a cosmic principle, Karma could be said to exist. Meaning: the books need to be balanced or there will be extra taxation or perhaps even investigation of fraud or tax evasion. On a personal level though, Karma is mainly a cultural concept that has seeped into the West from the East. The mere term thus becomes entangled in both religious and moral issues, which creates an unnecessarily complex overview. I would therefore like to substitute it in our context here with the term "Magicoin." Sure, "magical currency" could be another suitable term, but this is also semantically entangled with other kinds of concepts within the magical sphere (The "93" Current, the "Setian" ditto, etc).

In our Western sphere, Self and Will rule supreme. And this is as it should be: without self-knowledge and will, we get nowhere. Or perhaps at most shuffled around by others who are more eloquent in defining us and who thereby can use us for their own ends. But if Self and Will are there, firmly rooted within the individual, we have a good, solid foundation to learn about how magic (and life) works. If we stay on the level of "I want" without further understanding of genuine Magicoin principles, there will be debt. If we work with agents like spirits or other non-tangible, inner forces, we can only go so far with a steady flow of demands. Just as with credit cards.

It's almost easier to understand the Magicoin concept when looking at it outside the sphere of magic. Money and economics is one very clear-cut sphere, human relationships another. If we take something and don't pay, that's called stealing. If we use someone else indefinitely for our own ends, that turns into abuse and, very likely, confrontation. That's why we don't do those things if we see the big picture and understand our own position within it.

Why is the dilemma even there? Meaning, why is it that magicians in the Western sphere so seldom understand these basic principles? I think the problem is twofold. One is that magical practice is usually compartmentalized in time and space and seen as an activity separate from the overall flow of life. This is a big error. If magical practice is fully integrated in one's life, for instance by applying one's own terms and interpretations rather than rehashing traditional, dogmatic, symbolic and arcane ones (and thereby increasing the potential for a better understanding of the concepts), there won't even be any dilemma left. Hermes Trismegistus' dictum of "As above, so below" will rule on all levels, both outer and inner.

The second aspect is that I perceive that many young people begin with magical practice before they're fully individuated. That is, before they fully understand their own relationship to everyone and everything else. Magic is mistakenly regarded simply as something you *do* at certain times and spaces, not something you *are* 24/7 and wherever you go or stay. Magic is mistakenly regarded simply as something you do to achieve your own ends in fairly non-rational ways, *not* something that ties you together holistically with the universe.

It's a bit like cramming in school. Students can mechanically or automatically repeat what's been taught in class and thereby give a semblance of knowing. Which can, in bad schools, actually produce good grades. But these are grades that are misleading as indications of real understanding. Any challenging or unexpected question to the student will quickly reveal that it's just a matter of regurgitation or repetition.

By being, we carry potential. By doing, we achieve. But by achieving, are we always successful? What we do affects ourselves on the inner planes, and also the totality outside us. If we disregard any overall karmic concepts as being strictly "moral" ones, and instead just look to the economy of the processes, it is my experience that if there's a conscious and willed balance in the Magicoin books, there *will* be success.

It's always healthier to generate funds than it is to deal with credit. This is something most of us recognize from everyday finances. How we generate is by "offering" first and "asking" later. It's interesting to see how the word *offer* even ties in etymologically to this. To "sacrifice" means "making holy." The German word for a "victim" and for "sacrifice" itself is "Opfer" (in Swedish "offer", to sacrifice: "att offra", cf. "make an offer"). The word "victim" is originally Latin, and means exactly the same as in English. Its roots can be traced to a "sacrificed animal." Another synonym for something sacrificed is "hostia", as for instance in the "host" of the Christian communion. And as in the English "hostage", something or someone being offered in return for something or someone else.

If we ask first, and possibly ask without immediate payment, there will be debt, i.e. a credit situation. This is something young occultists seem to disregard as much as the overall culture seems to disregard it on the strict financial levels. In an entire economy of debt, no wonder people (and nations, even) become slaves as a result of their own bad choices.

An important question: Is magical success equal to the concept of profit? Meaning: If we generate more than what we spend, is that a sign of specific magical success? The answer is No. Profit and surplus are in our minds predominantly an economic, cultural concept within a tradition, not an existential given. Of course, one could argue that financial profit and its residues are necessary as status indicators and thereby of natural stratifying processes. However, the magical process is always an individual one. It can never be collective. Magical success equals the balancing of the individual Magicoin books. One exception would be when advanced magicians actually contain more Magicoin energy than they need for their own individual purposes. This can then be shared with others. If someone not advanced enough tries to do the same thing, there will be depletion within his or her own Magicoin system.

Goethe's *Faust* is an often referenced work of art in this regard, as is Marlowe's earlier play and a hundred different variants of the theme. Making a pact or a deal with the so-called Devil is merely succumbing to a credit-based slavery situation. The same goes for working within traditional esoteric systems where so-called external forces are called forth to presence. If and when the magician declares his or her will to the force in question, but forgets to explain the possible dividends or even to add a "please" after the declaration, then the odds are likely that the outcome will be more expensive than could ever be imagined.

What this means in real life is of course not that some occult force pops up at night and demands to be paid back in full or that some fantastic Devil tries to drag your soul to some monotheistic vision of Hell. But what it could mean is that you, after a successful ritual, find that its manifested goal may contain problematic aspects too, previously not considered. Had the pre-ritual overview been crystal clear (the equivalent of an economic budget that balances out), problems could have been foreseen and possibly dealt with before the ritual even. An example: You make a ritual to secure one more or less constant sexual partner. This manifests in a perfectly sexually compatible woman and she is very nice indeed. But she's also a human being with emotions and a will of her own that might not be compatible when she's making demands of a deeper relationship than merely carnal. Or that as a result of the volatile and intense lust she's able to provoke, all according to your fantasies, you make her pregnant.

Another example could be an even more youthful or naive one: A young magician wants a gadget that he can't afford right now and performs a ritual for the situation. The train of events leads to that a good friend of his, equally poor, actually steals two gadgets and gives him one. This could be seen as a beautiful and successful operation from the magician's perspective. However, the friend was caught on CC-TV and is later charged with the crime. The attraction of that gadget very soon loses its potency.

Much better to generate the energy needed oneself and then send it off on adventures of manifestation. If well-directed, it not only becomes an appropriate legitimate expense but also potentially an investment. Meaning, an expense that furthers the cause, broadens the base, facilitates creative expansion. In the example of the fencing young magician, things could have been changed for the better with mere expression of intent.

If he had integrated the expression of desire in a larger context of self-development for instance, in which the gadget could play a tangible, creative part, the result could have manifested in a different way. And his using the gadget lead to an improved skill rather than a bad conscience.

As in our normal economy, there is also a meta-level in the magic business. We normally talk about a stock market that trades in worth, loss and potential in existing companies. Translated into our own sphere of hocus pocus this would correspond to the lucrative area of magical books. They carry potential for change on their pages, and attract by symbolism, poetry, promises of power, etc. They deal with magic and they deal in magic. Thereby the entire meta-sphere of magical literature and its writers becomes the stock market of occultism. A speculation in worth and potential. If more people invest in one writer rather than another, even though these writers may be writing about the same kinds of magical phenomenon, then his or her value increases and even more investors show up. This could also strengthen related power structures such as magical groups or orders behind the writer in question, which could then be seen as an actual board (or an advisory one) for the writer/corporation in question.

When the Catholic Conquistadores entered Central America and were shocked by the human sacrifices performed by the Aztecs, they apparently forgot about the essence of their own religion. The Aztecs tried their best to appease their main sun god and other minor gods and goddesses by ritually killing human beings. In their own minds they succeeded, because the sun did come back. Every day, in fact. And crops and harvests were for the most part plentiful in that fertile region. So in a way they existed within a brutal and blood-soaked logic of success. The very same logic was then applied by the Conquistadores, who slaughtered and eradicated the Aztecs and their behavior for their own profit and for Catholicism. They also succeeded: the Aztecs were killed off and Catholic success and affluence followed. Meaning, the remaining converts could now instead partake of communion consisting of blood and flesh from the invaders' own sacrificial proxy: Jesus Christ.

Today, human sacrifice is not condoned, if we exclude fundamentalist muslim terrorists and some retrograde tribes in remote jungles. The challenge today, if we stick to our young hubristic Western magicians, is rather to deal with their culture of fragmentation and over-saturation. If we already have everything and still want more, wouldn't the most beneficent sacrifice have more to do with behaviors and attitudes rather than with tangible objects or life forms? Cleaning up internally first, so to speak? Getting rid of destructive behavioral patterns and shortsightedness? Sacrifice external pollution and internal malnutrition?

An interesting yet considerably more speculative area of magico-economic research could be whether the magical currency (NB, *not* "current") is exchangeable or universal. Would it for instance be meaningful to use Scandinavian heathen magic in central Africa or would one need to somehow exchange the terminology and the forces used for a successful operation? Would American Indian magic work well in Tibet? Aboriginal magic in the Vatican? Or vice versa?

Interesting things are also going on within the highly abstracted sphere of high finance in regard to Mother Nature's capital, which in many ways is permeated by powerful sources of magic. Where an old-fashioned economic thinking simply got what it wanted from the planet without returning anything at all (a very black form of magic) and thereby facilitated incredible fortunes out of many magical and sensitive ecosystems, today the phenomenon of "mitigation banking" is a new growth market in the undertow of ecological consciousness (or simply a bad conscience). It works like this: A bank buys a huge piece of land that needs protection for the sake of, for instance, bio-diversity. Rapacious corporations can then buy a small segment to exploit, quite expensively, and part of the bank's revenue goes to actual further bio-protection. It's a very strange set-up, almost illogical, but it's now making huge profits for all concerned. And yes, to perhaps a greater extent than in the recent decades, wildlife can now be better protected. But it does have a strange, almost eerie aftertaste. It's like a bank suddenly owning a previously raped woman, and now, in the name of her overall protection, sells long-term leases for her mouth and hands to her previous rapists. Translated into a magical set-up, it's like a mitigation made by a wise magician for an assortment of unwise magicians, who all want to have results immediately but cannot see the big picture or the role they play. They can use the force but only when sanctioned by some other magician who is thereby getting morally and inexorably entangled in whatever it is that's going on. A healthy set-up? I think not.

On a stricter and more concretely generative level, we can always return to the main mysteries of magic – the sexual ones – for both metaphor and concrete food for thought. The theory is usually divided into psychosexual and physical-residual parts. Isolationists say the creative force lies in one but not the other, and other, more holistically inclined theorists say it's a mix of both. That is, that the magical force lies in the ecstatic moment itself, which can be charged and directed. Or that the dissemination and direction of the ultra-proto-generative force in the physical sperm and egg is what matters. We will not delve into this fascinating mystery this evening, at least not on that level.

It's interesting to note though, that the physical sacrifice of sperm in ejaculation carries almost unlimited potential when it comes to generating new human life. Even if there is conception, that was made possible by the parallel sacrifice of a billion sperm-buddies. Male generative sacrifice is usually associated with intense pleasure. Female generative sacrifice is usually associated with intense displeasure. The sacrifice of an unfertilized egg in menstruation is not such an apparent joyous occasion, but it does facilitate the placement of new egg, ready and willing should a vital sperm drop by. Considering the potential these generative sacrifices contain, both as states of mind *and* body, both as ecstasies *and* physical residue, it's no wonder that they constitute prime magical currency. With this very basic insight in mind, it should be easy to see that a credit-based magical economy might not be the best place to begin your own magical career.

Essentially, it's very simple: plus and minus need to add up to zero, in magical operations and in life in general. That's quite enough. If we can learn to change from looking at "sacrifice" as a painful noun to looking at it as a pleasurable, constructive verb, we have come a long way.

THE BOOK OF THE SENTIENT NIGHT:
23 NAILS

Stephen Sennitt

INTRODUCTION

In March 1985, I performed an exercise in magickal evocation which resulted in daemonic experiences that have affected my life ever since. These experiences were accompanied by short, cryptic texts and sigils which I undertook to decipher and explore. This exploration had profound influence on my magickal praxis and research over the following decade, and more texts and related transmissions were intermittently forthcoming. These materials, communicated by a preternatural source of genuine provenance, as I came to believe, finally resulted in the creation of a personal grimoire, which I have here called *The Book of the Sentient Night*. The 'reception' of this text in February 1997 acted as the culmination of a particular cycle of my work as a Typhonian or Sinister magician and initiated a new phase, which is continuing to this day.

The exercise which took place in March 1985 was inspired by my readings about certain tunnels and guardians of the Qliphoth, as expounded upon by Kenneth Grant in his book, *Nightside of Eden*, (an extended commentary on *Liber 231*, a grimoire of weird provenance published by Aleister Crowley). The Qliphothic guardians I had been focusing on were Zamradiel and latterly Yamatu, where a formula associated with a specific kind of *karezza* (applying to magickal masturbation) can be utilized to exteriorize a sigilised desire in the form of a succubus, or shadow-woman. The arduous task of preventing normal orgasmic climax (whilst directing my concentration on the sigil I had created) and channeling the almost painfully ecstatic sensations to flow downwards, into the chakras in reverse order, finally terminated in the sought-after exhaustion which this type of karezza technique is meant to achieve.

In the resulting period of sleep, I had the tremendously vivid experience, engaging all the senses, of having prolonged coitus with an exceptionally sexually provocative and beautiful, aggressive female with animalistic characteristics – and at the climax of this encounter, I saw the sigil on a wind-blasted horizon, shining as bright as the sun at noon. In the dream-vision, I shielded my eyes until the glyph slowly sank out of sight. The sense of intense heat, sexual and physical, during this 'sunset' was searing; overwhelming. A short time after these events, I received a communication during an automatic-writing experiment that gave a curious design/sigil and the names Zomoz and Zorastar.

These names belong to an entity which presented itself to my astral vision as, most frequently, a raven; sometimes a tenebrous dragon-serpent with horns, and on only one occasion, but most vividly, as a spider-like creature which rested on a glowing, green, web-like grid at the top right-hand side of my field of vision. When the spider sensed I had apprehended it, there was a distinct move backwards and further to the right until it had disappeared from my field of vision. In an instant, the 'rays' of the web were shut off, like a pencil-thin beam of light disappearing when a powerful electric torch is switched off. (At that time, I had not encountered the writings of Michael Bertiaux on the Ghede family of spider Loas, also connected to the word 'Zom', but feel that these entities supplied the energies to facilitate the series of contacts I was undergoing).

By Hebrew gematria, Zomoz = 66, a number of the Qliphoth and The Great Work. Though ill-prepared intellectually to accept it, I felt intuitively that I was being prepared to encounter the daemonic presence known in magical tradition as the Holy Guardian Angel, and that Zomoz was the name He would forthwith use to communicate with me

The power and vividness of the trances continued unabated and the following weeks were fruitful. I was instructed about personal talismans via pictorial imagery which emanated from the raven-form of Zomoz in more dream-visions. A particularly striking communication resulted in the receiving of a Latin 'word': *Deademum.* Consulting a popular Latin Dictionary I broke the 'word' down into constituent parts, which provided for me an *ad hoc* analysis:

Dea = 'goddess' Demum = 'finally' (as in 'Time', after a long wait, etc.) De = 'of'

A message was implied in the communication; I considered that this was to come via the 'goddess of time/of the end of time'.

When this message arrived, I could not have been more surprised by its medium. Another friend, mostly disinterested and disconnected from my occult pursuits, received it in the middle of the night, awakening from a dream about a goddess in the form of a lioness; an event which cannot be played down, as the medium had absolutely no knowledge of the concepts in the communication, or of my recent activities, but felt it should be passed it onto me as a matter of importance. The transmission was written in the form of more 'pidgin' Latin (and Greek?) forming what I took to be a kind of black litany to the succubus/goddess I had encountered in my experiment:

Alre de Vide / en ust vallis / Coa / nilus / de dula / orum / est hedon(m)

Analysis: *Alre* (nourish) *de* (from) *Vide* (see) *vallis* (farewell, in 'strength') *coa (lustful woman – 'woman of ancient times') nilus* (River Nile) *dula* (scraper – sometimes as in 'abortionist') *orum* (via the mouth; speak/imbibe) *hedon* (pleasure, delight – Greek) / Hedom = Edom, the Biblical 'red land'.

Sometime after this, a further trance communication revealed the importance of the phrase OR-UM and its connection with the occult concept of Gold. The true Latin word is AURUM (Gold) but the spelling expressed in the ritual indicates further significance in relation to the sexual energies. In *Outside the Circles of Time*, Kenneth Grant relates

The Sigil of Samael   *Automatism*

the symbol of Gold with the physiological state necessary for the invocation of Ma'at, particularly in this sexual form as Sekhmet:

> "The Aeons of Set-Horus and of Ma'at are symbolised by the lioness Sekhmet who typified in Egypt the heat of sexual passion and the fire of strong drink…" However, considering the specific interpretation of the word we may conclude that the liquid ingested here is that the sexual fluids. In *The Magical Revival* Grant tells us: "Red, Black, Gold, are equivalent terms. The menstruum or vehicle of light (Gold) on the physical plane is blood, the liquid source of manifestation."

Compelled by further events around this period I decided to investigate the Names of Power and discovered the information which led to the current hypothesis. Analysis by gematria revealed a further received magickal formula, ZAMOAY = 65. Added to ZOMOZ (66) this gave 131 – the number of Samael. Gustave Davidson's *Dictionary of Angels* features a description of the angel ZAMOL, defining him as a form of Samael. This immediately struck me because I realised that the design I had drawn in the first automatic writing communication was a representation of this sigil in reverse, in similar fashion to the Qliphothic sigil of Yamatu:

As Guardian of the Abyss, Samael is the infernal archetypal aspect of the Holy Guardian Angel, the emissary of Set, in the sense that he guards the threshold to Chaos and His knowledge opens the Pit of initiation. His true invokation formula is explicated here, and this is the only known process of becoming his living Avatar.

Like Aiwass (of whom he is a form), he is the "Minister of Hoor-Paar-Kraat" (Satan), the messenger of the Hidden One and as such the key to the ultimate power of Chaos: realization of wisdom beyond form, time and space; the acceleration of evolutionary consciousness; the ability to create incarnate desires. Contact with this *Great Old One* eventually led to the reception of the transmission/personal grimoire which follows. Life has been tough, but not uninteresting, since its reception!

The Book of the Sentient Night: 23 Nails

Received 23 .02. 97
(23:00- 0:23 hrs)

0. Zorastar speaks to the Scribe.

1. I am the Eternal Seed Returning

sporing through the Silent Tunnels
that slither in the shadows
of Black Stars.

2. In the signal I am sending:
Seven Rays and Eight Rays
in lavender and blue
descending in hollow Black Flames
shot through with emerald.

3. Beyond the Night of Pan
and All conjectured Paths,
lies the Path of Return.

4. It is the Voice in deep caverns
driven into Sentient Night
like Nails into Flesh

5. The Radiating cry of Nepthys.

6. The Same Mouth lapping at vortices
into which life-blood drains.

7. Her red, ecstatic cries
Piercing through the Void.

8. Twenty-three Nails in the Returning Echoes –

9. Each Nail the Same Voice,
Yet changing pitch and resonance,
establishing a different nuance
from which emerge separate Piercings.

10. The Nails of Nepthys rend Sentient Night
into separate Kingdoms
and City-States of the Pit –
These undead aeons of the Red Land.

0. *Astraroz* Dances before the Scribe:

1. She smiles from a mirror.

2. She stands Behind the Image.

3. Her Secret token is a Feather
plucked from the Vulture –

4. A token to elicit cries of Ecstasy.

5.Her Star is Set astride the Tower,
Her Seven and Her Eight Balancing
the spheres' precarious alignment.

6. Her Six, the focus of the cry.

7. Her Nine, its' Expression
in Words of Power,
the *ululus* of Forgotten Selves.

0. *Azrasot* flows Outside the Higher Balance,
arousing the Vessels of Insatiable Lust:

1.Let this Star-Blood drain
into the Red Land,
the vessels which once contained it
are cracked
like the pierced flesh of ancient mummies,
Fetishes driven with Nails.

2. Titans are now vampires,
Sustenance forever draining away,
Nourishment the hollow dream
of ZADAGUA,
His Desert City arid in the Sentient Night.

3. NEMATI, Bird-Eating Spider,
Black City of Traps.

4.VULOA, Pyramid of the Dragon-Bird,
a Bird singing at the dead of night.

5. GANI-GEBA, cavern of the Abhorrent One,
the Hissing of the Desert Storm Outside.

6. KHRU, the dark pattern of the Star-Wells,
its' emerging vibration along the
carapace of the lattice, this
Sunken Realm without Location.

7. ZOMOZ is the Tower and the Crown,
the son of Arachne
whose Dais is the Hub of a million wheels
of Scarlet-Robed Figures in mindless orbit.

8. D'RUGHU, the Lizard crawler of Endless vortices.

9. ZOTHOMMOGA, the Dwellers in the Deep,
Spawn whose Dreams are Glimpses of the Ultimate.

10. ULULUS, the Forgotten One, the Nameless One,
Devouring the Image of the Beast.

11. These Eleven reflected by One,
exonerated by their Eleven refractions –
Into Light, in the Prism of the Paths.

12. The Sentient Night
is Ever Thus the Echo
of the Three-Fold Voice,
The Render of the Veil of Flesh.

PRELIMINARY COMMENTARY

PART I

0. Zorastar is my Daemon, HGA, call it what you will. He is Zoroaster, or Prometheus, wielder of Star Fire through the dynamism of CHESED (via TIPHARETH) to HOD. His mystic number is therefore 484, demonstrating the CHESED-HOD-CHESED 'Feedback'/circuit.

1. This communication comes via the underworld of Set.

2. Seven/Eight Rayed Star = 15 Rayed Star of the Goddess. The Black Flame is an eidolon of Ma'at.

3. I.E.: Beyond Binah, Chokmah into Kether; or beyond conjecture.

5. Nepthys, Egyptian Goddess, associated with the mouth and 'beth' a house or a palace (see Grant, *Outside the Circles of Time*, p.58; 113).

8. The number 23 signifies the unification of ALL 22 Paths of the Tree of Life, etc' (see Addendum).

10. Sentient Night = Nightside Consciousness. The red Land is Edom, abode of the Titans or Nephilim.

Part 2

0. Astraroz is an anagram representative of the goddess aspect of the Daemon, suggesting also Astaroth or Astarte, the-Star Goddess. Her mystic number is 575; this in relation to 'Balancing' 484.

3. Feather and Vulture are, respectively, 'Positive' and' Negative' images associated with Ma'at.

4. The vulture's cry of ecstasy = mu, the mother tongue.

5. The 'Tower' is the Path connecting HOD and NETZACH; the 'volatile' god, Set, who upturns expectations and destroys beliefs.

6. Six = TIPHARETH.

7. Nine = YESOD; the word 'ULULUS' means the 'howler' or to 'cry out' (ululate) creating the enlightenment of the 'Beast' which results from the Balancing of god and goddess energies at YESOD and TIPHARETH; understanding the Forgotten Ones via the illuminating consciousness of the Daemon. (Its negative formula is CACONOVAZ).

Part 3

0. Azrasot is an anagram of the first two names and represents their dissolution in to the Abyss. The name suggests Azathoth, a 'contradictory' concept of sentient, yet idiot, infinity or ultimate chaos from which manifests another Order of 'Being' altogether: the Nightside.

1. The 'vessels' are the 'unbalanced forces' of the Outside; which, in lore and legend, forever hunger to end their banishment from our universe.

2. ZADAGUA, Gematria = 23; the Path Beyond. Suggestive of Tsathogua, the Vampire Bat, and an infernal aspect of Saturn.

3. NEMATI = Nepthys as the spider goddess. Her number is 111; Set; the 'thick darkness'; web of the abyss.

4. VULOA = 45; Blood. The Vampire/Vulture Loa, or Soul-snatcher (Bird singing in the dead of night).

5. GEMI-GEBA = 70; the Eye of the Ghoul; 71; the number of LAM. Suggestive of Ganin-Gub (see Grant's *Nightside of Eden*).

6. KHRU = 231; the Number of the Book of Amenta, central to understanding The Sentient Night. Suggestive Of Cthulhu, the Locus/focus of Nightside Consciousness.

7. ZOMOZ = 66; the Number of the Qliphoth; this verse seems to describe the 'children of Da'ath', the Black Brothers.

8. DRUGHU = 213, part-metathesis of 231.

9. ZOTHOMMOGA = 124; a Number of the Aeon of Ma'at. The Spawn of the 'dreaming' Cthulhu.

10. ULULUS = 96; (Yesod & Tiphareth) a 'word' more than a 'name' as such - see note 7, part 2. Another associated name is CACONOVAZ (93) Thelema, or Will as the Beast – a Devourer of Self-within (Ego).

11. The Eleven reflections: the 'known' sephirah.

12. Describing the formulae of cosmic consciousness, emphasising the dissolution phase beyond the Abyss.

ADDENDUM: GENERAL NOTES.

The 23 Nails symbolism resolves in to concepts of Qabalistic tradition, regarding the 10 sephirah and Da'ath (= 11); their reflections, the 10 inverse sephirah (cities of Edom) and Da'ath (= 22); and the 1 True Path where All is resolved in 0 (= 23).

The Nails seem to pierce holes of Ingress/Egress in the system, refracting into Paths of Light and Shadow (see Grant's treatment of *Liber 231* (23 = 1) in *Nightside of Eden,* et al). Phenomena/Noumena 'bleed' from the 'wounds'. Their medium is Maat (Truth) as Nepthys, Her Double Tongue (um-mu) the Eater and Excreter of worlds. Her Word or Cry echoes through the Nightside Tunnels as glossolalia or howlings, echoing and re-echoing in a babble. Thus the *one* voice is lost in distortion until the echoes cease. Silence, and the illusion of consciousness is at the end. Part 1 = 11 verses; Part 2 = 8 verses; Part 3 = 13 verses = 32 verses / 23 in reverse.

We Ate the Acid:
A Note on Psychedelic Imagery

Henrik Dahl

"Symbols – symbols everywhere. All along my journey they flashed forth the apocalypse of utterly unimagined truths."
— Fitz Hugh Ludlow

Psychedelic art typically contains a number of recurring motifs. Examples include circles, spirals, eyes, concentric shapes, grids, landscapes, nudity, long hair, skeletons and mushrooms. Other common motifs are various kinds of non-human animals, vegetation, space scenery and mandalas. And when humans and objects are featured, they are occasionally seen in x-ray. Furthermore, psychedelic art is usually – but not always – characterised by intense, contrasting colours. There may also be a liquid quality to objects, where it looks as if they are melting. Obviously, these motifs and features are also included in many other artistic genres. Hence, in order to be defined as psychedelic, the motifs have to be combined and presented in a way that resonates with the psychedelic experience.

Why does psychedelic art nearly always contain this kind of imagery? Surely, there are numerous other motifs and features an artist could think of using. The images that one is exposed to while under the influence of psychedelics often display a huge variety, yet in the vast majority of cases the same motifs are used ad infinitum. For example, why is the eye such an omnipresent element in psychedelic art? Huge numbers of artworks, posters, book covers, album covers and leaflets feature the eye. To an outsider this could almost be seen as a pathological obsession. Although this piece is only a brief introduction to psychedelic imagery, it will hopefully spark some further interest in this fairly unexplored subject.

The psychedelic experience often produces deeply symbolic imagery, and naturally psychedelic art is usually packed with symbols. In the words of psychotherapist Maria Papaspyrou, "Entheogenic journeys are highly creative spaces. They 'speak' to us through symbols, images, and feeling states that are carried forward by visions" (Papaspyrou, 2014: 35). Before discussing the symbolic meaning of psychedelic imagery, a few words should be said about what defines a symbol. According to Carl G. Jung, the symbol indicates something vague or unknown. Writing in *Man and his Symbols*, the Swiss psychiatrist said that, "A word or an image is symbolic when it implies something more than its obvious and immediate meaning. It has a wider 'unconscious' aspect that is never precisely defined or fully explained. Nor can one hope to define or explain it." (Jung, 1968: 3-4). Jung was mostly interested in the symbols of dreams, which of course are produced during sleep. Imagery that is encountered while under the influence of psychedelics, on the other hand, is seen when fully awake, albeit mostly with eyes closed. This piece will take a look at symbols that appear in psychedelic art. But first a few words should be said about some of the many significant developments that have influenced or shaped psychedelic culture and, as a consequence, psychedelic imagery.

In order to acquire a better understanding of psychedelic imagery, one needs to look at psychedelic culture as a whole. Its history consists of a somewhat complex mix of cultural references, which are often filled with symbols and signs, many of which initially had little or nothing to do with psychedelics. Therefore, being a researcher of psychedelia simultaneously entails making research in several different fields such as anthropology, religion, history, the arts, the esoteric, psychology and medicine. Only by using this eclectic, interdisciplinary approach is it possible to reach an understanding of why a certain motif is used in psychedelic art.

It would be easy to think that psychedelic imagery as we know it from the 1960s and onwards appeared out of nowhere, as if the motifs and features were contained in the LSD molecule itself. Of course this was not the case. The origins of psychedelic art, as well as psychedelic culture as a whole, can be traced back to a number of culturally significant events, some of which took place many decades, even centuries, prior to the LSD counterculture of the 1960s.

When considering proto-psychedelic art and literature, it is not always known if psychedelics were an influence during the creation of a specific artwork or book. Obviously, there are many ways of reaching altered states of consciousness (ASC). Besides mind-altering substances, ASC can be reached through techniques such as meditation, breathing exercises or fasting, to name a few, and artworks inspired by non-psychedelic altered states can certainly come across as having been the result of someone taking psychedelics. When discussing artworks that have a psychedelic "feel" but probably did not involve any mind-altering substances, writers and researchers sometimes refer to these works as having a "psychedelic sensibility." The English poet and artist William Blake (1757-1827) is a perfect example of someone who made such works. Although there is no record of Blake using psychedelics, many people regard him as an important figure in the history of psychedelia. This is mostly thanks to Aldous Huxley, whose seminal 1954 trip report *The Doors of Perception* takes its title from a phrase in Blake's *The Marriage of Heaven and Hell*.

Psychedelic sensibility is also present in the Lebensreform movement of the late 19th and early 20th century. The lifestyle of these proto-hippies were linked to nudity, sexual liberation, organic farming, vegetarianism and long hair, which of course were also features of the LSD counterculture of the 1960s. Furthermore, psychedelic sensibility is found in the Art Nouveau movement (Masters & Houston, 1968: 110), which roughly coincided with the Lebensreform movement. Artists working in the Art Nouveau style used curved forms found in nature, typically forms resembling stems and blossoms. Several psychedelic artists in the 1960s counterculture were heavily inspired by Art

Nouveau. This was particularly evident when it comes to the poster art of the hippie era. Czech painter Alphonse Mucha was a huge influence. So much so that his posters reappeared in the counterculture where they were reworked and given a thorough psychedelic treatment. For example, Mucha's classic colour lithograph *Job* – a poster advertising a brand of cigarette papers – was used by Alton Kelley and Stanley Mouse in a 1966 poster promoting a concert at the Avalon Ballroom. Even though the latter features a colour scheme that is undoubtedly psychedelic, one could argue that Mucha's 1896 original is equally appealing to the art-loving psychonaut. In fact, Mucha's *Job* has several features that make it very similar to psychedelic art. The poster shows a woman with incredibly long flowing hair. She has an expression of contentment in her face and could easily be interpreted as being stoned. Of course cannabis smokers like to think that the cigarette in her hand is in fact a marijuana joint. Furthermore, framing the picture is a somewhat trippy zigzag pattern. No wonder the young San Francisco poster artists were magnetically drawn to Mucha.

Psychedelic imagery is arguably the result of many different cultural events and influences. Some of these – such as the works of poet and artist William Blake, Art Nouveau and the Lebensreform movement – have already been mentioned. Other examples include the children's book *Alice's Adventures in Wonderland* by Lewis Carroll, and early accounts of psychedelic experiences by the likes of Fitz Hugh Ludlow, Weir S. Mitchell and Antonin Artaud. Admittedly, the Surrealists and the Beats are also part of the story, and so are characters such as Jung and Aleister Crowley. In the 1950s, interest in altered states induced by psychedelics increased. An early pioneer when it comes to visual art was French artist and writer Henri Michaux, who made drawings while under the influence of mescaline and cannabis. Michaux's experimentation resulted in his book *Miserable Miracle*, which was originally published in French in 1956. Also deserving a mention is Austrian painter Ernst Fuchs, who found artistic inspiration from his peyote experiences in the 1950s. But the perhaps most influential events in western psychedelia of the 1950s were the release of Huxley's aforementioned book *The Doors of Perception* (1954), and the publication of R. Gordon Wasson's *Life Magazine* article "Seeking the Magic Mushroom" (1957).

The 1960s counterculture was shaped by many different characters and groups, including the Merry Pranksters, the Grateful Dead and the San Francisco poster artists, to name a few. Furthermore, it should be mentioned that the counterculture's interest in Eastern philosophy had an effect on psychedelic imagery. In particular, the Yin Yang symbol has been used in many artworks of the era. The late sixties also saw the publication of Carlos Castaneda's *The Teachings of Don Juan*, and it is safe to say that his book – regardless of what one may think of the accuracy of its content – helped create an interest in indigenous shamanism. This is still very much seen in today's visionary art movement. Another noteworthy event in the late sixties was the release of Crowley and Frieda Harris' *Thoth* tarot deck. Finished already in the early 1940s, the deck contains a huge number of symbols and many of its cards are very similar to psychedelic and visionary art. Moreover, the early seventies saw the release of *Be Here Now* by Ram Dass. In equal parts fascinating and peculiar, this hugely popular book is filled to the brim with psychedelic drawings.

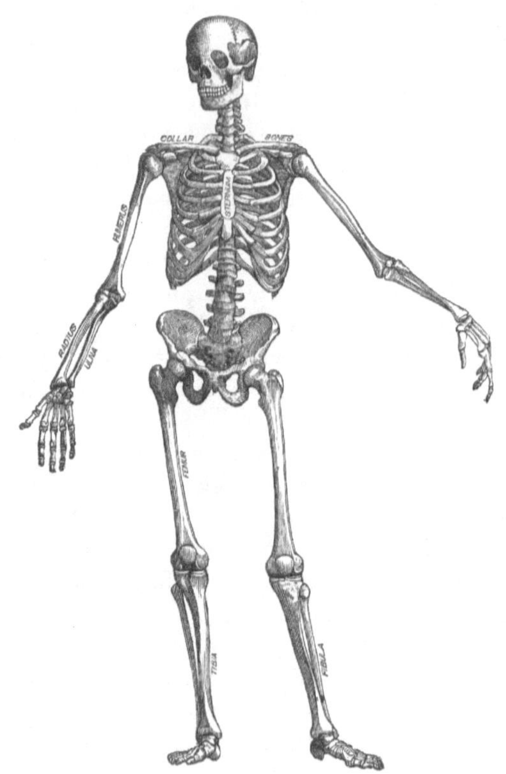

An early example of psychedelic art is seen in the work of artist Sherana Harriette Frances. In 1963, Frances took part in LSD therapy at the International Foundation for Advanced Study in Menlo Park, California. During her trip she experienced the dissolution of her ego, which she depicted in 18 ink drawings shortly afterwards. Her works – which are full of archetypes – are excellent depictions of the ego-loss (or "ego-death") that some people experience while on psychedelics. Praised by psychiatrist Stanislav Grof and others, Frances' drawings were included in her book *Drawing It Out: Befriending the Unconscious* (2001). Several of the motifs that were mentioned in the beginning of this piece are found in Frances' drawings. For example, in one of them, she is caught in a spiral together with five skeletons. In the drawing she is seen in the nude with her long flowing hair. As previously mentioned, spirals, skeletons, nudity and long hair are all common motifs in psychedelic imagery. Interestingly, it should be noted that Frances created her drawings several years before the appearance of the hippie movement with its psychedelic artworks, posters, album covers, light shows and films. In other words, her artworks were not influenced by the LSD counterculture of the mid to late 1960s.

The Skeleton symbolises death and mortality. Besides in Frances' drawings, the motif is seen in many psychedelic artworks including the widely reproduced "Skull and Roses" poster by Alton Kelley and Stanley Mouse, which was made as an advertisement

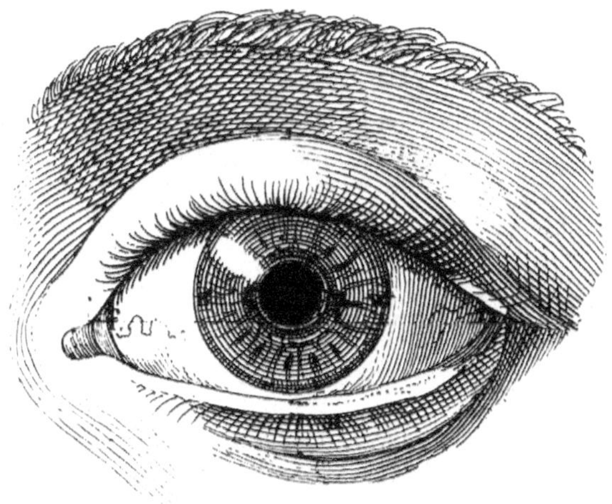

for a Grateful Dead show at the Avalon Ballroom in 1966. In addition to Kelley and Mouse's poster, skeletons and skulls are also seen in the works of Alex Grey. The latter is known for depicting humans in the x-ray style. X-ray depictions, which typically show inner organs and skeleton structures, are also seen in shamanic art all around the world (Halifax, 1982: 76). Writing in her book *Shaman: The Wounded Healer*, anthropologist Joan Halifax noted that, "The skeletonized shaman figure is the personification of death. At the same time, like the seed of the fruit after the flesh has rotted away, his or her bones represent the potential for rebirth" (Halifax, 1982: 76). In addition to the examples above, it is worth mentioning the death card in Crowley and Harris' *Thoth* tarot deck, which, naturally, features a skeleton.

Let us now consider one of the most common motifs in psychedelic imagery, namely the eye. The eye has great symbolic value. It can for instance symbolise omniscience, knowledge, the mind, and the all-seeing divinity. The single eye – which is how the eye is often depicted in psychedelic art – can symbolise enlightenment, eternity and the eye of God. Furthermore, in Buddhism we find the third eye of Buddha, which represents spiritual consciousness (Cooper 2013, 62). The eye has been present from the start in western psychedelic imagery. For example, John Woodcock's front cover design of the first edition of Huxley's *The Doors of Perception* features an illustration of three eyes, and since its release numerous book covers have included the motif in some way or another, a contemporary example being *Hallucinations* (2012) by Oliver Sacks, which features a single eye. A large single eye was also part of the cover design of The 13th Floor Elevators' seminal 1966 debut album *The Psychedelic Sounds of the 13th Floor Elevators*. As for painters working today, visionary artist Alex Grey often returns to the motif in his paintings. According to Grey, "The Eyes are wings of the Soul – they see us to Heaven" (Dahl: 2014, 96). Incidentally, it is worth noting that although most psychedelic visions take place behind closed eyelids, the eye in psychedelic art is almost always wide open.

Besides having great symbolic value, most people find the eye aesthetically appealing and the eye lends itself very well to artistic depictions, not least in a psychedelic context. The eye is no doubt one of Mother Nature's most fascinating creations, and staring into a pupil and the surrounding iris – incidentally a psychedelic artwork in itself – can be a captivating experience. Furthermore, it should be noted that the shape of the eye consists of an oval surrounding a circle. The latter, as will be discussed in a moment, is a motif that is recurring over and over in psychedelic art.

The circle is a universal symbol with many different meanings such as wholeness, the infinite and the Self. Seeing that it has no beginning or end, it can also symbolise timelessness (Cooper, 2013: 36). Psychedelic art typically contains concentric circles (i.e. circles that share the same centre point), and given their visually stimulating character they are highly suitable as motifs in psychedelic art. In nature, concentric circles are formed when a small stone or such is dropped into still water. It is fascinating to think that humans at the dawn of humanity saw the same concentric circles in water as we do today. One who often returns to the motif is American artist Fred Tomaselli. For example, concentric circles are seen in his artworks *Ripples-Trees* (1994) and *Abductor* (2006), which have been used on the cover of David S. Rubin's *Psychedelic* and Erik Davis' *Nomad Codes*, respectively. Incidentally, concentric circles are also found in several kinds of shamanic art, including peyote inspired yarn paintings by the Huichols in Mexico.

One who took interest in psychedelic imagery at an early stage was Heinrich Klüver. In 1926, while studying the effects of mescaline, Klüver noticed that it produced recurring geometrical patterns. Klüver gave them the name *form constants*. In addition to psychedelics, form constants may for example also be triggered by epilepsy, sensory deprivation, migraine headaches and fever. Klüver categorised four types of patterns: lattices, cobwebs, tunnels and spirals. Another term for such geometrical patterns is entoptic images. These animated "films" are obviously a source of inspiration to the psychedelic artist. For those not accustomed to the psychedelic experience, it is important to mention that entoptic images induced by psychedelics are very different from self-controlled fantasies or daydreams. Rather than being cooked-up, the imagery is presented to the psychonaut with little or no control over its content.

Continuing this brief exposition of psychedelic imagery, let us now turn to one of Klüver's form constants – the spiral. In her book *An Illustrated Encyclopaedia of Traditional Symbols*, J.C. Cooper says the spiral is "a highly complex symbol" that has been used since paleolithic times and appears in many different cultures. Among many things, the spiral is a symbol of the great creative force and the manifestation of energy. It also symbolises the realms of existence and the wanderings of the soul and its final return to the Centre (Cooper, 2013: 156). The spiral has a shape that makes most art and design look instantly psychedelic, and if one makes an internet search for spiral images one is bombarded with trippy results. Spirals are common on front covers in psychedelic literature. Presumably, the shape lends itself particularly well to the rather compact book format.

Long hair is seen in numerous psychedelic artworks, especially those made by the LSD counterculture. This is hardly a coincidence. Hair flowing loose – like the woman's hair in the previously discussed *Job* poster – symbolises freedom. Hair is also a symbol

of the life-force and the higher powers (Cooper 2013: 77). With this in mind, the popularity of long hair during the hippie era as well as among forerunners such as the adherents of the Lebensreform movement makes perfect sense. Moreover, hair is a distinct feature in an art project where an anonymous artist took LSD and drew eleven self-portraits over nine hours. During the trip the hair in her drawings changed character, e.g. spirals were added to her depictions, and, interestingly enough, her hair grew longer and became flowing and expansive (independent.co.uk).

The psychedelic experience is strongly linked to imagery that is intensely colourful, and psychedelic art often places great emphasis on recreating how colours are perceived behind closed eyelids while in altered states. Fascination with colours was seen already in the late 19th Century when westerners started to experiment with peyote. For example, in his classic 1896 trip report "Remarks on the Effects of the Mescal Button: An Experience with Peyote Extract," published in *The British Medical Journal*, Dr S. Weir Mitchell talks of "floating films of colour" and "gorgeous colour-fruits." Mitchell even stated that, "All the colours I have ever beheld are dull as compared to these" (erowid.com).

In a chapter titled "Of LSD, Eidetic Imagery and Eyeless Sight," published in his book *The Symbolism of Color*, the one time leading colour expert Faber Birren discusses how psychedelics can completely alter the way we see colours. Even though Birren comes across as somewhat ignorant when it comes to the counterculture (which he calls a "drug cult"), he was clearly very fascinated by the consciousness expanding effects of acid: "The amazing discovery was made that a fantastic world of color existed within the human psyche. It lay buried as if in a golden cask, and a drop of LSD opened it up and let its magic burst forth. Here the process of vision was reversed – it came from the inside out, not from the outside in" (Birren, 1988: 161-162). It is safe to say that colour is a hugely important aspect of psychedelic art, not least spiritually. In 1912, long before psychedelic art was a recognised artistic genre, Russian painter Wassily Kandinsky said that, "Colour is a power which directly influences the soul" (Kandinsky, 1977: 25). Presumably, many psychedelic artists would agree with the painter.

Psychedelic journeys are potentially therapeutic, even life-changing experiences, but the effects of psychedelics are sometimes too emotionally overwhelming. This situation may lead to a difficult experience (a so-called "bad trip"). In such cases psychedelic imagery may be perceived as highly unpleasant with many grotesque visions. However, it should be said that positive psychedelic experiences often include at least some dark elements too. Clearly, the presence of the latter does not make the journey any less valuable. On the contrary, getting through dark passages of a trip may prove to be highly transformative and healing. In fact, the psychedelic experience – just like life itself – contains both darkness and light. This duality is an aspect that has been known and acknowledged all along by writers and researchers in psychedelia. For example, when psychiatrist Humphry Osmond coined the term *psychedelic* in a correspondence with Aldous Huxley in 1956, Osmond described the psychedelic experience as a state where one may "fathom Hell or soar angelic". Interestingly, as will be touched upon in a moment, many artists working in the field of visionary art tend to focus mostly on positive psychedelic experiences.

Psychedelic art was established as an artistic genre in the mid to late 1960s (about a decade after the word "psychedelic" was coined). The first book on the style, simply titled *Psychedelic Art*, was published in 1968. Edited by Robert E.L. Masters and Jean Houston, the book provided important documentation of some of the psychedelic art of the counterculture era, and for decades it was the only major work discussing the genre.

When it comes to art that relates to the psychedelic experience, many people have started using the term *visionary art*. Although visionary art can seem more or less synonymous with psychedelic art, it should be mentioned that there are subtle yet important differences between the two. Visionary art typically places a strong focus on spirituality, and when it comes to artists working in the style today many take inspiration from ayahuasca shamanism. Furthermore, many visionary artists are very skilled painters, which may explain why there is a great emphasis on technical ability within the genre. Psychedelic art on the other hand tends to deal with a wider range of themes and usually comes across as less religious, and may include humorous, absurd or erotic elements. Historically, psychedelic art has involved several different techniques, which are not typically used by visionary artists. In addition to painting and drawing, techniques include collage, video, sculpture and light shows. Considering the differences between these two styles, it is unfortunate that psychedelic art and visionary art are sometimes believed to be one and the same.

A somewhat stern critic of visionary art is Finn McKenna, the son of legendary writer and "bard" Terence McKenna and ethnobotanist Kathleen Harrison. In a 2014 interview with Tao Lin of Vice Magazine, Finn McKenna describes the style as being "embarrassingly self-serious." In addition, he thinks visionary art has an over-emphasis on positivity, and as a consequence the style disregards the duality of darkness and light that is inevitably part of the psychedelic experience. "The scene is severely lacking in the irony, biting humor, and cosmic ridiculousness that Terence articulated," he says (vice.com).

One of the better-known psychedelic artists working today is the aforementioned Fred Tomaselli. Although some of his artworks may at first seem similar to visionary art, Tomaselli has an approach to psychedelic imagery that is very different from what is found among most visionary artists. According to art critic Ken Johnson, Tomaselli is a kind of pop artist that is toying with clichés of the psychedelic style (dosenation.com). Clearly, very few visionary artists would be described in a similar way. (This is not to say that artists working in the field of visionary art haven't produced excellent artworks.)

It may seem overly simplistic to lump together a dozen or so motifs and make the claim that they are the building blocks of psychedelic art. Needless to say, I am well aware that art can be much more complex and mysterious than what one may initially think. That said, the fact remains that numerous psychedelic pictures – whether they are contemporary art, graphic art or lowbrow art – contain the motifs and features that were mentioned at the beginning of this piece. Take for instance legendary poster artist Rick Griffin's front cover illustration of the 1969 album *Aoxomoxoa* by the Grateful Dead. Originally a concert poster, the artwork is one of the most memorable examples of psychedelic art from the counterculture era. Seen in the image is a warped landscape where its vegetation – which consists of motifs such as mushrooms and trees – is shown in x-ray. (Incidentally, the latter is a feature that was also seen on the cover of The Incredible String Bands' *The 5000 Spirits or the Layers of the Onion*, designed by Dutch design collective The Fool.) The lower part of Griffin's image features a skull, and right above it is a glowing sun that is being penetrated by what appears to be sperm. The shape of the sun and its variations in colours are made up of concentric circles. One of the strong points of the image is Griffin's exquisite lettering, which features a so-called ambigram. As is well known among Deadheads, hidden in the words "Grateful Dead" is also the phrase: "We ate the acid."

Interestingly, most of the motifs seen in psychedelic art of the 2010s are the very same as those used by earlier generations of psychedelic artists. This is evident in *Juxtapoz Psychedelic*, a book that presents several artists that can be categorised as being psychedelic. For example, Pearl Hsiung often includes concentric circles in her artworks; Oliver Hibert's paintings feature nudity and mushrooms; and the works of David D'Andrea include motifs such as the eye, non-human animals and skeletons. Incidentally, the latter admits to having a "love for eternal symbols" (Juxtapoz Psychedelic, 2013: 204). Of course one could say that psychedelic art of today is influenced by the counterculture of the 1960s. Undoubtedly, the motifs and features discussed in this piece became firmly embedded in people's minds during the hippie era, and have stayed that way ever since.

Psychedelic art – how fascinating as it may be – can only ever be a poor imitation of the psychedelic experience. This is not to say that such art is of inferior value. On the contrary, psychedelic pictures may play a hugely important role in a person's life. If anything, these artworks can be reminders of earlier life-changing visionary journeys, and being in the presence of psychedelic imagery on a daily basis can certainly be of help when it comes to integrating such experiences.

REFERENCES

—⚞— Birren, Faber, *The Symbolism of Color* (Secaucus, NJ: Citadel Press, 1988)

—⚞— Cooper, J.C., *An Illustrated Encyclopaedia of Traditional Symbols* (London: Thames & Hudson, 2013)

—⚞— Dahl, Henrik, "Visionary Design Through the Power of Symbolism: An Exposition of Book Covers in Psychedelic Literature", in *The Fenris Wolf 7* (Stockholm: Edda Publishing, 2014)

—⚞— DoseNation, "DoseNation 25: Ken Johnson, Psychedelic Art," 2013, http://www.dosenation.com/listing.php?id=8770

—⚞— Halifax, Joan, *Shaman: The Wounded Healer* (New York: Crossroad, 1982)

—⚞— Hooton, Christopher, "Artist takes LSD, draws herself over different stages of the 9-hour trip to show its effects," The Independent, 2015, http://www.independent.co.uk/arts-entertainment/art/news/girl-takes-lsd-draws-herself-over-different-stages-of-the-9hour-trip-to-show-its-effects-10474372.html

—⚞— Jung, Carl G. (Ed.), *Man and his Symbols* (St. Louis: Turtleback Books, 1968)

—⚞— Kandinsky, Wassily, *Concerning the Spiritual in Art* (New York: Dover Publications, 1977)

—⚞— Lin, Tao, "Psychedelic Drugs, Art, Music, and Other Drugs: An Interview with Finn McKenna," *Vice*, 2014, https://www.vice.com/en_uk/read/psychedelic-drugs-art-music-and-other-drugs-an-interview-with-finn-mckenna-815

—⚞— Ludlow, Fitz Hugh, *The Hasheesh Eater: Being Passages from the Life of a Pythagorean* (New Brunswick, NJ: Rutgers University Press, 2006)

—⚞— Masters, Robert E.L. & Houston, Jean (Eds.), *Psychedelic Art* (London: Weidenfeld and Nicolson, 1968)

—⚞— Mitchell, S. Weir, "Remarks on the Effects of the Mescal Button: An Experience with Peyote Extract", *Erowid*, 2005, https://www.erowid.org/experiences/exp.php?ID=42614

—⚞— Papaspyrou, Maria, "Femtheogens: The Synergy of Sacred Spheres", in *Psychedelic Press* UK 2014 Volume 5 (Falmouth, Cornwall: Psychedelic Press, 2014)

—⚞— Stouffer, Hannah (Ed.), *Juxtapoz Psychedelic* (Berkeley, CA: Gingko Press, 2013)

Robert Anton Wilson's Cosmic Trigger
and the Psychedelic Interstellar Future
WE NEED

Jason Louv

In 1977, Robert Anton Wilson's *Cosmic Trigger* predicted a utopian, space-faring, enlightened future. 37 years later, it's finally starting to show up.

In my second year of college, I bought a copy of Robert Anton Wilson's *Cosmic Trigger* at a New Age bookstore in downtown Santa Cruz.

It had a naked space goddess on the cover, and threatened to reveal the "Final Secret of the Illuminati." I read it in one sitting, and when I closed the book, I'd not only learned said group's final secret, I felt like I was one of the *inner circle*.

I immediately loaned it out, and watched it circulate among about a dozen people before vanishing into the Santa Cruz synchronicity vortex. Everyone I talked to had about the same experience.

Cosmic Trigger—a record of one man's journey into inner space—has been doing that, consistently, since its first publication in 1977. It's the Little Red Book for futurist mutants.

A Cosmic Trigger Warning on the Door to Chapel Perilous

Here's how it started: In 1962, 30-year-old Robert Anton Wilson was working as an assistant sales manager in Yellow Springs, Ohio, with a wife and four young children, when he decided to eat some peyote. As a hard-headed rationalist, Wilson was in for a rough ride: The cactus shredded his narrowband understanding of existence and his place in the universe.

Wilson walked straight through the now-opened doors of perception and into a decade and a half of exhaustive experimentation with willed brain change—encapsulating research into LSD, Aleister Crowley's Magick, Count Alfred Korzybski's General Semantics, Dr. John Lilly's sensory deprivation tank, conspiracy theories, Sufism, Buckminster Fuller, UFOs, Gurdjieff, Zen Buddhism and a lot more.

A collaborative partnership with Timothy Leary and a five-year stint as an associate editor at *Playboy* provided more fuel for Wilson's voyage, which culminated in the publication of *Cosmic Trigger*. The book is his first-person record of fucking with the settings of his own mind—all while maintaining a healthy degree of skepticism and empiricist rigor, as an antidote to the muddled thinking that blights the territory he was scouting.

Wilson's experiments convinced him that humanity's limitations are largely self-imposed, that "reality is always plural and mutable," and that if we were to just take off our conditioned blinkers of superstition and ideology, we could unlock our dormant Promethean intelligence, overcome our tribal conflicts and get our species off the planet. *Cosmic Trigger* ends far from Wilson's early rural peyote trips, with a vision of mankind colonizing the stars.

A recent flu afforded me the chance to re-read *Cosmic Trigger*, thirteen years after I first found it as a student. Those thirteen years had been occupied with my own stress-test of reality, including many of the avenues Wilson had explored, much of which I recorded in the books I published in my 20s. It was also a time in which I'd watched the utopian future promised by Wilson, Leary, Douglas Rushkoff, Ken Wilber and others utterly crash and burn. 9/11 *seemed* to kill the *Star Trek*-style future all the smart nerds had been working on, instead spawning a new dark age of religious fundamentalism and illiterate barbarism typified by Bush Jr. and the newly reactionary, compassionless, cocaine-fuelled hipster "counterculture" that sprouted up under his rule—followed by the Great Sleep of the socially progressive but rights-and-privacy-decimating, Facebook-hypnotized Obama years.

It was with the lingering weight of this decade-plus of disappointment that I expected to return to *Cosmic Trigger* and find that it had all been bongthink—but what I discovered instead was that most of Wilson and Leary's utopian predictions actually seem *well on their way to coming true*, if a bit later than the two men expected.

RAW was right.

SMI²LE

SMI²LE—a phrase coined by Tim Leary in the 1970s—stands for *Space Migration, Intelligence Increase, Life Extension*, and was his recipe for a working future.

RAW focused much of *Cosmic Trigger* on the SMI²LE formula, predicting that by the end of the 20th century humanity would be living in off-world O'Neill colonies, with greatly enhanced cognitive ability and lifespans extended by centuries or even indefinitely.

None of these predictions came true within Leary or Wilson's lifetimes—both men died, without any immortality pill in sight, in a post-Challenger era in which the US space program had wilted, and humanity was acting stupider than ever.

But 2014 is a different story. Although the same old "let's party like it's 1999" Crusader script keeps getting remade over and over, with better special effects each time, we're also starting to actually see some of the SMI²LE future show up.

SM—SPACE MIGRATION

Both Leary and Wilson strongly believed that humanity's destiny was post-terrestrial, and came to consider psychedelics and consciousness alteration as a kind of prepping for weightlessness—ways to prepare for outer space by exploring inner space.

RAW, in particular, saw a kind of *logos* of humanity's interstellar aspirations embodied in Jack Parsons, the legendary co-founder of Jet Propulsion Labs in Pasadena, who spent his days launching rockets and his nights excelling as a student of Aleister Crowley's occult system, hosting drug-fuelled orgies, conducting magical rituals, writing anarchist polemics and encouraging young science fiction writers like Ray Bradbury (and, unfortunately, L. Ron Hubbard, who later took Parsons for everything he had). Parsons blew himself up in 1952, at the age of 37, in a lab accident; his primary contributions to the world were the creation of JPL and the invention of solid-state rocket fuel, which was instrumental in getting the US to the moon.

For Parsons, like Leary and Wilson, there was no difference between pushing inner space boundaries and outer space frontiers—they were simply the Next Steps, ones that Parsons felt religious and political authority stood directly in the way of, an Inquisition just like the one that murdered fellow-traveler Giordiano Bruno in 1600 for suggesting that the stars were distant suns. Bruno, we must remember, was just as steeped in the occult as young Parsons—as were other scientific giants like Copernicus, Galileo, Kepler, Newton and many, many more.

In this light, Parsons looks less like a mutant and more like a stalwart upholder of the Western intellectual project. Parsons' seemingly disparate interests in space travel, Magick, drugs, sexual adventurism and science fiction, I will suggest, are really the same impulse—a *pushing at the edges of reality*. Parsons, like so many brilliant scientists and shamans before him, simply saw the edge of human endeavor and decided to *shove* it. This is the same spectrum of adventure that Leary and RAW consciously inherited, expressing the forward momentum of evolution as SMI^{2}LE.

What Jack Parsons began, Elon Musk may well end; he's now promising to put humans on Mars in a decade. The dream is not dead—it has, if anything, simply outgrown the American government. Space is for all—and while European Union, Chinese or Virgin Galactic bases on Mars may not fit with 1960s American patriotic fervor, what matters is that mankind gets off the rock.

As Earth closes in on its estimated carrying capacity of 10 billion humans (and that's only if we *all* live at developing world standards), space migration is the only palatable solution to the population and environmental crises. If we want to survive as a species, all forward momentum must go into space.

I^2—Intelligence Increase

Leary and Wilson spent much of their lives attempting to increase their intelligence, largely by torching their fixed models with entheogens. When used correctly, psychedelics can undoubtedly spark quantum leaps in cognition, wisdom and insight—and thanks to pioneering research from groups like MAPS, entheogenic substances are gaining broader acceptance for clinical trials, especially for use in treating PTSD and addiction. Recent data has even shown that psilocybin mushrooms may encourage the birth of new neurons. Leary, who was pursuing similar research at Millbrook before he was shut down, would have been proud.

While a perfect intelligence enhancer hasn't yet been found, the Internet is awash with close candidates—particularly the racetam family of nootropics and the eurogic drug Modafinil, which allows for long periods of wakefulness without the eroding effects of amphetamines. (The side effects, however, are unknown.)

And then there's the Luciferian ability of the Internet itself—which Leary tirelessly proselytized for in his last days—to create memetic hive minds that can exercise levels of intelligence beyond the capacity of the network's individual nodes, for good or ill. Wikipedia, Twitter and Reddit are all prime examples—as is 4Chan. The Web's acceleration of collective intelligence is hard to overestimate. Of course, a new Internet waits in the wings, and virtual reality, augmented reality and the Internet of Things will soon make the Web look parochial. Following on from there, the beginnings of *matter reassembly*, first via 3D printing and later by nanotechnology, may well make literal the alchemists' dream of erasing the gap between matter and spirit, by making the material world immediately and infinitely malleable by the whims of the human imagination.

I remain convinced that the metaphors of the occult, of the psychedelic experience and of inherited wisdom like the *Tibetan Book of the Dead* will be our only real guides for dealing with such a world.

LE—Life Extension

The Immortalist project keeps chugging along, having blossomed into transhumanism—a world now awash with venture capital and military contracts, which increasingly looks like either weapons R&D or a health care plan 99.9% of the population won't be able to afford.

On the life extension front specifically, we now have a vast array of promising leads into slowing the aging process, including caloric restriction, supplementation, hormone therapy, insulin growth factor restriction, stem cell therapy, therapeutic cloning, gene therapy and life extension drugs like Rapamycin and Metformin. Ray Kurzweil has stated that nanotechnology may make aging reversal possible by 2030 (around the same time as some experts' predictions of Mars settlement). It remains to be seen how quickly these technologies will progress, and how available they will be to the general population.

Starseed

Reality, ironically, can be crushing for people like Robert Anton Wilson. You keep peeling back your sense of the possible, dutifully scrubbing off the limitations of your model of the world, through psychedelics, spiritual practice, therapy, bodywork. Pretty soon you realize that nobody really has anything figured out, and that the whole damn thing is up for grabs—that, as RAW said, *reality is what you can get away with.*

You see that people are staring at the flickering shadows on the wall of Plato's cave. Religion, politics, media, social expectations, even language itself—it's all conditioning. And you see that all you have to do is turn around, away from the shadowplay you've been trained to see as reality, and you get to see the *infinity of the universe*, the night sky of billions upon billions of stars, distant galaxies, superclusters beckoning you to the galactic game of which the admission price is *admitting you know nothing.*

Jack Parsons expressed it so perfectly in his letters to Marjorie Cameron, his spiritual consort:

> "You bawl and weep to give up the ego, the greasy penny that you have been greedily clutching in your dirty little paw, and, behold, when you do it, it buys you a ticket to the greatest show on earth, with ice cream and cake free for ever."

But how heartbreaking it is to see all of that, as RAW did, and then turn back to witness humanity asleep in front of their televisions, murdering each other over ancient and incoherent books, tearing each other limb from limb over gender or race or class or what so-and-so said on Twitter instead of uniting as a whole. How heartbreaking it is to return to the zoo after seeing the stars.

Reading *Cosmic Trigger* again, I could only wish that Wilson had lived to see his utopian vision begin to come true, rather than exiting Earth in the final stretch of the Bush years. But like all great wizards and mentors, RAW left us in our darkest hour—not to abandon us, but because it was time for us to put what he had taught us to use, and bail our own asses out of the fire.

SMI²LE.

New Orleans Voodoo
– An Oddity Unto Itself

Carey Hodges & Chad Hensley

The word "Voodoo" is derived from a Dahomean word meaning *spirit* and it has been suggested that its use to describe a religious system originated in New Orleans.[1] The practice of Voodoo in New Orleans holds a mysterious and intriguing history. Voodoo has existed in the Crescent City and its surrounding areas since the arrival of the first African slaves in the early 1700s. However, the varied practices of Voodoo did not become organized until the appearance of the Saint Domingue refugees (between 1790-1840), who were fleeing a revolution in what is now Haiti. For a century the practice of Voodoo was a powerful force in the lives of many blacks and whites in New Orleans. This article will discuss the history of New Orleans' Voodoo, women's dominance in the religion, and race relations between the black and white practitioners.

The *Random House Unabridged Dictionary* defines Voodoo as a class of religious rites originating in Africa as a form of ancestor worship, practiced mainly by Negroes of Haiti and to a lesser extent by people in other West Indian islands and in the United States. Voodoo is characterized by propitiatory rituals and the use of the trance as a means of communicating with animistic deities.[2] Animism is the belief that natural objects, natural phenomena, and the universe itself possess souls and consciousness and may exist outside of the body.[3] Voodoo then is a folk religion combining aspects of Roman Catholicism from the slave masters with religions of the African tribes practiced by slaves brought to the New World.

The Louisiana slaves were unique in that the French Colony of Louisiana received most of its black slaves directly from Africa, and in particular, from only one region of Africa, the Senegambia, and often of a particular ethnicity, the Bambara.[4] This was a result of the fact that the privately-owned Company of the Indies had a trade monopoly in both Louisiana and Senegambia. Almost all slaves brought to Louisiana from Africa arrived within a twelve-year period following the founding of New Orleans. Very few slaves arrived to French Louisiana after 1731.[5] This allowed for a very distinctive slave culture to develop in Louisiana during the eighteenth century. A culture that would

---

1 Martinie, Louis & Glassman, Sallie Ann, *The New Orleans Voodoo Tarot* (Destiny Books, 1992), pp. 2-4.
2 *Random House Unabridged Dictionary*
3 Ibid.
4 Hirsch, Arnold S. & Logsdon J., *Creole New Orleans* (Louisiana State University Press, 1992), pp. 69-71. "The Formation of Afro-Creole Culture" Hall, Gwendolyn M.
5 Ibid.

become firmly established by the time the United States purchased the Louisiana Territory in 1803. This slave culture was based on a separate language community with its own folkloric, musical, religious, and historical tradition. This tightly knit, self-confident, self-reliant community survived, deeply influencing the peoples of all races and languages who lived among them.

Between 1790 and 1840 there was a large movement of refugees from Saint Domingue, fleeing the slave insurrection. In 1809 a number of Saint Domingue planters, who had refugeed in Cuba, were expelled and sought sanctuary in New Orleans. These white planters brought with them their slaves and a considerable population of free men of color. These free men of color, the *gens de couleur* as they were called by the French, were artisans, craftsman, and sculptors who added to the talent and literacy of New Orleans.[6] The free men of color were also some of the greatest practitioners of Voodoo and, along with the Saint Domingue slaves, helped organize the practice of Voodoo in New Orleans.

Until now Voodoo had scarcely been a dominant living force. It had continued to surface, but only to be suppressed with violence and discipline by the slave owners and city authorities. Plantations were widely separated, and the slaves of various estates did not often meet. However, old Negroes passed on a few of the superstitions, remembered the *gris-gris* magick (Voodoo powder made of herbs and alligator innards) known to their elders, never forgetting Voodoo.[7] But there was only an occasional Voodoo gathering until the arrival of the Saint Domingue slaves and free men of color. Additionally, in New Orleans the French Colonial Government's Black Code (*Code Noir*) had guaranteed the slaves basic rights including restrictions on physical abuse, rights to petition courts, and the obligation that slave owners provide for their spiritual needs.[8] Although the code was not followed completely, the latter allowed the slaves to attend white-controlled churches practicing the only religion allowed at that time, Roman Catholicism.

Slaves began meeting at dances and in "tin pan alleys" in such numbers that by 1817 the New Orleans City Council saw fit to set aside for purposes of crowd control a place for slaves to openly congregate.[9] The City Council also passed an ordinance to try to keep slave groups from meeting except on Sunday. The ordinance also designated the places were such meetings could be held. One such place, Congo Square, was chosen, and for twenty years slaves danced, sang, and performed Voodoo rites as curious onlookers watched in bewilderment. Congo Square was the area where the ramparts of the city once stood and (coincidentally?) is now the present location of the Louis Armstrong Park and Harrah's Gambling Casino.

Voodoo represented one of the few ways for blacks to gain economic and personal power during the racist and chauvinistic Southern Reconstruction. A number of blacks discovered this opportunity, the majority being women, and thus made a business out of Voodoo.[10] The last half of the seventeenth century brought with it the rise of organized

---

6 Garvey, Joan B. & Mary Widmer, *Beautiful Crescent* (New Orleans, 1990), pp. 55.
7 Tallant, Robert *Voodoo in New Orleans* (New Orleans, 1983), pp. 11-12.
8 Bodin, Ron *Voodoo Past and Present* (Lafayett, 1990), pp. 14-19.
9 Ibid.
10 Ibid.

Voodoo. After the Civil War and the Emancipation, the freed man went through economic hard times. Work was hard to find, and scarce funds focused attention on the all-powerful "root doctor" or "Voodoo Priestess" as the healer of diseases. This return to African tradition also helped shape nineteenth-century Louisiana Voodoo – Voodoo that involved close knit, anti-white characteristics in reaction to slavery and the emerging Jim Crow mentality that witnessed whites substituting hatred of blacks for the pre-Civil War pity of the race.[11] Under these conditions, Voodoo became more organized over the years and less Africanized in the context of the ever changing Louisiana black experience.

Voodooism seems to have been a matriarchy almost from its first days in Louisiana. The Voodoo King was always a minor figure, the only men of importance being the Witch Doctors. The King was probably changed from year to year as, in most cases, he was the current lover of the Voodoo Queen and chosen exclusively by her.[12] Women seem to have made up at least eighty percent of the practicioners and it was almost always the women who made up the white membership of the sect. The songs and chants used in old Voodoo rites are almost entirely about the Queens. A song given to a reporter of the New Orleans *Times-Picayune*, printed on March 16, 1924, reflects the dominance of the Queens in New Orleans Voodoo and boasts of their tremendous power. Originally sung in the *patois,* known as Creole, a few lines are given here in English: [13]

I – the Voodoo Queen,
With my lovely headkerchief
Am not afraid of Tomcat shrieks,
I drink serpent venom!

I walk on pins,
I walk on needles,
I walk on gilded splinters,
I want to see what they can do!

The Voodoo Queen, Marie Laveau, is the most famous of the Voodoo practitioners. So great was her influence among blacks and whites she became known as "The Boss Woman of New Orleans."[14] Marie Laveau, a free woman of color, was born in Saint Domingue in 1794 and came to New Orleans in 1809, one of the ten thousand whites and *gens de couleur libre* escaping the bloody aftermath of the slave insurrections in Haiti. She married Jacques Paris, a free man, and bore him fifteen children, including a daughter, Marie, who was her look-alike and would herself become a Voodoo Queen. Her daughter also helped to mythologize the legends of her mother, for the history of both Marie Laveaus have become entwined into a single entity.

---

11 Ibid.
12 Tallant, *Voodoo In New Orleans,* pp. 20-22.
13 Ibid.
14 Leavitt, Mel *A Short History of New Orleans.* (San Francisco, 1982), pp. 121-122.

It is not clear how Laveau actually became involved with Voodoo, but it appears that she may have been taught by "Dr. John" Montenet. There are also many legends surrounding Dr. John but it is known that the man wore only black, had numerous scars covering his face, and his home contained a bizarre collection of snakes, scorpions, and skulls.[15] Some claim that Dr. John was the first to blend Saint Domingue Voodoo with Catholicism. He possessed a spy system that consisted of black servants he paid off for information on their masters. He is said to have blackmailed blacks and whites from every level of society. Marie Laveau owes Dr. John for teaching her his elaborate spying system, for it was in this way that she learned things that would be to her profit. Her spy system was even more elaborate than her teacher's and, along with her hairdressing business, she learned the 'dirt' on the citizens of New Orleans, rich and poor.

In the process, Laveau put her unique stamp on Voodoo. Claiming her followers were Christian, Marie Laveau added statues of Saints, prayers, incense, and holy water (borrowed from the Catholic religion) to the traditional Voodoo rites, which already incorporated snakes, black cats, roosters, blood drinking, and fornication.[16] One of Marie's most infamous antics included dancing with her "venomous" twenty-foot snake named Zombi each June 24 in a sort of Walpurgis Night on the Bayou. She would behead live roosters, drink their blood, and cavort with half-naked *bamboula* dancers in an outdoor orgy that caused "thousands to shudder" at its animal intensity.[17] Marie also capitalized on the public's fascination with the Congo Square activities and opened up less sensitive Voodoo ceremonies to the public for an admission fee. New Orleans was divided in its opinion of Laveau; she was seen as both a devil witch and an angel of mercy. She nursed the wounded at the Battle of New Orleans and comforted yellow fever victims during numerous epidemics. She visited prisoners on death row, built a chapel for them, and decorated their cells.[18]

During Laveau's lifetime Voodoo became increasingly popular. Especially notable was the increased participation of whites in the practice, as was seen in the festivals of St. John's Eve held on June 23rd around Bayou St. John. "There are 300 Voodoos in the city," the *Times* editorialized on June 25, 1873. "They are presided over by a Queen... and amongst them are numbered at least ten [white] women who partake in their hellish orgies. There are about a thousand more [white women] who secretly have faith, and practice on the sly."[19]

But just twenty-three years earlier, the New Orleans newspapers had been defending Voodoo. In July of 1850 the *Weekly Delta* editorialized as being "inclined to question police rights to interrupt their [Voodoo] rites". This had been a response to an incident where police had arrested a large group of women – "white, black, and of mixed color", while they were gathering for Voodoo dance and proceedings. The arresting police officers described the rites they had witnessed as indecent and orgiastic in character. The arrested women summoned eminent counsel, who argued that voodoo practices were purely religious and that the law had no justification for its attitude toward them.

---

15 Ibid.
16 Bodin, *Voodoo Past and Present*, pp. 21-25.
17 Leavitt, *A Short History of New Orleans*, pp. 122.
18 Ibid. pp. 123.
19 Ibid. pp. 91.

The court, apparently bewildered at this, fell back on an ordinance forbidding the assembling of white women and slaves.[20] The New Orleans *Times* in August of 1850, described the arrest of fifty nude women, including several white women. The white ladies claimed that they had been unclad only because of the excessive heat and had been present only because they had all collapsed simultaneously on the doorstep of the Voodoo Priestess prior to the commencement of the ritual. The white women were fined and dismissed.[21]

The question of the legitimacy of the New Orleans papers must be taken into account. During this time, Voodoo was in everyone's attention and the topic of much discussion and gossip. One must not forget the consequences of exaggeration with regard to the validity of many of these stories and newspaper articles. However, the presence of white women at the Voodoo ceremonies was apparent, and the practice did have many white followers. Racial mixing had been apparent since early colonial times, due to the lack of white women in the area. Black and Mulatto women were taken as substitutes for lovers and wives throughout New Orleans history. The New Orleans area was also only livable on the limited areas of the natural levees. Therefore, people of all races and backgrounds were forced to live amongst each other in close settings. Cultural boundaries to a certain extent were forced open. This could be an explanation for the adoption of another race's or ethnic group's practices and customs.

New Orleans's unique history holds a sacred place in the formation and practice of the Voodoo religion. Thanks to the contributions of the Saint Domingue refugees, the practice of Voodoo became a powerful force in the lives of many New Orleans people. Furthermore, individuals such as Marie Laveau and Dr. John helped to popularize Voodoo in folklore and local history. The combined aspects of Roman Catholicism, African tradition, and animistic rites, all helped to shape Voodoo into a new religion and carve for it a special place in history that will continue to fascinate the serious occultist as well as the mundane modern man.

---

20 Tallant, *Voodoo In New Orleans* pp. 24.
21 Ibid.

Kabbalah references in contemporary culture

Alexander Nym

This text is based on a presentation delivered at the Jewish Culture Festival, Krakow, on June 30, 2014. Fraternal greetings and gratitude to David Tibet, Nikolas Schreck, Susanne Zeller and Peter R. Koenig for sharing information and providing input. Particular gratitude goes to Kornelia Binicewicz and Alexander Pehlemann for inviting me to Krakow and seeing after the administrative side of that prolific event. – A.N.

Some of you might remember when, in the late 90s, Madonna, the US popstar, released an album by the name *Ray of Light*. The famous "Queen of pop", known for her chamaeleonic changes in public image and infamous for absorbing various fashion trends, again appropriated an iconic popcultural mode of presentation: Henna tattoos, black hair dye and a rather sombre, darkish costume and set design accompanied her appearance in the promotional video of the single *Frozen*, a track that was subsequently also played in gothic and industrial clubs; places rather less well known for their fondness of mainstream pop music. However, Madonna's then producer William Orbit, veteran of the UK electronic dance underground, had succeeded in creating a sound that was appealing to both radio listeners as to rather sensitive and moody goth audiences. Along with this change in sonic and visual appearance, Madonna also made it known in interviews that her personal interests had begun to include mysticism, particularly the Jewish mystical tradition of the Kabbalah. In how far this interest exceeded the construction of a media savvy image to accompany and enhance the aforementioned album's subtext is difficult to gauge. What it achieved though, was the (re)popularisation of a subject shrouded in mystery and speculation, and one that had heretofore merely been hinted at by few and lesser known groups (with the exception of David Bowie, as we will see) most of which were operating within particular music genres far removed from mass media attention the likes of which Madonna attracted.

I'm not going to bore you with the long and winding history of the Jewish mystical system known as Kabbalah, but will focus on its more recent history in the popcultural context of the 20th century. Suffice to say that the Kabbalah dates back at least to the 14th century and is based on the idea that in Hebrew, letters correspond with numbers which in turn correspond with meaning, opening up virtually indefinite possibilities of combining words and meanings and interconnecting them based on their overall numerical value. Kabbalah's incursion into modernity was prefigured by French magician Eliphas Lévi (born in 1810 as Alphonse Louis Constant), who is regarded as the pioneer of the modern European occult revival. Not only because he introduced the Tarot card system and symbology into modern magic, but this will prove to be the Kabbalah's most important gateway into pop-cultural awareness. Even though Lévi himself wasn't Jewish, his pen name was an attempt to translate his given name into Hebrew. His writings were fundamental for the revival of magic(k) and occultism in the late 19th and 20th century and laid the foundation for the comparative study of mysticism as practised by the renowned Hermetic Order of the Golden Dawn (G.'.D.'.), which comprised quite a few influential writers, poets and intellectuals of their time amongst its ranks, such as Arthur Edward Waite (1857–1942), British-American author, Freemason and co-creator of the Rider-Waite Tarot deck, William Butler Yeats (1865–1939), Bram Stoker (1847–1912), Arthur Machen, Algernon Blackwood, Allan Bennett, who introduced Buddhism to the West, and of course the notorious magician Aleister Crowley, who would later found his own occult organisation, the A.'.A.'.

The G.'.D.'.s grade structure, which was taken largely from the Societas Rosicruciana in Anglia, consisted of paired numbers related to positions on the kabbalist Tree of Life. The first numeral indicated the number of steps up from the bottom (Malkuth), while the second numeral denotes the number of steps down from the top (Kether). Dion Fortune, member of a G.'.D.'. offshoot organisation called Stella Matutina, and founder of the Society of Inner Light, was not a member of the original G.'.D.'. She was a psychologist, writer and practicing occultist whose work *The Mystical Qabalah* (an introduction to hermetic Kabbalah first published in England in 1935) is regarded by some as one of the best books on magic ever written. Together with Lévi, Crowley and G.'.D.'. founder Samuel Mathers, she ranks among the foremost pioneers to reintroduce the hermetic Kabbalah into the resurgence of interest in spiritual matters in the West. Thus it comes as no surprise that Dion Fortune was directly referenced in late 20th century pop-culture several times. Besides lending her name to a Death Metal band in the early 1990s, *Dion Fortune* was also the name of a German record label of the same period, which was mainly conceived as outlet for occult-influenced gothic rock group *Garden of Delight*, abbreviated G.O.D. – the label also released a series of a half dozen compilation albums (which, hardly surprising, each but one featured G.O.D.), the 3rd of which has a track called *Dion Fortune* by electronic postpunks *The Cassandra Complex*. In this context, it is noteworthy that the band's mastermind Rodney Orpheus is a practicing member of the OTO, an occult temple founded in the 1920s in Germany, one of many which practically act as heirs to Aleister Crowley's philosophical legacy. The sleeve of the 1989 release *Satan, Bugs Bunny and Me* shows an adapted version of the seal of Aleister Crowley's own magickal order.

The first edition of their 1991 album *The War Against Sleep* included a free 3" bonus CD entitled *Gnostic Christmas*, which featured Aleister Crowley on the front, the OTO seal on the back of the sleeve, and Crowley's mottos "Do what thou wilt shall be the whole of the law" and "Love is the Law, Love under Will" next to the rim of the CD itself.

Yet this wasn't the first time Crowley's figure appeared in pop culture. The notorious English magician had previously been drafted by rock's most celebrated group *The*

Beatles as one of the iconic figures adorning their seminal album *Sgt Peppers Lonely Hearts Club Band* from 1968.

Crowley, who is regarded by many as the single most influential magician of the 20th century, was rediscovered by the hippy movement of the 1960s which adopted his liberal ideas and philosophy of Thelema. Anyhow, even though Crowley had a deep seated contempt for the book religions and was notorious for his mocking and spiteful remarks about Christians, Muslims and Jews, whose religions he regarded as enslaving and spiritually mutilating to humans, he was fond of Solomonic Magick and further developed the connections between the Kabbalah's Tree of Life and the Tarot cards according to the G∴D∴ theory of correspondence, the association of elements from diverse traditions such as astrology, geomancy, ceremonial magick, Kabbalah and so on. In order to understand his contribution to the universal application of the Tree of Life, let's take a closer look.

The Tree of Life is the central glyph in the Kabbalah, which in its blossoms represents various aspects of both psychic and materialist aspects of reality, according to the neo-platonic and hermetic schools. Kether, the crown, represents the initial manifestation of Light in extension, the creative monad or the seed of existence, and together with Binah and Chokmah forms the upper triad, a purely abstract and metaphysical concept of union dissolved into dichotomy, the dialectic of illumination through the synthesis of opposites. The flow of creative energy is pictured as descending from the crown of initial manifestation, Kether, through the multiple archetypal renditions of various aspects of existence down to Malkuth, the Kingdom, which represents the most dense manifestation of energy in form and matter. The tree is to be understood as a holistic and universal image, and idealised abstraction of reality divided into its various aspects of existence, be they mental or physical. Thus, the tree encompasses the totality of existence, and offers a visual structure of the pure concepts of which our understanding of reality is made up. Every aspect of existence could in theory be broken down into composites of the various conditions represented by the blossoms, or Sephiroth, and their relations towards each other. This is where the numerical aspect of the Hebrew alphabet comes in: The 22 connections or paths between the ten Sephiroth are represented by letters, thus numbers. According to the theory of correspondence, each of these 22 letters is associated with one of the 22 major Arcana of the Tarot, a concept introduced by Eliphas Lévi and further developed by Crowley, eventually resulting in the creation of his own deck of tarot cards designed by him and painted by Lady Frieda Harris. Together with the picture of Aleister Crowley on the *Sgt Pepper*-album, his ideas and writings were popularised by the 1960s counterculture and beyond, including the Tarot and its foundation/reflection in the Kabbalah. Both Tarot and Kabbalah appeared in occidental culture in the late middle ages, approximately in the 13th/14th century, and Lévi wasn't the only writer assuming they were related on levels not exactly obvious to the eyes and minds of the uninitiated. Due to the identity of meaning, numerical value, and scriptural as well as phonetic nature within the Hebrew alphabet, it offered itself naturally to hermetic philosophy which, according to occult history, dates back to ancient Egypt and was exported by Moses long before Hermes was said to have transmitted the Tabula Smaragdina,

However, for centuries both the hermetic as well as the kabbalistic secrets were closely guarded by initiates.

The film *Pi*, like the aforementioned *Ray Of Light* album also from 1998, represents a very different approach to the Kabbalah as a mystical system than that of Madonna's. Whereas Madonna incorporates what must seem like a superficial general interest in the esoteric seamlessly into her body of work, indicating the syncretistic nature of pop culture as a supermarket of ideas, *Pi* takes its time to explain the mathematical and numerical content of the Kabbalah's philosophy in several key scenes. Here, Hasidic Jews are depicted as traditional mystics attempting to extract the name of God from the Torah. *Pi*, which is famed director Darren Aronofsky's debut work, premiered at the Sundance film festival in January 1998 and saw a cinematic release about six months later in the United States, almost coinciding with *Ray of Light*. *Pi* is a film noir style paranoid thriller centred around mathematician Max Cohen who, while seeking to figure out the world formula to predict stock exchange rates, is sucked into power games of secret service techno-elites and Hasidic mystical Jews suspecting the 216-digit number his computer managed to print before burnout might perhaps be the number of god, Jehova's true name, coded by Kabbalists as Shemhamphorasch, or more exactly ShemHaMephorash. The film blends contemporary topics of Individual vs. Organisation and control, loss of identity and logical coherence in the face of mysteries both scientific and subtle. While the film uses stark black-and-white photography to create a detached effect, the sound design and music, along with the editing, were at the forefront of the burgeoning 1990s electronic music culture. Reputable names like *Orbital, Massive Attack, Banco de Gaia, Autechre* and *Aphex Twin*, among others, feature on the soundtrack, and the original epic Jungle/D'n'B score was composed by Clint Mansell, formerly of 80s New Wave/Indie band *Pop Will Eat Itself,* who went on to become a successful film music composer whose score for Aranofsky's next project, *Requiem for a Dream* (recorded with the *Kronos Quartet*), received worldwide acclaim and recognition. *Pi* not only combines the notion of centuries-old hermetic philosophy with modern-day information technology and power politics, with traditional Hasidic Jews competing with an unspecified yet threatening secret service, but underscores this combination (or juxtaposition, if you prefer) by applying effective use of a visual retro aesthetic complemented with an ultra-contemporary soundtrack. Nevertheless, while the depiction of the Hasidic mystical Jews may be persuasive, it also strikes the viewer as quite stereotypical, a notion balanced by Mark Margolis' portrayal of Sol Robeson, a wise fatherly figure referencing King Solomon not just in name.

Considering the overall influence of occult themes on pop music, the counterculture etc, especially in connection with Aleister Crowley, the G.'.D.'. and the OTO, it's almost surprising how few direct references to the Kabbalah there are to be found. In countercultural literature, the *Illuminatus!* trilogy by Robert Anton Wilson and Robert Shea is probably the most notorious example, as the novel is structured in 10 parts which are given the names of the Sephiroth. In general though, it is less openly referenced than indirectly hinted at as an abstract model and underlying universalist philosophy. As a signifier of a specific, mysterious aspect of Jewishness, or rather of Jewish mysticism, Kabbalism is mostly referenced by groups from the darker, occult-inclined segments of popular music like the Gothic/Industrial, (Dark) Ambient, and Metal genres, but certainly not limited to these. In the wake of the 1960s, Graham Bond, who claimed to be an illegitimate son of Crowley's, used many hermetic and esoteric references on his albums, and so did the highly productive singer/songwriter Bill Nelson. David Bowie, who was an immense influence on several generations of musicians, openly dabbled in magick at least from the early to the mid-1970s. There are references to the G.'.D.'. and being "immersed in Crowley's uniform" on his *Hunky Dory* album from 1971 (quote from the song *Quicksand*.) Another example is the line "Here are we, one magical movement from Kether to Malkuth" on *Station to Station* (from the heavily influential 1976 album of the same name), and the widely seen photos of Bowie drawing the sephirot and the reference to that practice in the song "Breaking Glass" from 1978: "Don't look at the carpet; I drew something awful on it".

Yet also during the supposedly less mystically inclined 1980s, a few instances of kabbalist influx into music culture can be found: In the wake of the occult phenomenon in the post-industrial UK underground music scene emerged *Current 93*, a group associated with the *Temple of Psychick Youth*, an organisation dedicated to exploring and reclaiming magickal, shamanic and initiatory techniques of consciousness alteration. The current in question was that of Crowley's Thelema, as the group's mastermind David Tibet was at the time a member of Kenneth Grant's Typhonian OTO, and liked to appear on records under the moniker of Christ 777, a direct reference to Aleister Crowley's book about the Kabbalah, *Liber 777*. The number 93, as in three times 31, is also a direct kabbalist reference and represents the numerical value of the kabbalist term LAShtAL, which also happened to be the title of *Current 93*'s first release, a recording of Crowley-inspired ritualistic music and sampling audio recordings of his. *Current 93* went on to become a widely acclaimed avantgarde group, severing all bonds to Crowley and the OTO no later than with 1987s tongue-in-cheek parody song *Crowleymass*. David Tibet, born David Michael Bunting, continued to professionalise his interest in the mystical and historical sides of world religions, studied Coptology and eventually became one of the few experts worldwide capable of translating ancient Coptic manuscripts. On *Current 93*'s 2014 album *I Am The Last Of All The Field That Fell*, the track *Kings and Things* contains a direct Kabbalah-reference:

> LOOKED AT HER BEAUTIFUL PROFILE
> AS SWEET AS ALL THE א ALEPHS א
> LUSTED FOR SMILES WITHOUT SHEEN
> WALL OR DROPS
> I COULDN'T BUY MY WAY OUT OF
> BRUISES BY THIS DATE
> QABALISTIC TRICKERY UNWORKS
> THE NATURAL DRAKBARK
> WHISKERED AND GLITCHING
> ELECTRONIC FACE OF HYMN HER

WHO IS YOUR NIGHT?
WHO IS YOUR OWN ANGEL?
WHO IS YOUR OWN NAME?

However, *Current 93* fans who got into the magickal messages of the group's early, Crowley- and OTO-inspired outlook, self-released a bootleg recording known as *Tetragrammaton*, the title itself and the number of copies (an edition of 418) being direct kabbalistic references. The record is a split LP with Italian ritual music and dark ambient outfit *Sigillum S*. The otherwise blank white cardboard sleeve carries a sticker displaying several Kabbalah-references.

Sigillum S's comrades of Italian group *Ain Soph* reference the Kabbalah in their name already, and have, in their output since the 1980s, turned from sinister avantgarde/ritualistic music to sunnier folk and classicist types of music. Irish singer/songwriter Sinéad O'Connor, who also went on to display a widespread interest in syncretist and so-called heathen belief systems, thanked her Kabbalah teacher Warren Kenton in the sleeve notes of her best known album, *I Do Not Want What I Haven't Got* from 1990, the title track of which was reportedly inspired by him. The note reads: "Special thanks to Selina Marshall + Warren Kenton for showing me that all I'd need was inside me." *Ambient Temple Of Imagination* (*ATOI*) was co-founded by Richard Sun, a Native American mystic, in 1992 in San Francisco and pioneered chill-out sound environments for raves around the Bay Area. With introspective chill spaces, ritualistic performance art, and spoken-word poetry, *ATOI* focused on the public ceremonial exploration of magick and sound. At the crest of what shamanic writer and consciousness explorer Terrance McKenna dubbed the "archaic revival", ambient and electronic music had arrived in the USA to revive and inspire the countercultural aspirations of young people in California and elsewhere, soon to be known as cybertribes, a term commemorating the reemerged tradition of tribal idea(l)s since the 1960s.

While *ATOI* used the Tree of Life and Kabbalah references, or rather their universalist notions, to combine with them a host of other more or less apocalyptic, futuristic and archaic ideas, to create an urban shamanic neo-primitivism centred on consciousness alteration, illumination, and ultimately tolerance and the idea of a peaceful syncretistic, inclusive spirituality through embracing the New Age of Kali Yuga, groups of other genres prefer the darker and gloomier aspects of the Kabbalah. They reference the Sefira of the abyss (Daath), or invoke the inversed, "evil" shadow Sefiroth known as Qlipoth. Thus, taking into account the "evil bias" within some subgenres of metal music, it is hardly surprising that there exist several songs by the title of *Qliphoth*, e.g. by the groups *Behemoth* and *Astaroth*, and a progressive death metal band from Atlanta/Georgia by the name of *Daath* (who are by far not the only ones using that word as part of a band name).

Italian doom metal band *Black Oath* released an album in 2013 called *Ov Qliphoth And Darkness*, which appropriates Aleister Crowley's unicursal hexagram as band logo, like *Current 93* used to do in the mid-1980s, and their habit of spelling "of" as "ov" is a direct reference to the aforementioned *Temple of Psychick Youth* and its founding fathers, the video- and hyperdelic avantgarde group *Psychic TV*, who in the 1980s were also infamous for twisting and tweaking language to uncover hidden layers ov meaning.

Yet, the association with the gloomier aspects of the Tree of Life (which, if inverted, would become a Tree of Death to a dualistic mind) seems rather popular in the metal subcultures, particularly in doom and black metal.

Another example for this is the 2013 album *Necrovision* by German oldschool black metal band *Darkened Nocturn Slaughtercult*, who admit to using occult philosophy, hermetic and kabbalistic teachings as the basis of what they refer to as "Necrocosm", which serves as the inspiration for the songs on *Necrovision*. Another recent group from the doom and black metal spectrum is *Ithdabquth Qliphoth* or *Hammer Ov Qliphoth* (I'm not entirely sure whether this is actually the same group or two different bands). Released on the Russian label *Thou Shalt Kill! Records* they feature, besides Kabbalah references in song titles, tracks titled *Monotheistic Supremacy* and *Your fucking creation is bleeding away*, which suggest a similarly spiteful view of monotheistic religions to Aleister Crowley's. However, let's turn our attention back to the less gloomy fields of mainstream pop so we needn't finish on a downer. A rather unexpected Kabbalah reference comes from German popstar Nena, known outside of Germany mainly for her early 1980s power pop hymn *Ninety-nine Red Balloons*, who directly referenced the Kabbalah by naming her 12th studio album *Chokmah* in 2001.

However, the title was chosen less for esoteric than for mundane reasons, namely the phonetic similarities between the Sefira's name and a line in the lyrics which translates as "this shocks my system". Besides the title, the esoteric references in both music and lyrics are less prevalent on the record, but would at least indicate some familiarity with the Kabbalah, even though that might have had to do with the mainstream presence of Hollywood-kabbalism in the wake of the success Madonna had had shortly before Nena began recording *Chokmah*. Besides these examples from pop, rock and subcultural music scenes, there are a number of explicitly kabbalistic compositions and recordings thereof, the best known being the compositions of Baal HaSulam. These are attempts at representing the transcendental and meditative aspects of spiritual insight and illumination through meditation on the Kabbalah and are thus not referencing the Kabbalah in a popcultural context but use it as the raw material for the compositions, which are arranged using the aesthetics of easy listening pop and jazz music.

In summary it can be said that the Kabbalah, as a philosophical toolkit as well as a mystical narrative and tool of magickal instruction, had ceased to be an exclusive signifier of Jewishness already by the dawn of the Renaissance. Considering that Cornelius Agrippa and other initiates had already been familiar with it prior to the occult revival in the 17th century, its proliferation outside of Jewish mystery schools probably began much earlier, even though its popularisation is clearly a result of the occult revival in Europe in the late 19th and 20th century, when comparative religious studies were conducted by hermeticists, gnostics and occultists from a variety of mystical backgrounds. From the 1960s onwards, it made its path into rock- and pop-culture, mainly through its associations with notorious figures like Aleister Crowley and his various musical disciples, and has since become both a Hollywood fad as well as a constant in the field of syncretist religious and mystical groups, leading to its incorporation into what might be generalised as modern Western occultism. Although rock and pop music displayed intense interest in all things esoteric, particularly in the wake of the 1960s (see for example the many direct astrological references in early recordings by both *Pink Floyd* and *Tangerine Dream*), there are hardly any isolated instances of blatant Kabbalism in pop culture, or works dedicated exclusively to this thematic complex. Whenever the Kabbalah is present, it is usually connected to other spiritual disciplines, philosophies or mystery schools, thus reprocessing its path from the once secret knowledge of a few sectarian groups to become a universally applicable metaphorical vehicle with the option of utilising a hypercomplex syntactical and numerical system which, through archetypal and physical correspondences, can interact, reflect and change the thoughts and contexts it is applied to.

While it may come as a bit of surprise, considering the Kabbalah's manifold means of contextualisation, and its poetic symbolism, that it has never been properly made the subject matter of a concept album, chances are that the Kabbalah will continue to inspire artists and mystics alike as a thought provoking and thought generating mode of perceiving and analysing the world and ourselves within it.

Recommended reading

—∿— Dion Fortune, *The Mystical Qabalah*, Aquarian Press 1987.

—∿— Peter R. Koenig, *The Laughing Gnostic – David Bowie and the Occult* (1996/2015), www.parareligion.ch/bowie.htm (last accessed December 23rd, 2015).

—∿— Israel Regardie, *A Garden of Pomegranates. An Outline of the Qabalah*, Llewellyn Publications 1985.

Standing in line

Zaheer Gulamhusein

Standing in line, out of our minds
Worship the warped lords of this Dark Age
Hands shape, shift lock and surround
To create a vortex of neon gnostic sound
Sucking out the final moments of linear time
Into the abyss, a perfect silent array of bliss

But still trying to conceive that once fateful combination
Visual saturation, twinned with sonic cosmological appreciation
The ripples of your shimmering mental manipulation
Enhance this kaleidoscopic foray into physiological experimentation
Haunted by the steps of your baneful maenad perversion
This new couldn't have felt more utterly ephemeral

Beyond the blurry forms and incessantly flashing lights
There could have been countless worlds beneath me
Uncontrollable contortions momentarily frozen on spectral moons
Played like detuned icy cold notes on a liquid horizon
Feels so disjointedly real, patched up emotions create insane melodies
The beating heart of this ticking anal clock cock sensation
Makes my heart stand unpleasantly still to attention

Poised against sunset bleached white stains of wilful preparedness
The moment your seed comes to its unavoidable fruition
That flesh on flesh, slippery analogue glossy wet VHS combination
With the ingestion of self begins the next +1 cosmic instalment
To the glitch filled screens and humming drone of my virtual sacrum
Every elegant and mundane move executed under your digital supervision

As the wolf lies down to rest

Carl Abrahamsson

Howling, growling
Bite by bite
Swallowing the whole
Of the sun
Immersion
Digestion
Regurgitation
Cataclysmic rejuvenation
Ragnarök
Smoke of Mirrors
Of deceipt
Massive destruction
As it opens its jaws
Fever, fire, fervour
We know not what we do
Yet we're against it
Instinctually apprehensive
Of the end
Unaware of its inherent beauty
The ultimate end of complacency
All feeling
All sentience
All violence
And re-evaluation, return, rebirth
Sharpen the fangs
On bloody insecurities
Chew them up
Spit out the ill-tasting
Swallow the nutritious
Morsels of though and action
Fervent shouts
Declaring war
And peace
The sun also rises

Welcome back: father, mother, child
In your pristine strength and heat
Replenish your life force
Repollinate earth and womb
The sun also rises
Chlorophyllic saturation
Chlorophallic satisfaction
Recreation is dead
Creation lives on
The permanent center of impermanence
Change, chew, choose
Digest well and use
Our new world
World of wonders
Magic and joy
As the wolf lies down to rest
The sun also rises

Ritual and Psychoanalytical Spaces as Transitional, featuring Sangoma Trance States

Vanessa Sinclair & Ingo Lambrecht

The ritual takes us out of our day-to-day lives, creating space where we are able to create, giving us an opportunity to invent our lives the way we might imagine them to be. The space created in the analytic session is much the same – a transitional space where one is taken out of one's daily routine for 45-50 minutes or a variable length of time depending on the analyst's orientation. This ritual may occur once, twice or three times per week; classical analysts see patients four to five days, while Sigmund Freud sat with his analysands six times a week. A ritual extraction from the daily narrative, a time when one may rewrite one's story by venturing back into it, following different avenues of thought, pathways meandering through the unconscious, striking various nodal points, signifiers sliding into one another, splintering off into varying but concurrent realities.

D.W. Winnicott championed the idea of the transitional space, positing that this space is necessary for creation to occur. It is the space of play, art and sublimation, sexual exchange and experimentation. Rituals create a transitional space. The traditional idea of ritual is that it encourages mastery through repetition. As the movements and patterns become more familiar they require less conscious thought, which allows for a space wherein consciousness may develop a further reach, a longer leash. One can see this familiarity in the tools utilized in the creation of such spaces across cultures and spiritual traditions. The use of fragrance, oils, incenses, the burning of resins or herbs, the quality of light whether it be candlelight or time of day – the first rays of morning, the last of twilight or the night stars. Chanting, song, drumming, movement and ecstatic dance are also often part of ritualized settings.

However, another view that I would like to illuminate is that it may be through the impossibility of repetition itself that true transition is found. It may not be the mastery of repetition that matters but rather the space that is created via the difference. You see, when we engage in what is proposed to be a repetition of a previous act it highlights the differential (Zupancic, 2008), for no act can ever be repeated precisely. There will always be a shred of difference. When tracing and retracing, the lines will never exactly match up. And even if they somehow do, the time, place, circumstance, mindset of the facilitator will always be different. And in this slice of imperfection separation occurs; and in this separation, the space for creation. Life. Nothing can be created if there is no void to fill. Repetition is un-exact and therefore creates small deviations, differences where change may come into play. Small cuts, spaces that open potential for something new, which then in turn alter the system. In this light, repetition may be seen as the scaffolding of the creative space. Perhaps the familiar elements that we find across cultures enable us to erect this scaffolding so that the unfolding of creation may take place.

This idea runs parallel with the concept of the cut-up, which also creates a gap, a space. When most think of the cut-up, they think of the cutting up and reassembling of words, language – the cut-ups of the Dadas, Brion Gysin and William S. Burroughs. But these artists also cut up tapes, sounds, images, photographs, and eventually thoughts, concepts, minds. Cutting one piece out of its prescribed position and re-animating it in a new way, giving it new life. When we take the time out to perform a ritual or attend the next analytic session – when we exit our daily program – we're cutting ourselves out of our daily narrative. The space created creates space so when we re-enter the scene, re-turning to the day-to-day, we've created room for something new to transpire. A cut, a slice, opening a gap, creating space that we may utilize to re-program ourselves, inventing ourselves the way we wish to be rather than the way we're destined to be based on our upbringing, parents, social conditioning, societal standards. This act creates room for our Will, and the practice of this repeated ritual has a cumulative effect.

Another aspect of this work is the altered state of consciousness that is created during both ritual and psychoanalytic treatment. It could be said that altered states of consciousness coincide with acts that occur in transitional spaces, during the creation of art, play, sex. I would argue that in analysis, not only the analysand but the analyst as well experiences an alternative state of consciousness. Some have called it a state of detached awareness or listening. I find that in this state, the signifiers of the analysand's speech tend to jump out more, like shining gems. And no matter what is happening in my own life, no matter what trials and tribulations I might be facing, I am able to separate myself and move into a different space upon entering the consulting room. My consciousness changes, and I am able to detach myself somewhat from my ego and reflect what the other requires.

Amongst the shamanic traditions of many indigenous people, mind and space are closely related as a transitional space. Different from religious rituals, in which the form of the ritual is the meaning, in shamanic rituals, the form not only holds meaning but also creates a transitional space to alter consciousness. It in fact is a part of the technology that alters the mind. For this article I will hold the somewhat contentious position compared to anthropologists who seek narrower definitions that common to most shamanic traditions across the world is the shifting of the mind in some sense, even if the specific rituals are different (Walsh, 2007; Winkelman, 2010)

It is true that repetition is never just the same, and that is especially true in shamanic rituals. The repetition of ritual is in fact more like stepping into a field of resonance, the repetition becomes the ground upon which flight occurs and new forms appear. This is true for music, art, psychoanalysis and altering consciousness. I will draw upon my own experiences and interviews from powerful shamans or *sangomas* in South Africa (Lambrecht, 2014) to highlight some of the thoughts in this paper.

Whereas rituals become interpreted historically by British anthropologists as reflecting social systems, French anthropologists find symbol systems and cosmologies

(Peek, 1991). Here I wish to make more use of Foucault's notion of creation of a self through the positive power-knowledge relations (Foucault, 1977) in regard to consciousness. Through the repetition of discipline, such as in rituals, a new self is established - be it in the breaking down of the tiny steps of action in order to shoot a gun, be it in the supervisory gaze in a panopticon (as prison system with a central observer looking into the cells) that creates an internalized feeling of guilt and self censorship, be it in the discipline of free association and interpretation in the psychoanalytic session, or in the shamanic ritual – a new and different self emerges. New sense of self is moulded through discipline of repetitive actions and meanings, that through time access increased positive effective power, that enhances knowledge, be it in terms of military capacity, a psychoanalytic self knowledge, or a shamanic mind trance state. The ritual is that space where power and knowledge through repetition and resonance establishes a productive self and identity. These identities are never fixed; they remain productive and transitional.

It is impossible in this article to fully articulate the trance states of sangomas. Trance states, what I have called the *amadlozi* trance state, during a sangoma dance ritual occurs in the presence of vigorous drumming, a specific form of dance, a dress code, and the presence of the community, which in fact provides the edges of such a ritualized space. The community functions as a holding, container or a secure base (Winnicott, 2005; Bion, 1977; Bowlby, 1969). It functions much like an Ancient Greek choir (observer, commentator, record keeper). There are certain effective technologies that induce a shift of mind. Already in the sangoma hut before going out to fulfill the ritual, dressing in certain garments starts the process. The memory of certain burning herbs, the repetitive singing begins to create the space of the familiar, the repetition as comfort, beguiling in its calling. The relentless and repetitive drumming begins to entrance; the rhythm captures you, not in an intellectual way of meaning but as a lived experience of resonance, trapped and held, embraced and pushed forward to that threshold. As you begin to dance, your body knows through its practices in the past those same steps, over and over it allows you to suddenly go into an inner space, a transitional space, that in my experience was like a dark funnel, a threshold that then suddenly opens you up to the landscape of visions or the whispering of ancestral voices. The ritual has then performed its transitional function, the community can now hold and benefit from the results of the altered state of consciousness, be it healing or knowledge.

Given the unique minor details of rituals and disciplines, it is therefore important to be specific. Psychoanalytic sessions are different from other psychotherapy sessions and will produce a certain state of mind; equally shamanic rituals will affect certain alerted states of consciousness. I can only provide brief sketches of trance states of sangomas here that are more carefully and respectfully explored in my study (Lambrecht, 2014). To give an example, I will choose a sangoma trance state that I have called the *amadkhosi* trance state during divination. The reason for choosing this specific sangoma trance state amongst the four I have established in my research is that it may be closest to a psychoanalytic space, allowing for a certain degree of similarity.

For sangomas, the experience of trance states are directly related to the presence of ancestors. So whilst dancing and trancing during a specific ritual, the ancestor is directly embodied in this altered state of consciousness or trance state, whereas during divination or consultation, the ancestors are described as being 'out.' No embodiment takes place, but the voice of the ancestor becomes an inner articulation as opposed to an outer expression; it traverses the inner mind spaces of the sangoma. The *amakhosi* trance state seems less obvious and definitely less theatrical or public in its nature. My teacher, Daniel, and those sangomas gathered around him at that time, considered this *amakhosi* trance state more important than the *amadlozi* trance state. "It is not the dancing that counts, but whether you can see, hear *bhula* (divine) and heal others." (Lambrecht, 2014, p.112)

To provide some necessary context, the most common method of divination involves the divining dice (in Sotho: *ditaola*), the so-called 'bones'. Different cultures have different tools to create the symbolic event, such as the Runes, the Tarot, or the I Ching. South African sangomas use divination to diagnose illnesses and recommend medicines, the coming of rainfall and the outcome of battles can be predicted, as well as being able to find lost or stolen objects. A set of bones will usually be made up of the astragalus (ankle) bones of sheep, cattle, antelope, baboon or antbear, and sometimes wild pig. It may also include objects such as seashells, coins, dice or strangely shaped stones. Fundamental to the complete set of bones are four bones, or small ivory tablets, which are at times triangular or quadrangular in shape. One face of each is incised with dots or lines, while the other face is plain. The dots or lines of each of the four signify the adult male, the young boy, the adult woman and the young girl respectively, therefore representing the whole family unit (Hammond-Tooke, 1993).

Sangomas have noted that the ritualised aspect of the *amakhosi* trance state during divination is supportive of entering this trance state. The enquirers can be an afflicted person, his or her family members or even neighbours of the afflicted person. The sangoma sought out should not reside too close in order not to have access to local gossip. They sit down in the sangoma's hut while she squats opposite them. Some *impepho* (herbal medication) may be lit. Between them lies a grass mat upon which the divination bones are thrown. The fees for divination are not viewed as payment for services but as a gift to the ancestors. It can take various forms: food, meat, sheep, chicken, some cloth, and of course money – in my experience the common form of the gift. The money is folded up and slid under the mat.

After this transaction, sometimes, the bones are shaken out of the bag onto the mat, where they are blessed with snuff. The sangoma chants a praise to her ancestors, the chant she uses to identify herself and ask the bones for help. The bones are then collected up in both hands, the sangoma strikes them together then throws them onto the mat, and the interpretations of the fall begin. Sometimes she takes them straight into her hands. She begins to call upon her ancestors in the form of a prayer. She asks the patient his or her full name, which is included in the call to the ancestors. She might also request the patient to blow on the bones in her hands.

Importantly, she has no prior knowledge as to why the patient is sitting there silently. Thus the first throw of the bones is to establish the reason for the patient's visit. As the bones are scattered across the mat and begin to settle into a meaningful pattern, the sangoma gazes silently at them, sometimes listening to her own body for the sympathetic pain. The usual method of informing the client of the outcome of a fall is the *Vumisa* method. The sangoma is expected to make statements, followed by her exclamation of the words *Vumani Vho!* (Agree then!). After this exclamation, the client and her support people clap their hands or click their fingers saying, "*Siyavuma!*" (We agree!). If a point was established to the satisfaction of the client then they would say, "*Phosa ngemva*" (Put it behind you). If the sangoma was wrong, they would say, "*Asiva*" (We do not hear) (Hammond-Tooke, 1993, p.190).

I recall how my teacher got into this singsong voice and became rhythmic in his words and exclamations. The clients would answer with *Siyavuma*, and he would begin again, and thus the client's affirmations would confirm him, in fact at times speed up his utterances. A back and forth would develop between him and the client, who became the chorus to his prophetic voice. The tension would rise, the rhythm sometimes speed up; my teacher was entranced, and in fact so were all in the room through our participation.

If the sangoma has correctly established the reason for the patient's visit, it means she is worthy of her craft – a worthy healer who can be trusted, for she has passed the test. It is accepted that despite a successful reading, patients go for second and often third opinions to check out the diagnosis and remedies. This shows the community is not necessarily naïve or blindly faithful.

Attempts have been made to understand the divinatory process as a psychological and transferential process (the diviner in dialogue with the client) or as involving psychic elements (trance states). It is also deemed to be a synchronistic process understood in Jungian terms in which two acausally related events are considered to be meaningful (Parkin, 1991). My teacher told me that a sangoma must never talk to others about a patient's divination session, similar to the confidentiality code of psychoanalysts. The teacher pressed on me never to treat serious ailments or bewitchment of my own family, for the sangoma's own feelings become involved. And if the sangoma is seriously ill, another one should be sought out. My teacher was therefore fully aware of transference and its ramifications. I certainly agree with the statement that often patients or clients continue talking "long after the divining and prescribing are done. This is when the sangoma becomes both priest and counselor. Who else, after all, do these people have to talk with?" (Arden, 1996, p.143). I have witnessed this on many occasions.

Specifically in terms of the *amakhosi* trance state, and similar to the psychoanalytic session providing a different ritualized space as a cut away from normal life, "all the drama of divination serves to move the participants out of their normal mode of thinking, shaking them up in order to change their minds because their current understanding of the situation is inadequate" (Peek, 1991, p.205). The sangoma becomes both the messenger and the interpreter, and does so by entering a trance state, not so different from the psychoanalyst in her reverie, an altered state that allows for the oracular words of interpretation to emerge.

Similar to the reverie and mindful presence of the psychoanalyst, the sangomas in my research spoke of creating ritually an inner quietude of the mind – a state of silence and relaxation allowing the ancestors to direct and support a trance state. One sangoma stated that one way of transitioning is to slow down the breathing as part of the induction process. One summarised all the trance inductive techniques in her statement: "Yes, when I am throwing the bones [...] the time you have put on your hair and your bag of bones, put on your things, taken your snuff, before that you must be quiet, silence, and I burn *impepho* (herbal medication), quietly without speaking. After that I take my snuff, and in seconds or a minute I talk to my ancestors, I pray." (Lambrecht, 2014, p.242)

Briefly then, divination as knowledge becomes further translated into power through the social position of the shaman as an advisor or consultant (Blier, 1991), as much as a psychoanalyst is the holder of the ritual in the analytic space. So divination produces meaning within a history. It re-authors and re-moulds the client's narrative in a whole system of symbolic and relational networks, not so different to the oracular analytic space.

In this trance state for the sangomas, the ancestors are supportive and quiet. They whisper answers, they suggest and nudge with intuition and insight as the flow of information becomes fluent and graceful. The sangoma can often begin to access knowledge that is not dependent on the bones. As some sangomas in the study reported, they stop using the bones as a trigger for their accurate knowingness. They begin to achieve a flow of knowledge in a trance state that transitions from the positions of the 'bones' to other inner spaces. Such spaces allow the presence of ancestral voices, who are subtle but present. The sangoma is supported with the openness of mind, a reverie and transitional space so often reported by psychoanalysts.

For sangomas, concentration is focused on the bones, and at the same time there is an openness of mind, which allows the *Gestalt* of meaning to emerge. Psychoanalysts use the imagery of dreams and the words from the altered state of free association to allow meaning to arise. This concentration of the mind, this attentive stance, is held lightly, without tension. From my experience, as soon as tension occurs the trance state is lost. It needs a light touch, so the inner silent space can be reached where knowledge, voices and images begin to flow. This focus on the emptiness of the mind means a blank canvas of the mind is sought, upon which the ancestors whisper and sculpt thoughts in the minds of the sangoma. Some sangomas give themselves over to this mind space to such an extent that in effect they find it difficult to remember what was said during the divination, a space of no memory, no ordinary knowing. Sangomas then claim it was their ancestors who spoke. I certainly can also attest to such transitional experiences in divination.

Similarly, when I sit in my psychoanalytic practice, I become aware of my body, the same posture, the sudden silence of my mind. Bion (1977) is right — the dark threshold of not knowing, not remembering or desiring, is a transitional space for the psychoanalyst to enter to allow, In this very repetition, forms of new life and knowledge to emerge. My body and mind shift through repetition of the ritual of analysis, the same room, the same time, the same person, into a creative space where healing may occur. I speak, much like a shaman, an oracle, sometimes things come out of my mouth that I was not aware of, a flow of words seem to make sense beyond my own comprehension. It is only possible if I allow this to occur with a more subtle mental space that shamans know in their ritual of divination where the mind is altered in a quieter, gentler, but nonetheless profound manner. Again the shamanic consultation around divination is very often ritualized, and different to religion, it does not merely repeat meaning but rather actively produces new knowledge, relevant and personal to the client. Similar to a shaman, I am at times not sure in the session who is speaking, where it comes from, and I am also not sure it matters, as long as the knowledge is effective and helpful in a ritualized safe space of reverie.

References

— Arden, N. (1996). *The Spirits Speak: One Woman's Mystical Journey into the African Spirit World.* New York: Henry Holt & Company.

— Bion (1962/1977). *Learning from Experience.* London: Karnac Books.

— Blier, R. (1991). Diviners as Alientists and Annunciators among the Batammaliba of Togo. In Peek, P.M. (Ed.) *African Divination Systems: Ways of Knowing.* Indianapolis: Indianapolis University Press, pp. 73-90.

— Bowlby, J. (1969). *Attachment and loss.* Vol.1 Attachment. New York: Basic Books.

— Foucault, M. (1977). *Discipline and Punish.* London: Penguin Books.

— Hammond-Tooke, D. (1989). *Rituals and Medicines: Indigenous Healing in South Africa.* Johannesburg: AD. Donker/Publisher.

— Hammond-Tooke, D. (1993). *The Roots of Black South Africa.* Johannesburg: Jonathan Ball Publishers.

— Lambrecht, I. (2014). *Sangoma Trance States.* Auckland: AM Publishing.

— Parkin, D. (1991). Simultaneity and Sequencing in the Oracular Speech of Kenyan Diviners. In Peek, P.M. (Ed.) *African Divination Systems: Ways of Knowing.* Indianapolis: Indianapolis University Press, pp. 173-189.

— Peek, P.M. (1991). African Divination Systems: Non-normal Modes of Cognition. In Peek, P.M. (Ed.) *African Divination Systems: Ways of Knowing.* Indianapolis: Indianapolis University Press, p.193-212.

— Walsh, R.N. (2007). The World of Shamanism: New Views of an Ancient Tradition. Woodbury: Llewellyn Publications.

— Winkelman, M. (2010). Shamanism: A Biopsychosocial Paradigm of Consciousness and Healing. Oxford: Preager.

— Winnicott, D.W. (1971/2005). Playing and Reality. London: Routledge.

— Zupancic, A. (2008). *The Odd One In: On Comedy.* Cambridge: Massachusetts Institute of Technology.

Listening to the Voice of Silence
– A Contemporary Perspective on
the Fraternitas Saturni

Hagen von Tulien

Part One:
An Abbreviated History of the Fraternitas Saturni

The Fraternitas Saturni (The Brotherhood of Saturn) was founded on the 8th of May in 1926 in Berlin, and still exists today. Candidates who prove themselves willing and prepared to follow the Saturnian path to the higher development of mankind are initiated after a one-year probationary period (novitiate), thus becoming a brother or sister of the Order.

The Fraternitas Saturni emerged from the Rosicrucian influenced Pansophia Lodge, which was officially dissolved on Holy Thursday in 1926. The Lodge's secretary, Berlin author and bookseller Eugen Grosche (better known as Gregor A. Gregorius), was one of the founding fathers of the FS and its first Grand Master.

As an outcome of the Weida Conference in 1925, the future founders of the Fraternitas Saturni adopted the Law of Thelema as the Law of the New Age, but refused to recognize Aleister Crowley's spiritual or organizational leadership. The phrase "Mitleidlose Liebe" (which could be roughly translated as "Compassionless Love") was added to the Law, which expresses a type of love free from sentimentality and conditioning.

The Fraternitas Saturni was and still is a mystical-magical and enlightened Order dedicated to the Gnosis of Saturn, which means the pursuit of occult knowledge in the spirit of the Saturnian/Uranian era.

Initially a ten-degree grade scheme was followed until the early 1960s, when a thirty-three degree system was adopted, that is still in place today. Some of these degrees are earned through work and the acquisition of specific knowledge, while others are honorary and degrees of high distinction.

The core element of Saturnian work is the dark light of the Great Demiurge Saturn, the Guardian of the Threshold. Initiates on the Saturnian path endeavor to polarize human existence ever higher, with the help of the Brotherhood's egregore, GOTOS.

GOTOS means "Gradus Ordinis Templi Orientis Saturni", it is the daimonium and magical force field of the FS, its interface to the sphere of Saturn, and at the same time its 33rd degree.

The unique qualities of the Fraternitas Saturni have attracted the interest of serious occultists right from the start, which is evident in the names of its members: Rah Omir Quintscher, Albin Grau, Karl Spiesberger, Guido Wolther and Frater UD are just a few examples of significant names.

Albin Grau was a German artist, architect and occultist, and the producer and production designer for Murnau's movie "Nosferatu" and other UFA movies. Alongside his accomplishments in film, he expressed his creativity in the occult magazine "Saturn-Gnosis", a highly acclaimed Lodge publication of the Fraternitas Saturni under the direction of Gregor A. Gregorius.

Another publication was the "Blätter für angewandte okkulte Lebenskunst", a series of documents that was published on a monthly basis after WWII continually for over thirteen years. Numerous isolated publications of FS members continue to enrich and cultivate the occult scene today.

Parallel to the Saturnian influx of utmost wisdom and clarity, the Uranian influx of openness to new impulses can be felt in more negative manifestations time and again as well. Thus the history of the FS also manifests as a history of internal conflict (schism of 1964-69), split-offs (Ordo Saturni, 1980) and new groups created by estranged brothers (GAG, 1997; merger with the FS in 2003).

The Fraternitas Saturni is particularly noted for the vast magical expertise of its members: The magical/mystical practices of the ancient Greco-Roman mysteries, Hermetic traditions, the Knights Templar, Rosicrucianism, Freemasonry, Alchemy, astral magic and Luciferian gnosis are all practiced alongside O.T.O. Sex Magic, Esoteric Voudou, Tibetan Yoga and other systems.

The FS works in the crystal clear light of Saturn, pursuing, comprehending, achieving and examining magical-mystical enlightenment, and then passing down this knowledge within the tradition of the Order true to the Saturnian principal, in a focused and concentrated manner. In the spirit of the Great Demiurge, the Saturnian Sorcerers of the FS practice their own specific Saturn Yoga, as pioneers of the New Age and seekers of eternity.

DE PROFUNDIS CLAMAVI AD TE DOMINE

Sanctus Saturnus

Highest of the seven Archons,
creating the world
from the cosmic Void of Chaos,
manifesting and crystalizing
manifold forms
in infinite abundance.

Sanctus Saturnus

Guardian of the keys
to below and beyond,
abiding at the threshold
to the deepest depths
and the highest heights,
the crossroads
of brilliance and darkness,
of being and eternity.

Sanctus Saturnus

Never-ending change
gives permanent birth to eternity
in the infinite Here and Now,
decay of the old,
emergence of the new,
perpetual play
from the Great Demiurge.

Sanctus Saturnus

The crystal-clear impetus
of the dawning aeon,
the true momentum
of esoteric evolution,
the coming-into-being
of individual Dasein,
erecting transcendental
progression.

Sanctus Saturnus

O Lord of the plethora,
open the way
and the gate of creation
to accomplish
the reincarnation
into cosmic consciousness.

Sanctus Saturnus

All contemplation
will end in silence,
the end
will be the beginning,
an entry
into transmogrification.

Sapienti sat.

Part Two:
The Concept of Saturn in the Fraternitas Saturni

The true nature of Saturn remains relatively unknown to the general public today. Traditional astrology treats Saturn as the typical bad boy – the personification of true evil who brings nothing but pain and suffering and is often equated with none other than Satan himself. Saturn boiled down to astrological terms is not much more than a conglomeration of unpleasant words.

Modern esotericism unfortunately presents a greatly distorted and simplified image of Saturn as well. This outdated image is mainly based on the departing Age of Pisces, which has been marked by the growth of monotheistic religions and dominated in particular by the influence of Christianity.

However, the Fraternitas Saturni views itself as the pioneers of the New Age, the Age of Aquarius, and both are marked by Saturnian and Uranian elements. Consequently the Brotherhood of Saturn views Saturn as a neutral principle, neither good nor evil, that manifests in numerous forms. One of the Brotherhood's primary tasks is to introduce its neophytes to Saturn's true nature and character, and to open the door to its diversity. Through the intense study of Saturn and the work with its principles, one is able to recognize the numerous ways in which Saturn can significantly manifest in one's life. As the Great Demiurge, the Guardian of the Threshold, the Master of Time, and the Master of Order, Saturn is able to convey gnostic insight, and this key element is a particular feature of the Fraternitas Saturni.

Saturn as the Great Demiurge

Saturn is the principle of centralization and crystallization. Here it is manifested in its aspect of the great form-giver who creates out of the massive abundance of his power by molding and casting forms. The Fraternitas Saturni recognizes him as the Demiurge, the Creator or Craftsman who shapes the four-dimensional space–time continuum.

But the universe that he represents is not static; it is made of pure energy. As an energetic universe it pulsates with lights and sounds that are in constant change and fluctuation, and the flowing form is reflected in the ceaseless fluctuation and constant change of things.

Thus the seemingly rigid nature of Saturn is indeed merely a superficial viewpoint, and below the surface it will reveal a pulsation of force fields. But unfortunately man's limited perception is designed to perceive the world as merely material, physical, and with solid consistency. As a result of this dual thought process, we are constantly drawing descriptive relationships between subjects and objects. Our perception forms our everyday consciousness through which we continually create, define and structure the world around us anew every single day. In turn, this process establishes the impression of reality that we perceive. On the earthly plane, Saturn is merely a planet whose position in the solar system has been clearly defined by astronomers and is visible to the naked eye in the night sky.

Saturn as the Guardian of the Threshold

Classical astrology defined Saturn as the outermost boundary of the discernible solar system. Beyond that stretches the infinite space of the night sky, known as Nuit according to the ancient Egyptian religion. Today we are well aware that there are other planets in the solar system beyond Saturn, yet Saturn remains the "Guardian of the Threshold". So what significance does this hold for the Fraternitas Saturni today?

In order to answer that, we first need to define the word "threshold". A threshold is the sill of a doorway that separates two rooms. Saturn guards the threshold between the world of form and the infinite space that lies beyond it. More specifically, Saturn is manifested as the threshold that separates form from the emptiness of space. Gnostics describe this empty space as Pleroma, the world of fullness, which expresses the state of emptiness that holds all potential. It is this source of unlimited potential that Saturn uses to create form. This threshold divides the endless omnipotent Pleroma from the numinous material world of shortcomings and deception, the physical world of time and transience.

Saturn as Master of Time

Saturn is often depicted with a scythe and an hourglass to express his role of master of time and time expired, or death.

Our linear perception of time is an expression of our inner conceptual limitation. After all, in altered states of awareness it is possible to experience a four-dimensional reality. We are then able to perceive how each and every object stands in relation to one another – not only in space, but also in time. The apparent separation of past, present and future is based on self-deception since we cannot perceive the coexistence of time in everyday consciousness. Coexistence means the single moment in the present where the past and future are united as one.

Time is one of the great mysteries and the gnosis of time magic is one of the highest endeavors of the Saturnian path. If we can succeed in realizing the experience of coexistence and to stabilize this within ourselves, this would expand our range of action to seemingly infinite dimensions.

Saturn as the Master of Order

Saturn's severity, hardship and adversity are generally perceived by man as unpleasant burdens that bring nothing but difficulties and problems. But Saturn's constraints bring long-term liberation through the release of attachment, the release of the things that bind us, and the release of thought concepts.

Yet Saturn challenges us in another way. He shows us our weaknesses and unresolved tasks and urges us to settle matters that we have successfully managed to avoid so far. Through compassionless love, Saturn holds a mirror to our face so that we can see what needs to be done. This is why the Saturnian Path may be particularly difficult in the early stages. The neophyte may be confronted with problems and tasks that were thought to have been long resolved. But Saturn will find your weakest spots and challenge you to face those weaknesses.

FURTHER ASPECTS OF SATURN

SOL IN SATURNUS

Polarity is the manifestation of opposites or contrasting principles. The fact that nothing can exist without its polar opposite is expressed in the concept of Yin and Yang. The same type of polarity also exists between the Sun and Saturn. On a planetary level, the principles of Sol and Saturn represent the innermost and outermost borders of our solar system. While the Sun is the life-giving power that draws everything centripetal into its center, Saturn is the centrifugal, counteracting force. The interaction of these two powers creates balance and stability.

Therefore Saturn is the opposite of the Sun, which is why the core of Saturn is solar and the core of the Sun is Saturnian. Sol in Saturn, Saturn in Sol.

SAT – PURE AND TRUE ESSENCE OF BEING

"Being" is the omnipresent form of all manifestation. It is described in the Vedanta in Sanskrit as "sat", the seed syllable of Saturn. Sat is the pure essence of being, a state that excludes nothing, not even nothing itself. Sat is therefore inseparably connected to pure consciousness ("chit") and forms a unity with it. There is no opposite of being and every attempt to identify sat with something would reduce it to a mere object.

Sat is the state of awareness that encompasses everything, and nothing may be added or subtracted from it. Sat is self-existing and has no beginning or end since it exists beyond the concept of time. It is infinite, beyond form and object. Sat can be defined as an infinitely illuminating empty awareness that is hidden deep inside every one of us.

Sat forms the basis of interaction between Nuit (the infinity of space, emptiness) and Hadit (centralization, form) and Ra Hoor Khuit (dynamic force, movement). Sat, the pure essence of being, is the nucleus of the process that the Fraternitas Saturni describes as the "crystallization of the self".

THE SHADOW OF SATURN

Shadows are created where light is absent. The shadow of Saturn is the area that is not illuminated by the light of Saturn, or the Demiurge's Luciferian aspect of illumination. It is characterized by ignorance, disorientation and self-deception and represents the part of our soul that contains all things repressed and aspects of ourselves that we have not yet acknowledged or accepted.

Old publications of the Brotherhood refer to this area as the "lower octave" of Saturn. The Fraternitas Saturni today prefers to call this the "shadow" since it corresponds to the psychological concept of the same name as defined by C. G. Jung.

The shadow is the dark side of the soul, the undiscriminating and underdeveloped mental and emotional characteristics that are generally repressed. Jung defined two types of shadows: the personal shadow, containing the psychological constraints of the individual, and the collective shadow, which is already a part of man's collective consciousness. Everyone carries a shadow and the more it is ignored, the blacker and denser it becomes. According to Jung, the shadow is prone to projection and thus a personal inferiority is perceived in others as a moral deficiency.

In Western religions, the dark side of the self is called evil and is personified by Satan. In contrast, the Fraternitas Saturni views evil not as a principle in itself, but rather as the result of what we experience and bring about ourselves. Suffering is based on the contradictions between man and the world, the conflict between what we want and what actually happens. The powerlessness that results from our defeats is perceived as painful and sorrowful. The cause of this powerlessness, however, lies in ignorance, attachment and negative emotions that create the false impression of a self that exists separately from the world around us. This is the objective of Saturnian crystallization – dissolving this feeling of separateness and the false view of things that it creates.

SATURN AND LUCIFER

Old publications of the Brotherhood describe Lucifer as the "higher octave" of Saturn that brings the light of insight. The saturnal gnosis of the Fraternitas Saturni views Lucifer as the Great Demiurge's aspect of enlightenment, which is expressed in Lucifer's name meaning "bringer of light". This angel of light represents the rebellious aspect of Saturn; after all, separation from the all-encompassing unity is what enabled the cosmic process of individualization in the first place. Following this separation, the act of creating the universe began, which was carried out by Saturn as the Demiurge.

The Luciferian aspect of Saturn manifests in each and every one of us on a daily basis. Because Saturn compels us to face our personal attachments, entanglements and philosophical and ideological concepts, he helps us to free ourselves from these burdens and rid ourselves of everything that is unnecessary. Saturn achieves his work through crystallization. This begins with disillusionment and revelation because clarity free of self-deception is the start of every crystallization process. Therefore his symbol is the philosopher's stone, the ultimate goal of an alchemistic process, symbolically represented by a diamond.

The Fraternitas Saturni does not, however, achieve freedom and liberation through abstention and retreat, but rather through action. Overcoming personal limitations and constraints and inner conflict are the driving forces along the Saturnian path. Therefore concepts such as self-discipline, consequence, perseverance, seriousness and patience reflect core Saturnian characteristics.

Another aspect of Saturn is the ability to create distance. When Saturnians sometimes isolate themselves from the world for a period of time, it is not a means of escape, but rather to give Saturn room to unfold and create space for crystallization. The saturnal process of crystallization is unique to the path of Saturn. This path leads to freedom and insight that the Fraternitas Saturni describes as Luciferian gnosis.

The above illustrates just some of the abundant aspects of Saturn as acknowledged by the Fraternitas Saturni. However to recognize Saturn in its entirety means to dare to actually cross his threshold and be willing to relinquish everything that defines us as human beings. Saturn works in silence and he can be expressed in nothing but silence. And the voice of that silence is the counsel of those on the Saturnian path.

NOTES

Concept, editorial work, illustrations by Hagen von Tulien.

"Part One - An Abbreviated History of the Fraternitas Saturni" based on an article by Felix Wolf (as translated from the original German by Melinda Kumbalek), revised and extended by Hagen von Tulien.

"De profundis clamavi ad te Domine" by Hagen von Tulien.

"Part Two – The Concept of Saturn in the Fraternitas Saturni" is based on an internal publication of the Fraternitas Saturni and has been loosely translated and paraphrased by Melinda Kumbalek.

Many of the ideas and concepts that are of great significance and unique to the Fraternitas Saturni (e.g. the concept of "Mitleidlose Liebe / Compassionless Love", and the Order's egregore GOTOS) could only be touched on in this article and require further explanation, which may transpire at a later date.

Infectious Hoax:
Robert Anton Wilson reads H.P. Lovecraft

Erik Davis

Many creative thinkers and esoteric practitioners have critically engaged the matter of Lovecraft, but for my money few are as inventive and perspicacious as Robert Anton Wilson. Wilson also began his engagement with the weird fiction master in the nineteen-sixties and early seventies, when Lovecraft criticism was in its infancy. Admittedly, Wilson largely corralled his intellectual appreciation for Lovecraft in his own works of fiction, in which the genre of horror only plays a minor role. Indeed, Wilson claims that he never considered Lovecraft's writings "horror fiction" because they never scared him. "I regarded them as a special kind of prose-poetry that lifts the reader into a perspective far, far beyond human prejudice, a perspective in which Earth and its denizens are very unimportant, virtually accidental parts of the cosmic drama."[1] That said, when Wilson personifies cosmic and inhuman forces in *Illuminatus!*, a masterpiece of high weirdness written with Robert Shea and published in 1975, or in 1973's pulpier *The Sex Magicians*, he turns as often as not to Yog-Sothoth and other gruesome creatures that Lovecraft invented as part of the artificial mythology of cosmic outsiders famously dubbed the "Cthulhu mythos."

Wilson wove Lovecraft's beasties into his fictions in part to continue the intertextual game started by Lovecraft and his *Weird Tales* cronies in the early thirties, in which a shared network of references to gods and grimoires subtly thickened the "what if" ontology that sprouted up between the tales. In his work with Shea, Wilson was already using similar referential strategies to develop the quality of quasi-reality that characterizes the occult and political conspiracies that charge *Illuminatus!*, with its clever mix of fact and fiction. These strategies were also heavily influenced by the Discordian Society founded by Greg Hill and Kerry Thornley, and which similarly played with fact, fiction, irony, and belief. At the same time, Wilson brought a more distinctly literary sensibility to the Discordian game. Indeed, Wilson was not just a good reader of Lovecraft, but an insightful student of the whole tradition of weird and gothic fiction that Lovecraft helped focus and cohere in his own 1927 critical account of the supernatural tale.

In fact, though *Illuminatus!* is usually classed (rather poorly) as "science fiction," it is perhaps better seen as a countercultural and conspiratorial reformulation of the *weird tale*, a pulp form that derives some of its peculiar frisson by, as we will see, making the reader ever so slightly paranoid. Secret societies are, in the light of *Illuminatus!*,

---

1 Robert Anton Wilson, *Cosmic Trigger II: Down to Earth* (Tempe, Ariz.: New Falcon Publications., 1991), 172.

weird societies. In *Illuminatus!* we are even told that Bavarian Illuminati head Adam Weishaupt performed rites so bizarre that the resulting "psychic vibrations" bounced off every sensitive mind in Europe, directly generating such literary mutants as Lewis's *The Monk*, Maturin's *Melmoth the Wanderer*, Mrs. Shelley's *Frankenstein*, and DeSade's *One Hundred Twenty Days of Sodom*—most of which play key roles in Lovecraft's own history and establishment of the weird tale in his *Supernatural Horror in Literature* (1927).

For of course it is Lovecraft that deserves pride of place here in this etiology of the weird. Blending elements of classic fantasy, pulp horror, and the emerging logic of science fiction, the central bulk of Lovecraft's tales are characterized by a fascination with the dialectics of madness and knowledge; a pantheon of bizarre extraterrestrial pseudo-gods who are essentially inimical to human life; and an anxious concern with human degeneration and the corrosive call of the primitive. In Lovecraft's mature work, supernaturalism is replaced with a *weird naturalism*: magic, whether learned or atavistic, unleashes prehistoric and cosmic powers rather than mystical hierarchies of angels or devils.

Lovecraft first makes this naturalistic move in his 1928 story "The Call of Cthulhu," wherein he reframes the archaic gods worshipped by vodoun initiates and remote "Eskimo wizards" as extraterrestrial or inter-dimensional beings. Paralleling Theosophy's mythological histories of earth, and anticipating Erich von Daniken's "ancient astronaut" theory, Lovecraft's deep history suggested that the savage mysteries that animate the most primitive human cults encode actual truths about the cosmos, including dimensions of reality—like Minkowski spacetime and the non-Euclidean geometry used to describe it—that early 20th century astrophysicists were only beginning to understand. In contrast to the supernaturalism of ghost stories or the gothic tales he began his fiction career with, the metaphysical background of Lovecraft's mature horror is thus a kind of science fiction whose "cosmic indifferentism" reflects the atheistic materialism that Lovecraft professed at great and sometimes hectoring length in his letters and popular press articles. But even as Lovecraft embraced the disillusioning powers of science, he also pessimistically anticipated science's ultimate evisceration of human cultural norms. His weird tales were imaginative diversions from this nihilism, but the amorality of their cosmic monsters reflected it as well, as did the quasi-journalistic realism that Lovecraft brought to many of his greatest works. Lovecraft was no Romantic, in other words, and the dialectic that his work and thought stage between realism and metaphysical wonder helps explain why he was so important to Wilson and other more-or-less skeptical voyagers into psychedelia and the high weirdness of the counterculture.

One of the best ways into this dialectic of imagination and doubt is through the literary historian Michael Saler's important notion of "disenchanted enchantment." In his book *As If*, Saler describes how Anglo-American readers and writers in the late nineteenth century began turning to works of fiction that combined the pleasures of the marvelous—already found in the Aesthetic and decadent writers of the time—with the rhetoric of reason and objectivity that such writers rejected on principle. H. Rider Haggard's enormously popular *She*, which came equipped with maps, chronologies, and doctored photographs and other documents, is Saler's classic example of how writers came to combine imaginary exotica with the armature of rationality—a process that, as Alex Owen and others have argued, also characterizes important aspects of the contemporaneous occult revival. According to Saler, this self-reflexive form of enchantment "delights without deluding," as readers come to enjoy their fictions "as if" they were real, but only in so far as this conditional state is clearly bounded by what Saler calls the "ironic imagination." In magical terms, we might say that the ironic imagination is *apotropaic*. Armed with the disenchanting powers of ironic distance, adults could "reside safely within carefully mapped geographies of the imagination without compromising their reason—going native, as it were—because the necessary distinction between fantasy and reality was securely reinforced through the distancing power of irony."[2]

In other words, the texts of "disenchanted enchantment" embrace the imagination as a pleasurable portal to worlds at once wondrous and stimulating, but they do so without relying on the metaphysical substance the animates the central current of Romanticism or the metaphysical claims of, say, Theosophists. In contrast to the hieratic and earnest sensibility of the nature poet or occult mystagogue, Saler's "as if" texts instead emphasize "the provisional, the contingent, and the artificial."[3] Which brings us back to Lovecraft. Indeed, one of the more remarkable statements of such disenchanted enchantment found in Saler's book comes from a celebrated 1930 letter by Lovecraft to his friend, the California weird fiction writer Clark Ashton Smith:

> [I get a] big kick . . . from *taking reality just as it is*—accepting all the limitations of the most orthodox science—and then permitting my symbolizing faculty to *build outward* from the existing facts; rearing a structure of *indefinite promise and possibility* . . . But the whole secret of the kick is that I know damn well it isn't so. I'm probably trying to have my cake and eat it at the same time—to get the intoxication of a sense of cosmic contact and significance as the theists do, and yet to avoid the ignorant ostrich-act whereby they cripple their vision and secure the desiderate results.[4]

Note that here the ironic imagination takes its pleasures, its *intoxication*, partly through its almost perverse proximity to religion. In the classic terms of the history of religion, we might say that the ironic imagination enjoys the sacred but only at the cost—often exuberantly paid—of its profanation. Cosmic promise and possibility are, in the end, nothing but a tease that produces an ultimately demotic pleasure, a big kick, a cheap thrill—and a sober and rational morning-after.

Indeed, it is no accident that Lovecraft uses the term "intoxication", since nothing ironizes the numinous metaphysical imagination of romantics or mystics so much as the recognition of how mere pharmacology can so impressively mimic or model such sublimities. For Walter Benjamin, the energies released from such "profane

---

2 Michael T. Saler, *As If: Modern Enchantment and the Literary Pre-History of Virtual Reality* (Oxford; New York: Oxford University Press, 2012), 29.
3 Ibid, 33.
4 H.P. Lovecraft, *Selected Letters III: 1929-31*, ed. August Derleth and Donald Wandrei (Sauk City, WI: Arkham House, 1976), 193; cited in Saler, 31.

illuminations" contained the seeds of real historical (ie dialectical) possibility; for a lot of heads and freaks in the counterculture, profane illuminations were also big kicks. As such, we need to underscore an important and underplayed vein of disenchanted enchantment within the occultural milieu of the sixties and the seventies. Both the authors and fans of *Illuminatus!*, for example, wanted to have their occult-conspiratorial cake and eat it too—a sensibility that many readers brought to texts that were themselves not ironic. Many readers and seekers might take Von Daniken or Yogananda extremely seriously, but many others read these books more or less as they would read Lovecraft— for an imaginative or rhetorical rush made more delicious or perverse by its proximity to a religious "structure of indefinite promise" provided by the author's own (perhaps dissimulated) stance of sincerity. Whatever "secrets" might be revealed through such esoteric readings are, in this modern context, inextricably bound up with the other "secret" Lovecraft mentions above: the secret that the reader knows damn well it isn't true, a secret that itself must itself be temporarily secreted for kicks to be had.

This is why Lovecraft, when discussing the methodology he brought to bear on his fiction, invoked the language of the hoax. In the same letter to Smith cited above, in which he characterized his attitude as that of the "hoax-weaver," Lovecraft described his method: "One part of my mind tries to concoct something realistic and coherent enough to fool the rest of my mind & make me swallow the marvel."[5] Lovecraft developed this dialectical hoaxing, which served as an important literary model for Wilson, through a variety of tactics. One was the language of realism Lovecraft developed in his mature writing, which restrains the feverish rhetoric of the macabre for a more transparent language that, while not without its purple blooms, often lies closer to reportage, scholarship, and nonfiction essay.

More notably, Lovecraft's fictions developed a collective "virtual" consistency through a webwork of invented place-names, creatures, and book titles that would recur across many stories (although some of these appearances are themselves notably inconsistent). Even more importantly, Lovecraft turned this world-building into a shared collective practice. He encouraged his fellow *Weird Tales* writers to drop the names of his grimoires and beasties into their fictions, something Lovecraft himself also did when he edited and ghost wrote stories for clients. "I think it is rather good fun to have this artificial mythology given an air of verisimilitude by wide citation," he noted in one letter.[6] Lovecraft would also return the favor, as writers like Robert E. Howard and Clark Ashton Smith made their own contributions to the growing lore— what later writers called the "Cthulhu Mythos" but which Lovecraft referred to more lightly as his "cycle of synthetic folklore" (*SL* 5.16) or simply "Yog-Sothery."[7] These tactics recall the important changes that the Discordian Society went through in the late sixties, when Greg Hill transformed his and Kerry Thornley's project into POEE, the Paratheo-Anametamystikhood Of Eris Esoteric, a collective insider game of invention

---

5 Ibid.

6 Ibid, 166.

7 Following Lovecraft's death, August Derleth, who founded Arkham Horror largely to publish the work of his friend and mentor, coined the term "Cthulhu Mythos" to describe this shared fictional universe, which Derleth and others in the Circle continued to elaborate and extend, often by forcing the Lovecraft Circle's enigmatic cluster of possibilities into a polished and, in Derleth's case, explicitly moralistic system.

and self-reference that played with the form of the literary hoax, using false letterheads, invented societies, and other paradoxuments. Needless to say, both the Yog-Sothery of the Lovecraft group and POEE marked Wilson's practice.

One fine example of Lovecraft's interweaving of social and invented worlds is his 1936 tale "The Haunter of the Dark," the last independent story he wrote. The hero of the tale is a young writer of fantastic fiction named Robert Blake, who is a stand-in for Robert Bloch, a young *Weird Tales* contributor who had placed a Lovecraft-like figure in a story published the previous year. In "Haunter," we read of Blake's exploration of an abandoned Providence Free-Will church once occupied by the Church of Starry Wisdom. This cult used a Shining Trapezohedron to communicate with extraterrestrial beings, one of whom, we are led to infer, spells the end of poor Blake. Blake's researches, however, are substantially bibliographic. In his first visit to the Church, Blake discovers a copy of Lovecraft's most famous invented book, Abdul Alhazred's dread *Necronomicon*, along with an encrypted record book and other hoary tomes, including texts—like von Junzt's *Unaussprechlichen Kulten*—that were invented by Lovecraft's pals (in this case, *Conan* creator Robert E. Howard). Blake later figures out that the record book is written in Aklo, an obscure language first mentioned in an 1899 story by the British supernatural horror writer Arthur Machen. In other words, in this and other stories, Lovecraft casts his referential web back in time, taking in early writers of supernatural horror and thereby charging the genre itself with an intertextual "virtual" reality, a sort of secret tradition constructed backwards through time.

Perhaps the most surprising title included in the list of Blake's finds is the *Book of Dzyan*, which is an actual book—sort of. Madame Blavatsky's monumental *The Secret Doctrine*, one of the most influential texts of Theosophy, is an elaborate commentary on the *Book of Dzyan*, whose stanzas she claimed to have stumbled across while studying in Tibet. Though some passages may have been cribbed from the Rig Veda, the book is largely believed by scholars to be the product of Blavatsky's considerable imagination. That said, it is a *different kind* of invented book than the *Necronomicon*, not simply because we are given a good deal of its contents, but because the speech act that frames it does not depend on fictionality. Indeed, like so many important esoteric texts, the *Book* stands somewhere between (or beyond) the polarities of fact and fiction, and derives its authority from neither.

As Dan Clore notes, Aleister Crowley recognized this paradox in his review of another fabricated Blavatsky text, *The Voice of the Silence*. Crowley declared the book "better than 'genuine,' being, like *The Chymical Marriage of Christian Rosencreutz*, the forgery of a great adept."[8] Crowley's reference here is to one of the early Rosicrucian texts, whose appearance in the seventeenth century inspired the creation of actual Rosicrucian orders, but which was admitted by its author to be a *ludibrium*, or "trivial game". Similarly, the *Book of Dzyan* can be seen as a *ludibrium*, or, perhaps with more earnestness, a Tibetan *terma* text—in other words, a text that derives its authority from both the visionary imagination and its recursive enframing within a spiritual discourse or tradition. And like *The Chymical Marriage*, Blavatsky's *Voice of the Silence* and *The Secret Doctrine* proved

---

8 Cited in Dan Clore, "The Lurker at the Threshold of Interpretation: Hoax Necronomicons and Paratextual Noise," in Joshi, S. T, *Dissecting Cthulhu: Essays on the Cthulhu Mythos* (Lakeland, FL: Miskatonic River Pres, LLC., 2011), 105.

enormously influential. Especially with her antediluvian history of the earth's fabulous races and civilizations, Blavatsky provided the basic motifs and themes for copious New Age cosmologies and UFO revelations (including von Daniken's astronaut archaeology). Moreover, Blavatsky's wild and rather science-fictional lore, with its tales of Atlantean sex magicians, giant Lemurian apes, and liberating rebel angels, also influenced both weird fiction writers and the tangled Atlantean backstory of *Illuminatus!*

All of which is to say that the Lovecraftian line between the substance of fictions and the forgeries of adepts had already grown mighty hazy by the time Wilson and Shea started to play the game. Adding a cosmic (and comic) dimension to conspiracy culture, the two authors cast the extraterrestrial entities of the Cthulhu mythos as the ancient inhuman intelligences that guide and interact with the Illuminati. Wilson and Shea call these entities the *lloigor*, a term not used by Lovecraft himself but invented by two later Mythos writers, which already ropes us into the collective dimensions of the hoax. In *Illuminatus!*, Shea and Wilson use this para-fictional web to round out or even counter the historical claims of existing conspiracy theories with a fictional if still conspiratorial game of Yog-Sothery, a now thoroughly collective body of metafictional lore they also intelligently—and sometimes disturbingly—extend. Indeed, one of the most sober moments of the book involves a *lloigor*. Throughout most of the novel, Yog-Sothoth remains imprisoned in a Pentagon-shaped building, but late in the text he temporarily possesses the body of one of the Illuminati leaders and speaks. For once in the novel, the authors' words are not leavened with much humor. "The voice was like crude petroleum seeping through gravel, and, like petroleum, it was a fossil thing, the voice of a creature that had arisen on the planet when the South Pole was in the Sahara and the great cephalopods were the highest form of life."[9] The simile here is rich and timely, both for the seventies and today: modern petroleum-based civilization is in essence a Lovecraftian pact with the dead monsters of the past.[10]

For the most part, of course, Wilson and Shea make their Lovecraftian moves in the more metafictional mode of the ironic imagination. In a few flashback sequences, we meet Lovecraft himself in the nineteen-twenties, and the episodes suitably mix fact and fiction.[11] This Lovecraft is a strict materialist, but he is being threatened by mysterious cultists who object to him revealing their secrets—secrets that the author claims he simply cribbed from books written by "mental cases" and stored in the library of Miskatonic University, a faux institution that itself appears as part of the Cthulhu Mythos. "Remember what happened to Ambrose Bierce," threatens one anonymous letter, referring to the mysterious 1913 disappearance of the California fabulist Ambrose Bierce, who also invented terms—like Carcosa and Hali—that were reused by the fantasist Robert Chambers, who was, as noted, an important node in Lovecraft's literary web.[12] Another one of the cultists warns Lovecraft that the powerful occult societies

---

9 Shea and Wilson, 648.

10 For a theoretically sophisticated contemporary spin on petroleum necromancy, see Negarestani, Reza, *Cyclonopedia: Complicity with Anonymous Materials* (Melbourne: Re.press, 2008).

11 Including H.P. Lovecraft as a character or direct reference within Cthulhu Mythos stories is a time-honored tradition. See "Lovecraft as a Character in Lovecraftian Fiction", in Robert M. Price, *H.P. Lovecraft and the Cthulhu Mythos*, (Mercer Island, WA: Starmount Press, 1990), 32-36.

12 Shea and Wilson, 181. "Carcosa" also made an appearance in the first season of the HBO series *True Detective* (2014).

of the day have for the most part left him alone only because the readership of pulp magazines is so small. However, the source cautions, the situation is not likely to last as the genres of fantasy and science-fiction themselves begin to take off.

Along with thickening the implications of the Cthulhu Mythos lore, Wilson and Shea also put their own kind of pressure on Lovecraft's famous claim that the weird tale should be crafted with "the care and verisimilitude of an actual hoax." For this statement is more curious than it at first appears. As Clore explains, hoaxes cannot be presented *as* fictions and remain "genuine" hoaxes. But neither can fictions be presented as hoaxes and remain mere fictions. In some cases, the ironic imagination that surrounds fictions that traffic with verisimilitude creates the *impression* of a deeper veil, a second-order or "inverse" hoax, one that masks truth as the surface fiction. "The usual hoax: fiction presented as fact," says *Illuminatus!*, which derives far more power from the opposite conspiratorial possibility: "fact presented as fiction." The pretense of such a presentation must at once be veiled and clever enough to stir a deeper order of pattern recognition, so that a "structure of indefinite promise and possibility" looms between and the lines and stories. Here is where so many of the later Cthulhu Mythos writers, notably August Derleth, go wrong: they define and systematize the mythology, whereas it is precisely the contradictions and enigmas of the Lovecraft Circle's referential game that keeps the structure indefinite, but still structurally *growing*, and therefore still "building outward" rather than simply slotting into a particular imaginative logic.

An even more infernal elicitation of pattern recognition undergirds the dialectics of knowledge and insanity that characterize so many Lovecraft stories, and that also serve to draw the reader into the plot. As readers, we follow bookish and blinkered protagonists as they piece together alien and bizarre implications from quotidian fragments of evidence and experience, usually drawn from texts and dreams. As they proceed, they form incomplete patterns of possibility whose more ominous import we readers invariably recognize before the doomed characters do. David E. Schultz explains the resulting reader response: "The reader of Lovecraft's stories realizes that horror lies beneath the revelation. But as one closes the pages of the story just read, one realizes that a greater horror has not been stated…In our enlightenment, we have been drawn into and forced to become part of the horror and we are helpless to retreat." [13] At times in his letters, Lovecraft claimed that he was "of course" not interested in *actually* fooling his readers with his invented mythology. But critics rightly contest this claim.[14] To use the term anachronistically, Lovecraft was something of a mindfucker.

Perhaps the greatest irony of Lovecraft's Yog-Sothery was how a game of esoteric hoaxing designed by an arch skeptic came to be appropriated by practicing occultists in the latter third of the twentieth century. Though the story is now well-known, it is worth recalling here. The first visible signs of the emergence of Lovecraftian ritual magic occurred, perhaps coincidentally, while Shea and Wilson were first composing *Illuminatus!* and can be traced to the British magician Kenneth Grant. Writing for *Man,*

---

13 David E. Schultz,, "From Microcosm to Macrocosm: The Growth of Lovecraft's Cosmic Vision", in Lovecraft, H. P, David E Schultz, and S. T Joshi, *An Epicure in the Terrible: A Centennial Anthology of Essays in Honor of H.P. Lovecraft* (Rutherford [N.J.]; London; Cranbury, NJ: Fairleigh Dickinson University Press ; Associated University Presses, 1991), 214.

14 See Clore, op cit.

Myth and Magic in 1970, and two years later in his 1972 book *The Magical Revival*, the renegade British Thelemic magician Kenneth Grant argued that Lovecraft was linked to actual traditions of ancient and contemporary magic through, of all things, his sleeping mind. Grant's story has good factual roots: Lovecraft was an extraordinary dreamer, whose unusually vivid, often nightmarish, and intensely detailed dreamlife directly influenced his fiction (the name *Necronomicon*, for example, came from a dream). According to Grant's writings, Lovecraft's dreams were esoterically objective; as such, *The Necronomicon* is a "real" book tucked away in the Dreamlands that Lovecraft's waking mind was too hidebound and timid to accept. Continuing to play the cross-referential game, Grant was particularly keen on lining up curious similarities between names, like Yog-Sothoth and Crowley's Sut-Thoth.

The year 1972 also saw the publication of Anton LaVey's *The Satanic Rituals*, a companion text to the Church of Satan leader's popular *The Satanic Bible*. The book includes two Lovecraftian rites written by LaVey's deputy Michael Aquino, the "Ceremony of the Angles" and "The Call to Cthulhu." In his introduction, Aquino legitimizes the occult appropriation of Lovecraft along much less supernaturalist lines than Grant, emphasizing instead Lovecraft's amoral philosophy and the subjective, archetypal, and possibly prophetic power of fantasy. This argument accorded with the language of "psychodrama" that LaVey himself offered as a non-supernatural explanation for the transformative power of blasphemous ritual. Within the Church of Satan, LaVey also founded an informal "Order of the Trapezoid" whose name was inspired in part by the "shining trapezohedron" in "The Haunter of the Dark."

To be sure, the Lovecraftian currents within contemporary occult practice sometimes veer towards esoteric kitsch, becoming at once silly and overly ponderous. But as Tim Moroney put it, in appropriating the skeptic's work, "they have committed no category error." [15] In other words, the warrant for the occult appropriation of Lovecraft is there for all to see, for it lies in the intertextual, metafictional, and imaginal dynamics of the texts themselves. The central Lovecraftian theme that critic Donald Burleson identifies as "oneiric objectivism"—that the dreamworld is real—becomes, as we see with Grant, the central vehicle for occultist legitimization. From this perspective, occultists impose a second-order level of objectivity onto the textual circuit that Lovecraft himself established between his actual dreams and his (meta)fictional worlds. Lovecraft himself noted this very logic in a letter pointed out by Robert M. Price: "Who can disprove any… concoction [of the imagination], or say that it is not 'esoterically true' even if its creator did think he invented it in jest or fiction?"[16] However, what is more interesting than oneiric objectivism from Wilson's more "skeptical" purposes is the LaVeyan approach, which requires no essentialist substantiation for the game beyond the psychodynamics of the play itself. From this perspective, Lovecraftian occultists are simply culture makers who have accepted the literary invitation to enter and extend the intertextual network of the Mythos and its flirtation with another order of veiling and representing reality. In the occultist version of the game, however, players place their bets on the element of

15 Tim Maroney, "Introduction" in Tim Maroney, ed;, *The Book of Dzyan* (Oakland, CA: Chaosium, 2000), 56.

16 Lovecraft, *Selected Letters* III, 326. Cited in Robert M. Price, "Demythologizing Cthulhu," in Joshi, S. T, *Dissecting Cthulhu: Essays on the Cthulhu Mythos* (Lakeland, FL: Miskatonic River Pres, LLC., 2011), 123.

verisimilitude within the framework of the "hoax." Within the circle of the ritual, or the referential network of texts, a different mode of ontology is allowed to take shape, one that "has a life of its own."

We all know this clichéd phrase, but perhaps we have not taken it seriously enough. For what does it really mean to say that a fiction has a life of its own? Playfully making a move himself, Michael Saler notes that, in Lovecraft's brief "History of the *Necronomicon*", the writer characterizes the dreaded tome as a translation of an earlier Arabic text called *Al Azif.* Saler notes that Lovecraft derived this Arabic title from Samuel Henley's notes to William Beckford's weird masterpiece *Vathek.* But Saler also jokes that Lovecraft may also have been alluding to Hans Vaihinger's text *The Philosophy of "As If"*, which was first translated into English in 1924. A post-Kantian thinker, Vaihinger argued that a great many concepts in science and rationalist philosophy—the atom, say, or the infinitesimal, or even Kant's *Ding-an-sich*—are simply fictions that we treat "as if" they were true in order for us to get on with our practical business in the world of sensation and moving bodies. Vaihinger was no irrationalist; as a pragmatist, he rejected the great doubts of philosophical skepticism, and maintained that there was a crucial difference between such useful fictions and true scientific hypotheses in that the latter can be rigorously tested experimentally. However, Vaihinger's notion of "as if" fiction as a "a more conscious, more practical and more fruitful error" has applications beyond the philosophy of science, particularly in psychology and literature; he also helps lend theoretical heft to Nietzsche's idea of necessary fictions.[17] Vaihinger also introduced the important idea that "as if" fictions, like hypotheses before they are experimentally proven, create an irritable tension in the mind. In most minds, this disturbance naturally seeks the equilibrium of settled reality provided by the interconnection of facts. When this "as if" tension collapses, in a mind or a scientific enterprise, fictions become dogmas and facts, *as if* becomes *because.*

Wilson was not a systematic thinker, either temperamentally or conceptually. As such, much of his thought (and occult practice) addressed conceptual models as "as if" fictions running on a "maybe logic" whose results must ultimately judged by their pragmatic or experiential effects. In technical terms, we might say that Wilson put forward a skeptical empiricism that framed both ontological and epistemological questions in pragmatic, pluralist, and radically constructionist terms. Wilson sometimes characterized his view of reality as a "neurological model agnosticism," as explained in the preface to the 1986 edition of *Cosmic Trigger*:

> the only 'realities' (plural) that we actually experience and can talk meaningfully about are perceived realities—realities involving ourselves as editors—and they are all relative to the observer, fluctuating, evolving, capable of being magnified and enriched, moving from low resolution to hi-fi, and do not fit together like the pieces of a jig-saw into one single Reality with a capital R.[18]

---

17 The quotation is from Vaihinger, Hans, trans. C. K Ogden, *The Philosophy of 'As If', a System of the Theoretical, Practical and Religious Fictions of Mankind,* (London; New York: K. Paul, Trench, Trubner & Co., Ltd.; Harcourt, Brace & Company, Inc., 1924), 94. For Nietzsche's concepts, see *Beyond Good and Evil,* 4.
18 Robert Anton Wilson, *Cosmic Trigger I: Final Secret of the Illuminati* (Phoeniz, AZ: Falcon Press, 1986), iv.

Here Wilson calls for a fallibilist sort of "meta-programming" that deploys concepts but keeps moving forward by remaining open to the rupturing power of personal experience, including occult and paranormal experience. This radical empiricism, riding the line between inner and outer worlds, then becomes an operational vehicle of insight, revision, invention, and play. Though in some ways echoing New Age discourses that were emerging in the seventies, Wilson's theory is bound up with a practice that is both libertarian and, in an ethical, almost utilitarian sense, hedonistic. So on the one hand, Wilson called for a "guerrilla ontology" that critiqued, rejected, and made fun of the normative discourses or "reality tunnels" that dominate and constrict modern society, cultural behavior, and individual psychology. On the flip side, he trumpeted the creative, expansive, and ultimately mystical possibilities of self-reflexive reality-construction, a practice that remained open to a universe whose possibilities are not compassed by the settled human mind, but which also gleefully embraced the generative power of fictions.

Wilson's stance helps us identify an important current of modern occult practice, not just among Lovecraftian occultists but by other practitioners who work and play with the "as if" fecundity of fictions. These include Discordians and any number of self-conscious esoteric bricoleurs, including one crew who proved very influential on Wilson. The New Reformed Orthodox Order of the Golden Dawn was a vital Northern California Pagan tradition whose followers described themselves in one 1972 publication as "an assemblage of natural anarchists, bootstrap witches and alienated intelligentsia."[19] The phrase "bootstrap witches" here referred to the fact that, unlike the Gardnerian and related Wiccan traditions that had been imported into the States from the United Kingdom, the California group openly acknowledged that their practice began, not with an "authentic" transmission or hidden ancestral tradition, but rather with art, fiction, play, and experience. The origins of the order lay in a class taught at San Francisco State by the poet and film-maker James Broughton, whose assignment to create a ritual inspired Aidan Kelly, Glenn Turner, and others to begin a collective process of creative invention. Sampling different literary and mythological traditions, and pulling themselves up by their own "bootstraps", the crew transformed themselves in short order into a living occult current whose practitioners took the sometimes astounding results of their magical performances seriously as well as playfully.[20] After one particularly powerful early ritual, Kelly realized "that the Craft could be a religion for us skeptical middle-class intellectuals."[21] Wilson and his wife Arlen later joined two NROOGD spin-offs, the Stone Moon coven and the aptly named Moebius Circle.

The evident occult power of such fictional bootstrapping adds another twist to Saler's notion of "disenchanted enchantment." For Saler, disenchanted enchantment is an attitude modern readers learn to bring to their fictions so that they can enjoy the fantastic satisfactions of the imagination while refusing the credulity associated with religion and superstition. However, something additional seems to happen when this

---

19 Adler, *Drawing Down the Moon*, 162

20 Kelly, a PhD, would also go on to produce scholarly research that effectively destroyed Gardner's claim that his texts were products of a living but hidden witchcraft tradition. Kelly's social history of the NROOGD is contained in Aidan Kelly, *Hippie Commie Beatnik Witches* (Tacoma, WA: Hierophant Wordsmith Press, 2011).

21 Kelly, *Hippie Commie Beatnik Witches*, 23.

same general attitude is brought to bear on religious or esoteric practice by practitioners themselves. In contrast to Saler, we might call this skeptical or constructionist magical pragmatism *enchanted disenchantment*. Put into practice, in other words, an ontologically deflated and constructivist attitude paradoxically "boots up" entities that demand room to breathe beyond the safe circle of irony or even "play". In the words of the philosopher and sociologist of science Bruno Latour, such beings are asking for their own sort of ontological pasture. Here, then, is another secret: sometimes ontology, a being's claim to being, does not appear already existent but is instead *produced*.

Latour, no occultist, explains this process using the rather ugly term *instauration*, which is his attempt to improve on the well-worn notion of "construction". What Latour wants to do is to move beyond the usual social constructionist position that holds that social facts are "merely" constructed through human cultural processes and therefore have no ultimate ontological weight. Instead, Latour wants to describe those acts whereby a process of construction produces a kind of being that can now make its own claims on us. "The act of instauration has to provide the opportunity to encounter beings capable of worrying you," he writes. These are "beings whose ontological status is still open but that are nevertheless capable of making you do something, of unsettling you, insisting, obliging you to speak well of them."

Appropriately for us, Latour introduces his notion of instauration with the example of fictions. When Balzac writes that he has been "carried away by his characters", Latour thinks we need to pause and seriously consider the enigmas involved in the work of fabulation, through which one's actions make "others" get moving. When an author's characters take on a life of their own, we have the doubling that Latour calls, in French, *faire faire*: "but now the arrow can go in either direction: from the constructor to the constructed or vice versa, from the product to the producer, from the creation to the creator." Latour insists that this oscillation is part of the phenomenon itself, even if authors like Balzac are misspeaking, or succumbing to Romantic cliché. Yes the author is making it up, but something also escapes, and flickers beyond the circle of the subject it nonetheless depends upon. This is the flickering that takes place in what the philosopher and schizoanalyst Felix Guattari calls those "incorporeal domains of entities we detect at the same time that we produce them, and which appear to have been always there, from the moment we engender them."[22]

Latour also reminds us that, though the world is saturated with such "beings of fiction", and indeed unimaginable without them, our usual modern and materialist story divests them of any ontological substance. Fictions are pregnant nothings, unlike rocks or the second law of thermodynamics. However, this ignores what Latour calls the *exteriority* we find among beings of fiction, or what Lovecraft readers might call *outsideness*. However enigmatic the causal act of instauration or creative bootstrapping is, it remains a two-way street. Such beings not only appear in the imagination, or even deeper, but they offer us an imagination we would not have without them. As Bach fans we not only receive the master's music—we also receive the very *capacity* to appreciate Bach's music. As such, we creators and nonetheless subject to fictions in that we win our subjectivity from them.[23]

---

22 Guattari, 17.
23 Latour, 241.

Still, even as these beings of fiction impose themselves on creators as well as fans, they remain delicate constructions, "composites", as Delezue and Guattari would say, that depend on our own practice and attention. "They have this peculiarity, then: their objectivity depends on their being reprised, taken up again by subjectivities that would not exist themselves if these beings had not given them to us."[24] Latour acknowledges just how peculiar this line of thinking is, at least from the perspective of science and so much modern thought. "It's weird, yes," he writes, using *bizarre* in French, but this weirdness inherently already appears "in the art and manner of what exists." To the objection that all this weirdness simply proves that we only "imagine" these beings, Latour asks us instead to reframe the act of imagining as a relational ontology. It is simply part of the nature of fictional beings—Castaneda's Don Juan, Madame Bovary, Conan the Barbarian—that they need us to keep them going even though we are part of their invention. "We are part of their trajectory, but their continuous creation is distributed all along their path of life, so much so that we can never really tell whether it is the artist or the audience that is creating the work."[25]

Needless to say, Latour's "weird" ideas are particularly appropriate to the matter of Lovecraft's and Wilson's artificial mythologies. Instauration, however lame a term, helps us understand both the constructive contributions of fans and readers, and the networks that form both the content and the context of the literary game of Yog-Sothery. But Latour's notions are also extremely helpful in lending substance to the bootstrap witchery of NROOGD, the Discordians, and left-hand occultists working in a Lovecraftian vein. Like fictions, religion is constructed, but it is no *mere* construction. The "as if" is a springboard for real encounter, a delicate key that opens a Pandora's box. As Jose Ferrer notes, "Spiritual knowing is not a mental representation of pregiven, independent spiritual objects, but an *enaction*, the 'bringing forth' of a world or domain of distinctions cocreated by the different elements involved in the participatory event".[26] These "different elements" are material as well as psychological, and form what Latour would call a network. And the similarity of such networks in spiritual and literary practice suggests a conclusion of sorts: the beings encountered in religious experience are inextricable from beings of fiction, but are in no more *mere* fictions than fictions themselves.[27]

The weird slippage between fictions and supernatural beings is one of the central themes of Wilson's *Cosmic Trigger* (1977), which describes how the surreal conspiracies of *Illuminatus!* began to take over the author's real (albeit pretty far-out) life. Though the Cthulhu mythos itself was not central to the network that Wilson traces, the Lovecraftian game of intertextual invocation that he played in *Illuminatus!* remained a crucial meta-

---

24 Latour, 242.

25 Latour, 242 3.

26 Ferrer bases his claim on enactionist modes of cognition developed by Francisco Varela, Evan Thompson and Eleanor Rosch. These in turn draw heavily from the autopoetic systems theory described in an earlier chapter. See Jorge Ferrer, "Spiritual Knowing as Participatory Enaction," in Jorge N. Ferrer, and Jacob H Sherman, *The Participatory Turn Spirituality, Mysticism, Religious Studies* (Albany, NY: SUNY Press, 2008), 137.

27 Indeed, one of the reasons that Lovecraftian magic has come to play such an important role in the conceptualizing of "hyper real" religion today may lie in the fact that the beasties are so nasty that their capacity to unsettle us is simply much harder to deny than with more pacific entities.

model for intensifying the weird ontological dynamics of fictions through occult and psychedelic explorations. The important lesson here is that ontology is polyphonic, situational, emergent, and relational.

As Hagbard Celine explains in *Illuminatus!*, "When you're dealing with these forces or powers in a philosophic and scientific way, contemplating them from an armchair, [the] rationalistic approach is useful. It is quite profitable then to regard the gods and goddesses and demons as projections of the human mind or as unconscious aspects of ourselves. But every truth is a truth only for one place and one time, and that's a truth, as I said, for the armchair. When you're actually dealing with these figures, the only safe, pragmatic, and operational approach is to treat them as having a being, a will, and a purpose entirely apart from the humans who evoke them. If the Sorcerer's Apprentice had understood that, he wouldn't have gotten into so much trouble."[28] But though Wilson presumably understood this lesson, having allowed Celine to speak these words through his own hand, he still found himself in some rather remarkable forms of trouble.

---

28 Shea and Wilson, 599-600.

II. Land

N.

The House of God is
a strange palace
       and she looked beneath her chin -
the white silken robe
blackened and heavy,
riveted by a fervid flame.
      A fever from the skies!
      A rain of lust from Eden!
And drops of sweat cut-trace
the neck, and abet
the self-rising leaven
rolling even to the fold of her breast.

It was night
and she had already poisoned herself
by Romeo's bane,
      and it was taking effect
in the swamp and the hot
to the point of a budding not.

Oh dead Aphrodite!
Without a soft spot,
beneath. No stars, no stars!
where she was the strongest now a weakling
lies
– attempting to sigh.

One heavy breath
after another,
she gathered herself into her hold
and a soft breeze blew
to throw the mind in – and into the sacerdotal mold.
Of a storm the breath spoke
as she reached deeper and down

in her, somnambular lungs -
every pore was a door
a stretched sail on the wind
and every little hair was a ground.
... for the whole world to yell
for the whole world to yell!
"LAND!"
"LAND!"
"LAND!"

Neo-Chthonia

Kadmus

"I exhort you, daimon of the dead [and] the necessity of death which has happened in your case, image of the gods, to hear my request…"[1]

"Once sacrilege against God was the greatest sacrilege, but God died, and thereby the sacrilegious died too. Sacrilege against the earth is now the most terrible thing…"[2]

I. Revival

There seems to be a revival afoot; in some occult circles one hears talk of little else. It can be characterized in various interconnected ways, the most common of which is as the "Grimoire Revival".[3] From the viewpoint of Chaos Magic it can be seen as a revival of the so-called spirit model of magic in opposition to the previously more popular psychological model. Related to these two is recent extensive interest in *The Greek Magical Papyri* (henceforth called PGM) and careful studies by initiates into Afro-Caribbean religious and magical practices[4]coupled with an increased interest on the part of non-initiated occult practitioners. I've even heard it characterized, positively, as the return of superstition.[5]

As a lifelong practicing ceremonial magician and a professor of philosophy I would like to analyze as carefully as possible the implications and aspects of the different threads of this ongoing revival in order to envision its unique content and both metaphysical and practical implications for occultism in general. My central claim is that the one

---

1 *The Greek Magical Papyri in Translation* Hans Dieter Betz ed. (henceforth PGM) LI 1-5.

2 *Thus Spoke Zarathustra* Graham Parkes trans. p. 12

3 See, in particular, Jake Stratton-Kent's *Encyclopedia Goetica* published by Scarlet Imprint.

4 See the extensive work of Nicholaj De Mattos Frisvold including his *Exu & The Quimbanda of Night and Fire, Pomba Gira & The Quimbanda of Mbumba Nzila, Palo Mayombe: The Garden of Blood and Bones* all from Scarlet Imprint as well as *Obeah – A Sorcerous Ossuary*, and *Kiumbanda, A Complete Grammar of the Art of Exu.*

5 Just as important as newly published books, occult blogs and online discussions have contributed greatly to the development of the would-be revival and my own perspectives upon it. There are too many such blogs to mention, but I would be remiss if I did not mention the excellent work on the PGM at "Voces Magicae," "The Valentines: black magic, rock and roll, sex" along with a few brief but decisive online discussions with Ryan Valentine throughout the years, "Dionysian Atavism," Jason Miller's "Strategic Sorcery," Jesse Hathaway's "Serpent Shod," and Gordon White's "Rune Soup."

thread connecting all these elements is the thoroughly chthonic character of each of these developments, a claim that isn't strictly unique to me but rather is derived from my reading of Jake Stratton-Kent's incomparable *Encyclopedia Goetica*. I do hope to unify and expand upon several suggestions made elsewhere with several unique and, I feel, decisive insights of my own. At the most basic level my question is what it means for there to be a uniquely chthonic occult revival and what the chthonic insight can provide to the occult community and, indeed, contemporary society at large.

The grimoire wing of the revival consists of an ever-widening group of occultists and scholars dedicating careful attention to the full expanse of the grimoire literature understood as a viable and vital framework for a complete occult practice. This is in sharp contrast to the way the grimoires were treated in the Victorian occult revival where they most often played an auxiliary role, only a very few were focused upon (mostly *The Sacred Magic of Abramelin the Mage* and the so called "greater" and "lesser" keys of Solomon), and most others were written off as evil, dark, or low magic.

By and large most practitioners of contemporary grimoire magic approach it in terms of the independent and real existence of the spirits in question, even if when engaged in metaphysical speculation they are willing to side with the psychological model that would understand the spirits as manifestations of buried aspects of the individual or trans-individual psyche. In other words, the operative mode of grimoire practice is a realist one in which the spirits are presumed to be independent active entities.

It is this respect for the reality of the spirits, whether in practice alone or theory as well, that provides an easy and vital bridge between European and Afro-Caribbean traditions in which the spirits are understood to be not just independently operative but the main teachers of the tradition's wisdom and practices. It is this aspect of learning directly from the spirits rather than from texts, human teachers, or standing traditions alone that provides the impetus of growth and vitality that make Afro-Caribbean traditions so much more vital than the frequently hidebound nature of Eurocentric practice. Afro-Caribbean vitality consists of at least two main characteristics, specifically their widespread influence and importance for their home cultures at large and their ongoing growth and alteration via the agency of the spirits themselves. In light of these aspects they are also extensively practical traditions aimed at the addressing of worldly troubles and the improvement of the lives of their communities. The connection between the grimoire revival and the Afro-Caribbean traditions is made easier through the recognition that the very grimoires the revival seeks to rehabilitate have long been respected and used in the Afro-Caribbean context. In this, as in most things, the Afro-Caribbean traditions are far ahead of Eurocentric occultism and their living traditions are a fair model for the goal of the revival.

The lynchpin of the entire revival is, arguably, the increased appreciation of the role played by *The Greek Magical Papyri* in the western occult traditions. What has facilitated the possibility of any goetic or grimoire revival is the recognition that the grimoires are not, not originally and not essentially, books of Christian, Jewish and Arabic magic aimed at the inappropriate manipulation of angels and demons for worldly ends. Instead, the frequent overlap of aspects of the grimoires and the late antique papyri reveals both a surface and deep connection between western occultism and ancient paganism.[6] It is this appreciation for the central practical and textual line from Ancient Greece, Rome, Egypt and the Near East to early modern Europe that provides the clearest chthonic aspect of the revival.

II. Chthonian Metaphysics and Theology

To understand the nature and goal of the revival it is necessary for us to ask what it means for something to be chthonian. In its original Ancient Greek context it first meant dealing with those things on the earth and under the earth. When applied to gods and spirits, however, it came to mean two things. First, it meant the gods and goddesses of the earth, most particularly the pre-Olympian Titans. Second, it was connected with Hades and the pantheon of the underworld. These meanings, in turn, connected the chthonic with the generally dark anti-Olympian forces and the dead. This is largely the connotation it has retained, having come to be connected with the demonic or satanic once monotheistic religions claimed mastery over much of the earth. This, however, changed some of the most important aspects of the chthonic.

The chthonian, I would like to suggest, consists of several elements: a truly polytheistic metaphysics and epistemology in contrast to the often hard to see but all-pervasive monotheism; an anti-dualistic worldview; a world-focused ontology. Beyond these points it also has traditional historical connections with magic in contrast to established religion, as well as a focus on popular concerns and culture in contrast to the aristocratic or state adopted norms. Finally, the dead have always played a central role in chthonic worldviews and are beginning to do so again.

Although most people are familiar with the theological differences between the belief in many gods and the belief in the existence of one, people seem far less cognizant of the deeper implications and influences of the metaphysics embodied by each belief. We can understand the pervasiveness of monotheistic metaphysics and the promise involved in moving beyond it by understanding monotheism as consisting of two primary myths. These are the myth of unity and the myth of substance each of which involves prioritizing the One as ultimately superior and prior to the Many. Epistemologically this provides the basis for the belief that Truth is One, that there is some one potential accurate description of all of reality, which empowers the rejection of diverse or contradictory aspects of experience, belief, or life. This then leads to the myth of unity, the idea that all the diverse elements of any given subject of discussion can eventually be united and, in being united, reduced to some one principle. Unity and reduction go together, in this way, in an inextricable tangle. Each event has but one ultimate explanation. There can be only one right way of life, belief, or government. All gods are one God and all truths one Truth. The list of unifying and reductive principles go on and on, in each case lessening our grasp and appreciation of the full richness of life, reality, and experience. The myth of substance is connected to the reductive impetus embodied in the myth of unity insofar as it proposes the ontological idea that

---

6 To mention perhaps the least example, *The Eighth Book of Moses* which is an important grimoire largely overlooked in Eurocentric traditions but essential for many Afro-Caribbean traditions appears in two different ancient forms in the PGM.

all things must be grounded in, or made of, some one thing.

Polytheism is productive rather than reductive. Its gods are children of other gods and, often enough, half-breeds and bastards. Zeus is a third generation patricide, and yet is king of the gods. His priority comes not from being first, or being most fundamental, unified, or basic. His priority is in being most complex, the richest outcome of a long line of organic growth and differentiation. Indeed, the entirety of the cosmic forces of polytheism fit into a framework of production and differentiation. A polytheistic metaphysics and ontology understands reality as consisting of an ever-widening collection of differences without underlying unity. The related epistemology is one that seeks to increase the depth and complexity of understanding while appreciating the impossibility of ever reducing, dismissing, or unifying to One Truth the inescapable richness of existence.

There is one final aspect of the ascendency of the One over the Many that needs be taken into account. Where one has posited one truth or ultimate good the world nicely arranges itself into two camps. There are those who stand with and for the truth and those who are either in error or fight in favor of falsehood. The ethical and ontological implications of this are clear. Reality is divided into Good and Evil, whether Evil is understood in terms of privation as simply a lack of Goodness or is understood as a positive powerful force or entity. In this way, transforming the chthonic into the monotheistic demonic does indeed deprive it of a key aspect of its nature. Within a truly polytheistic view there is what is helpful and dangerous, what is creative and destructive, what is bright and what is dark, and so on but none of these overlaps with a standard of Good and Evil. The destructive might be dangerous, or the dark unhealthy, but not all destructive, dangerous or dark things are unnecessary or to be rejected. Reality has many aspects, some more pleasant than others, some more friendly to the aims of humanity than others, but none are open to rejection in the global manner of monotheistic ethics and its related ontologies.

These points form the necessary background of a chthonic view, and I feel are more than enough to recommend it to us especially when political and cultural concerns are taken into account, but are not yet sufficient to make the chthonic clear. The chthonic is derived from a division within the polytheistic framework. The Norse had their divisions between Asgard and the domain of the light elves versus the lands of the giants, dwarfs, dark elves and dead. The Greeks and Romans had their Overworlds and Underworlds, their Olympus and Hades. Based on this we can set up a contrast between the chthonic and uranic, the earthly and heavenly. Yet this distinction would be insufficient, as I hope to demonstrate.

We might be better served in thinking of the anti-chthonic as the pure, rather than the heavenly. Well before there was the monotheistic concept of evil as revolt against the ruling One, and therefore as sin, evil was identified with a more material basis – namely contamination and defilement.[7] Impurity, rather than guilt, was understood as the mark of this type of evil. We get very close to understanding this contrast, between the pure and the defiled, when we consider the role of the monstrous in ancient religions. In Celtic legend we have the one eyed, and often one legged, Fomorians.

---

7 See Paul Ricoeur's excellent *The Symbolism of Evil* for an extensive discussion of this point.

These were ancient gods often representing some sort of monstrous inhuman danger and power that predated Celtic culture proper. In Norse legend we have the giants and in Greek legend the Titans, again each older than the ruling powers. In each camp we find deformity and non-human characteristics. Many armed, many headed, having too much or too little of what would make a divinity parallel to humanity. These harbingers of danger are, at the same times, the representatives of impurity and defilement. The Olympian or Uranic is not, then, so much identified by its location in the heavens but rather by its sublime purity and beautiful perfection, order, and balance. This is all the more clear when we notice that the chthonic strain in Greek culture, for example, often identified solar deities as themselves being chthonic. We might also consider the role of Osiris in Egypt as clearly chthonic and yet not exclusively and not at the exclusion of him from the state respected pantheons. The order represented by the Uranic is, of course, not to be understood yet in terms of monotheism's positing of an unchanging perfection and oneness. This would appear most strongly first in Platonism and Neo-Platonism. Rather, Uranic perfection is a human perfection that can go along with the various misdeeds of Olympian divinities. The key is that the Uranic represents a system of purification and perfection arrived at through the forces of order while the chthonic was the realm of the more chaotic, mixed, diverse and impure forces. These distinctions can be found in Hellenistic Greece, for example, as a precursor to the insights of Plato and later Neo-Platonism and appreciating the role they play in the pre-Socratic context provides us with an understanding of the cultural and religious impetus that led to the development of monotheism very largely through the influence of Platonic thought.

But the Olympian/Chthonic divide was not the first form the Chthonic took, any more than the end state of our views of the Fomorians represents the role these divinities and entities always played in Celtic and pre-Celtic culture. Indeed, the ascendency of purity was historically a political move used to bolster specific social and political types of order. In Ancient Greece, for example, the Olympian pantheon was a reworking of older religious practices and myths and was used to unify the new social and political form of the city-state.[8] In this regard, the Olympian or Uranic gods tend to be aristocratic while the chthonic traditions and practices are more populist and maintain this popular vitality even after later religious reforms are championed by the state. This is why things are nowhere near as clear and simple in the ancient world as might be expected from my previous discussion. The Olympian gods maintain much of their chthonic aspects and Hades, in fact, is part of the Olympian order. The overlaps and confusions found in the Ancient Greek context are mirrored in many other ancient pagan cultures and reflect almost universally a contrast and conflict between older practices and myths which favored the chthonic and, indeed, seem to recognize little else. Newer ones seem to present an ideal political order as a repression of these earlier chthonic influences.

A fair illustration of this point can be seen in one of the standard versions of the myth behind the founding of the Oracle of Delphi. Delphi had always housed an oracle but originally it was a thoroughly Chthonic one, ruled over by an earth goddess frequently represented by a giant serpent. Eventually Apollo came along, slew the

---

8 On this, see Jake Stratton-Kent's *Geosophia*.

serpent, and stole the oracle from the earth goddess. On one level the playing out of the Uranic versus Chthonic Greek religions is very clear here, but on deeper levels things are, of course, more complex than they seem. The nature of Delphi was a unification of both the chthonic and uranic, as found in the dual process involved at the oracle where a female priesthood would become inspired (according to some accounts by the fumes rising from the earth) and speak in tongues while a male priesthood would interpret the chaos of the intoxicated speech into ordered and comprehensible language and meter. Here chaos and clarity combine to give birth to a riddle, for every prophecy was a riddle. So, Delphi was more a harnessing of the chthonic than a dominating of it. But, more than this, Apollo himself had transformed from an earlier god of war and disease – a thoroughly chthonic god – to an Olympian god of the sun, music, and prophecy. The dual nature of Delphi, then, mirrors Apollo's own history.

Already in the privileging of purity the ancient pagan world was on its way to monotheism, for with the concept of purity comes a world rejection that prefigures the concept of transcendence. Purity and transcendence alike lead to the immovable perfection of the One and the rejection of the many and the mixed. The Chthonic, then, will be those aspects of pagan pluralism that, at the same time, reject transcendence in favor of a focus on the world in all its complexity and "impure" mixing. It is here that the key mark of the Chthonic comes into play, it is thoroughly *this-worldly* such that even the afterlife is lived through and in communion with this one. The underworld is part of this world, as indeed the overworld is, and the spirits are real worldly entities not metaphysical essences escaped beyond the veil of the material. The spirits are with you and around you, and the otherworld is a place you can go to as part of this world rather than one requiring high mystical transcendence arrived at through purity.

The thoroughly chthonic nature of the worldview expressed in the *Magical Greek Papyri* has provoked much speculation. The editor of the latest English edition of the *PGM* speculates that we see in these texts a new religion that syncretizes the numerous Mediterranean and Near Eastern religions while casting them all in chthonic terms.[9] This view, however, fails to fully appreciate both the chthonic basis of Ancient religions which is so often covered over by later developments and the thoroughly mixed and syncretic nature of these religions. Pagan cultures have by and large been the ones voracious for the experience and use of foreign gods, and no matter the culture much of their practices and divinities have at one time or another been foreign. The *PGM* is, indeed, thoroughly chthonic and makes clear why the chthonic nature of a thing goes beyond some simple contrast between earth and heaven. The sun god Helios, who features extensively in the *PGM*, is a fully chthonic god there. He traverses the heavens, surely, but in doing so he rules over plagues and floods, over earthquakes and the dead. He transforms from hour to hour from one animal to another and, in short, is thoroughly of a mixed "monstrous" and impure nature while remaining this worldly rather than transcendent.[10]

We have illuminated aspects of the chthonic via attention to the monstrous but

---

9 PGM p. xlvi

10 For a detailed analysis of the nature of Helios in the PGM see Eleni Pachoumi's "The Religious and Philosophical Assimilations of Helios in the Greek Magical Papyri" in *Greek, Roman, and Byzantine Studies* 55 (2015).

we can make the intimations thus far presented clearer through reference as well to the animal. Consider the concept of divinities in Egyptian and much Ancient Middle Eastern religion. There we find divinities represented not as exclusively or primarily human but rather as blended animal and human hybrids. We see similar aspects of this in Native American and African cultures where some divinities take specific animal forms or are mixed with these forms. Here we strike upon a key aspect of the chthonic not yet fully addressed, namely its recognition of the spirits and gods as frequently foreign to human life and concerns. When one recognizes divinity in animal form, rather than the idealized humanity of anthropomorphic gods, one recognizes that the forces and realities of the universe are not to be understood or measured on a human scale. They can be dealt with, but not necessarily as one deals with one's neighbor, boss, or mother. Otherness is one of the defining marks of the chthonic, otherness to standard human life, which will come to be equated with evil once monotheism has thoroughly anthropomorphized the cosmos into nothing but a stage for humanity with a dominant model of what humanity should be. The chthonic, then, embraces the world without forcing it into a human mold or appealing to a life-denying escape through transcendence.

The chthonic, as this-worldly and non-anthropomorphic, provides a unique position for the spirits of the dead. The dead represent the link between the disconcerting chthonic gods and the everyday lives of people. They exist as a bridge between the human and Other. As such they are at the very center of any system intended to work with the realm of the chthonic. We should not, then, be surprised that one of Christianity's main attacks upon traditional folk religion and magic was to isolate people from connections with the dead and especially their ancestors.

The chthonian revival, then, consists in this re-emergence of early modern grimoire magic, understood in the light of *The Greek Magical Papyri*, and influenced through lessons learned from Afro-Caribbean occult traditions. Each of these elements includes, and indeed requires, a central role for the dead as the bridge or mediators between the human and the chthonian. It is an anti-anthropomorphic tradition open to the Otherness of reality with a pluralistic metaphysics and epistemology rejecting the rule of the One. Insofar as this is the case, it is also a rejection of "purity" in preference for complexity, richness, and diversity. Considering the horrific roads down which the metaphysics and politics of unity, absolutism, dualism, and purity have lead us, especially during the last century, it may just be a much-needed counter-force to the flaws from which our culture has too long suffered.

III. Transcendent Anthropomorphism and the Psychological Model

The metaphysical revolution involved implicitly in the chthonian revival also involves a rejection, I would argue (and perhaps be alone in arguing), of occultism's other great champion of the impure and diverse – specifically Chaos Magic. Chaos Magic's focus on the role of belief along with its related interest in "reality tunnels" and "paradigm piracy" derives from the anthropomorphic and anti-realist heart of modern science that is ultimately based on a subjectivist metaphysics grounding a skeptical epistemology

Despite modern claims to the contrary, every epistemology or method of gathering and justifying knowledge is first grounded in pre-emptive assumptions about the reality to be investigated, and modern scientific epistemology is no different. Put simply, modern science was grounded on the basic assumption that we are minds isolated within our bodies and interacting with an external world via the dubious but correctable means of our senses. Beliefs are the isolated pictures we form about the veiled reality hidden outside of our minds. The key thing to realize about this metaphysical picture of isolated minds interacting with external things is that it is thoroughly anthropomorphic insofar as it assumes, in a good Kantian form, that we are actively crafting beliefs (or being provided with them by other humans) that we then test against our sensory experience of the world. Beliefs, then, are human creations somehow other than the realities they concern. If we make sure to stress the Kantian position that we can only see and experience through the lens of our concepts and beliefs, in other words that our ideas are used in organizing and structuring any possible experience we could have, then we arrive at the idea of reality tunnels and the primary role of belief in the creation of reality-as-experienced.

The anthropomorphism I would like to focus on here is two-fold. It consists, first, in the claim that we are somehow isolated from reality through a veil of ideas and the senses and, second, of the related claim that ideas and beliefs come primarily from active imposition by our minds. This is anthropomorphic because, even as it assumes external reality is decidedly non human, it also assumes that all possible and actual experience and knowledge is thoroughly human. We can know and experience nothing that we do not first create. To connect back up to Chaos Magic, one way to understand this point is to see that even when a series of potential models for understanding magic or experience in general is offered, the underlying justification for offering such a series of models through which one can move is already based on the psychological model. Spirits, energy, information and so on are first and foremost, from this view, psychological posits on the part of active isolated human cognition, which is what alone allows us to choose amongst them and move from one to another. In this way it is clear that Chaos Magic as most often formulated is not neutral at all when it comes to metaphysical conceptions of the human place in the world; rather, there is a specific concept of a humanity trapped within its own head that can't be avoided at the base of its epistemology.

While modern science displaced humanity from being the center of reality in one sense, by recognizing that the sun and not the earth is the center of our planetary system and later locating our system in a backwater corner of a mid-sized galaxy amidst countless others, its epistemology eventually took revenge by repositioning the human mind at the center of a skeptical anti-realism. To the ancients, however, ideas were not subjectively posited but rather externally imposed by the world including its divinities and spirits. Beliefs were no different. This is, of course, the original meaning of the idea of "inspiration." As its etymology attests, it was literally a "breathing in" of the divine into humanity. Moments of courage and insights alike were external gifts from the gods. An anti-subjectivist epistemology doesn't, of course, require a belief in spirits and divinities as the work of numerous Twentieth-Century philosophers have pushed in this direction through exploring epistemologies in which the world directly provides us with ideas and beliefs without the need for divinity.[11] However, a fully chthonian framework can't, I feel, fail to oppose modern subjectivism with a refreshing belief in humanity's unity with the world. From this view beliefs and ideas are aspects of our experience of reality rather than lens or frameworks overlaying them. They may be better or worse aspects, ones which are more or less useful or distorted by other aspects, but they are still directly experienced aspects nonetheless. Modern epistemology is not just founded, however, on an anthropomorphism whereby the world is presumed to only appear in terms of human beliefs and concepts, but rather is also the last fragment of transcendence remaining following the death of the monotheistic god. At one time, we were understood, as in Plato, to be transcendent spirits housed in material bodies. Long after this view had been largely rejected the epistemology of the mind's distance and difference from the world around it remained, and remains still, in our myths of cognitive isolation and active conceptualization.

IV. Conclusion

Though the topic has not been exhausted, I hope that this sketch has made clear at least some of the unique aspects of a revival of the chthonic and what promise it holds for an occult culture that has been, perhaps too long, elitist. More than that, it should be clear that the chthonic revival has significant insights and resources to offer our societies and times in general. A living tradition focused upon and committed to this world that has escaped from the trap of dualistic battles between good and evil and poisonous obsessions with purity; a harkening to the voices of the dead for the improvement of the distressed world of the living; a pluralistic vision of the richness of existence that refuses to reduce the complexity of reality; a looking away from humanity's self-obsession in recognition of the Otherness of the world we inhabit and the entities with which we engage – it may just be that all of this and more is at least possible with this new revival. So, to paraphrase the quotations with which I opened this piece, I exhort you, daimon of the dead and the necessity of death, image of the gods, hear and grant my request that sacrilege against the earth be now the most terrible thing!

---

11 See, for example, the work of Martin Heidegger, Hans-Georg Gadamer, Hubert Dreyfus, and John Mc-Dowell to name just a few.

A Fragment of Heart

A contribution to the Mega-Golem

Kadmus

Something stirs –
Where once rivers flowed,
Where the ghosts of trees rest
Unremembered.
Something wakens –
From concrete
Once mossy banks,
And blinks.
It cherishes –
How the crows used to gossip in the branches
Just so,
And the stones of the river winked
With hidden quartz.
It shelters –
The echoes of days without time
When walks went on forever
And we watched clouds play tag
With our backs bruised with grass stains.
Something smiles –
Where slim stalks will grow
And angry voices will rise in joy
To demand life for the earth
The voiceful wind
The wine dark sea
The shivering wave
The silken sky
Once more.
Something remembers –
The songs we will strike
Like bonfires
In the fields at the end of history.
You can hear its voice calling us together

Hidden in the folds of the breeze
In the corners of the night
When no tread paces.
"Golem?" it asks,
"Call me Hope."

THE ONE TRUE CHURCH
OF THE DARK AGE OF SCIENTISM

Stojan Nikolic

"Atheists are of three kinds.

The mere stupid man. He has found out one of the minor arcana, and hugs it and despises those who see more than himself, or who regard things from a different standpoint. Hence he is usually a bigot, intolerant even of tolerance.[1]

The despairing wretch, who, having sought God everywhere, and failed to find Him, thinks everyone else is as blind as he is, and that if he has failed—he, the seeker after truth!—it is because there is no goal. In his cry there is pain, as with the stupid kind of atheist there is smugness and self-satisfaction. Both are diseased Egos.[2]

The philosophical adept, who, knowing God, says "There is No God," meaning, "God is Zero," as qabalistically He is. He holds atheism as a philosophical speculation as good as any other, and perhaps less likely to mislead mankind and do other practical damage as any other. Him you may know by his equanimity, enthusiasm, and devotion.[3]

There is a fourth kind of atheist, not really an atheist at all. He is but a traveler in the Land of No God, and knows that it is but a stage on his journey—and a stage, moreover, not far from the goal. This atheist, not in-being but in-passing, is a very apt subject for initiation. He has done with the illusions of dogma. He is tired of theories and systems of theology and all such toys; and being weary and anhungered and athirst seeks a seat at the Table of Adepts, and a portion of the Bread of Spiritual Experience, and a draught of the wine of Ecstasy."

– Aleister Crowley, "An Essay upon Number", *Equinox Vol. I No. 5 (Temple of Solomon the King)*

And finally, at the beginning of the 21ˢᵗ century we witnessed the appearance of a new,

---

1 Mr Daw, K.C.: M'lud, I respectfully submit that there is no such creature as a peacock.
2 Oedipus at Colonus: Alas! there is no sun! I, even I, have looked and found it not.
3 Dixit Stultus in corde suo: "Ain Elohim."

fifth kind of atheist, or rather, an entirely new combination of the aforementioned three kinds. They call themselves "new atheists" and they represent a growing movement, politically opposing organized religion, but also culturally stigmatizing all forms of spiritual pursuits as irrational and anachronistic. Many have categorized them simply as anti-theists. I further categorize them by borrowing a term from Robert Anton Wilson's "New Inquisition": "fundamentalist materialists."

Socio-politically, new atheists can be viewed as an expected, and I would add: much needed and long overdue reaction to the threat of a second connection between Church and State, mostly in the US, with the revival of Creationism and other religious schools of "intelligent design." Considering the rise of "political correctness", (self) censorship and "newspeak", being outspoken about something, or anything, is surely better than being a hypocrite. Furthermore, the hijacking of Islam as an ideological basis for terrorist attacks and suicide bombings further underpinned the new atheists' arguments. As such, they overlap with the secular humanism movement, particularly in rejecting religious dogma as the foundation of morality and decision making. However, it should be noted that secularism needs to be disarticulated from any atheism for a variety of reasons. First and foremost, these two -isms are simply not synonyms. One concerns itself primarily with politics, the other with (anti) metaphysics. At its core, secularism is deeply suspicious of any entanglement between government and religion. true secularism is a proponent of religious freedom as well as freedom from religion.

Socio-culturally, new atheists approach the understanding of reality from a purely rational, scientific standpoint, claiming the "God Hypothesis" is a valid scientific hypothesis, having effects in the physical universe, and like any other hypothesis can be tested and falsified. The new atheists believe science is now capable of investigating at least some, if not all, supernatural claims, thus dismissing all other arguments as pseudoscience and superstition. Moreover, they have engaged in a series of logical disproofs of the existence of a God in their campaigns to reduce the influence of organized religion and spirituality in the public sphere, attempting to promote some kind of a cultural change. This also comes as a predictable reaction to the eclectic new age movement, the most recent form of Western esotericism that blossomed during the hippie era.

But, instead of a purely intellectual movement, this activism often comes across as just another form of proselytizing, suggesting a paradoxical "evangelical nature" of new atheism. It assumes that it has a Good News to share, at all cost, for the ultimate future of humanity, by the conversion of as many people as possible. Part of being this kind of atheist is to preach to the heathen masses and seek to save them from their false gods by converting them to the Truth. Agreed, considering the alternatives, liberal societies are well worth defending. But there is no reason for thinking these societies are the alpha and omega of a species-wide secular civilization the kind of which evangelical atheists dream. The struggle for secularism ultimately requires more liberalism, not more atheism or any other -ism for that matter. New atheists can in fact be viewed as mirror images of their counterparts, the religious fundamentalists – intolerant and discriminatory to the point of bigotry. Hence their routine breaches of social etiquette as they go around bullying people that they are deluded, their interest in seeking out and creating conflicts that will lead to media publicity, thus leveraging their relatively small numbers into greater public attention and fostering the perception that they are the legitimate representatives of unbelievers in general. No wonder they have been called "militant atheists."

It is the opinion of this author that objective science is simply incompatible with prejudice and dogma. However, by assuming a dogmatic approach to the old debate, new atheism degenerates into some sort of blind faith, or perhaps even religious zealotry in materialistic rationalism, rejecting metaphysics as a viable tool for understanding the nature of being, discarding all criticism and claiming some kind of monopoly on truth. New atheism is awash with intolerance and new atheists are simply too emotionally involved to be objective, not understanding the cognitive dissonance between their real world actions and their thoughts, ideas, and beliefs about atheism.

In addition, logical positivism, which held the position that only statements verifiable either logically or empirically are cognitively meaningful is now philosophically bankrupt. There is also the epistemological problem of scientism – the idea that our only way of knowing anything properly is the (natural) scientific method, a position classical atheism was at great pains to avoid given its unsound philosophical grounding. Trying to treat religion as a whole as a scientific hypothesis which scientific methods could disprove is disputable. Science cannot actually refute the supernatural claims of religion because those claims are beyond its remit. Science is an epistemology restricted to naturalism, so all it can do is say what can and cannot happen according to our best understanding of physical laws. Magicians would say that this is simply "mixing of the planes." Science and religion ask different questions about different things. Where religion addresses ontology, science is concerned with ontic description. Indeed, it is their austere abdication of metaphysical pretensions that enables the sciences to do their work. On the other hand, religion, or spirituality in general, greatly depends, or at least it should, on the willed suspension of disbelief.

Back to the ideological framework of new atheism, we have identified a metaphysical component: "there is no supernatural or divine reality of any kind;" an epistemological component: "religious belief is irrational;" and finally we come to the moral component: "there is a universal and objective secular moral standard." At this point, the dread specter of relativism tends to be raised. Doesn't talk of plural moralities mean there can be no truth in ethics? If you set aside any view of humankind that is borrowed from monotheism, you have to deal with human beings as you find them, with their perpetually warring values. This isn't the relativism celebrated by post-modernists, which holds that human values are merely cultural constructions. Universal values don't add up to a universal morality. Such values are very often conflicting, and different societies resolve these conflicts in divergent ways. Religion is one of them and as such is definitively human. Though not all human beings may attach great importance to it, every society contains practices that are recognizably religious. Invariably the new atheists claim to be followers of Darwin, yet they never ask what evolutionary function this species-wide phenomenon serves. There is an irresolvable contradiction between viewing religion naturalistically – as a human adaptation to living in the world – and condemning it as a tissue of error and illusion. What if the upshot of scientific inquiry is that a need for illusion is built into in the human mind? If religions are natural for humans and give value to their lives, why spend your life trying to persuade others to give them up? Rejecting religion is no sure path to virtue; it is more likely to lead to complacent self-regard, or ideological arrogance.

New atheists are scientists who really understand almost nothing about philosophy, yet engage in philosophical arguments as if they were experts. In this light, new atheism's disdain for the discipline of the philosophy of religion looks like hubris or even anti-intellectualism. A community that vocally calls for critical thinking would enjoy critical examinations of how it could do better, or at least it would welcome such criticism. Instead, new atheists seem to think being rational means agreeing with them in all matters great and small and if you don't then you're irrational. The overall perception of new atheists is that they have gotten themselves into the movement to indulge in their feelings of superiority to those they disparage as stupid. They give out little impression that they are interested in the kinds of ongoing introspection and self-suspicion that are invaluable to personal growth. Instead, they are just there to throw rocks at the retards, often with no understanding of the complexities of history, culture, psychology, literature, art, anthropology, sociology, or contemporary geopolitical and socioeconomic forces. New atheists should not hold an entire religious community responsible for the actions of governments and fundamentalist state religions, and still they somehow manage to turn their contempt for religion into a contempt for the religious, at a time when reactionary bigotry is gripping both America and Europe. The problem with their response is not one of factual inaccuracy but rather of a profound lack of empathy for the subjective importance of faith. This does not automatically exclude the possibility of religious criticism but it renders strident criticism counter-productive for both sides of the argument.

Logically speaking, an absence of faith is just that; it does not imply active promotion of unbelief, nor does it involve challenging the spiritual beliefs of others. Why waste time and energy debating the existence of something that supposedly does not exist? If new atheists sincerely believe that the main problem is their opponents' nonacceptance of factual truth or evidence, why do most of them appear to limit the confrontation to organized religion or spirituality in general? Humans hold all kinds of irrational beliefs about reality and the world – including ideas that are possibly more harmful to humanity than religious ones. Culture is after all nothing more than some set of arbitrary illusions that we all subscribe to in varying degrees and forms. For example, what about the delusion that socialism is somehow sustainable, the myth of democracy, extreme left or right wing politics, the global brainwashing into acceptance of consumer utopia? The point is that dogma and ideological indoctrination are not restricted to religion. Humans do not need religion to be unreasonable; it would appear that we can get along being quite unreasonable without it. It is curious how society manages to tolerate people who hold irrational views about politics, foreign policy, economics, and cultural traditions. Yet new atheists do not seem so bothered about those ideas, and often manage to respect them.

Returning to the beginning; in his "New Inquisition" Robert Anton Wilson said that " the fundamentalist materialist - either out of ignorance of philosophy or out of sheer bravado or out of blind faith - proclaims that materialism is the One True Philosophy and that anyone with doubts or hesitations about it is insane, perverse or a deliberate fraud. This One True Philosophy is the modern form of the One True Church of the dark ages... The fundamentalist materialist is the modern idolater, he has made an image of the world and now he kneels and worships it. Fundamentalist science is similar to other fundamentalism, lacking humor, charity and some measure of self-doubt, it behaves intolerantly, fanatically and savagely to all heretics... The New Fundamentalists are firmly entrenched in power structures everywhere in the modern world and really act like a New Inquisition toward those who reject their Idol."

Admittedly, he used this rhetoric in an overly dramatic way and while I do not share his passion for conspiracies, the most recent acts of censorship and in fact slander against Rupert Sheldrake[4] left me seriously disappointed and concerned. Perhaps not as concerned as I would be if I were a contemporary of Wilhelm Reich, but would our shelves of religious, spiritual and "occult" books be burnt in a Dark Age of scientism? Would anyone be allowed to speak out against the materialistic dogma?

The dark ages are a symbol of asserting a false light in whatever day and age. If science is a willingness for the uncovering of truth, then to love the truth is not to own, define or control it, but to be free in the identification of such delusions enough to discern one from the other and be open to it. Yet if science in the true sense stops being a movement of living curiosity and degenerates into scientism, it will eventually become entangled in its own inflated ego, or sense of itself as power unto itself. Thus we will confuse the 'working models' with Reality. Nevertheless, even if enough people share the same psychological bias, even if they have a 99% consensus, they will hold no more validity in the uncovering of truth than a 'loner' who would dare to step out or not be silenced by the 'consensual reality'. If it were otherwise, the Sun would still be revolving around the Earth.

A humbler, inclusive and much more participative appreciation of consciousness itself, and human consciousness as a construct within it, remains available for a curiosity to challenge the 'truths' that exhibit qualities of fear, guilt and control mentality. Robert Anton Wilson spoke of a reality labyrinth, where "existence [is] regarded as a multiple choice intelligence test; the sum total of reality-tunnels available to an open minded or non-Fundamentalistic human at a given time and place."

> "...there are still people who believe that sane science has at least a friendly greeting for Atheism and Materialism in their grosser and more militant forms."

> – Aleister Crowley, "Science and Buddhism", *Collected Works Vol. II*

---

4 TEDx Whitechapel, January the 13th 2013 e.v.

The Labors of Seeing – A Journey Through the Works of Peter Whitehead

Miguel Marques

According to José Saramago, a word can only be explained by other words.[1] Words as defined by words... Like variations on a theme. Have you ever noticed how often we start with "Look!" when we want somebody to understand something, to really capture the meaning of what we say? As if to break from the mold that words put us in, one would need the help of images. Camelia Elias reminds us that images are subjective. As fluid as our perception.[2] Maybe that's why that in his work Peter Whitehead, noted cineast, falconer and novelist has given so much importance to images. And maybe, when I set out to write this text about it, I tried to focus on his novels. On the safety of words. The prospect of having something objective to write about.

If words can only be defined by other words, any attempt to describe Whitehead and his work will, necessarily, fall short. William Burroughs does shine some light on this little conundrum, by declaring words to be images.[3] An idea that Whitehead himself reminds us about when he writes "Hieroglyphs. Images which embody meanings that only later become words. Places and objects and creatures that double for words".[4] By thinking in images and with images, but mainly communicating with words, we're assuming that words could be used as a first approach... As a sort of concrete language that somehow points us to the right direction. A first step into comprehending something more vast. WORDS that somehow can become a SWORD and cut everything unnecessary. But also implicit through pataphysics is another association: WORDS / WORSD / WORST.

By comparison, images would be the better medium. "In the beginning was not the WORD. There was something which preceded it. The polymorphous, polytheistic goddess. In the beginning was the IMAGE. I MAGE. EYE MAGUS. Image-ination. Haunted words. Subverting words with fairish meanings. Seeing ghosts in words. Allowing the ghosts to emerge and haunt reason away like the fleeting fragile threatening phantom that it is."[5] Here, then, is the first invitation that Whitehead extends. To look at the body of his work and see for ourselves what it is about. To perform an AUTOPSY.

---

1 José Saramago, *A Viagem do Elefante*, Caminho, 2008 Lisboa. (English version, *The Elephant's Journey*, 2011, Vintage).
2 Camelia Elias, *Marseille Tarot: Towards the Art of Reading*, p. 18, EyeCorner Press, 2015
3 William Burroughs, "The Electronic Revolution", reprinted in *The Job*, Penguin Books, 2008.
4 Peter Whitehead, *Bronwgate*, Hathor Publishing, 1999, p. 152.
5 Ibid, p. 229.

A word that comes from the Greek *autopsia,* which means "seeing with one's own eyes." To perform an autopsy, then, is to dig for hidden riches, but more importantly, to use our own capacities to analyze what's before us and draw our own conclusions.

Looking at the whole of Whitehead's work is a little like looking at a tree. A Noh-tree, or Whitehead's guide to his work.[6] A mind map, where every subject leads to other subjects which lead to other subjects into an ever-expanding system. We could start at its root, and build from there. But at each branch, a question would arise: "which path do we take?" Better then, to follow a different approach; to take Whitehead's lead and look at images. At the images he himself selected when asked to describe what his work was about.[7] To start as he started and build our own narrative from there.

A stone carved with the image of a falcon, symbolizing Horus, on a pedestal, while in the following image we see Isis, in the form of a falcon, hovering over Osiris' body. His opening statement then, the myth of Isis and Horus. ISIS or I SEES, goddess of Nature, Fertility and Magic, attempting that most powerful of actions: to return her dead dismembered husband, Osiris, to life. We all know the story: having successfully reunited all but one of the scattered pieces of her dead husband, Isis goes about to re-create the last missing piece, a crystal phallus so that Osiris can come back to life. She then assumes the form of a falcon and stands there, hovering, as she is magically impregnated. And thus, Horus is created.

As perhaps Isis first foresaw, so too we no longer see Osiris, now god of the underworld, but something new. A god of fire, commonly associated with the sky, war and hunting. More than just a resurrection myth, what we have here is a re-creation story. The coming back of an entity, gone to the nether realms, bringing with it knowledge and the gift of vision. His very name, *hr.w*, which not only means falcon, but also seems to mean "*the one who is above.*"[8] In truest shamanic tradition, we have here the coming back of the/a Spirit, his body broken and shattered by the vicissitudes of real events. By escaping reality, he ascends from *chronos* - the time measured by a "chrono-meter"; the sequential time and the time that marks the erosion of everything - to *kairos*, or the time of personal realization; that supreme moment beyond current events. By returning to the *chronos*, the Shaman descends again to our reality, bringing with him the tools to address the problems he first was faced with. Transformed through the forces of Nature, he comes as a problem-solver, as a healer, his journey through the nether realms allowing him to see not only the linear, concrete space-time continuum, but also everything that is beyond it. He brings a new perspective, gained by superimposing both images, divine and concrete, in the same structure, in a way not too dissimilar to a hologram. Or perhaps, a HALLOW GRAM...

Is this experience, then, a return to Nature? One could say that. In our lives, it's easy to get lost in the endless stream of tasks and commitments that we have to perform. As Agustina Bessa-Luis once wrote, "each individual has a limited room to operate and his brain works on a small circle of observations; its evolution, restricted to what

---

6 *Nohzone* site, http://www.nohzone.net (last accessed March 1st, 2015).
7 Peter Whitehead, "Seeing Through Stone: Image Montage", in Drake Stutsman (Ed.), *Framework*, 52, Nr. 2, pp. 959-974, Wayne State University Press, 2011.
8 Meltzer, Edmund S. Meltzer, "Horus", in D. B. Redford (Ed.), *The ancient gods speak: A guide to Egyptian religion*, Oxford University Press, 2002, New York.

surrounds it and the nearest exterior factors."[9] Such is the realm of rationality and concrete reality. Society, with all its precepts, succeeded only in developing an artificial world, outside the biological rhythms of Nature. But, as Agustina also tells us, "reason is a recent acquisition of the cerebral functions and it's easily eclipsed, even if only for a few moments." What the Isis and Horus myth tells us, is that by returning to Nature, by embracing Nature, we can transcend our view of reality. In a way, this shamanistic experience, as with all true magical experiences, dumbs us down. It dumbs us down on Science, and Art, and Culture. It allows us to let go of all societal restraints and look at things with a new pair of eyes. The same pair of eyes we had with us before our education, our introduction to Society's ways started.

This idea of isolation of Society to approach the *kairos* experience often appears in Whitehead's work. It is usual to see characters retreating from their current world in order to pursue a quest that mirrors a need for knowledge. Such is the case of Raymond Faulkner, who retreats to an isolated house, in the company of Nora and Anna, to reconstruct a particularly important psychoanalytic case study (*Nora And...*).[10] Or of Matthew Sutherland, asked by two girls, Cindy and Georgina, to investigate the disappearance of psycho-pharmacologist John Faulkner, in the novel *The Risen*.[11] In Brontëgate, we follow the the story of the disappearance of Michael Schlieman, sent to the North of England, to record the conversations of Princess Diana, but more interested in unwinding the mysteries of the Brontë sisters. The investigation of Schlieman's disappearance is narrated in the Nohzone texts, a trilogy consisting of four titles: the novel *Terrorism Considered as One of the Fine Arts*, the e-books *Nature's Child* and *Girl in a Train*, and the meta volume *And Death Shall Have No Domain Name*. The first three novels, each giving us a version of the same story, and from which arises the forth novel, *And Death Shall Have No Domain Name*. We're in Durrell territory, here: *The Alexandria Quartet*, which follows a similar path. And again, we're reminded of the myth of Isis and Horus... In order to understand the story before us, we have to put its pieces together and then, through the use of our Imagination, our IMAGE-NATION put the novel together.

The same puzzle solving motive can be found in Whitehead's other books. Electronic texts left by John Faulkner, in *The Risen*; the letters and annotations that are scattered in *Nora And...* or the dreams and visions which populate the Milton Crookshank novels. In each case, the puzzle demands from the main character that he transcends his rational thinking. Just like Isis had to create a fictional/magical artifact, if our characters want to have any chance of success, they must also take a leap of faith and incorporate any resource that's available, whether they are dreams, drug-induced hallucinations, voices from ghosts and spirits, *et cetera*. In their own way, each character has to go from facts, or FACTION, to FICTION and back again. Or, to put it in another way, to be able to see both externally and internally. To embody Horus and his all-seeing eye.

In his essay on Whitehead, James Riley calls to attention the importance of Whitehead's views of Tiresias and Oedipus.[12] How Whitehead saw Oedipus as a limited

---

9 Agustina Bessa-Luis, *Antes do Degelo*, Guimarães Editores, 2004, Lisboa (English translation by the author).
10 Peter Whitehead, *Nora And...*, Brookside Press, 1990.
11 Peter Whitehead, *The Risen*, Hathor Publishing, 1994.
12 James Riley, "The Technology of Myth: Peter Whitehead as Novelist", in Drake Stutsman (Ed.), *Frame-*

man, capable only of seeing only what was in front of him and how Sophocles' *Oedipus Rex* was, "in reality", about the discovery, by Oedipus, of that higher realm from which he could perceive everything. Riley points out, as did Whitehead on his film treatment of Tiresias,[13] that even though Tiresias was blind, he was the only one that could get to the truth. And further states that the punishment Oedipus inflicts upon himself is not really a punishment, but a way to transcend his own limitations in order to reach (TOO RICH) a higher realm of vision. A realm that only Tiresias' presence seems to suggest. His mutilation is then nothing else than his way to open his third eye and start his Shamanic experience.

This relationship between Tiresias and Oedipus is one of the core themes in *The Risen,* probably the central work in Whitehead's *oeuvre.* The book starts with three different events all occurring simultaneously, even if in different eras. At the same moment that crystallographer Matthew Sutherland (a variation of Sunderland, or SUN UNDER LAND) is starting an X-ray diffraction experience on a pyramid-cut crystal, John Faulkner (or FALCONER) *"physicist manqué, alias John Raymonde"* (RAY WORLD) swallows a new psychedelic drug called *Tiresiamine* in the form of a pyramidion-shaped crystal, just as a door that leads to the "hidden chamber in the Great Pyramid of Pharaoh Cheops where the secret library of Imhotep was hidden was being branched by light and time and unenlightened man."

In common to these three events, the pyramid: a symbol commonly associated with burial practices. But also, the place where pharaohs would start their journey into the after-life. A symbol of passage, of re-awakening. Of resurrection. The pyramidal prism, we are also told, with which the ancient Egyptians created holograms. Or the same pyramidal prism that Newton used to disperse white light into its different components... A combination of several radiations with different wavelengths. And right from the beginning of the book, we witness the clash between two different perspectives: Modern Physics and Ancient Egyptian mythology; New and Old Knowledge; between the Profane, Outside World and the Sacred, Inside World.

It is noteworthy to point out how the very name of these two characters already hint at their part in the novel. John Faulkner as The Falconer, the representative of Horus. He is in the process of being awakened, of undergoing the shamanistic journey when the novel starts, thereby dis-appearing from our concrete reality. And Sutherland, the one who will discover Egyptian culture and, in a way, a whole world that complements the one he was living in. The one who shall arise.

The Risen gives us the trajectories of these two characters: of John Faulkner through the disks he leaves behind, loaded with texts and information that Sutherland must decode, under-stand and assimilate. If he wants to find out what really happened to John Faulkner, he will have no choice but to follow in Faulkner's footsteps, to attune to Faulkner's way of thinking. To harmonize. Like two waves that interfere constructively. Sutherland must make the leap from the hard/cold/concrete scientific arena where he lived into the unpredictable, strange world of magic. For this to work, he will have to find a scientific view of magic.

---

work, 52, Nr. 2, pp. 799-818, Wayne State University Press, 2011.

13 Peter Whitehead, "Tiresias, Film Treatment, 1985" in Drake Stutsman (Ed.), *Framework*, 52, Nr. 2, pp. 759-769, Wayne State University Press, 2011.

In a sense, this initiation is to be made public. To be shared. It feels like an account of something that might have happened to Whitehead. However, it is Whitehead himself that warns us when he writes, *"Just fiction. I always say this so that anything can be subsequently denied to those who assume that to write fiction means you live it too. You know, stories that I invent."*[14] The story does tell us of a scientist that received a Shamanic call. In a way, it does mimic the story of Whitehead's life, a young Science student at Cambridge who one day comes face-to face with a stone image. A ST. ONE image. The face of an Egyptian princess, believed to be princess Meritaten. An encounter that, according to Whitehead, profoundly changed him[15] and defined the remaining of his life. That showed him what would be his path of integration. Interestingly enough, such a meeting occurred in a museum, that modern home where the ancient gods can shine their light and wisdom, under the guise of "Art", and "Culture", to whomever wants to hear them... See them... And experience their teachings.

In *The Risen*, as in his other books, there's a constant feel of an autobiographical voice. However, at the same time, the author tries to keep its distance... As if more important than to look at his particular experience, we should instead pay attention to what he is telling us. To follow in his footsteps, yes, but according to our own pace and our own sensibilities. In a sense, it's almost as if he's telling us to look at the characters as an alter-ego. A doppelganger. He is telling us to trust the story, but not the storyteller. From FACTS to FICTIONS and back again.

To follow his example, one only has to escape from this world. To break out from the Iron Prison, as Philip K. Dick would put it[16], or Rationality, if we follow Whitehead's terminology, and finally mend that distance that separates us from Nature/Wholeness/the *Kairos* experience. If Reason closes the Third Eye, we escape by going in the other direction. We already turn to magic in our everyday lives, by creating complex virtual worlds/fictions/parlor tricks whose main purpose is to convince us that we can indeed live in the concrete world, to make it bearable. "Have you ever had the impression you're creating reality the way they used to improvise those really low budget, and I mean *low* budget movies? Like they used *real* places to shoot it?"[17]

In his work, Whitehead suggests that we should use the same resources to live magically, to walk between Worlds and like Tiresias, like Horus if you like, to become aware of the ground we step on. To again paraphrase Camelia Elias, "Walking between worlds is not a question of what we believe, but rather a question of what we practice. If we practice awareness of our expectations, and of how each world behaves according to our expectations - be it this world physical or metaphysical - then we get a lot more out of it than if we merely speculated on the conditions for the existence of each of these worlds."[18]

To achieve this, we each should find our own personal story. The search for the "I."

---

14 Peter Whitehead, *Brontëgate*, Hathor Publishing, 1999, p. 1.

15 Peter Whitehead, "Head of an Arnana royal female, possibly Meritaten", in http://www.fitzmuseum.cam.ac.uk/gallery/hiddenhistories/biographies/bio.html?/inspiration/whitehead (last accessed February 28rth, 2015).

16 Philip K. Dick, *Valis*, Vintage, later edition, 1991.

17 Carmen St. Keeldare, *The Booker Prize Fix: Pulp Election*, p. 46, BlueDove Publishing, 1996.

18 Camelia Elias. "The Arts of the Night: Circumventing the Sign", *in* Todd Landman (Ed.), *The Magiculum*, pp. 124-147, EyeCorner Press, 2014.

Or the EYE. Those images, characters, gods and myths that totally haunt us, and come to understand them. To view our lives as a re-enactment of that same myth. Fortunately, we don't have to be as literal as Oedipus. Some people do it with drugs. Some with meditation. Some need to go through complex rituals, while others simply have to whirl and dance. Because, in the end, it's about that image that lingers in our mind long after the show is over. It is about ourselves.

The Conception of Number
According to Aleister Crowley

Renata Wieczorek

In the first chapter of *Liber AL vel Legis* there is a mysterious sounding thesis (AL I:4) that says: "Every number is infinite, there is no difference."

In this paper I would like to analyze Crowley's commentary to it published in *Liber 777*[1] in order to show that his approach to the conception of number presupposes interesting and unorthodox meta-mathematical, as well as philosophical theories that anticipate some of the achievements and discoveries of modern science and mathematics. It gives some insight into the concept of infinity, an idea that was widely discussed by various philosophers and mathematicians, and as such, it is worthy of study from a philosophical perspective. I discuss philosophical implications of Crowley's understanding of the two conceptions (number and infinity) which may result in a better comprehension of the actual mathematical infinity. I also give a short study of mathematical and other formal languages as tools for modeling some aspects of physical reality, especially those characterized by variation and change.

The conception of number from Pythagoras to Crowley

Mathematicians and philosophers differed on the nature and existence of mathematical objects, including numbers. Some of them, like Pythagoras and Plato, believed numbers "dwell" in the realm of ideas. Gödel and Cantor maintained that numbers and other mathematical objects exist independently of the human mind and are, in a way, "things". Others, among whom we find Dedekind, Gauss and Kroenecker, claimed that they depend mostly on human cognitive activity and as such should be treated as products or constructions of the mind.

According to Pythagoras and his followers, numbers were the essence of existence, the rulers of forms and ideas; laws of mathematics indicated laws of nature. They treated numbers as spatial quantities, forces that existed and acted in the world, not only abstract ideas as they seemed to be understood by Plato.

However, while incommensurable quantities were discovered, the belief that the physical world reflects the realm of real numbers became difficult to maintain. The discovery is ascribed to Pythagoras and his followers, though they preferred to keep it in secret since it obviously didn't fit with their philosophical, mystical and religious system

---

1 A. Crowley, *Liber 777 and Other Qabalistic Writings of Aleister Crowley*, Appendix B, *What is a "Number" or a "Symbol"?*, Weiser Books, Boston, MA/York Beach, ME, 1986, p. 127-137. The paper was first published in 1912.

of beliefs. This problematic issue, together with some difficulties with understanding the conception of infinity, resulted in replacing numbers with geometrical figures and operations upon them. Numbers started to be seen as segments made of units by finite addition.

Nonetheless, the accepted idea of mathematics was basically that a number is merely a term in a series homologous in character. Mathematical arguments and definitions were based on conception which admits the identity of 2 plus 1 and 1 plus 2. In other words, according to the "orthodox" mathematical approach, every number was no more than a statement of relation.[2]

According to Crowley, the nature of every number is a thing peculiar to itself, a thing inscrutable and infinite, a thing inexpressible, even if we could understand it. In his words, a number is an unique and necessary element in the totality of existence.[3] Any number possesses an infinite variety of powers to transform any other number, even by a primitive process of addition. We observe, he says, also how the manipulation of any two numbers can be arranged so that the result is incommensurable with either, or even so that ideas are created of a character totally incompatible with our original conception of numbers as series of positive integers. We obtain unreal and irrational expressions, ideas of wholly different order, by a very simple juxtaposition of such apparently comprehensible and commonplace entities as integers. Every number is a thing in itself possessing an infinite number of properties peculiar to itself.[4]

Numbers relate to each other (though these relations are in fact only illusory) in complicated and incomprehensible (for a finite mind) ways: the quantity of properties that enables a given number to interact with other numbers is infinite.

UNRAVELING THE MYSTERY OF INFINITY

The microcosm is an exact image of the Macrocosm; the Great Work is the raising of the whole man in perfect balance to the power of Infinity.[5]

Infinity has played a key role in the conceptual development of mathematics. The need to carry on infinite processes of reasoning or arithmetical procedures with infinite quantities has been the basis for many achievements in mathematics and science. The concept and its enigmas and profound questions implied by them have played an important role in the formulation of the conceptions of Euclid, as well as these of Russell, Gödel and Cantor.

Infinity can be understood as a process, a state or a mode of reasoning. It refers to something *without any limit* but the Latin term *infinitas* from which it is derived can be translated as "unboundedness". In mathematics, infinity is often treated as if it were a number (i.e., it counts or measures things: "an infinite number of terms") but it is not the same sort of number as the real numbers. In number systems incorporating

---

2 A. Crowley, *Liber 777 and Other Qabalistic Writings of Aleister Crowley*, Appendix B, *What is a "Number" or a "Symbol"?*, Weiser Books, Boston, MA/York Beach, ME, 1986, p. 129.

3 Ibid., p. 135.

4 Ibid., p. 134.

5 A. Crowley, *Magick In Theory and Practice*, 1929, chapter 0.

infinitesimals, the reciprocal of an infinitesimal is an infinite number, i.e. a number greater than any real number. During the late 19th and early 20th centuries many ideas related to infinity and infinity sets were formalized by Georg Cantor. In the theory he developed, there are infinite sets of different sizes (called cardinalities). For example, the set of integers is countably infinite, while the set of real numbers is uncountably infinite. In Cantor's system of transfinite numbers the first transfinite cardinal is *aleph null* ($\aleph_0$), the cardinality of the set of natural numbers.

The philosophy of mathematics discriminates between two types of infinity: actual and potential. Both types are connected with the conception of infinite sets. The latter kind of infinity (potential) is described as inflation of a finite number (set) above (or beyond) finite boundaries or diminishing below any finite limit. Actual infinity is a set that is unchanged, fixed and determined while transcending every finite set. Cantor distinguished three kinds of actual infinity: (1) absolute actual infinity, (2) infinity that can be found in the actual world, and (3) mathematical infinity which we can encompass with abstract thought. The first kind of actual infinity Cantor named God and claimed it is transinfinite, incomprehensible with ordinary thought and incomparable with the mathematical infinity, in which he did not agree with earlier theories of Bolzano, who believed the Absolute Infinity can be connected with mathematical truths and understood by means of reason.

Crowley's conception of infinity seems to be neither purely of Cantor's nor Bolzano's type, though perhaps joining the two into a new synthesis. He reveals his thoughts in a symbolic and mystical language rather than by using purely mathematical concepts, so that it is difficult to translate his conception into a more "scientific" way of speaking. The real difficulty, however, is rather the limitations of the human capacity of reasoning and necessity to transcend reason itself in order to "catch" the meaning of Infinity.

In *Liber Legis*, the central text of the Thelemic system developed by Crowley, infinite space is called the goddess NUIT, while the infinitely small and atomic yet omnipresent point is called HADIT.

These two are unmanifest. One conjunction of these infinites is called RA-HOOR-KHUIT, more correctly, HERU-RA-HA, to include HOOR-PAAR-KRAAT, a unity which includes and heads all things.

In Crowley's words, this profoundly mystical conception is based upon actual spiritual experience, but the trained reason can reach a reflection of this idea by the method of logical contradiction which ends in reason transcending itself. An immeasurable abyss divides the truth from all manifestations of Reason or the lower qualities of man. In the ultimate analysis of Reason, we find all reason identified with this abyss. Yet this abyss is the crown of the mind. Purely intellectual faculties all obtain here. This abyss has no number, for in it all is confusion.[6]

It is worth noting that two infinite sets can be in such a relation to each other that each element of one of them can be paired with an element of the other. No element remains unpaired and elements in pairs do not repeat (the imagination is isomorphic), yet one of the sets contains the other as its proper part. This property was discovered by the ancient philosopher Proclos and was used (probably independently of this early

---

6 A. Crowley, *Magick In Theory and Practice*, chapter 0.

discovery) to define infinite collection in the 20th century by Richard Dedekind.

If we take into consideration that, according to Crowley, NUIT can be understood as infinite "space" containing all possibilities (compare Wittgenstein's *Tractatus Logico-Philosophicus*[7]) and HADIT as an infinitely small point containing all within, this mystical vision seems to be very close to what philosophers and mathematicians have tried to show or describe by means of rational thought and formal language. It is worth mentioning that a similar idea seemed to be shown in an artistic, hence non-propositional way, in the *Vierge Ouvrante*.

Infinity can be represented in many ways. It seems that on some level of (infinite) abstract thought it loses all qualities comprehensible to human reason. It is what apparently Cantor meant by the concept of absolute actual infinity (God). It must be remembered however that for him this kind of infinity was totally beyond any thought. Bolzano tried to "tame" infinity and claimed the actual absolute infinite set (which he also identified with God) can be understood in terms of mathematical infinity, hence he seemed to say human reason is capable of "catching" the true meaning of the former kind of infinity.

For Crowley, Absolute Infinity, which seems to be in a way identified with the mystical cabbalistic conception of Nothing(ness), is neither beyond the ability of thinking and understanding, nor is it to be understood in terms of "ordinary" mathematics. Mathematical concepts can only serve as a "ladder" that enables transcending reasoning and seeing the world (infinity) as it is. It is what Ludwig Wittgenstein meant in his *Tractatus*. Some things can be *shown*, never *said* (described by means of concepts). However, Wittgenstein, in the mystical part of his book, recommended keeping silence when we reach truths transcending the intellectual way of comprehending. Crowley does quite a contrary yet very similar thing: he says it is possible to "translate" our transcendental understanding back into "ordinary" language – it even should be done, contrary to what traditional mystics say[8] – but this interpretation will always serve only as a sign leading beyond the limits of reason.

According to Crowley, our detailed, scientific and everyday knowledge is so contemptibly minute, that it is hardly worth reference, save that our shame may spur us to increased endeavor. The knowledge we should strive for is very general and abstruse, of a philosophical and almost magical character: this consists principally of the conceptions of pure mathematics. It is, therefore, legitimate to say that pure mathematics is our link with the rest of the universe and with "God."[9]

THE LANGUAGE IN WHICH WE DESCRIBE/CREATE THE WORLD

The original formulation of infinitesimal calculus by Isaac Newton and Gottfried Leibniz used infinitesimal quantities. In the 20th century, it was shown that this treatment could be put on a rigorous footing through various logical systems, including smooth infinitesimal analysis and nonstandard analysis.

Calculus and analysis as a systematization of the study of infinity as a process are

---

7 L. Wittgenstein, *Tractatus Logico-Philosophicus*, Kegan Paul, Trench, Trubner, 1922.
8 Compare A. Crowley, *Little Essays Toward Truth*, London 1938.
9 A. Crowley, *Magick In Theory and Practice*, 1929, chapter 0.

powerful tools for modeling the aspects of physical reality that are characterized by variation and change.

However, it must be remembered that the language we use to describe the world is as much a tool for description as for creation. If we additionally consider that within mathematics or any other science we have many theories, sometimes incompatible with each other, the question of knowing the truth (the *only* true description or theory) starts to become problematic. We always act within a conceptual framework or a scheme and answers to our questions, no matter how profound or basic, seem determined by the very framework we use, as much as by the nature of the "world" we describe (and hence, create, in a way). There can't be a "more/less true" framework or scheme. Formal languages and the frameworks they offer are tools, conventions, and as such can't be valued as true or false; their only value is being useful.

Crowley's approach seems to be very similar. He says mathematical and other (semi) formal languages, including that of cabbalistic systems, are conventions – we should ask if they serve well for pragmatic ends, not whether they are true or false.

We use the instrument of science to inform us of the nature of the various objects which we wish to study, but our observations never reveal the thing as it is in itself. They only enable us to compare unfamiliar experiences with familiar experiences. The use of an instrument necessarily implies the imposition of alien conventions. When we say that we see a thing, we only mean that our consciousness is modified by its existence according to a particular arrangement of lenses and other optical instruments, which exist in our eyes and not in the object perceived.[10]

Mathematical theories are based on a set of propositions called axioms which are neither justified or proven. For a long time it was believed that Euclidian geometry was the true system, perfectly describing physical reality. Immanuel Kant even claimed Euclidian geometry is *necessarily* true. In the 19th century the claim was questioned by discovery of non-Euclidian geometries, which rejected the axiom system of Euclidian geometry. Bolyai, Lobatschewsky, and Riemann have shown conclusively that a consistent system of geometry can be erected on any arbitrary collection of axioms. It was proven that the new geometries not only make consistent and coherent systems but are very useful tools for description of phenomena within Einstein's theory of relativity. The philosophical question was posed: which of the geometries is *true*? However, this question seems to be a profoundly wrong one. One geometry can't be "more true" than another, for the simple reason that each of them is consistent and coherent and we have no means (they would imply "a view from nowhere" – from outside of *any* of the systems) for deciding which of them represents truth. Geometry is a tool of description. When we wish to describe solid macroscopic objects, we use Euclidian geometry which proves to be the best to this end. If we want to give a description of events in Einstein's theory, it is better to choose non-Euclidian geometry. The systems are incomparable and their value rests in their usefulness. Hence, they do not offer true (or false) descriptions of the world, either. The descriptions should be seen for what they are: means of coordinating phenomena.

---

10 A. Crowley, *Liber 777 and Other Qabalistic Writings of Aleister Crowley*, Appendix B, *What is a "Number" or a "Symbol"?*, Weiser Books, Boston, MA/York Beach, ME, 1986, p. 136.

As Crowley says, it is commonly imagined, by those who have not examined the nature of the evidence, that our experience furnishes a criterion by which we may determine which of the possible symbolic representations of Nature is the true one. They suppose that Euclidian geometry is in conformity with nature because the actual measurements of the interior angles of a triangle tell us that their sum is in fact equal to two right angles, just as Euclid tells us that theoretical considerations declare to be the case. They forget that the instruments that we use for our measurements are themselves conceived of as in conformity with the principles of Euclidian geometry.[11]

We accept a given convention to quantitatively describe the world. If we take a look at the history of mathematics, science and philosophy, we will see a huge amount of incompatible theories and languages which deliver views from different perspectives. To ask which of them is "true" is like demanding a meaningful answer to the question "what is good for humanity?"[12]

The situation is inconvenient though if we take into consideration that many philosophers, scientists and mathematicians believed mathematics is the key to understanding the mystery of the Universe and God. The God Himself has been believed by many to be a Great Mathematician. Does Crowley's investigation reject this absolutist approach to mathematics? It doesn't seem so. He says, as mentioned earlier, that pure mathematics is our link with the rest of the universe and with "God". He also claims that each number is unique and absolute. The nature of every number is a thing peculiar to itself, a thing inscrutable and infinite, a thing inexpressible, even if we could understand it.[13]

This approach is close to that of the intuitionists, who say that mathematics as we know it – a system of symbols, axioms and theorems created by mathematicians – and mathematical *thought* are two different things. For the latter, mathematical language is only an imperfect means of expression. Here we have a distinction between rational a way of expression and inexpressible thought that "reaches" the "real" or true content. Thus the symbol (symbolic language) is a means for showing what can't be said and makes it possible to reach beyond its outward appearance. It is also a tool for translating into language comprehensible to the intellect the signs of what can be truly seen only in a way that transcends the latter. Hence mathematics is the key to understanding – if we treat it as a symbol system that opens the higher realms of knowledge.

As Crowley puts it, the situation is even more complex if we take into consideration that the apparatus of human reason is simply one particular system of coordinating impressions; its structure is determined by the course of the evolution of the species. It is no more absolute than the evolution of the species. It is no more absolute than that the mechanism of our muscles is a complete type wherewith all other systems of transmitting force must conform. Equally, of course, we have no means of knowing what we really are. We are limited to symbols. And it is certain that all our sense-perceptions give only partial aspects of their objects. Sight, for instance, tells us very little about solidity, weight, composition, electrical character, thermal conductivity,

---

11 Ibid, p. 132.
12 Comp. Nelson Goldman, *Ways of Worldmaking*, Hackett Publishing Company, Indianapolis, 1978.
13 A. Crowley, *Liber 777 and Other Qabalistic Writings of Aleister Crowley*, Appendix B, *What is a "Number" or a "Symbol"?*, Weiser Books, Boston, MA/York Beach, ME, 1986, p. 135.

etc., etc. It says nothing at all about the very existence of such vitally important ideas as heat, hardness, and so on. The impressions which the mind combines from the senses can never claim to be accurate or complete. We have indeed learned that nothing is in itself what it seems to be to us. The universe may contain an infinite variety of worlds inaccessible to human apprehension. Yet, for this very reason, they do not exist for the purposes of the argument. Man possesses, however, some instruments of knowledge; we may, therefore, define the Macrocosm as the totality of things possible to his perception. As evolution develops these instruments, the Macrocosm and the Microcosm extend; but they always maintain their mutual relation. Neither can possess any meaning except in terms of the other. Our "discoveries" are exactly as much of ourselves as they are of Nature. America and electricity did, in a sense, exist before we were aware of them; but they are even now no more than incomplete ideas, expressed in symbolic terms of a series of relations between two sets of inscrutable phenomena.[14]

<h2 style="text-align:center">On the lack of difference</h2>

According to Crowley, each number is unique and absolute. Its relations with other numbers are therefore in the nature of illusion. They are forms of presentation under which we perceive their semblances; and it is to the last degree important to realize that these semblances only indicate the nature of the realities behind them in the same way in which the degrees on a thermometric scale indicate heat.[15] We have no means of determining the difference between any two numbers, except in respect of a particular and very limited relation. We may also observe that each number, being absolute, is the centre of its universe, so that all other numbers, so far as they are related to it, are its appendages. Each number is therefore the totality of the Universe, and there cannot be any difference between one infinite universe and another.[16]

Gottfried Leibniz, one of the co-inventors of infinitesimal calculus, speculated widely about infinite numbers and their use in mathematics. To Leibniz, both infinitesimals and infinite quantities were ideal entities, not of the same nature as appreciable quantities, but enjoying the same properties.

Leibniz also claimed that the totality of existence consists of monads, and each of them is a separate universe. Each monad contains within itself all possibilities; each is an image of the whole Universe. The only "difference" between monads is that for each monad, different possibilities become actual. It makes us see them as different, though in fact there is no difference. There is no difference also because every monad is a separate Universe, a "thing in itself", so its relations with other monads are only illusion.

The idea that each element, no matter how small and "unimportant", contains within itself an image, or pattern, of the whole world, appears not only in philosophy and poetry, but also in very serious mathematical theories of fractal geometry discovered not so long ago.

<hr>

14 A. Crowley, *Magick In Theory and Practice*, 1929, chapter 0

15 A. Crowley, *Liber 777 and Other Qabalistic Writings of Aleister Crowley*, Appendix B, *What is a "Number" or a "Symbol"?*, Weiser Books, Boston, MA/York Beach, ME, 1986, p. 135-136.

16 Ibid., p. 136.

The structure of a fractal object is reiterated in its magnifications. Fractals can be magnified infinitely without losing their structure and becoming "smooth"; they have infinite perimeters – some with infinite, and others with finite, surface areas. One such fractal curve with an infinite perimeter and finite surface area is the well-known Koch snowflake or Sierpinski's triangle and carpet.

It is believed that the whole world may be of fractal nature – each element or fragment of it contains within itself a "notation" of all the rest that enables it to "re-create" the rest. Consider modern genetics.

Thus, if, according to Crowley, each number is the totality of the Universe[17], there cannot be any difference between them. There is no difference between one infinite universe and another.

Crowley's account seems to assume that:

1) Everything that exists is a reflection of everything else that exists.
2) Everything that exists contains a pattern of everything else that exists.
3) Each element is unique yet has its share in (and with) everything else.
4) If we look closely enough, we will see all.

Liberating our minds from the bondage of reason, and contemplating the world in its infinite aspects, we gain share in Infinity.

---

17 Ibid., p. 136.

FRAGMENTS OF FACT

Orryelle Defenestrate Bascule

The apparent friction betwixt fact and fiction is in fact a fiction
And in fiction a fact
The apparent friction betwixt fact and fiction is in fact a fiction
Instead a frisson twixt fact and fiction
May factualize fictions
And fictionalise the facts
A fusion twixt fact and fiction Is liable to warp our diction
And cause confusion with concrete illusions
Tangible tangents and graspable wraiths
The fusion of fiction and fact
Is certainty's faith?

This belief in either friction twixt fact and fiction
Or in fusion twixt fact and fiction
Creates opposing factions
Of fragmented faith
But whereas the friction's a fact to the fickle factitious
The pernicious fixaters of fiction-fact fusion depict
This fraction as merely a faction of fict
A fission twixt fact and fiction
Can fuse the facts with impossible acts
Confusing the factions which insist on distinction twixt faction and fict

Fragments of fact Keep things the way they are
The demons of stasis Bind us in our places So we cannot act
Beyond our allotted part
Whereas figments of fiction
Are like pigments of a pact
With an Angel of Art

Of course if we *fractalize* these fragments of fact
And figments of fiction
In a fact-fiction frisson fission
Of fact-fiction fragrant figment-fragment tangible illusion and vagrant cohesion

We might fact-fiction-fractal-fragment-fracture our brains
(So lets just stop there and play some music...)

We might fact-fiction-fractal-fragment-fracture our brains
(So lets just stop there and play some music...)

Conscious ExIt

Derek R. Seagrief

"Beyond living and dreaming there is something more important – waking up."

Uranus – the Awakener

That we have entered the 2000 year period known as the Age of Aquarius must be rather obvious to all, since we are currently exposed to such a great intensification of everyday living, experiencing a concentration of three days' experience into one single day. Our Baptism into the Aquarian vibration radically changes life on planet Earth and our human consciousness. In this article I want to share some of my astrological research regarding planetary patterns on the Death horoscope. My focus will be primarily the appearance of the planet Uranus and the sign Aquarius. Why?

Uranus reflects our capacity, as human beings, to attune ourselves to the larger system, and the sudden recognition of this bigger universe often has the effect of shattering our existing world-view. As we shall see through the astrological examples in this article, the strong presence of Uranus or the sign Aquarius on the Death chart, and related to the radix patterns, invites this accelerated awareness or what I am describing as a "conscious exit". For the evolved, the movement at death is towards freedom and liberation from the restrictions of the physical form – and an eagerness to meet soul friends awaiting on the other side. As long as human beings have recorded their perceptions, they have described some kind of cosmic order. Uranus initiates us into the Mind of God.

In the area of life ruled by the house in which Uranus is placed, we all long, consciously or unconsciously, to be Prometheus, the ancient Greek culture-Hero who brought to our world the gift of fire – enlightenment. It is because there is a promethean spirit within the individual, that is impelled to strive toward a different, freer place in a different, freer world. This spirit perceives society as imperfect and in need of change and reform, and the individual will seek, consciously or unconsciously, to be part of the vanguard which ushers in new social possibilities.

The current seven-year transit of Uranus through Aries (2011-2018) continues to encourage us to be ourselves, to individuate continually and to recognize that our uniqueness is an essential trait that we must nurture, support and express whenever possible.

Conscious Birth and Conscious Exit

When transit Uranus moved into opposition to my natal Leo Sun I was experiencing my 50th year and had my first child. It was a revolution and a radical change of lifestyle becoming a father. Then within a time frame of exactly seven years, less one day, my first and my third child were born in the sign of Pisces.

All three children started their existence on planet Earth through water-birth at home, a wonderful alternative method of natural birth, involving both father & mother, in sharp contrast with today's hospital system. This is suggested through my natal placement of Uranus in the water sign Cancer opposing my Capricorn Ascendant. Throughout my life I have often done things different than the norm, so becoming a father at a relatively late age was just another chapter in this continuing journey. When asked the inevitable question about "why so late", I often automatically replied that it was because I had truly met the right woman. But then I started to add that one of the greatest gifts that we as parents can bestow upon our children is the fact that we are "conscious parents", self-aware and integrated with body, heart, mind and soul.

I have been an enthusiastic promoter of "conscious birth" these past 12 years, so it was almost predictable that I would ultimately find myself progressively more involved with the opposite side of the equation - "conscious death" or "conscious exit", the title of this article.

It is an unfortunate fact in society that both the miracle of Birth and the Great Adventure of Death has been reduced to a material event.

We are two-fold beings, at once human and divine, finite and infinite, dualistic and non-dualistic. On one hand we have a body and a personality which change, that age, that experience happiness and pain, and eventually die. We also are pure consciousness, living spirit, deathless, the subject that experiences our body and mind as objects. We live in a society preoccupied with the body and the personality, with that which dies. Death becomes the enemy.

One appropriate task as our years roll by on planet Earth is to recognize life and death as a unity. One's own life may be seen in a greater context, and patterns which escape our notice earlier now become vividly apparent.

So, to the extent you or I have been able to bear the brilliant light of love, of joy, the totally open heart while still alive, then dying will simply be another moment of resting in this light.

To the extent we turn away from love and pull back with fear in our separateness, then dying will come too soon and be too terrible to face.

Now is the moment to awaken. Live consciously – die consciously.

Aquarius and radioactivity

The location of Aquarius as the eleventh sign of the zodiac indicates that it governs the eleventh House affairs. Realisation of ideals, bringing the far-away future nearer is the keynote of the house and the sign. One can therefore state that as the future unfolds more and more people will recognize the goal of a "conscious exit", which is the cooperation between the everyday personality and the universal spirit. Spiritual astrology asserts that our 2000 year passage through the vibration of Aquarius makes us "radio-active". The phenomena of radioactivity transcends form.

There is a sudden hastening of the evolution of human consciousness in all planes, as we transcend time and space. Humanity is gaining mastery over the physical plane and steps into the mysteries of space. And with this comes an extraordinary birth - a *new science of immortality is in the making,* as we practice conscious living and dying.

While the conscious mind is asleep, we can learn things and receive instructions and training through inner group contacts. The future promise is that we can live in the state of *Samadhi* while being active in all levels of objectivity inclusive of our duties towards our fellow-beings. *Conscious existence* of man in all planes simultaneously is the definition of this new yoga.

URANUS-PLUTO CONJUNCTION AND SQUARE ASPECT

The current Uranus-square-Pluto signature in the heavens is a powerful and transformative 14-year period (2007-2020) which we could paraphrase into simple keywords – *Awakening* (Uranus) *to the Underworld* (Pluto).

The Underworld, which belongs to Pluto, is anything that lies beneath the surface of life or the everyday world. From this zone issue forth all those things we regard as dark and dirty, deep and intriguing, horrific and unmentionable, compelling and profound, occult and shamanic, creepy and crawly, gothic and ghastly. When the great Awakener Uranus logs onto Pluto's site, we really are forced to wake up and have a good look at his "Face" – at what we and life are like deep down.

We must accept that there are "dark forces" and identify what to do to make something positive out of the situation – which means to accept and understand what the "dark" is all about. At its most basic this Uranus-Pluto process is waking up to the very existence of the subconscious mind – for that is what the underworld simply is in modern terminology.

The actual discovery and naming of the subconscious was, after all, made by Sigmund Freud during the Uranus-Pluto configuration of 1896-1907. Our current *Awakening* to *Transformation* involves a personal journey into our own darkness – wherein lies your own truth. And for me, this is our challenge – to unfold a new perception on the phenomena of change and death. Uranus is the ultimate Sky God and Pluto Lord of the Underworld, so we are in a process of a radical reworking of our collective attitudes and beliefs about Heaven and Hell and the Afterlife.

About 30 years ago the conscious dying movement was born in the modern West. Basically, conscious dying is the process of utilizing the dying process as an opportunity to become more present and loving, an opportunity for profound healing, for spiritual awakening. Eastern traditions, such as Hinduism and particularly Buddhism, as well as shamanic traditions, have clear teachings that guide the dying to a conscious and graceful death. In the West however, this wisdom was lost in the rush to industrialization and modernity.

For much of the 20th Century, death was almost completely denied in the West.

Things began to change in the late 1960s when we experienced the conjunction of Uranus and Pluto in the zodiacal sign of Virgo – sign of body-mind relationship and healing. The pioneering work of "grief therapist" Elisabeth Kubler Ross was published and the first hospice opened in London. Before the modern hospice movement – dying with dignity – death was denied. Dying was about the body only, so the mind and the spirit were avoided. The main benefit of the hospice movement and of the work of Elisabeth Kubler Ross was that death could be discussed, psychological issues were addressed directly, families could find closure, and people could make the best of a bad situation.

It is appropriate that the soul called *Elisabeth Kubler-Ross*, who personally liberated thousands of patients from the fear of death and nothingness, whose life work has positively influenced millions in the collective, should exit when transit Sun and Uranus were in dynamic opposition aspect, and the Death Ascendant at zero-degrees Aries was exactly conjunct her natal Uranus at 29½-degrees Pisces.

YOGANANDA'S EXIT

In Hinduism, the state of mind of the dying person is considered to be of utmost importance to their ultimate destiny – their next incarnation. Like *The Tibetan Book of the Dead*, the Indian classic *The Bhagavad Gita* declares that the frame of mind in which you put yourself at the moment of death will determine the state into which you enter at death. Technically this means our journey through the *Bardo* states, or the dimensions in-between lives. To know how a man dies, one teacher writes, is to know the man.

This proper frame of mind is not attained suddenly near the last hour before death, rather, it is cultivated during the life. The emphasis is placed on cultivating throughout life a state of mind which will be stabilized in the Real, the true self which is not subject to the death of the body or other changes in the physical world.

Zen Buddhist Masters are known to say to their students: "Why do you want to know what will happen to you after you die? Find out who you are NOW!"

Yogananda is celebrated as a beloved World Teacher, one of the greatest emissaries to the West of India's ancient wisdom. His life and teachings continue to be a source of light and inspiration to people of all races, cultures and creeds. You have probably read his classic book (*Autobiography of a Yogi*) but do you know how he died?

His physical death came on March seventh, 1952 during an evening banquet in Los Angeles, California, to honour India's ambassador to the USA. It was a sudden death, which came while reciting his own poem "My India." He entered into *Mahasamadhi, a conscious exit of the spirit from the body.* And what an amazing choice of exit, reading his own devotional poem, full of his ecstatic relationship with India! And if you had a choice (which you do) – how would you like to exit from the physical plane?

20 days later, according to a signed statement from the medical doctor, "….no physical disintegration was visited upon his body….it was apparently in a phenomenal state of immutability." This is what happens when the level of integration between the outer and inner vehicles is so intimate.

Yogananda was encouraged to pursue his own spiritual path at an early age. By age eleven he was having mystical experiences. His spiritual quest led him to Swami Sri Yukteswar in 1910 and for the next years he studied under this Master's loving discipline. Then one week after his Guru died, one the 19th of June 1936 at three pm Bombay time, his teacher came to him in a vision and gave him a tour of the Astral and Casual planes. Astrologically, transit Uranus was moving into opposition aspect to Yogananda's natal position of Uranus in Scorpio, while transit Jupiter, known as the Explorer or Traveller, the "Guru" in Sanskrit, was conjunct his natal Venus in Sagittarius. His Guru did indeed give him a glimpse of the Cosmic workings!

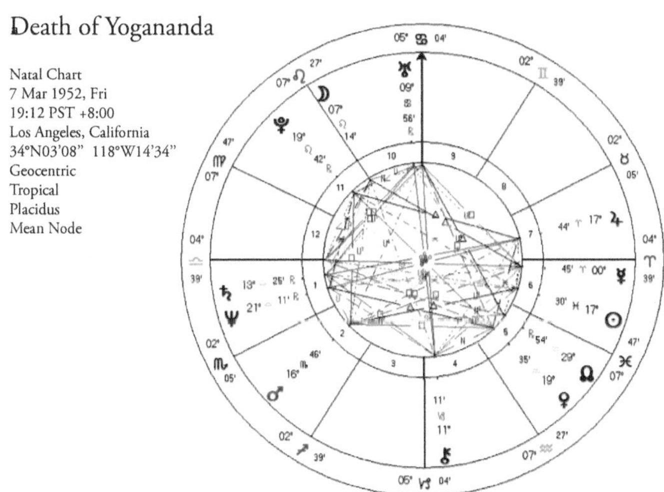

Death of Yogananda

Natal Chart
7 Mar 1952, Fri
19:12 PST +8:00
Los Angeles, California
34°N03'08" 118°W14'34"
Geocentric
Tropical
Placidus
Mean Node

If you look at his natal chart, Uranus is conjunct the South Node in third house Scorpio. The suggestion here is that he had already become liberated in past lives.

In my book *The Astrology of Death – Entry & Exit: Your Birth & Death Horoscope*, published in Swedish 2012, I emphasize the significance of the zodiac sign on the Descendant as symbolic of the death – and its planetary ruler as always being strongly present in the exit from the physical dimension. This is so because if the Ascendant represents the moment of birth then the opposite point is the moment of death or disembodiment. Dying is the personal experience of letting go of the physical body and become senseless.

In Yogananda's radix it is 29-degrees of Aquarius which occupies the seventh House cusp. On his Death horoscope it is transit Uranus at ten-degrees Cancer which occupies the highest point, the culminating Midheaven at five-degrees Cancer, and forms the opposition aspect to his natal Capricorn Sun. Planets at the top of the chart suggest a highly developed sense of full expression, as this represents the noon station of the Sun's journey, it's highest point of influence during the day.

There is also the exact contact between the transit nodal Axis at 30-degrees Aquarius-

Leo, passing through his natal horizon line. Birth and Death had already become a Unity before his physical exit.

A PERSON'S TRUE DESIRE IS REVEALED AT DEATH

Emanuel Swedenborg, who lived from 1688 until 1772, was born in Stockholm. The parallels between the afterlife experiences of Swedenborg and near-death experiences are quite remarkable. So remarkable in fact that Dr. Raymond Moody's ground-breaking book on near-death experiences, *Life After Life*, has a section where those parallels are specifically discussed.

In his search to locate the human soul and prove its immortality, Swedenborg went through various transcendent religious experiences which begun in 1743. He wrote a series of 30 volumes describing that Heaven & Hell are not places, but states of being.

Swedenborg's journey into the afterlife provides more than just a glimpse into the exciting journey awaiting us all – it gives a very clear picture. He writes that after death, people are their desire, or their *strongest desire*, which is a similar teaching to that of the East. Everyone has a number of desires, but they all go back to the strongest desire which makes them one, or taken all together, compose it. Taken all together, they make up a kind of kingdom, also called dimensions or planes of being. As astrologers we can state that the horoscope pattern at death becomes at the same time that of the birth into the spiritual realms.

These teachings make it clear that whatever our mind focuses upon, we become, or get to experience. Therefore the soul within will utilize any life experience in order to awaken us, which is the significance of us becoming clearer in our brain cells before we leave the physical plane. This is our conscious goal of increased livingness.

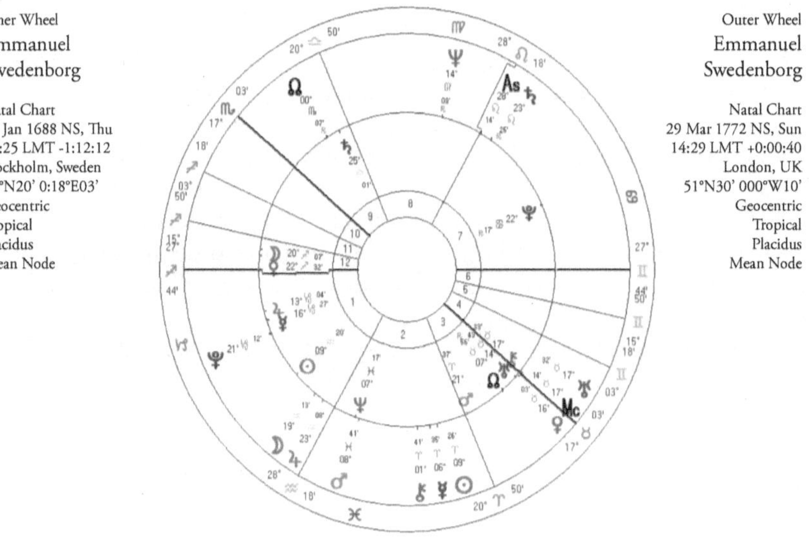

Swedenborg was born a first House Sun Aquarian with Uranus placed at the bottom of his chart, conjunct his Taurus fourth house cusp, yet technically still within his third house.

With his scholarly interests, he established Sweden's first scientific journal and anticipated a number of modern inventions, including prototype submarines and aeroplanes. He also published works on cosmology, chemistry, physics, the circulation of the blood etc.

He accurately predicted the time of his own death, the 29th of March 1772. He died in London aged 84, significantly during his Uranus return. Transit Uranus was not only *exactly* conjunct his natal fourth house angle, traditionally representing "end of life conditions", and just three degrees from its radix placement – but on the Death chart this placement reveals Uranus having reached the top of the chart, the Taurus Midheaven. From birth – with Uranus at the IC angle – to death, with Uranus at the opposite MC angle, this man's spinal axis had been activated by kundalini rising and he was free to explore the universe. This was indeed a "conscious exit."

The Uranus Return, which occurs at 84 years, is not guaranteed for us all. Although statistics keep changing and we are living longer now than we did a decade ago, we still cannot assume that we will reach this ripe age. Uranus is the first transpersonal planet that we can experience within our physical body. The next planet is Neptune but with its cycle of 146 years this is far beyond the human lifespan. Yet it is the presence of Uranus at the time of death that can offer us a sense of larger cosmos, which provides a new perspective on death and a new sense of one's role as part of that greater unity.

PAST AND CURRENT EXAMPLES

Carl Jung was born with an Aquarian Ascendant and Uranus eleven-degrees from a conjunction with his Leo Sun, yet exactly in square 90-degree aspect to his Taurian Moon. These liberating contacts speeded up his awareness of the masculine (Sun) and feminine (Moon) centers within the psyche. He emphasized the modern *path of self-individualization*. He died in 1961 at 85 years of heart (Sun) and circulatory troubles (Uranus) as transit Uranus at death had returned to its natal placement and was forming the opposition aspect to transit Saturn in Aquarius.

When the great Danish Cosmologist, *Martinus*, died in March 1981 age 91 – the death horoscope reveals Uranus three degrees from the Sagittarian Ascendant, with an exact Jupiter-Saturn conjunction culminating on the Libra Midheaven. His continuing journey, education and exploration of the higher worlds was clearly shown, as well as his enthusiasm to embrace the ever-present reality of the Cosmic now. The death chart becomes the template for determining the future incarnation. The advantage of having a "conscious exit" becomes clear to the evolving soul-personality.

Aleister Crowley's death chart I wrote extensively about in *The Fenris Wolf 6*. Was his death at the age 72, a "conscious exit"? Born with an exact Uranus-Saturn opposition at birth, co-rulers of his seventh and eighth Houses, he died when both transit Saturn and Uranus were significantly positioned. Transit Saturn was moving through the sign Leo, forming the conjunction to his natal Uranus and opposing his natal Saturn in

Aquarius. At the end he was experiencing increased isolation, "…with nothing but pipe and wit", going through a series of detachments from the physical plane. Destiny was knocking at his door, while transit Uranus in Gemini, was forming the dynamic square aspect to both his natal Pisces Moon (past) and his progressed Virgo Ascendant (future). Professional astrologers will quickly see the significance of these contacts to promote Crowley's liberation (Uranus) from form (Saturn) and provide the Magus with a conscious exit.

Nelson Mandela has become a household name. Born into the family sign of Cancer, it is significant that he had been a controversial figure for most of his life. The South African anti-apartheid revolutionary and politician served as President of South Africa from 1994 to 1999. He was the first black South African to hold the office.

He was born with natal Uranus situated in its own sign at 27-degrees Aquarius, significantly placed within his seventh House and opposing his Leo Ascendant.

His rebellion ultimately led to democracy – but before that he was arrested and put into prison in 1962 as transit Uranus reached his Leo Ascendant and formed the opposition to its natal placement. Right-wing critics denounced him as a terrorist and communist sympathiser. Mandela served no less than 27 years in prison. The four planets in his 12th House, that department of life that connects us with the institution of prisons and imprisonment, including his Cancerian Sun, led to a lifetime in prison – yet when he emerged, he became the founding Father of the new nation.

He died at 95 years, and the death chart shows transit Uranus within one degree of his Aries Midheaven, the top of his chart and transit Saturn exactly conjunct his Scorpio Moon.

Just as the previous examples of Yogananda and Emanuel Swedenborg, with transit Uranus on the Midheaven in their Death charts, Nelson Mandela is another clear example of a conscious exit.

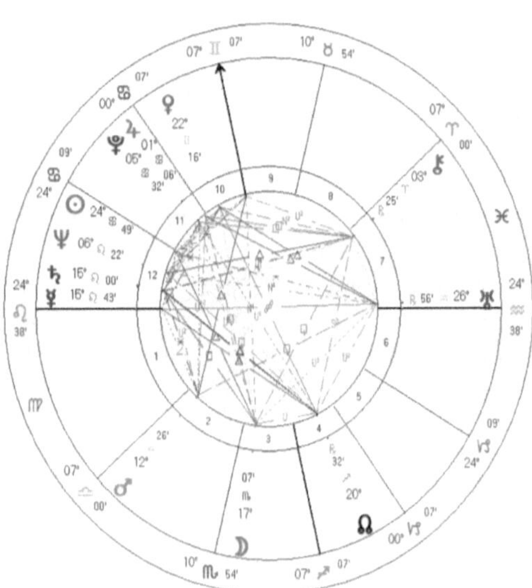

Nelson Mandela

Natal Chart
18 Jul 1918, Thu
08:45 EET -2:00
Umtata, South Africa
31°S35' 028°E47
Geocentric
Tropical
Placidus
Mean Node

Leonardo da Vinci is celebrated as a Renaissance man, a genius, centuries ahead of his time. Scientific Saturn, representing the "Golden Age" was elevated in Libra upon his Midheaven at birth. Death came in his 67th year as transit Saturn was exactly in opposition to his natal Uranus, while transit Uranus had just passed his natal Taurian Sun and was in exact conjunction to transit Mercury (Descendant ruler) and the transit Sun (eighth house intercepted sign Leo). Again and again in these examples we see how the Lord of Time and Fate – the planet Saturn – joins together with the planet of Liberation – Uranus – to give birth into the spiritual dimensions. Leonardo was well aware of the approaching opportunity for cooperation with the soul's intention. His too, was a "conscious exit."

Edgar Cayce, the famous *"Sleeping Prophet"*, was a unique personality who in his trance state entered into the Cosmic Bank or Akashic records with his eighth house Pisces Sun and left humanity with a huge range of psychic readings that he gave to thousands of clients.

Cayce urged us to recognize that what we are today is the result of what we have done about our ideals and our knowledge of God (or the Creative Forces) in past lives.

Born with Uranus exactly on the birth position of his 21-degrees Leo Ascendant – this pattern was repeated upon his exit from the physical plane, because at death transit Uranus was a few degrees from a Gemini Ascendant on the Death chart, with the sign Aquarius culminating at the Midheaven.

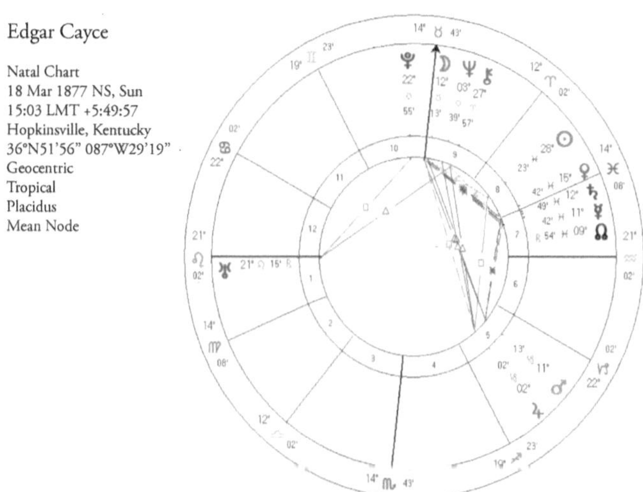

Edgar Cayce

Natal Chart
18 Mar 1877 NS, Sun
15:03 LMT +5:49:57
Hopkinsville, Kentucky
36°N51'56" 087°W29'19"
Geocentric
Tropical
Placidus
Mean Node

The remarkable teacher *Krishnamurti* continues to fascinate seekers of truth with his core teachings around the theme of freedom – a very typical Uranian theme. Hailed by the Theosophical leaders as the new World Teacher or *Matreya*, he announced his break with the Theosophical Society in 1929 before an audience of thousands.

His belief was that "truth is a pathless land" and taught a doctrine of independent salvation by right conduct. Tradition and doctrine might be barriers to personal progress, for each person must find their own path and their own link with the infinite.

He was born, as you can imagine, with a very strong Uranian presence – Aquarius rises, 20-degrees on the Ascendant, with Uranus placed in ninth House Scorpio forming the opposition aspect to a third house Taurian Sun – the planetary ruler of his Leo Descendant. He was a revolutionary teacher and set up educational centers for young people in India, UK and USA, which was another way of honouring this third-ninth house axis – the *educational axis* on the horoscope.

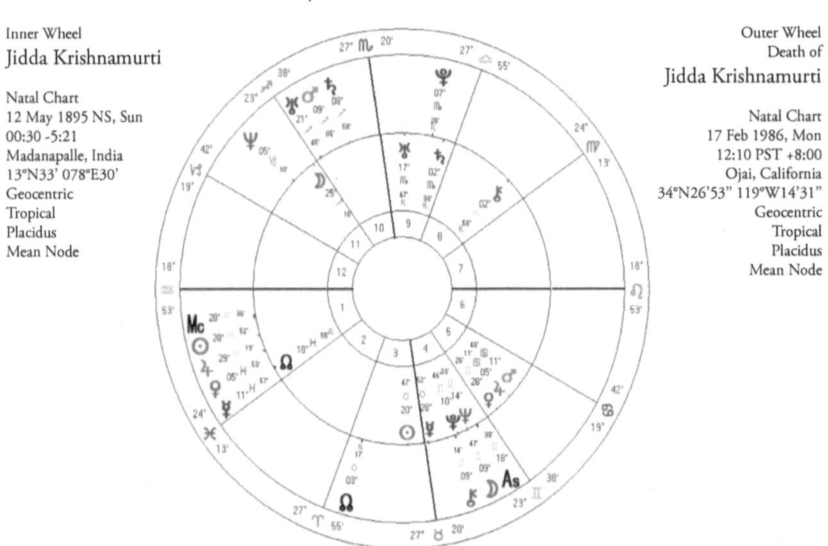

On his Death horoscope we see transit Sun at 29-degrees Aquarius was exactly conjunct both the Midheaven and Jupiter, while transit Uranus formed the opposition aspect to the Gemini Ascendant. This was indeed a conscious death and fast exit to the higher worlds.

Krishnamurti was himself a synthesis of East and West, born a Brahmin to a Hindu mother and Theosophist father. Detachment, a very Uranian-Aquarian word, was a highly developed attribute of this teacher, one of whose books is entitled: *Freedom from the Known*. He never "prepared" for a lecture and often would sit in silence for a period of time before speaking, apparently tuning into his audience and what the message would be for that occasion. This form of telepathy is characteristic of developed Uranian personalities.

THE EGO AND SELF-INDIVIDUALIZATION

We cannot really make sense of Uranus in the birth chart without looking at the Sun and Saturn as well, because these two are, in a way, the brackets around the individual's personality. These are the two planets most concerned with ego and ego-development, and because of this they are the vessels for containing, grounding and individualizing the outer planets. In the natural Zodiac we can see this relationship shown by the polar signs of Leo-Aquarius and Cancer-Capricorn. Saturn co-rules Aquarius. He is the son and castrator of Uranus in myth. They are intimately linked and inseparable, and this is reflected in their joint rulership of Aquarius.

The Sun is also intimately linked and inseparable, because it is solar fire that Prometheus steals, and this is reflected in Leo's natural opposition to Aquarius. Each needs the other – they are two halves of the same story.

The polarity of Uranus-Saturn shapes and moulds our solar and lunar consciousness. When you explore the prominence of Uranus and the sign Aquarius in these examples of "conscious exit", you will also recognize the significant role that Saturn also plays in the birth and death chart. As you might know from any practical work with astrology, the planets act as a "team of energies."

Let us redefine our commitment to the Aquarian goals of no-more-automatic-pilot as we embrace a more conscious living and our soul destiny – *a conscious exit!*

By This, That

– A spin on Lea Porsager's Spin Φ

Kasper Opstrup

"For I, being a woman, lust ever to mate myself with some beast. And this is the salvation of the world, that always I am deceived by some god, and that my child is the guardian of the labyrinth that hath two-and-seventy paths. Now she is gone."

– Aleister Crowley, Bou-Saada, December 2, 1909. 4:50–6:5 p.m.

Reciting the PUSSY invocation, the Furry Quantum Pussy – an invisible agent of Chaos – stands with a foot and a half in the shadows, surrounded by dark matter and hidden particles. The Pussy is there, and it is not. Summoned by the voices emanating from the quantum device known as H@t (#Blavatsky, #Besant, #Bohr, #Merkel), the Pussy fully enters the room. It circles in on the sigil made out of steel beams, laying on the floor, that conjured its essence to begin with. In order to open up horizons that were thought closed, it bows before the sigil in the sign that it, and only it, may know.

Purring with resistance, the Spin Φ in which the Pussy is spun is language and its accompanying barrage of images; the control system with which we are conditioned, our vehicle for thought, a crowned virgin riding upon a bull, a moonrise at midnight. The illusion becomes real when you accept it. A simple method to break with the language of control is through a Rimbaudian derangement of the senses: from stroboscopic lights and sensory withdrawal to breathing techniques, alcohol and psychedelic drugs, there are many methods to enter new states of consciousness.

Out of time and into space, language – instead of operating by linear and causal communication – suddenly operates by quantum leaps between association blocks, nodes in a fragmented web where everything and everyone is entangled but where there is never a proper path. Overflowing with meaning, it becomes an unknowable object.

By rearranging the relations between text, image and content this entanglement – between words, worlds and we's – opens up speculative techniques to intervene into the present with, forging new relations to both past and future. By intervening on the level of myth-making the techniques often consist of strange and unutterable speech acts. Instead of inhabiting the equilibrium of a Joycean chaosmos, a tiny, unstable cosmos, clinging to the edge of total chaos, is temporarily occupied. Communicating in incantations, these acts conceal what they exhibit while operating on multiple levels. It is chaos as a fog of war.

A hidden Spin Φ on this flight from reason can be traced back to the beginnings of the modern occult imaginary. The occult is that which makes sense of the unknowable and the inexplicable. From the mid-19th century the Western esoteric traditions began to incorporate elements from Eastern traditions. This alchemical wedding found new forms in Theosophy and the Hermetic Order of the Golden Dawn, movements that along with Spiritualism kickstarted an occult revival which has only grown stronger and more popular since.

Theosophy – whose dominant figure was the Russian spirit medium Madame Helena Petrovna Blavatsky, or HPB as she was known to her followers – was a mix of secret chiefs, cosmic evolution and prehistoric civilisations. It synthesised the world's religions, suggesting that Christ, Buddha, Lao Tzu and others were all equal masters, while promoting a fascination with non-Western cultures such as Egypt, India and Tibet. It introduced Hindu and Buddhist ideas about reincarnation and karma to the Occident, as well as ideas about the astral body and the astral plane. Although the occult would be associated throughout the 20th century with reactionary tendencies, in the 19th century it was bound up with progressive politics like women's rights and colonial self rule – as can be seen with Annie Besant, HPB's successor as leader of the Theosophical society, who was a Fabian suffragette.

If we think of the occult imaginary as a kind of psycho-politics where the contested area is not only a physical terrain but also a state of consciousness, the occultural techniques and the (aesthetic) derangement of the senses become methods of escape from conventional ways of thinking and seeing, vehicles for the exploration of areas of mind heretofore unknown. By experimenting with how to force the hands of chance and break the laws of probability by will alone, the techniques become means to escape the mechanisms of control, to transcend the biological trap of duality as well as to obtain the ability to rewrite one's own past.

In Theosophy, this is expressed in thought forms, an energy that can be programmed to carry out particular tasks. In the occult traditions following the Hermetic Order of the Golden Dawn – a magical order, founded in London in 1888, with roots in rosicrucianism and freemasonry that would go on to inspire Wicca and Thelema – it is expressed through sigils, a quantum hack of both mind and matter through a type of performative art that is not meant to be seen. Like the artist, the occult practitioner wants to occupy our minds and is fully aware that the universe is a measureless domain of resonating frequencies which requires an observer for sub-atomic particles to come into existence.

On the creation and use of sigils for conjuration, information can already be found in the works of Heinrich Cornelius Agrippa (1486–1535), but the way it has been practiced in more pragmatic DIY occultural milieus from the 1980s onwards – by chaos magicians like the Illuminates of Thanateros (who counted writer William S. Burroughs as a member) or the post-modern pranksters from the Temple ov Psychick Youth (TOPY) – goes back to one person in particular: the English proto-surrealist painter Austin Osman Spare (1886–1956).

Spare's fundamental insight was that our ideas shape the world we observe. To tap into this, he developed an occult system, the Zos-Kia Cultus. Seeing the world corresponding to the laws of quantum physics as formulated by Niels Bohr or in Heisenberg's uncertainty principle, Spare wanted to shape it by governing energy, using drawing and painting as the medium of control. He developed a method – sigilisation – that treats cultural production as a technology for spell casting in that the act of magic becomes indistinguishable from creating the piece of work. At its most basic level, sigil magick consists in the creation of a magically charged symbol but it can take the form of collage, sculpture, video, writings, and various other media.

For Spare, the form was an individual 'alphabet of desire' which incorporated elements of the sacrificial use of blood and saliva as well as yogalike postures to intensify the experience of making the sigil. Sigilisation requires a masturbatory intensity of concentration, maybe more pleasurable than the art itself since the process is the product. The artwork or object created to act as a receiving vessel or talisman for the desired is a by-product.

A quick how-to for the curious: write down the object of desire and erase all vowels, leaving only a string of consonants. Squash the string down, throw out or combine lines, play with the letters, and end up with an appropriate looking glyph/sigil. In order to charge it, concentrate on its shape and evacuate all thoughts. These no-mind states can be reached in a number of ways, such as fasting, spinning, fear, sex, intense exhaustion, but the preferred way is that of sex magick (which stems from tantric yoga but was popularised by Crowley and the OTO). A very basic form available to us all is masturbation. You masturbate and at the moment of orgasm, or just before, you project the image of your chosen sigil in your mind's eye. According to adepts one does not need to believe in it since it has nothing to do with faith. If it is done, it works.

Since the spiritual rebellion of the Beats and the counter-culture of the 1960s occult ideas have been ubiquitous. Today's occulture is as much a product of punk, Fluxus and Mail Art, plus a century of quantum weirdness and speculative genre fiction from H.P. Lovecraft to Robert Anton Wilson and Terence McKenna, as it is of the esoteric tradition proper. The double strain from Blavatsky and the Golden Dawn *via* the Ordo Templi Orientis (OTO) and the Order of the Silver Star (A∴A∴) of which Spare was a probationer looms large, though.

In the penultimate Spin Φ, it is the morning of the magicians and we must all become sorcerers. In order to survive a catastrophic future horizon where the Angela Merkels of a world governed by political Spin Φ seem hellbent on reproducing the disaster that produced the disaster, our mental jiu-jitsu must take the form of tactical magick, utilising the ability of fragments randomly juxtaposed, of collage, assemblage and montage, to make it possible to tell one's own stories and, thus, shape the perception of reality. It requires a link to the past and a vision for the future where the purpose of prophecy is not to be right about the future but to act upon the present. It is a technology to change the world by re-wiring the collective subconscious where the use of occult language also is a sign of defiance, challenging the religious edifice of the social structure one is against. This is not a matter of claiming that history is only made up of stories we tell ourselves, but simply that the logic of stories and the ability to act as historical agents go together. Politics, art, myths, forms of knowledge construct fictions – material rearrangements of signs and images that influence the relationships between self and world.

The occult yearning for a unified field theory has a ring of quasi-science to it that opens it up for creative confabulation. Whether we are talking about environmental, social or mental ecologies, occult techniques have become a staple of many self-help books since. Technologies aside, it is a re-occurrence of the age old heretical battle cry that god is within you and without you; that paradise can be built on Earth in our lifetime. As the occult imaginary has do to with change, mutation, evolution, chance experiments and new formations, it is inherently political. But rather than anything recognisable within the terms of parliamentary politics, it transcends traditional categories. It asks more questions than it answers while psychogeographically exploring the meeting point where inner and outer reality at once blend, stumble, synthesise and crash together in unresolved #purradoxes.

Greyhounds of the Future

Genesis Breyer P-Orridge

Memory is a clock
The aging mechanism of the mind
Memory is a clock
The aging mechanism of the mind
Mechanism... mechanism
Turning gears... rocking... interlocking
Memories clocking
The aging mechanism of your mind

Memories tell us one thing
Everything must go
Memories tell us one thing
Everything must go
Memories tell us one thing
Everything must go
Memories tell us one thing
Everything must go

Everything must go

Nothing matters but the end of matter
Nothing matters but the end of matter
Nothing matters but the end of matter
Nothing matters but the end of matter

Be afraid to a point of formlessness
Be terrorized by a point of soundlessness
Be ex-dream to a point of powerlessness

Be afraid to a point of formlessness
Be terrorized to a point of soundlessness
Be ex-dream to a point of powerlessness

Be ex-dream
be ex-dream

Once upon a time there was a garden
This garden was destroyed by Word
Destroyed by language
Language became the first memory
Time was set in motion at this point
But the garden did not exist within TIME
Or language
It was an experiential neural projection
A Cathedral that worshipped its occupant
And that was your soul
Your s o u l
Your S O U L

The only thing you've got

And your soul, well it represented the MIND
The mind preset without light
And there was nothing to reflect... no mirrors, nor shape
Nothing to fix this paricular Dreeeeeam

And you've got no anchors
You don't know where you are
You don't know if you're really existing or you've
Blown everything and you've got to become a Star star star

Nothing matters but the end of matter
Nothing matters but the end of matter
Nothing matters but the end of matter
Nothing matters but the end of MATTER

We are born sounds
Made names

Trapping matter with language

We perpetuate our tyranny
And drown in a flood of SPECULATION
A false communication hahahaha

Do you want to be Immortal, reborn, outside of time ?

Come on child
Come through me

We must look for ways to transmit infinite alternative "realities"
And then maybe you have a choice of reality
You wanna stay alive
You wanna STAY alive
You don't really want to die...
So make it REAL
Make whatever it is real
M O R E REAL than anything emasculating
That we inherit
Ohh you've not yet been corrupted have you?
Trivialised have you?
Lost in belief have you?

Ahhhhhh you're in OUR singularity now

Nothing matters but the end of matter
Nothing matters but the end of matter
Nothing matters but the end of matter
Nothing matters but the end of MATTER

Every inherited moral construct
Every society every techno-patriotic political system
Betrayers of trade unions... believe us it exists
It exists... but it must be D E S T R O Y E D
As fast as its possible
You know... YOU know we make S P A C E !
Make space to be space

Memory is a clock
The aging mechanism of your mind
YOU can set the alarm

Memories tell us one thing
This thing must go
Memories tell us one thing
This thing must go
Memories tell us one thing
This thing has to go

Mass belief
Mass belief

Mass belief
Mass belief

Are you listening well?
Names are given in order to control
Names are given in order to control
Listen carefully
To reduce to comprehend the forces of nature
To demonstrate ownership and failure
This is the place to come
This is the race of the Greyhounds of a Future
G r e y h o u n d s of the Future
The race to name
The race to name O U R... strategy
Strategy
We poor have grown to be richhhhh
And the rich have grown to be poor
AGAIN

Know that to re-enter immortality
We must ourselves become un-nameable
And we're emptied of all sense
Just peeping

Memories tell us one thing
Everything must go

Memories tell us one thing
Everything must go
Memories tell us one thing
Everything must go
Memories tell us one thing
Everything must go

Contributors

Vanessa Sinclair, Psy.D. is a psychoanalyst based in Stockholm, who sees clients internationally. Her books include *Switching Mirrors* (Trapart Books, 2016), *The Fenris Wolf 9* (Trapart Books, 2017) co-edited with Carl Abrahamsson, *On Psychoanalysis and Violence: Contemporary Lacanian Perspectives* (Routledge, 2018) co-edited with Manya Steinkoler, and *Scansion in Psychoanalysis and Art: the Cut in Creation* (Routledge, 2020). Dr. Sinclair is also a founding member of Das Unbehagen: A Free Association for Psychoanalysis. She hosts conferences and events internationally, and is the host of the Rendering Unconscious Podcast. For more information, please visit: www.drvanessasinclair.net.

Frater Achad (Charles Stansfeld Jones, 1886-1950) was an occult writer and a favoured disciple of Aleister Crowley's. He worked with the orders A∴A∴ and Ordo Templi Orientis, predominantly in Canada. Achad wrote several books on magic and the Qabalah: *The Chalice of Ecstasy, The Egyptian Revival,* and *QBL,* to mention a few.

Timothy O'Neill, b. 1951, A.B., U.C. Berkeley, Art History 1973 B.F.A., San Francisco Academy of Art College, 1979. Has been published in *Apocalypse Culture; Secret and Suppressed; Popular Alienation; Occulture, Steamshovel Press, Leonardo,* and worked as a staff writer at *Gnosis* magazine for ten years. He is a long-time member of Yogoda Satsanga and AMORC. He is currently working in San Francisco as a Performance Artist, musician, painter and writer interested in the Gnostic tradition.

Nina Antonia is the author of four acclaimed biographies; 'Johnny Thunders – In Cold Blood' 'The New York Dolls – Too Much Too Soon' 'Peter Perrett – The One & Only' and 'The Prettiest Star'. She has lectured at Tate Liverpool, enjoyed a retrospective at the Barbican and has appeared in two lauded documentaries: 'Arthur Kane New York Doll' and 'Looking for Johnny.' She has also contributed to Mojo, Uncut and Classic Rock. Her first book 'Johnny Thunders – In Cold Blood' is the subject of a forthcoming feature film. Ms Antonia lives in London where she is currently working on supernatural fiction, having made her debut in esoteric literature with the publication of a short-story in the Egaeus Press anthology 'Soliloquy For Pan' in 2015. For more information please contact ninaantonia@talktalk.net

Aki Cederberg is a writer, musician, filmmaker and traveler, based in Helsinki, Finland. He has written about esoteric subjects for various publications and given numerous lectures. His first book was published in Finnish language and is titled *Pyhiinvael-*

lus: Matkalla Intiassa ja Nepalissa ("Pilgrimage: Journeys in India and Nepal", Salakirjat, 2013). An extended, English language edition of the book is currently in the works. Cederberg has been part of several musical groups, including Halo Manash and Maa, with whom he has recorded and toured extensively. He is a part of the podcast Radio Wyrd (radiowyrd.fi). Recently, he narrated and acted as main character in the feature documentary film *Instrument of Himmler*. He has a Bachelor of Culture and Arts (directing and scriptwriting) and works in writing and film production. Currently, Cederberg is exploring and writing about various pre-christian spiritual traditions and holy sites in Europe, which is the subject of his next book. The book will be accompanied by photographs taken by his wife, Justine Cederberg. Interested publishers are encouraged to contact: cederbergaki@gmail.com www.akicederberg.com

MICHAEL MOYNIHAN was born in New England in 1969. He is an artist, musician, author, editor, and occasional winemaker and bookbinder. He has traveled and performed music on both coasts of the USA, in European countries from Portugal to Russia, as well as in Japan. His award-winning non-fiction book *Lords of Chaos* (co-written with Didrik Søderlind; 2nd edition, Feral House, 2003) has been published in nine languages. His work as a translator includes the book *Barbarian Rites: The Spiritual World of the Vikings and the Germanic Tribes* (Inner Traditions, 2011) by Hans-Peter Hasenfratz. He co-edited and contributed to *American Grotesque*, a major monograph on the photographer William Mortensen (1897–1965), an early twentieth-century pioneer of grotesque and occult imagery, and also edited the new edition of Mortensen's classic handbook *The Command to Look: A Master Photographer's Method for Controlling the Human Gaze* (both published by Feral House, 2014). He is the co-editor (with Joshua Buckley) of the book-format journal *TYR: Myth—Culture—Tradition*. With his wife Annabel Lee he also runs the small independent publishing venture, Dominion Press, which has produced works by Stephen Flowers, Hans Bellmer, John Michell, and Joscelyn Godwin in limited hardcover editions (www.dominionpress.net). Email: himilkraft@comcast.net

FRIEDRICH HIELSCHER is extensively introduced in the article by Michael Moynihan in this issue.

ORRYELLE DEFENESTRATE-BASCULE is an esoteric artist in many media, including painting, writing, sculpture, sound and performance art. His 'Tela Quadrivium' series of alchemical art books are published by Fulgur Limited (final volume 'Distillatio' published 2015); his text-based book 'Time Fate and Spider Magic' by Avalonia Books (UK), and The Book of Kaos Tarot from iNSPiRALink.Multimedia Press. He is the writer-director of Australian-based Metamorphic Ritual Theatre Company who have presented many major original productions based in (and updating/mutating) various ancient mythos, and he often performs and exhibits internationally. His work engages with connecting the subconscious and conscious through employment of magical and mythical symbols and archetypes, as a part of the vanguard of current resurgence in esoteric arts balanced between the conceptual and the emotional-aesthetic.

ZBIGNIEW LAGOSZ is a graduate of Krakow's AGH University of Science and Technology with a Ph.D. in Religious Studies from the Jagiellonian University with the dissertation on Aleister Crowley's Influence on the esoteric movements in 20th-century Poland. In over 30 academic articles on esoteric and occult traditions, his principal research interests focus on the spiritual orders in 20th-century Poland and the figure of Czesław Czynski. He is also interested in altered states of consciousness as they intersect with the latest technological developments. He's been an international boxing referee since 2000.

GARY LACHMAN is the author of more than a dozen books charting the meeting ground between esotericism and culture, including the highly praised *Secret Teachers of the Western World* (Tarcher/Penguin 2015). Other titles include *Aleister Crowley: Magick, Rock and Roll, and the Wickedest Man in the World* (Tarcher/Penguin 2014), *Turn Off Your Mind: The Mystic Sixties and the Dark Side of the Age of Aquarius* (Disinformation 2003), *The Secret History of Consciousness* (Lindisfarne 2003), and *Politics and the Occult* (Quest 2008). He is a regular contributor to *Fortean Times, Independent on Sunday, Guardian, LA Review of Books* and other journals in the UK and US. He lectures frequently in the UK and Europe. In a previous life, he was a founding member of the rock group Blondie, and in 2006 was inducted into the Rock and Roll Hall of Fame. www.garylachman.co.uk

CARL ABRAHAMSSON (b. 1966) is the editor of *The Fenris Wolf* and the founder of The Institute of Comparative Magico-anthropology. He likes to write and read, take an occasional photograph and at times converse with the audio structure spirits. He is also a film-maker, predominantly with the documentary series *An Art Apart*. www.carlabrahamsson.com, www.trapart.net

BISHOP T OMPHALOS A.K.A. KJETIL FJELL is an aspirant to the A.'.A.'. and serves as a Sovereign Grand Inspector General and Bishop of the O.T.O. His professional background is within neuropsychological assessments and research. E-mail: omphalos111@gmail.com.

KENDELL GEERS changed his date of birth to May 1968 and lives between Johannesburg and Brussels. He made a name for himself as an socio-political, cultural-activist, artist and animist claiming the necessity of relational ethics in a spiritual engagement through art. His performances, sculptures, videos, installations and photographs question manichean visions of the world, by calling us to a reversibility of values. His raw language explores the boundaries of art and what is permissible, provoking and arousing intense feelings of desire and danger, seduction and repulsion.

JOHAN NILSSON is a Phd candidate at the University of Lund where he is writing his doctoral thesis about the image of Chinese religion in late 19th and early 20th century occultism. His research interests include the 19th century occult milieu, its engagement with modernity and entanglement with Asian religions, popular culture, 20th century new religious movements, and the historiography of the academic science of religion. As an independent publisher Nilsson released the first ever Swedish translation of the *Chaldean Oracles* (translated by Ola Wikander). Finally, he has written (and sometimes published) on such diverse subjects as the sacred hermaphroditism of Thomas Lake Harris, the lore and etiquette of the 19th century opium den and the image of the cat in the lyrics of alternative music group Current 93.

GORDAN DJURDJEVIC is a contributor to the anthologies *Aleister Crowley and Western Esotericism* (Oxford University Press, 2012) and *A Rose Veiled in Black: Art and Arcana of Our Lady Babalon* (Three Hands Press, 2015). He is co-editor, with Henrik Bogdan, of the collection of essays *Occultism in a Global Perspective* (Acumen, 2013; Routledge, 2015), and the author of *Masters of Magical Powers: The Nath Yogis in the Light of Esoteric Notions* (VDM, 2008); *India and the Occult: The Influence of South Asian Spirituality on Modern Western Occultism* (Palgrave Macmillan, 2014); and, with Shukdev Singh, *Sayings of Gorakhnath: Selected Translations from the Gorakh Bani* (Oxford University Press, forthcoming).

ANTTI P. BALK, a Finnish philosopher and historian, is best known as a translator and publisher of Thelemic literature. Author of *Saints & Sinners: An Account of Western Civilization* and *Balderdash: A Treatise on Ethics*. He lives in Tenerife, Spain.

STEPHEN SENNITT is best known as the editor and publisher of the innovative occultzine *NOX* (published from 1986-1991). He has written many articles/essays and several books on esoteric themes, including *Monstrous Cults* and *Liber Koth*. An acclaimed collection of his weird fiction was published in 2004 by Headpress, entitled *Creatures Of Clay & Other Stories Of The Macabre*. Contact Stephen at: s.sennitt[@]btinternet.com

HENRIK DAHL is a journalist and critic specialising in psychedelic culture and art. He is the editor of The Oak Tree Review, a website featuring interviews and essays on psychedelia and the 1960s counterculture. Dahl is also a regular contributor to Psychedelic Press UK. In 2012, he was a guest editor of Swedish literature and art magazine Papi, editing an issue on intoxication. Before becoming a journalist he studied social anthropology and art history at Lund University. Dahl lives in Malmö, Sweden.

JASON LOUV is an author, journalist and esoteric teacher. Among his published books are *Generation Hex, Ultraculture Journal, Thee Psychick Bible* with Genesis Breyer P-Orridge, *Hyperworlds Underworlds* and, most recently, *The Angelic Reformation*, about the occult legacy of John Dee and the Enochian system. He has written for *VICE, Boing Boing*, blogs at Ultraculture.org, and teaches classes on magick at Magick.Me.

CHAD HENSLEY is a skilled reporter on cultural extremes in music and art. A Bram Stoker Award-nominated author, Hensley saw several years of his writing on underground subjects published as *Eso Terra: The Journal of Extreme Culture*, through Creation Books in 2011. In 2014, Camion Noir published the French language version of the book. His non-fiction credits include *Apocalypse Culture 2, Terrorizer, Metalion: The Slayer Mag Diaries, Spin, Rue Morgue, Hustler*, and *Juxtapoz*. His fiction and poetry have received honorable mentions in Year's Best Fantasy and Horror. His poetry book *Embrace the Hideous Immaculate* was published in 2014 by Raw Dog Screaming Press and is available at Amazon. See his writer's page at http://www.esoterra.org/editors.htm. He currently lives in San Diego, California.

Carey Hodges runs Last Hurrah Records, a vinyl-only label specializing in combining heavy music with exciting visuals in order to create a single focus of sound and style at www.lasthurrahrecords.com. Her non-fiction credits include Fizz magazine and Morbid Curiosity.

Alexander Nym is a cultural analyst and theoretician, editor and writer, vocalist and voice actor, presenter and promoter. Primary research field is the various manifestations of (counter-)culture in film, literature and "underground" art and music in the 20th century and beyond. Regular public appearances as presenter, lecturer, panelist or performing artist. Editor of *Schillerndes Dunkel* (2010), a reference book covering the so-called "Gothic" subculture from the 70s to the present. Other publications include *Black Celebration* (2011, co-edited by Jennifer Hoffert), and contributions to *State Of Emergence* (Poison Cabinet 2011) about the NSK State phenomenon, as well as editing German editions of books about the controversial groups Laibach (Ventil 2013) and Death In June (Ploettner 2012). He holds a diplomatic passport of NSK State in Time and is co-founder and speaker of the Leipzig-based association "Collective for transnational art & culture" which is engaged in promoting exhibitions and presentations. See www.nsk-lipsk.de and www.nsk-folk-art-biennale.org

Zaheer Gulamhusein is a student of esoteric spirituality, with a specific interest in Neoplatonic Theurgy. He writes widely on the subject and has had several articles published. This piece is an attempt to articulate the mode of interaction between statue and theurgist at the climax of ritual, via the medium of poetry. Zaheer also produces electronic music as XVARR (forthcoming LP: *Beyond Illuminism*) and lives in London with his wife Eliza.

Ingo Lambrecht, Ph.D., is a clinical psychologist and psychoanalytic therapist for over twenty years, and has practiced in South Africa and New Zealand. He works in the public sector and has a private practice. Besides his PhD in psychology and MA in Comparative Literature, he has been the clinical leader of the Child and Adolescent Mental Health Service in Hawke's Bay (HBDHB) in New Zealand. In Auckland, he worked as a senior clinical psychologist with people struggling with severe psychosis and for years been working at a specialist service for personality disorders. Currently he is providing clinical leadership at Manawanui Maori Mental Health Service (ADHB). As a clinical advisor to He Kamaka Oranga (Maori Health Service, ADHB), he is a consultant and project leader on the integration of various Maori mental health services. He has presented internationally, and lectured widely on the complex clinical work regarding the cultural-clinical interface for indigenous people. He has also published various book chapters, and is the author of *Sangoma Trance States: Exploring Indigenous Consciousness Disciplines in South Africa* (2014) that weaves personal experiences of being trained as a sangoma, a South African shaman, together with the complex relations of clinical psychology, anthropology, and indigenous knowledges.

Hagen von Tulien (born 1961 in Berlin, Germany) is a contemporary artist and occultist. With about 40 years of intense magical theory and practice, he has specialized in creating art as an expression and manifestation of magical states of awareness and its use as an esoteric tool. He is working in a variety of media including pen and ink, paper cut, collage and digital formats. Hagen was forever following his spiritual and occult vocation. This resulted in his interest and engagement in various esoteric and hermetic traditions. He delved into realms of knowledge and culture, including systems of yoga, most Western magical traditions and orders/fellowships such as AMORC, the OTO, 'The Temple ov Psychick Youth' and several others. He also immersed himself deeply into the teachings and practices of the Nath and Kaula magicians, as transmitted in the works of Sri Dadaji Mahendranath. Throughout the 1990s Hagen was a key figure in the Magical Pact of the Illuminates of Thanateros (I.O.T.), serving as its section head for Germany. He is currently a Master-Initiate of the Fraternitas Saturni (F.S.) and an empowered adept of the Voudon Gnostic Current, focused on deeply researching the Saturnian and Voudon Gnosis. As a Gnostic Bishop of the Ecclesia Gnostica Spiritualis (ordained by Michael Bertiaux), Hagen von Tulien is dedicated to manifesting the supreme and divine Gnosis Aeterna within himself while assisting others on their own path to kosmic freedom and liberation. He also holds a position as tutor and facilitator at Acranorium College. Art and magic are the two founding pillars upon which his life and experiences are built.

Erik Davis is an author, podcaster, lecturer, and award-winning journalist based in San Francisco. His wide-ranging work focuses on the intersection of alternative religion, media, an the popular imagination. He is the author, most recently, of *Nomad Codes: Adventures in Modern Esoterica.* He also wrote *The Visionary State: A Journey through California's Spiritual Landscape*, and *TechGnosis: Myth, Magic, and Mysticism in the Age of Information*, which has been translated into five languages and was recently reissued by North Atlantic Books. He also wrote a short critical volume on Led Zeppelin. His essays on music, technoculture, and spirituality have appeared in dozens of books, and he has appeared in numerous documentaries, including *The Source Family* and *DMT: The Spirit Molecule.* He explores the "cultures of consciousness" on his weekly podcast *Expanding Mind*, on the Progressive Radio Network. He graduated from Yale University, and recently earned his PhD in religious studies at Rice University. www.techgnosis.com

Kadmus is a life long practicing ceremonial magician with a long standing relationship to the ancient Celtic deities. His interests and practice are highly eclectic (including Chaos Magic, Qabalah, Thelema, several forms of mysticism, and Goetia) but a deep commitment to paganism is the bedrock upon which they all rest. Kadmus is also a ongoing contributor to the website "Gods and Radicals" as well as a published academic with a Ph.D. in philosophy teaching at the college level. You can find some of his reflections on the occult at: http://starandsystem.blogspot.com/ or look him up on twitter at: @starandsystem

Stojan Nikolic is a Thelemite and a medical doctor with a Masters in neurophysiology aspiring towards specialization of psychiatry. He enjoys observing the social and societal manifestations of the New Aeon, and cultural phenomena in particular. As a libertarian he leans strongly towards the Austrian school of economics.

Miguel Marques comes from Portugal and has mostly devoted himself to chemistry, music, and the tarot. He has regularly contributed papers to tarot magazines and conferences and more recently to the Pop Culture Grimoire Vol. 2 and the portuguese musjc project Moon(in)Motion. He can be reached at mmarques.comsciencia@gmail.com

Renata Wieczorek is a professional philosopher. She specializes in philosophy of science and theory of knowledge but her interests encompass a wide range of subjects, from Russian mysticism to higher mathematics. Her family lives in Zakopane and she was raised there during summer vacations and climbed the Tatra Mountains from her early childhood.

Derek Seagrief has written the book *The Astrology of Death: Entry & Exit – Your Birth & Death Horoscope*, published in Swedish 2012 by Ica Bokförlag (as "Dödens Astrologi: Entré och Sorti – Ditt Födelse & Dödshoroskop"). To contact the author: Email: derek@seagrief.com Website: www.seagrief.com

Kasper Opstrup is a writer and researcher of radical culture. For many years, he was a member of the Copenhagen based art collective 'floorless' and he holds a PhD from the London Consortium. His book, *The Way Out – invisible insurrections and radical imaginaries in the UK Underground 1961-1991*, is forthcoming on Minor Compositions in 2015.

Genesis Breyer P-Orridge (1950-2020) is a multiversal, polymathic, pandrogenous artist-magician of legendary stature.

Ray O Neill – *Double, Double, Toil and Trouble: Psychoanalysis Burn and Surrealism Bubble*, Derek M Elmore – *Dreams and the Neither-Neither*, Julio Mendes Rodrigo – *Rebis, the Double Being*, Eve Watson – *Bowie's Non-Human Effect: Alien/Alienation in The Man Who Fell to Earth (1976) and The Hunger (1983)*, Carl Abrahamsson – *Formulating the Desired: Some similarities between ritual magic and the psychoanalytic process*

Carl Abrahamsson – *Editor's Introduction*, Vanessa Sinclair – *Polymorphous Perversity and Pandrogeny*, Charles Stansfield Jones (Frater Achad) – *Alchymia*, Tim O'Neill: *Black Lodge/White Lodge*, Nina Antonia – *Bosie & The Beast*, Aki Cederberg – *Festivals of Spring*, Michael Moynihan – *Friedrich Hielscher's Vision of the Real Powers*, Friedrich Hielscher – *The Real Powers*, Orryelle Defenestrate Bascule – *Ear Horn: Shamanic Perspectives and Multi-Sensory Inversion*, Zbigniew Łagos – *The Figure of the Polish Magician: Czesław Czynski (1858-1932)*, Gary Lachman – *Rejected Knowledge: A Look At Our Other Way of Knowing*, Carl Abrahamsson – *Intuition as a State of Grace*, Bishop T Omphalos – *The Golden Thread: Soteriological Aspects of the Gnostic Catholicism in E.G.C.*, Kendell Geers – *iMagus*, Johan Nilsson – *Defending Paper Gods: Aleister Crowley and the Reception of Daoism in Early 20th Century Esotericism*, Gordan Djurdjevic – *The Birth of the New Aeon: Magick and Mysticism of Thelema from the Perspective of Postmodern A/Theology*, Tim O'Neill – *The Derleth Error*, Antti P Balk – *Greek Mysteries*, Carl Abrahamsson – *The Economy of Magic*, Stephen Sennitt – *The Book of the Sentient Night: 23 Nails*, Henrik Dahl – *We Ate the Acid: A Note on Psychedelic Imagery*, Jason Louv – *Robert Anton Wilson's Cosmic Trigger and the Psychedelic Interstellar Future we need*, Carey Hodges & Chad Hensley – *New Orleans Voodoo: An Oddity Unto Itself*, Alexander Nym – *Kabbalah references in contemporary culture*, Zaheer Gulamhusein – *Standing in Line*, Carl Abrahamsson – *As the Wolf Lies Down to Rest*, Vanessa Sinclair & Ingo Lambrecht – *Ritual and Psychoanalytical Spaces as Transitional, featuring Sangoma Trance States*, Hagen von Julien – *Listening to the Voice of Silence: A Contemporary Perspective on the Fraternities Saturni*, Erik Davis – *Infectious Hoax: Robert Anton Wilson reads H.P. Lovecraft*, N – *II. Land*, Cadmus – *Neo-Chthonia*, Kadmus – *A Fragment of Heart: A contribution to the Mega-Golem*, Stojan Nikolic – *The One True Church of the Dark Age of Scientism*, Miguel Marques – *The Labors of Seeing: A Journey Through the Works of Peter Whitehead*, Renata Wieczorek – *The Conception of Number According to Aleister Crowley*, Orryelle Defenestrate Bascule – *Fragments of Fact*, Derek Seagrief – *Conscious ExIt*, Kasper Opstrup – *By This, That: A spin on Lea Porsager's Spin*, and Genesis Breyer P-Orridge – *Greyhounds of the future.*

Carl Abrahamsson – *Editor's Introduction*, Sara George & Carl Abrahamsson – *Fernand Khnopff, Symbolist*, Sasha Chaitow – *Making the Invisible Visible*, Vanessa Sinclair – *Psychoanalysis and Dada*, Kendell Geers – *Tu Marcellus Eris*, Stephen Sennitt – *Fallen Worlds, Without Shadows*, Antony Hequet – *Slam Poetry: The Warrior Poet*, Antony Hequet – *Slam Poetry: The Rebel Poet*, Genesis Breyer P-Orridge – *Alien Lightning Meat Machine*, Genesis Breyer P-Orridge – *This Is A Nice Planet*, Patrick Lundborg – *Psychedelic Philosophy*, Henrik Dahl – *Visionary Design*, Philip Farber – *Higher Magick*, Kendell Geers – *Painting My Will*, Carl Abrahamsson – *The Imaginative Libido*, Angela Edwards – *The Sacred Whore*, Vera Nikolich – *The Women of the Aeon*,

Jason Louv – *Wilhelm Reich*, Kasper Opstrup – *To Make It Happen*, Peter Grey – *A Manifesto of Apocalyptic Witchcraft*, Timothy O'Neill – *The Gospel of Cosmic Terror*, Stephen Sennitt – *Sentient Absence*, Carl Abrahamsson – *Anton LaVey, Magical Innovator*, Alexander Nym – *Magicians: Evolutionary Agents or Regressive Twats?*, Antti P Balk – *Thelema*, Kjetil Fjell – *The Vindication of Thelema*, Derek Seagrief – *Exploring Past Lives*, Sandy Robertson – *The Fictional Aleister Crowley*, Adam Rostoker – *Whence Came the Stranger?*, Emory Cranston – *A Preface to the Scented Garden*, Manon Hedenborg-White – *Erotic Submission to the Divine*, Carl Abrahamsson – *What Remains for the Future?*, Frater Achad – *Living In the Sunlight*, Genesis Breyer P-Orridge – *Magick Squares and Future Beats*

Carl Abrahamsson – *Editor's Introduction*, Frater Achad – *A Litany of Ra*, Kendell Geers – *Tripping over Darwin's Hangover*, Vera Nikolich – *Eastern Connections*, Carl Abrahamsson – *Babalon*, Freya Aswynn – *On the Influence of Odin*, Marita – *Runic Magic through the Odinic Dialectic*, Aki Cederberg – *Afterword: The River of Story*, Shri Gurudev Mahendranath – *The Londinium Temple Strain*, Gary Dickinson – *An Orient Pearl*, Derek Seagrief – *Aleister Crowley's Birth & Death Horoscopes*, Tim O'Neill – *Shades of Void*, Nema – *Magickal Healing*, Nema – *A Greater Feast*, Philip Farber – *Sacred Smoke*, Robert Taylor – *Death & the Psychedelic Experience*, Michael Horowitz – *LSD: the Antidote to Everything*, Alexander Nym – *Transcendence as an Operative Category…*, Carl Abrahamsson – *Approaching the Approaching*, Renata Wieczorek – *The Secret Book of the Tatra Mountains*, Sasha Chaitow – *Legends of the Fall Retold*, Sara George & Carl Abrahamsson – *Sulamith Wülfing*, Robert C Morgan – *Hans Bellmer*, Genesis Breyer P-Orridge – *Tagged for Life*, Carl Abrahamsson – *Go Forth and Let Your Brain-halves Procreate*, Anders Lundgren – *Satanic Cinema is Alive and Well*, Anton LaVey – *Appendices*

Carl Abrahamsson – *Editor's Introduction*, Jason Louv – *The Freedom of Imagination Act*, Patrick Lundborg – *Such Stuff as Dreams are Made of*, Gary Lachman – *Secret Societies and the Modern World*, Tim O'Neill – *The War of the Owl and the Pelican*, Dianus del Bosco Sacro – *The Great Rite*, Philip H Farber – *Entities in the Brain*, Aki Cederberg – *At the Well of Initiation*, Renata, Wieczorek – *The Magical Life of Derek Jarman*, Genesis Breyer P-Orridge – *A Dark Room of Desire*, Genesis Breyer P-Orridge – *Kreeme Horne*, Ezra Pound – *Translator's Postscript*, Stephen Ellis – *Poems for The Fenris Wolf*, Hiram Corso – *Mel Lyman*, Mel Lyman – *Plea for Courage*, Gary Dickinson – *The Daughter of Astrology*, Robert Podgurski – *Sigils and Extra Dimensionality*, Frater Nigris – *Liber Al As-if*, Peter Grey – *The Abbey Must be Built*, Vera Mladenovska Nikolich – *A Different Perspective of the Undead*, Kevin Slaughter – *The Great Satan*, Lionel Snell – *The Art of Evil*, Phenex Apollonius – *The Quintessence of Daimonic Ipseity*, Phanes Apollonius – *Infernal Diabolism in Theory and Practice*, Anonymous – *Falling with Love: Embracing the Infernal Host*, Lana Krieg – *Sympathy with the Devil: Faust's Infernal Formula*, Carl Abrahamsson – *State of the Art: Birthpangs of a Mega-Golem*, Carl Abrahamsson – *Hounded by the Dogs of Reason*

THE FENRIS WOLF 4 (2011)

Carl Abrahamsson – *The whys of yesterday are the why-nots of today*, Hermann Hesse – *The Execution*, Fredrik Söderberg – *Black and White Meditations 1-23*, Peter Gilmore – *Every Man and Woman Is a Star*, Peter Grey – *Barbarians at the Gates*, John Duncan – *Hallelujah*, Ramsey Dukes – *Democracy Is Dying of AIDS*, Tim O'Neill – *The Technology of Civilization X*, Thomas Karlsson – *Religion and Science*, David Beth – *Bloodsongs*, Payam Nabarz – *Liber Astrum*, Hiram Corso – *Unveiling the Mysteries of the Process Church*, Jean-Pierre Turmel – *The Pantheon of Genesis Breyer P-Orridge*, Kendell Geers – *The Penis Might Ier Than Thes Word*, Z'EV – *The Calls*, Robert Taylor – *Dreamachine: The Alchemy of Light*, Phil Farber – *An Interview with Terence McKenna*, Phil Farber – *McKenna, Ramachandran and the Orgy*, Thomas Bey William Bailey – *The Twilight of Psychedelic America?*, Ernst Jünger – *LSD Again/Nochmals LSD*, Baba Rampuri – *The Edge of Indian Spirituality*, Aki Cederberg – *In Search of Magic Mirrors*, Carl Abrahamsson – *Thelema and Politics*, Carl Abrahamsson – *Someone's Messing with the Big Picture*, Carl Abrahamsson – *An Art of High Intent?*, Carl Abrahamsson – *A Conversation with Kenneth Anger*

THE FENRIS WOLF 1-3 (1989-1993-2011)

Carl Abrahamsson – *Editor's Introduction*
Carl Abrahamsson – *'Zine und Zeit (2011)*

THE FENRIS WOLF 1 (1989)
John Alexander – *The Strange Phenomena of the Dream*, Helgi Pjeturss – *The Nature of Sleep and Dreams*, Tim O'Neill – *A Dark Storm Rising*, Carl Abrahamsson – *Inauguration of Kenneth Anger*, Carl Abrahamsson – *An Interview with Genesis P-Orridge*, William S Burroughs – *Points of Distinction between Sedative and Consciousness-Expanding Drugs*, Carl Abrahamsson – *Jayne Mansfield: Satanist*, TOPYUS – *Television Magick*, Anton LaVey – *Evangelists vs The New God*

THE FENRIS WOLF 2 (1990)
Lionel Snell – *The Satan Game*, Carl Abrahamsson – *In Defence of Satanism*, Anton LaVey – *The Horns of Dilemma*, Genesis P-Orridge – *Beyond thee Valley ov Acid*, Phauss – *Photographs*, Jack Stevenson – *15 Voices from God*, Jack Stevenson – *18 Fatal Arguments*, Tim O'Neill – *Art On the Edge of Life*, Terence Sellers – *To Achieve Death*, Stein Jarving – *Choice and Process*, Tim O'Neill – *Under the Sign of Gemini*, 93/696 – *The Forgotten Ones In Magick*, Tim O'Neill – *The Mechanics of Maya*, Coyote 12 – *The Thin Line*, Genesis P-Orridge – *Thee Only Language Is Light*, Jack Stevenson – *Porno on Film*, Carl Abrahamsson – *An Interview with Kenneth Anger*

THE FENRIS WOLF 3 (1993)
Jack Stevenson – *Vandals, Vikings and Nazis*, von Hausswolff & Elggren – *Inauguration of two new Kingdoms*, Tim O'Neill – *A Flame in the Holy Mountain*, Frater Tigris – *A Preliminary Vision*, Carl Abrahamsson – *The Demonic Glamour of Cinema*, William Heidrick – *Some Crowley Sources*, Peter H Gilmore – *The Rite of Ragnarök*, ONA – *The Left-Handed Path*, Zbigniew Karkowski – *The Method Is Science...*, Fetish 23 – *Demonic Poetry*, Ben Kadosh – *Lucifer-Hiram*, Freya Aswynn – *The Northern Magical Tradition*, Anton LaVey – *Tests*, Austin Osman Spare – *Anathema of Zos*, Rodney Orpheus – *Thelemic Morality*, Nemo – *Recognizing Pseudo-Satanism*, Philip Marsh – *Pythagoras, Plato and the Hellenes*, Terence Sellers – *A Few Acid Writings*, Hymenæus Beta – *Harry*

severely Satanic headaches – many of which he originally helped create... Easier said than done! Satan's love of the ambitiously mischievous humans is challenged as his own "Team Apocalypse" fervently sets to work. But as the world begins to change quickly and dramatically for the better, a new question arises: can God and his suspicious Archangels really be trusted in this cataclysmic, cosmic undertaking?

CARL ABRAHAMSSON: MOTHER, HAVE A SAFE TRIP

Unearthed plans and designs stemming from radical inventor Nikola Tesla could solve the world's energy problems. These plans suddenly generate a vortex of interest from various powers. Thrown into this maelstrom of international intrigue is Victor Ritterstadt – a soul searching magician with a mysterious and troubled past. From Berlin, over Macedonia, and all the way to Nepal, Ritterstadt sets out on an outer as well as inner quest. Espionage, love, UFOs, magic, telepathy, conspiracies, LSD, and more in this shocking story of a world about to be changed forever...

"It's a thrilling roller coaster ride through psychedelic adventures, juicy romantic interludes, metaphoric dreamscapes, high Himalayan yoga enclaves, telepathic portals, 60's flashbacks, magical constructs, secret government pursuits and many more twists that kept all three of my eyes open. It's a story that you'll definitely want to keep non-stop reading, which I enthusiastically recommend."
 – George Douvris, Links by George

"*Mother, Have A Safe Trip* is a highly entertaining and thought-provoking novel. Chock-full of psychedelia, the book is also a much welcome addition to the far too few fictional works published dealing with psychedelic culture."
 – Henrik Dahl, Psychedelic Press

"The dialogues are great. But it's too short. I wanted more."
 – Genesis Breyer P-Orridge, Artist

"It's a wonderful read. A lovely book."
 – June Newton/Alice Springs, Photographer

CARL ABRAHAMSSON (ED.): THE MEGA GOLEM: A WOMANUAL FOR ALL TIMES AND SPACES

An anthology of texts and images constituting the current Corpus of the Mega Golem – the talismanic being/sentience created by Carl Abrahamsson in 2009. With contributions by Carl Abrahamsson, Vanessa Sinclair, Kadmus, Gabriel McCaughry, and others.

VANESSA SINCLAIR: SWITCHING MIRRORS

Switching Mirrors is an amazing collection of cut-ups and mind-expanding poetry by Vanessa Sinclair. Delving into the unconscious and actively utilising the "third mind" as developed by William S Burroughs and Brion Gysin, Sinclair roams through suggestive vistas of magic, witchcraft, dreams, psychoanalysis, sex and sexuality (and more). Causal apprehensions are disrupted by a flow of impressions that open up the mind of the reader. What's behind language and our use of it? What happens when random factors and the unconscious are given free reign in poetic form? *Switching Mirrors* is what happens.

Vanessa Sinclair (ed.): Rendering Unconscious
– Psychoanalytic Perspectives, Politics & Poetry

In times of crisis, one needs to stop and ask, "How did we get here?" Our contemporary chaos is the result of a society built upon pervasive systems of oppression, discrimination and violence that run deeper and reach further than most understand or care to realize. These draconian systems have been fundamental to many aspects of our lives, and we seem to have gradually allowed them more power. However, our foundation is not solid; it is fractured and collapsing – if we allow that. We need to start applying new models of interpretation and analysis to the deep-rooted problems at hand.

Rendering Unconscious brings together international scholars, psychoanalysts, psychologists, philosophers, researchers, writers and poets; reflecting on current events, politics, the state of mental health care, the arts, literature, mythology, and the cultural climate; thoughtfully evaluating this moment of crisis, its implications, wide-ranging effects, and the social structures that have brought us to this point of urgency.

Hate speech, Internet stalking, virtual violence, the horde mentality of the alt-right, systematic racism, the psychology of rioting, the theater of violence, fake news, the power of disability, erotic transference and counter-transference, the economics of libido, Eros and the death drive, fascist narratives, psychoanalytic formation as resistance, surrealism and sexuality, traversing genders, and colonial counterviolence are but a few of the topics addressed in this thought-provoking and inspiring volume.

Contributions by Vanessa Sinclair, Gavriel Reisner, Alison Annunziata, Kendalle Aubra, Gerald Sand, Tanya White-Davis & Anu Kotay, Luce deLire, Jason Haaf, Simon Critchley & Brad Evans, Marc Strauss, Chiara Bottici, Manya Steinkoler, Emma Lieber, Damien Patrick Williams, Shara Hardeson, Jill Gentile, Angelo Villa, Gabriela Costardi, Jamieson Webster, Sergio Benvenuto, Craig Slee, Álvaro D. Moreira, David Lichtenstein, Julie Fotheringham, John Dall'aglio, Matthew Oyer, Jessica Datema, Olga Cox Cameron, Katie Ebbitt, Juliana Portilho, Trevor Pederson, Elisabeth Punzi & Per-Magnus Johansson, Meredith Friedson, Steven Reisner, Léa Silveira, Patrick Scanlon, Júlio Mendes Rodrigo, Daniel Deweese, Julie Futrell, Gregory J. Stevens, Benjamin Y. Fong, Katy Bohinc, Wayne Wapeemukwa, Patricia Gherovici & Cassandra Seltman, Marie Brown, Buffy Cain, Claire-Madeline Culkin, Andrew Daul, Germ Lynn, Adel Souto, and paul aster stone-tsao.

Sir Edward Bulwer Lytton: Vril – The Power of the Coming Race

Sir Edward Bulwer Lytton's cautionary tale of occult super-powers and advanced subterranean cultures have fascinated readers since 1871. Part early science-fiction, part educational tract, part occult romance, *Vril* keeps spellbinding readers thanks to its wide range of themes and emotions, as well as its thrilling sense of adventure.

A curious man descends into a mountain through a mine and experiences far more than he bargained for. Deep inside the mountain lies a completely different world. Its inhabitants, the

Vril-ya, are human-like but physically superior and philosophically more advanced. They live in harmony made possible by their wisdom but also by the powerful and potentially destructive magical energy they call "Vril."

The impressed yet terrified visitor is allowed to stay and learn more about their ancient and advanced culture, something very few visitors have – it seems that all the previous adventurers have been mercilessly disposed of by the Vril-ya...

This edition includes an introductory essay by Swedish author Carl Abrahamsson.

MORE INFORMATION CAN BE FOUND AT OUR WEB SITE: WWW.TRAPART.NET

www.ingramcontent.com/pod-product-compliance
Lightning Source LLC
LaVergne TN
LVHW091657190726
843493LV00001B/41